'While victims of political violence and terrorism are frequently centred in politicians' speeches and media headlines, Will McGowan provides us with the first book-length and empirically rich study of survivors' experiences. By building relationships of longstanding trust with his interviewees, the author has brought their stories of political violence and its aftermath to light, in this sensitive and nuanced inquiry. This methodologically rigorous and theoretically informed book fills a notable gap in Political Science, Criminology and Sociology – acquainting us, for the first time, with the making of "resilient" survivors, as well as the loss that pervades their recovery'.

Charlotte Heath-Kelly, Professor of
International Security, University of Warwick

'Will McGowan's book offers a deeply original engagement with the pervasiveness and power of "resilience" in contemporary discourse on political violence. The conceptual sophistication he brings to this discussion is enviably complemented by its empirically rich engagement with the voices and views of victims of violence. The book makes for fascinating reading, and fully deserves the attention and audience it will no doubt receive'.

Lee Jarvis, Professor of International Politics,
University of East Anglia

'McGowan's book provides a clarion bell for understanding the hotly contested concept of resilience. Drawing on firsthand experiences of the survivors of political violence and terrorism, this book delivers thoughtful, balanced and much-needed clarity for researchers, policy-makers and activists interested in understanding *what* resilience is, *where* it is found – and *how* the survivors of suffering and injustice make use of it'.

Simon Green, Professor of Criminology and
Victimology, University of Hull

Victims of Political Violence and Terrorism

This book examines the survivors of political violence and terrorism, considering both how they have responded and how they have been responded to following critical incidents. As this work demonstrates, survivors of comparatively rare and spectacular violence hold a mirror up to society's normative assumptions around trauma, recovery, and resilience.

Drawing on two years of observational field research with a British NGO who work with victims and former perpetrators of PVT, this book explores contested notions of 'resilience' and what it might mean for those negotiating the aftermaths of violence. Examining knowledge about resilience from a multitude of sources, including security policy, media, academic literature, and the survivors themselves, this book contends that in order to make empirical sense of resilience we must reckon with both its discursive and practical manifestations.

An accessible and compelling read, this book will appeal to students and scholars of criminology, sociology, victimology, criminal justice, and all those interested in the stories of survivors.

William McGowan is a Lecturer in the School of Justice Studies and member of the Centre for the Study of Crime, Criminalisation and Social Exclusion (CCSE) at Liverpool John Moores University.

Victims, Culture and Society

Concerns about victimisation have multiplied over the last fifty years. *Victims, Culture and Society* explores the major concepts, debates and controversies that these concerns have generated across a range of disciplines, but particularly within criminology and victimology. As the impacts of globalisation, the movement of peoples and the divergences between the Global North and Global South have become ever more apparent, this series provides an authoritative space for original contributions in making sense of these far-reaching changes on individuals, localities and nationalities. These issues by their very nature demand an interdisciplinary approach and an interdisciplinary voice outside conventional conceptual boundaries. *Victims, Culture and Society* offers the space for that voice.

Each author adopts a strong personal view and offers a lively and agenda-setting treatment of their subject matter. The monographs encompass a transnational, global or comparative approach to the issues they address. Examining new areas of both empirical and theoretical enquiry, the series offers the opportunity for innovative and progressing thinking about the relationship between victims, culture and society. The books will be useful and thought-provoking resources for the international community of undergraduates, postgraduates, researchers and policymakers working within the broad field of victimisation.

Edited by: Sandra Walklate, University of Liverpool, UK and Monash University, Australia

Kerry Carrington, Queensland University of Technology, Australia

Women, Rape and Justice: Unravelling the Rape Conundrum
Jan Jordan

Victims of Political Violence and Terrorism
Making Up Resilient Survivors
William McGowan

For more information about this series, please visit: www.routledge.com/Victims-Culture-and-Society/book-series/VICS

Victims of Political Violence and Terrorism

Making Up Resilient Survivors

William McGowan

First published 2022
by Routledge
4 Park Square, Milton Park, Abingdon, Oxon OX14 4RN

and by Routledge
605 Third Avenue, New York, NY 10158

Routledge is an imprint of the Taylor & Francis Group, an informa business

© 2022 William McGowan

The right of William McGowan to be identified as author of this work has been asserted in accordance with sections 77 and 78 of the Copyright, Designs and Patents Act 1988.

The Open Access version of this book, available at www.taylorfrancis.com, has been made available under a Creative Commons Attribution-Non Commercial-No Derivatives 4.0 license.

Trademark notice: Product or corporate names may be trademarks or registered trademarks, and are used only for identification and explanation without intent to infringe.

British Library Cataloguing-in-Publication Data
A catalogue record for this book is available from the British Library

Library of Congress Cataloging-in-Publication Data
Names: McGowan, William (University lecturer), author.
Title: Victims of political violence and terrorism: making up resilient survivors / William McGowan.
Description: Milton Park, Abingdon, Oxon; New York, NY: Routledge, 2022 . | Includes bibliographical references and index.
Identifiers: LCCN 2021049968 | ISBN 9780367722463 (hardback) | ISBN 9780367722470 (paperback) | ISBN 9781003154020 (ebook)
Doi: 10.4324/9781003154020
Subjects: LCSH: Victims of political violence. | Victims of terrorism. | Resilience (Personality trait)
Classification: LCC HV6431 .M424 2022 |
DDC 362.88/9317–dc23/eng/20211015
LC record available at https://lccn.loc.gov/2021049968

ISBN: 978-0-367-72246-3 (hbk)
ISBN: 978-0-367-72247-0 (pbk)
ISBN: 978-1-003-15402-0 (ebk)

DOI: 10.4324/9781003154020

Typeset in Bembo
by Newgen Publishing UK

For Derry

Contents

Acknowledgements	xi
Introduction	1

PART I
Resilience as Discourse and Practice — 17

1	Setting the Scene of the 'Terror–Trauma–Resilience' Nexus in the 21st Century	19
2	To Survivors Themselves: Why, Where, and How to Study Survivors of Political Violence and Terrorism?	47

PART 2
Turning Points and Processes of Resilience — 79

3	'Resilient' to What? Mapping the Impacts of Political Violence and Terrorism	81
4	Sources of Resilience for Survivors	105
5	Exploring Temporalities of (In)Security and Resilience	132

PART 3
Repurposing Resilience — 161

6	Temporality, Resistance, and Solidarity: The Making and Moulding of Resilient Survivor Communities	163
7	Am I Invictus?	188

x Contents

Conclusion   213

Methodological Appendix   233
Index   255

Acknowledgements

This book and most of the material that fills it originally took shape as a doctoral thesis which I finished back in 2018. Reading over my acknowledgements from that work now, just three years later, it feels strange in some ways to be rewriting them. As many writers will identify with, 'acknowledgements' are often one of those awkward 'odd jobs' left until last, bringing back all sorts of memories of the times, places, and people that made the work what it is for various reasons. It certainly feels that way for me. Despite the fundamental gist of the work remaining the same, this book is a different piece of work, completed in a different environment, and with a very different set of imperatives accompanying it. The many debts of gratitude associated with my PhD work still stand and those people, primarily though not exclusively based in Liverpool, know who they are. I would, however, like to extend my deepest thanks and appreciation to a number of people who have either been integral to my thinking and general commitment to finishing the book since finishing my thesis, and/or whose support and input has been so essential to the completion of the work as a whole, then and now, that a restatement of thanks is warranted.

I am extremely grateful to both the Tim Parry Johnathan Ball Foundation for Peace, Warrington, and to all of their participants, who gave up so much of their time to talk to me on numerous occasions during the research and who shared such deeply moving and personal stories of their lives. Many of these people do not feature directly in the book but all shaped and influenced my fieldwork and ongoing reflections in ways that they will not necessarily appreciate. I owe a particular debt of gratitude to Donna Craine, Jo Dover, Terry O'Hara, Nick Taylor, Ann Beswick, Harriet Vickers, Anne Walker, and Lee Lavis.

I was incredibly fortunate to have benefitted from the inimitable supervision of Sandra Walklate and Gabe Mythen during my PhD, whose enthusiasm for the project, ongoing advice, and dedication to keeping me focused were invaluable. I would also like to thank Lee Jarvis and Barry Godfrey for reading an earlier iteration of this work so generously and who saw a book in it long before I did. A number of other people, whose ongoing enthusiasm for my work since completing the original project, have given me the much-needed impetus and confidence to see this book through. This enthusiasm has taken various and varied forms, including professional guidance, moral support, critical and intellectual debate, and, above all, friendship. They are Emma Murray, Christian Perrin, Lizzie Cook, Will Jackson, David Whyte, Vickie Cooper, Andrew Kirton, Roy Coleman, Zoe Alker, Giles Barrett, and Janet Jamieson. Lindsey Metcalf and the Shut Up and Write regulars at LJMU – Úna Barr, Hilary Currin, Kym Atkinson, Helen Monk, Katie Tucker, Katherine Harbord, Jodie Hodgson and Joe Sim – played a big part in keeping me motivated just when I needed it most. There are, of course, so many more people that I have drawn support and inspiration from in my working life beyond trying to get this book finished. We need our mates and good colleagues more than ever to bounce off and lift our spirits and I feel so fortunate to have had them as a sounding board throughout the process of putting this book together.

I would like to acknowledge financial support from the Economic and Social Research Council who funded this project through a +3 studentship at the University of Liverpool between 2014 and 2017. I also received Researcher Development Funding from the University of Liverpool, which allowed me to share my findings more publicly with the Foundation for Peace and many of the same participants whose stories you will come across in this book. A workshop held at the Foundation in Warrington towards the end of 2019 entitled *Making Sense of the Past in the Present: Findings and Futures for Survivors of Violence and Conflict* certainly helped to firm up some of the ideas presented here in dialogue with staff and survivors at the charity. It should go without saying that all faults with the work are, of course, all my own.

You can never dictate or even forecast the reception a work will receive but I must say a huge thanks to Maria Follett at Liverpool John Moores University for drawing my attention to some internal funding from the university which has enabled me to publish this book under an Open Access Creative Commons license. I hope this will encourage anyone with an interest in the subject matter to access and share the book, including those who contributed to it or who have had similar experiences, those working with survivors in a supportive capacity, or scholars and policymakers who might otherwise have been unable to read it as easily. Jessica Phillips and Tom Sutton at Routledge have also been fantastic and made the process far smoother than I anticipated.

My deepest love and thanks go to both my immediate and extended (and extending!) family for making this whole journey possible, especially to Mum, Dad, Alex, Tora, Aunty Sandy, and the Newton McGowans, for supporting me every step of the way. A very special loving thanks go to Samantha Fletcher, who listened, read, questioned, and encouraged, pushing me towards the finishing line amidst everything else that this whirlwind past couple of years has thrown our way, while simultaneously writing her own book. At the centre of the whirlwind, a loving little smiley thanks goes to Feddy, whose arrival hastened the completion of this book in the most wonderful way possible.

Introduction

'Resilience' has become something of a 21st-century buzzword in social and environmental policy fields as diverse as ecology, urban planning, economics, and security, also featuring prominently in clinical psychology, counselling therapies, and popular self-help discourse. It has attracted widespread usage and sparked considerable controversy within social science and beyond. It is now a commonly used epithet within many political institutions, reflecting the seemingly universal appeal and purchase it has had within social policy and among the political class. Globally mediated phenomena, from terror attacks to controversial political events to public health pandemics, have seen discursive appeals for resilience across this diverse and vast qualitative terrain, yet all are implicitly said to exist: resilient systems, resilient communities, resilient subjects. Yet, how do we know 'resilience' when we see it? How do we go about researching it? What does this contemporary precedent of 'resilience' thinking reveal about everyday politics and, more specifically, about the everyday politics of trauma and memory? In short, what do we know about the reality of 'resilience'?

This book takes resilience as its point of departure and return as a ubiquitous, much used concept that is nonetheless poorly understood and which remains less often subject to critical, empirical scrutiny by advocates and critics alike who more frequently tend to present it as a fait accompli. Its discursive deployment in relation to counterterrorism, radicalisation, and security as a more 'positive' development to the negative and defensive category of risk superficially encourages the building of robust community structures, preparedness amongst emergency responders, and the capacity to 'bounce back' in the event of security emergencies and terrorist attacks. This drive to 'build resilience' is manifest in policy responses that operate at micro, meso, and macro levels, ranging from exhortations for citizen policing to community-based projects to challenge extremism, and national appeals to 'pull together' to combat terrorism. Setting these apparent shifts in framing to one side momentarily, might we ask a deceptively simple question instead: how have people who have survived political violence and terrorism (PVT) coped, or not, with the harm such critical incidents produce? What are the factors influencing this?

DOI: 10.4324/9781003154020-1

2 Introduction

I focus on terror attacks and their aftermaths here because they are quintessential examples of individual and personal traumas which are often invoked to garner and mould particular kinds of collective action (McGowan, 2016). Declarations of 'our' ability (whoever this 'we' is) to 'bounce back', or of 'keeping calm and carrying on', have become almost stock responses from mainstream media and policymakers. But what is the relationship between the lived experiences at the heart of such tragedies and these wider sentiments? Drawing on fieldwork at an NGO in the UK offering support to survivors of PVT, subsequent in-depth interviews with some of these survivors and staff, and recent responses to terror attacks in the UK by government, media and communities, this book explores this political and conceptual controversy by drawing out some of the specificities at play when victims of traumatic violence share their testimonies.

This research began in 2014 at The Tim Parry Johnathan Ball Foundation for Peace (FfP), an organisation that works for peace and non-violent conflict resolution and provides needs assessments and support to survivors of PVT in the form of their Survivors Assistance Network. The incidents bringing survivors to this NGO span a diverse time and place range, including both institutional violence committed 'from above' (e.g. the shooting of innocent protestors by the British military in Northern Ireland in 1972), as well as anti-institutional violence 'from below' (e.g. the 2005 London bombings) (Ruggiero, 2006: 1). While the spectacle of 'terrorism' feeds into a whole host of public fears and anxieties, often harnessed by media and state actors to justify the ceaseless 'war on terror', survivors with first-hand experience of violence perpetrated by both state and non-state actors have a regrettably intimate vantage point from which to reflect on such issues. Through a close reading of participant's narratives, the work maps a range of impacts of PVT, details the 'resilience resources' (Overland, 2013: 204) survivors have drawn on in traversing this suffering and loss, and highlights a temporal complexity to survivors' narratives typically rendered over within counterterrorism and security policy discourses espousing notions of citizen resilience and empowerment.

Focusing on how individuals have coped in the face of personal injury and devastating loss, this book not only explores 'resilience' as an organising metaphor for pre-emptive action and preparation against future shocks (as it is typically framed within social and security policy), but also as a human response to the short- and long-term aftermaths of past harm and trauma. Recognising that our responses to adversity are enacted in the present, within various touching distances and reference points to the past, and with shifting emphases placed on the future, a much messier, complex and interesting portrait appears of 'the resilient survivor'.

Rather than confirming or challenging the veracity of existing resilience policies or theories, this book simply attempts to show that there are many different ways of being a person. We live in an era obsessed with entrepreneurial soul searching, self-optimisation and demonstrable strength in the face

Introduction 3

of adversity, which both encourages and warns against the power of disclosure. Yet given the fact that every single voice represented within these pages could be said to have responded to harm and injustice 'resiliently' at some point, even while their experiences, histories, and responses differ so markedly, how are we to make sense of this pervasive and catch-all concept? If, as Aristotle once declared, 'a friend to all is a friend to none', with resilience offering so broad an umbrella that it is rendered meaningless, then the story will have to stop here. But, of course, we are not passive objects who remain indifferent to the ways our experiences are packaged and classified. In this case, harm and suffering is silenced at times, reified and magnified at others, with varying accents placed on survivors' strength and agency. How, then, are we to approach such unstable phenomena?

Making Up Resilience

'Resilience' divides opinion. Many compelling critiques discard it out of hand for its supposed nihilism, vacuity, or for the depoliticising powers it is said to possess. Many more sing its praises for its restorative, regenerative, or empowering potential. A frustrated few of us, keen to explore the reality in between, take this controversy itself to be an interesting manifestation of a much broader set of methodological and political contentions. As Humbert and Joseph (2019) rightly highlight, research to date has left much space to explore the practical manifestations of resilience, including its relationship with neoliberalism, indigeneity and, of course, competing definitions. Not everyone is interested in conceptual conflict. An emergent, but disparate, number of books and articles similarly interested in exploring 'practices of resilience' (Cavelty, Kaufmann and Kristensen, 2015: 3) often begin by acknowledging its sprawling, messy and contested nature, precisely in order to quickly move on to the 'real task at hand' of working with specific data and away from what they see as abstract or polemic generalisations. This book takes a slightly different approach insofar as both contested but abstract struggles over discursive meaning *and* observable insights derived from situated local practice are deemed equally important, with each finding their way into my analysis.

While resilience continues to enjoy an intriguing, contested, and often irritating adulation through self-help 'mediums' (a homonym readers will have to negotiate for themselves!), it has become equally pervasive because of its deployment in policymaking language. Commenting on this 'rise of resilience', Chandler (2014: 3) states: 'the key aspects that define resilience approaches to policy-making are methodological assumptions about the nature of the world, the complex problem of governance, and the policy processes suitable to governing this complexity'. The original impetus for setting out on this research journey was to investigate how closely this burgeoning policy concept seemed to adhere to lived experience using empirical insights drawn from survivors of PVT. Surely, abstract sounding descriptions about 'complexity governance'

4 Introduction

would prove irrelevant? As time wore on, however, I became more interested in the extent to which these somewhat abstract generalisations and the lived experiences of people going about their lives might be mutually altered over time rather than unconnected. Later chapters show how the data collected illuminate a range of broader issues than those associated with resilience, but it is nonetheless this 'stretchy' and 'pervasive' concept (Walklate, McGarry and Mythen, 2014: 410) which provides a point of departure and return throughout the book.

On the one hand, then, we have a somewhat esoteric, though undoubtedly significant, shift in policy thinking. 'Resilience research' typically begins by acknowledging its omnipresence and diversity, often pointing to a confusing and abstract conceptualisation of a broader set of governing rationalities (Chandler, 2014: 203). Until we flesh these out with examples of more tangible, specific practices, we can say little about the form 'resilience' is said to be taking. Purely theoretical work focusing on resilience often appears anxious to iron out its conceptual ambiguity, exemplifying simultaneously the promise and futility claimed by its proponents and critics alike.

On the other hand, the word resilience remains an ordinary member of the English language with relevant everyday use value in all sorts of contexts. If readers bring to bear familiar connotations of the word, they are likely to arrive at fairly ordinary ideas, certainly more mundane than theoretical problems in 'the governance of complexity' (Chandler, 2014). Often, the use of the word 'resilience' within psychological studies of coping, healing, and positive adaptation sound much more akin to this ordinary and familiar everyday use than studies of political governance and even carry a ring of linguistic convenience. Clinical psychologist George Bonanno, one of the pioneers in bringing about a focus on 'resilience' to studies of trauma, loss and bereavement, places a striking lack of importance on clarifying 'resilience' or even insisting on its use at all, suggesting that its use is merely coincidental with a range of familiar, positive attributes or outcomes. Describing positive outcomes to trauma, as opposed to 'chronicity', by which he means 'long-lasting mental health problems after highly aversive events', Bonanno (2012; emphasis added) goes on to explain: '[…] but you'll notice that the most common response is down there in that spot [signalling to a section on his graph showing a majority (36–65%) of people classified as exhibiting "mild disruptions in normal functioning" after these highly aversive events] that we [clinical psychology] weren't sure about – that's what I'm calling here resilience, you can call this anything, call this a stable trajectory, healthy functioning – the word resilience is not really necessary, "*cos this is really an empirical finding*"'. Self-evident, perhaps even objective. Out there in the world, just waiting to be discovered, collected, and measured. Unlike the anxious search for clarity emanating from theoretical debates about resilience, here we see a positive nonchalance toward its very use in a context that we might readily ascribe it some importance and conceptual purchase.

This book is neither anxious to arrive at a position of theoretical clarity nor disinterested in whether resilience has a specific form. Contra Bonanno, empirical findings cannot be divorced or isolated from the ways in which we gather or describe them, and there certainly are valid reasons for wanting to think carefully through why we choose these words over others. This, in fact, is crucial if we are to arrive at a more holistic picture of what resilience might mean or whether it resonates in practice. Eponymous 'resilience' research, discourse, policy, and popular and clinical literatures, in addition to the viewpoints of survivors themselves, all need to be taken into account.

There is an inevitability and even a weariness surrounding resilience, including the rifts alluded to above, leaving some 'exhausted by its ubiquitous weight and the chains it places around all our necks' (Evans and Reid, 2015: 154). But when phenomena in the human sciences seem inevitable, they also make for fascinating cases of what philosopher Ian Hacking (1995, 2002) refers to as 'interactive' or 'human kinds' (this will be explained more fully in Chapter 2). Distinguishing 'human kinds' from 'natural kinds' has been integral to Hacking's notion of 'making up people', which he has used to make sense of various changing phenomena including mental health classifications, child abuse, suicide, autism, obesity, and many more besides (Hacking, 2007). Rather than some inherent fascination with any one of these topics' specific qualities, they all provide interesting case studies 'in classifications of people, in how they affect the people classified, and how the effects on the people in turn change the classifications' (Hacking, 2007: 285). This 'looping effect' and the dynamics between classified people and their actions allow us to think about how people are constituted as certain kinds of people, at certain points in time – in short, what 'makes them up'? If we were to separate them purely for heuristic purposes, this is an approach that places equal and iterative importance on discourse and practice (notwithstanding the problems such a reduction invites) (Hacking, 2004).

Approaching the problem of resilience in this way requires that we take it seriously. Hacking's work provides as much mileage for making sense of 'the resilient terrorism survivor' *idea* (sketched out in Chapter 1) as it does the direct accounts of survivors of terrorism explored later. This book focuses predominantly on the latter, or what Hacking (1997) deems the 'object' under study, but as something surely connected to the 'idea' (Hacking, 1997) of 'the resilient terrorism survivor' which, as Chapter 1 argues, pervades the present conjuncture. This tapestry of work has repeatedly opened up fruitful lines of inquiry within the data and resonated strongly with the twin problem posed by making sense of tangible, empirical social action against an emergent and shifting discourse of resilience. It does not and cannot, however, make good all of the project's methodological shortcomings (see, for example, McGowan, 2019, 2020; McGowan and Cook, 2020). The following note on theory and method, along with Chapter 2's more detailed explanation, will have to suffice

6 Introduction

in guiding readers through subsequent data analysis chapters before these methodological shortcomings are picked up again more decisively at the end of the book.

Though finding value in Hacking's work on 'making up people' and other associated ideas, this book cannot claim to offer anywhere near as thoroughgoing account of 'the resilient survivor' as Hacking's own genealogies do, but it is hoped that this book can at least introduce new readers to his body of work and act as an invitation for them to explore some of his ideas for themselves.

A Note on Theory and Method

This is a book about resilience that draws on the experiences of a small group of survivors to explore this idea. As stated above, it maintains that ideas such as 'resilience' oscillate between more or less discursive, practical, structural and subjective terrains, picking up new meanings as they go and producing shifting manifestations over time and space. The book does not offer a 'theory of resilience', but a discussion and analysis of resilience as an incredibly popular and contested term and concept, and a survey of where these different meanings of resilience resonate or jar with survivors' experiences. It is not written in order for its findings to be applied to larger groups of people or survivors recovering from events elsewhere around the world. It is, however, written as an invitation for like-minded scholars or practitioners who are working with or researching survivors (of PVT, in particular, but not exclusively) to compare and contrast their findings with those described here. Chapter 7, in particular, presents an ideal-typical constellation of resilience and one way we might group the kinds of resilience found within the preceding analysis, but this represents just one possible arrangement of my findings and, as ever, this arrangement must be approached critically by readers who are encouraged to scrutinise its curation.

As with most qualitative projects, the primary data and empirical findings discussed here form only part of the broader argument being made. As well as not developing a new theory of resilience, the work should also not be viewed as a substantive case study example of a particular phenomenon being used to champion a specific method over all others. In fact, the reverse is almost true in that the methods used to attain and present survivors' experiences are woefully inadequate for representing anything like their reality. The methods used to attain the primary data at the heart of the book emerged out of a combination of practicability, convenience, opportunism and, above all, ethical considerations. While I remain agnostic in hindsight about the place of interview data and the narratives we might extract from them (see McGowan and Cook, 2020), there are two points I would like to make about this agnosticism. Firstly, I believe research findings such as those which involved people who gave their time so freely, generously and openly should at the very least (and this is a relatively low bar but nonetheless an important starting point for researchers) be shared directly with those same people at the earliest opportunity and that this

Introduction 7

should take priority over compiling what are often predominantly academic outputs (such as the book you are reading). The primary data in this book was collected mostly between 2014 and 2017 and, I am pleased to say, the findings were presented at a participatory workshop entitled 'Making Sense of the Past in the Present' at the Foundation for Peace in Warrington in November 2019. This event and many related communications with its participants were key in affirming earlier interpretations of the data and in shaping the arguments put forward in this book.

Secondly, misgivings one may have at times about relatively grandiose ideals of representing 'reality' as best we can may easily, though inappropriately, seem dismissive of survivors. Put another way, survivors' experiences and the academic task of describing survivors' experiences in our research outputs are often sadly far from one and the same. This is not to acknowledge that many academics are survivors who also write about their experiences, including through participatory action research where original experiences and their dissemination ARE more mutually inclusive, nor is it to argue that we actually attempt to separate who we are as people from our participants. A compassionate politics requires the contrary. But my concern in these introductory remarks is simply to emphasise that our findings should be methodologically 'scrutinizable', regardless of their sensitivity. This links to the first point – a set of findings that have been first presented back to participants as soon as is practicable after their collection, prior to publication, seems more open, ethically speaking, to free critique. This sense of 'doing right' by participants is not without its issues but it does make a case that early dissemination of our interpretations to our participants, in turn, adds methodological rigour by allowing us to treat such data as accurate, transparent and *relatively* comprehensive (though see McGowan and Cook, 2020) as far as its collection is concerned which renders any subsequent critique surely more robust.

Finally, and more fundamentally, is a concern over how reliant we are becoming, particularly through ostensibly critical spaces within disciplines and sub-disciplines such as politics, sociology, criminology, victimology, human geography, international relations, among many others, on the seemingly unbridled sense of epistemic virtue often problematically attributed to the panacea of 'lived experiences'. This inexorable rise has not been helped, arguably, by social science's mass turn in recent decades to what is typically termed 'narrative analysis' (Riessman, 1993, 2008; Elliott, 2005). As a book both motivated and supported in large part by narrative, by stories, it might seem odd to begin with such a cautionary and even scornful comment. But there is sometimes confusion here. 'Narrative analysis' implies a thoroughgoing method of investigation ('the analysis' part), but often reveals itself to be an empirical object of interest ('the narrative') for the analyst. Certainly this book, in the main, tends heavily towards the latter, providing only ideal typical themes (Psathas, 2005, see also Methodological Appendix) from broader transcribed interview narratives, rather than a sustained analysis of the narrative form such interviews took (as might be found in conversation analysis, linguistics, or some critical discourse analysis, for example). Nevertheless, the following sentiments of philosopher Rick Roderick (1993) in his now-classic *The Self Under Siege* lecture series provide a useful description of what is deemed interesting and significant about narratives for my purposes here:

> I'd like to argue in a strong sense that every one of us has some kind of theory of what we are as a person. Now by that I don't mean a really highly developed theory like one in quantum mechanics or anything like that. I may only mean a narrative story, something that connects, or attempts to connect, the various, disconnected episodes in our lives, something that gives us a reason to think we are the same person today that we were yesterday in some important sense, even if that sense only means that you've still got the same driving license. In some way we want to have a narrative about our lives, about ourselves. We want them to mean something, in short.

This presents quite a broad, but coherent, sketch of what we might mean when we talk about narratives. Note, however, that Roderick says nothing of 'lived experience', or of the relationship between the narratives we use to navigate life events and the facticity of those events. Nor does he say that we can use narratives to grasp some sense of ontological reality in others. I use narratives and imply certain 'lived experiences' from them with these omissions firmly in mind.

I also urge readers working with 'narratives' and who elevate 'lived experience' to an almost sacrosanct epistemic status to bear two related problems in mind. Firstly, there is often a close alignment made between 'lived experience' and discourses of self-help, including 'resilience', which do not automatically disempower but which often rely on negative freedoms and individualised approaches to empowerment. Secondly, methodologically, I do not think that we can use this kind of data in order to make ontological claims equivalent to, or even reliably representative of, survivors' firsthand experiences (McGowan, 2019; McGowan and Cook, 2020). To claim we can is an epistemological fallacy but one which nevertheless goes unchallenged in much social research drawing on narratives or their analysis. Rather, these survivors' perspectives are presented in relation to particular projections of what can or cannot, or rather what do and do not, appear to constitute 'resilience' in popular and political imaginaries contemporarily.

Structure of the Book

Part I Resilience as Discourse and Practice

In pursuing the lines of enquiry alluded to above, Part I of the book, 'Resilience as Discourse and Practice', lays the foundations for such an analysis. Chapter 1 sets the scene of the 'terror–trauma–resilience' nexus in the 21st century. Taking

Introduction 9

an already ample and valuable genealogical literature on resilience as a point of departure (see, *inter alia*, Walker and Cooper, 2011; Joseph, 2013; Evans and Reid, 2014; Zebrowski, 2016; Michelsen, 2017; Bourbeau, 2018), it focuses attention more specifically on the ubiquity of resilience in relation to PVT in what we might dub the 'Civil Contingencies era' (particularly since the early 2000s). While 'resilience' is frequently paired, implicitly and explicitly, with various antonyms across different areas of social policy, 'trauma' is frequently invoked – clinically and culturally – in the aftermath of terrorist attacks. Whether 'resilience' and 'trauma' represent true binary opposites remains a moot point and is not the focus of the chapter. Rather, it is argued that contemporary discourses of resilience have attempted to foster some sort of collective identity at communal and national levels (*qua* Bean, Keränen and Durfy, 2011) against the backdrop of collective trauma (*qua* Alexander, 2012) – both real and imagined. In addition to this declared stoicism, which as the chapter shows has also been written into critical incident recovery and counterterror preparedness legislation, a large and diverse corpus of work has studied the propensity of individuals who have been exposed to critical incidents such as terror attacks to recover and respond 'resiliently'. Taking these heterogeneous approaches seriously, it is argued that psychology's relative monopoly on empirical studies of such victimisation – coupled with an abundance of theoretical and polemic exchanges about resilience discourse, which fail to observe practical specificity – leave a noticeable lacuna for sociologically informed narrative research to fill.

Before subjecting questions of resilience to this closer empirical scrutiny, Chapter 2 asks how, why, and where we might study survivors of PVT. Addressing these issues, respectively, the chapter provides a way of traversing the vast and complex definitional terrain of PVT. It then argues that victims and survivors of such violence represent important actors with regrettably intimate vantage points from which to reflect directly on the experience of feeling, witnessing or suffering PVT and its aftermath. Despite this, they are often selectively overlooked in both mainstream political discourse and 'critical' studies of PVT where their views or narratives may be unpalatable to the prevailing or aspirational worldviews of relevant actors, including political elites. Connecting this chapter with the first, it is argued that the philosophical ideas of Ian Hacking (2002, 2004) concerning language, action and historically dynamic ontology offer valuable provocations for thinking about resilience from a number of simultaneous angles.

Part II Turning Points and Processes of Resilience

Part II of the book, 'Turning Points and Processes of Resilience', leaves the world of theorising, policy mantras and methodology momentarily behind in order to focus on the voices of survivors themselves. Of course, staying true to the principles outlined above, none of these things truly *can be* left behind. They shape and mould the very context in which such voices were solicited. Those voices, after all, were solicited by me. But the chapters that sit there speak far less ambiguously about the matter at hand than I ever could. Chapter 3 is the first of these chapters, predominantly driven by qualitative in-depth interview data, which are written and structured in a way that aims to give maximum voice and space to the narratives of participants from the original study. This chapter specifically maps out some of the major impacts of PVT as articulated by survivors themselves. This includes a range of direct impacts on individual survivors, including physical injuries and their manifestation over time, short-term emotional responses such as anger, and the bereavement and grief experienced by those who have lost loved ones. The chapter also documents the indirect impacts experienced by survivors and their families, such as the longer-term emotional responses of fear, anxiety and hypervigilance, lasting consequences for personal relationships, and the challenge of unwanted media attention. While this reads as a standalone chapter, it also 'sets up' the question of how survivors have negotiated these harms and challenges.

Exploring the supposed character of resilience mooted in Chapter 1, yet here supported with more practical and empirical specificity, Chapter 4 presents the main sources of support, strength and coping mechanisms – in short, the major 'resilience resources' (Overland, 2013: 204) – harnessed by survivors as they have traversed the impacts highlighted in the previous chapter. This includes a heterogeneous mix of individual character and outlook, economic factors such as victim compensation, communal support systems such as religion and solidarity with fellow survivors, and practice-oriented support strategies including therapy and counselling, peace and reconciliation activities, and indeed engagement with the Foundation for Peace charity. This chapter makes good a significant gap in the existing literature by contributing its findings against a surprising dearth of empirical studies focused on practices of resilience among survivors of PVT.

Recurring attention is drawn to the issue of temporality within both social policy discourses around resilience and critical social science literatures deconstructing them. As Chapter 1 explained, the former tends to project and foster an imagined preparedness to catastrophic future adversity, which the latter often point to for examples of responsibilisation and the reaffirmation of liberal self-sufficiency in the face of dwindling State welfare and social solidarity. Valuable as these critiques are, they tend to focus rather narrowly on resilience as a discourse of futurity. Widening this focus from imagined future catastrophe to include actual harms rooted in the past and permeating the present is a central and recurring aim of the book. As such, Chapter 5 explores some of the temporal differences evident between participants, how and why certain survivors seem to articulate their experiences in more or less retrospective or prospective ways, and some of the drivers underpinning these differences. This includes whether violence was perpetrated 'from above' (as in the case of Bloody Sunday in Derry, for example) or 'from below' (as in the case of 7/7, for example) in terms of State involvement, whether these events were afforded clear and transparent inquests, the role of justice and peace campaigning, and how injuries and memories of events from the past intermingle with everyday activities in the present to produce different temporal 'shapes' to survivors' outlooks.

Recognising the difficulty and potential reductionism of bringing all individual narratives to the fore thematically, this chapter considers the issue of temporality – an area both underexplored empirically in existing studies of resilience and of great significance within the data – by presenting two comparably in-depth, ideal-typical case studies from the interview sample. This affords the reader a deeper insight into the lives of Anne and Kevin, a couple whose daughter Lauren was killed by a suicide bomber on the London underground on 7 July 2005, and Chandani, who survived a car bomb explosion outside a London department store in December 1983. Ostensibly, while Anne and Kevin have reached a point in their journey since losing Lauren where they now refuse to dwell on the past, Chandani has had to confront, and been confronted by, the past as an inevitable consequence of changes to her practical, everyday lifestyle – changes often beyond her immediate control.

These two cases illustratively represent distinct poles in a collection of narratives about traumatic memories. They are presented as such, not to suggest mutual exclusivity or one-directionality, but rather to give some impression of scale between discrete empirical cases (Psathas, 2005: 156). In delving into a smaller number of cases in greater depth and detail, this chapter explores survivor's 'testimony as data' (McGarry and Walklate, 2015) in a way that evocatively and vividly impresses both the long-term deleterious impacts of, and ongoing variegated responses to, the harms of PVT through a closer engagement with survivor's biographies.

Part III Repurposing Resilience

Part III of the book makes the circular journey from the narrative data back into the crowded and noisy milieu of 'resilience' sketched out in Part I, where academics, policymakers, clinical therapists, and politicians fight it out across eponymous terrain. Chapter 6 returns to some of the gaps highlighted and questions posed in Chapter 1 in light of the preceding analysis. It argues that greater attention be given to the interconnected issues of temporality, resistance, and solidarity for anyone wanting to make better sense of how 'resilient survivors' and 'resilient communities' – whatever they are; whatever we deem them to be – become constituted through the diverse mix of discursive naming, on the one hand, and the actions of those subjects in question, on the other. In short, returning to Hacking (2002), how they are made up; what is it that makes them up?

From Chapter 1, readers will recall that resilience is typically understood as a prospective or future-oriented phenomenon within both security-based policymaking and, concomitantly, theoretical critiques of resilience as

12 Introduction

a governmental logic of social control and responsibilisation. This seemingly inevitable and linear framing of temporality is rendered more complex when considered against the backdrop of participants' narratives. Following this discussion, attention is turned to resistance, contestation and anger – a primary emotion among those reported by participants within previous chapters. In particular, the claim that resistance and resilience are necessarily antithetical to one another is revisited and problematised in light of that analysis.

Finally, Hacking's (2002) guiding notion of 'making up people' is employed to consider a more dynamic way in which we might understand the constitution of 'community' than is often envisaged in much of the resilience literature. 'Community' is a central concept around which policymaking ideals of 'resilience' are applied. This application intensified in the UK under the 'Big Society' agenda of the 2010 government (Mythen and McGowan, 2018: 373) and has been a discursive answer to growing levels of economic exclusion, precarity, and insecurity ever since. Yet community, as with the issues of time and emotional solidarity, often receives only cursory or taken-for-granted engagement in this context, which, it is argued, produces a simplistic rendering and reductive account of power. Recent examples of how the kinds of resilience talked about in Chapter 1 have been enacted in practice, both real and imagined, can be seen in relation to a whole host of diverse phenomena through groups and movements such as the Manchester Bee, Survivors Against Terrorism, #JeSuisCharlie, among countless others, as well as commonly reported simulated terror attack training in public spaces around the world, all engaging in their own way some projected vision of shared morality and collective effervescence. To step away from PVT for a moment, the global COVID-19 pandemic of course furnishes a whole range of examples of its own when it comes to adversity, uncertainty, material inequalities, and the associated production of 'resilience' (both real and imagined). These all, in their own ways, some driven by love, solidarity, and common experience, others driven by division, suspicion, and retreat, represent the stuff of so-called resilient communities. Reflecting on the data analysed and commenting further on the Foundation for Peace as a 'resilient survivor community' case study, the issues of time, emotional solidarity, and community, considered collectively, produce a more complex and fluid picture than one inferred from comparatively prescriptive accounts of resilience. In working through these interconnected points of critique, this chapter contributes to growing and emergent debates around resilience and time (see Schott, 2015), the political status of resilience vis-à-vis resistance (see Michelsen, 2017), and resilience and community (see Wright, 2016; Zebrowski and Sage, 2017).

Rather than representing the same themes discussed in previous data-led chapters, Chapter 7 extrapolates the implications those themes and data have for how resilience is framed and understood in the context of trauma, harm, victimisation, and recovery. This underscores the real diversity of how people may respond to serious harm and bereavement, giving useful direction to researchers and practitioners alike. Participant's understandings of overcoming or negotiating adversity are grouped into five main categories. These categories are not the specific sources of support described in previous chapters but rather predominant or overriding ways in which overcoming adversity was framed. These categories include resilience as: (1) *Reformulations of Self or Experience*; (2) *Group solidarity*; (3) *Tacit peer support*; (4) *Transcending the past*; and (5) *Resisting injustice*. Each coheres in different ways with a range of impacts of political violence described in Chapter 3 and the sources of support covered in Chapter 4 but each are amalgamations of participant narratives, observations made during fieldwork, and iterative readings of the data vis-à-vis the resilience literature (Tavory and Timmermans, 2014). While Chapters 3–5 present the data analysis of participants' direct personal experiences ('the specific'), the understandings of resilience presented in Chapter 7 result from comparative and conceptual grouping ('the general'). Responding to Anderson (2015), the 'specific' and 'general' referred to here refer to the direct 'objects' of study versus the 'idea' of resilience as contested by a range of policymakers and academics, respectively (*qua* Hacking, 1997).

The second half of this chapter turns our attention to the thorny question of victim-centred policymaking, including the potential policy-relevance of critical studies of PVT and the perennial risk of political co-option this carries. Following this discussion, which clarifies the conditions upon which policy engagement occurs, it highlights six key recommendations for policymakers and practitioners to focus on, directly based on the findings of the present and preceding chapters. These centre on: (1) *A Duty of Care for the Media*; (2) *Information Sharing Among Emergency Services*; (3) *Languages of Recovery within Victim Support Policy*; (4) *Victim Compensation*; (5) *Fostering Survivor Solidarity and Peer Support Programmes*; and (6) *Coroners and Inquests*. Several of these findings speak to prominent issues raised in recent reports into events such as the Manchester Arena and Westminster Bridge attacks here in the UK, as well as ongoing developments relating to the Covid-19 public health pandemic, thus drawing out the broader relevance of these findings to events which have occurred since this fieldwork was undertaken.

The final chapter is an important summary of the book, restating the necessity and desire to explore the multiple and contested dimensions to resilience, rather than simply discarding it or focusing myopically on only one of its sides. This has been far from easy. Here the book takes a step away from its subject material and casts an eye back over the research trajectory leading to its culmination. Five years ago, Reghezza-Zitt and Rufat (2015: 201) argued that 'resilience is buzzing to the point of becoming a victim of its own success' and, while it may be odd to think of victimisation as a term of relevance to ideas and concepts themselves, this nevertheless offers useful pause for thinking through the relative place and value of resilience for making sense of real victim's experiences. In addition to reflecting upon not only the experience and, at times, the difficulty of researching a so-called in vogue buzzword (Reghezza-Zitt and Rufat, 2015: xiii) at the height of its political and academic ascendency to date in the

14 Introduction

social sciences, I critically consider whether notions such as harm, coercion, agency, and freedom offer somewhat less ambiguous starting points for thinking through these experiences. This discussion accompanies a reiteration of some of the problems of researching survivors in an environment where talk of both victimisation and trauma are ubiquitous. In doing so, the chapter poses some of the methodological tensions and limitations around (mis)representation. Finally, the book concludes by providing future trajectories to be developed in this area of research which link back to the discussions provided in Chapters 6 and 7.

While discussions in Part III of the book ultimately tie the front and back of the work together, synthesising insights derived from the data presented in the middle chapters of Part II with theoretical issues mapped out at the very start in Part I, each chapter hopefully has something to offer as a standalone read. The book does not necessarily have to be read in the order it is written and hopefully I have sufficiently signposted links with earlier and later chapters for readers to easily navigate the work in a way that best makes sense to them. To aid this even further and hopefully provide greater transparency to my work, I have also included a Methodological Appendix chapter at the end of the book which contains, among other things, more information about my research questions, fieldwork, some reflections on the ethical considerations associated with the project, and some brief 'pen portraits' of my participants and the circumstances leading them to the Foundation. This will be particularly useful, I think, for readers working their way through the interview data presented in Chapters 3–5.

My greatest hope, regardless of the conceptual significance made here or there, to this or that aspect of the field and its ongoing research into resilience, is that I have fairly represented the voices of the survivors who relayed their experiences to me, giving their time so generously. Without their time, enthusiasm, and critical insights, I would never have come to ask the kinds of questions that I have over time. Whether I have satisfactorily answered them remains a moot point and, of course, the many and varied faults within the work are my own.

References

Alexander, J.C. (2012) *Trauma: A Social Theory*. Cambridge: Polity Press.

Anderson, B. (2015) What kind of thing is resilience? *Politics* 35(1): 60–6.

Bean, H., Keränen, L. and Durfy, M. (2011) 'This is London': Cosmopolitannationalism and the discourse of resilience in the case of the 7/7 terrorist attacks. *Rhetoric & Public Affairs* 14(3): 427–64.

Bonanno, G.A. (2012) *George Bonanno: Measuring human resilience*. Available at: www.youtube.com/watch?v=M-W7wJlB6Y8 [Accessed 03/04/2019].

Bourbeau, P. (2018) A genealogy of resilience. *International Political Sociology* 12(1): 19–35.

Cavelty, M.D., Kaufmann, M. and Kristensen, K.S. (2015) Resilience and (in)security: Practices, subjects, temporalities. *Security Dialogue* 46(1): 3–14.

Chandler, D. (2014) *Resilience: The Governance of Complexity*. London: Routledge.

Elliott, J. (2005) *Using Narrative in Social Research: Qualitative and Quantitative Approaches*. London: Sage.

Evans, B. and Reid, J. (2014) *Resilient Life: The Art of Living Dangerously*. Cambridge: Polity Press.

Evans, B. and Reid, J. (2015) Exhausted by resilience: Response to the commentaries. *Resilience: International Policies, Practices and Discourses* 3(2): 154–9.

Hacking, I. (1995) *Rewriting the Soul: Multiple Personality and the Sciences of Memory*. Princeton, NJ: Princeton University Press.

Hacking, I. (1997) Taking bad arguments seriously. *London Review of Books* 19(16): 14–16.

Hacking, I. (2002) *Historical Ontology*. Cambridge: Harvard University Press.

Hacking, I. (2004) Between Michel Foucault and Erving Goffman: Between discourse in the abstract and face-to-face interaction. *Economy and Society* 33(3): 277–302.

Hacking, I. (2007) Kinds of people: Moving targets. *Proceedings of the British Academy* 151: 285–318.

Humbert, C. and Joseph, J. (2019) Introduction: The politics of resilience: problematising current approaches. *Resilience: International Policies, Practices and Discourses* 7(3): 215–23.

Joseph, J. (2013) Resilience as embedded neoliberalism: A governmentality approach. *Resilience: International Policies, Practices and Discourses* 1(1): 38–52.

McGarry, R. and S. Walklate. (2015) *Victims: Trauma, Testimony and Justice*. London: Routledge.

McGowan, W. (2016) Critical terrorism studies, victimisation, and policy relevance: compromising politics or challenging hegemony? *Critical Studies on Terrorism* 9(1): 12–32.

McGowan, W. (2019) Performing atrocity: Staging experiences of violence and conflict. In R. Lippens and E. Murray (Eds.) *Representing the Experience of War and Atrocity*. Cham: Palgrave Macmillan. pp.203–25.

McGowan, W. and Cook, E.A. (2020) Comprehensive or comprehensible experience? A case study of religion and traumatic bereavement. *Sociological Research Online* DOI: 10.1177/1360780420978662.

Michelsen, N. (2017) On the genealogy of strategies: Resilience in the revolution. *Resilience: International Policies, Practices and Discourses* 5(1): 61–77.

Mythen, G. and McGowan, W. (2018) Cultural victimology revisited: Synergies of risk, fear and resilience. In S. Walklate (Ed.) *Handbook of Victims and Victimology*, 2nd edition. London: Routledge. pp.364–78.

Overland, G. (2013) *Post Traumatic Survival: The Lessons of Cambodian Resilience*. Newcastle upon Tyne: Cambridge Scholars Publishing.

Psathas, G. (2005) The ideal type in Weber and Schutz. In M. Endress, G. Psathas and H. Nasu (Eds.) *Explorations of the Life-World: Continuing Dialogues with Alfred Schutz*. Dordrecht: Springer. pp.143–69.

Reghezza-Zitt, M. and Rufat, S. (2015) *Resilience Imperative: Uncertainty, Risks and Disasters*. Oxford: Elsevier.

Riessman, C.K. (1993) *Narrative Analysis*. California: Sage.

Riessman, C.K. (2008) *Narrative Methods for the Human Sciences*. London: Sage.

Roderick, R. (1993) *Rick Roderick on the masters of suspicion*. Available at: www.youtube.com/watch?v=4wetwETy4u0&list=PLA34681B9BE88F5AA&index=1&t=3s [Accessed 28/06/2021].

Ruggiero, V. (2006) *Understanding Political Violence: A Criminological Analysis*. Maidenhead: Open University Press.

Schott, R.M. (2015) 'Not just victims … but': Toward a critical theory of the victim. In H. Marway and H. Widdows (Eds.) *Women and Violence: The Agency of Victims and Perpetrators*. Basingstoke: Palgrave Macmillan. pp.178–94.

Tavory, I. and Timmermans, S. (2014) *Abductive Analysis: Theorizing Qualitative Research*. Chicago: The University of Chicago Press.

Walker, J. and Cooper, M. (2011) Genealogies of resilience: From systems ecology to the political economy of crisis adaptation. *Security Dialogue* 42(2): 143–60.

Walklate, S., McGarry, R. and Mythen, G. (2014) Searching for resilience: A conceptual excavation. *Armed Forces & Society* 40(3): 408–27.

Wright, K. (2016) Resilient communities? Experiences of risk and resilience in a time of austerity. *International Journal of Disaster Risk Reduction* 18: 154–61.

Zebrowski, C. (2016) *The Value of Resilience: Securing Life in the 21st Century*. London: Routledge.

Zebrowski, C. and Sage, D. (2017) Organising community resilience: An examination of the forms of sociality promoted in community resilience programmes. *Resilience: International Policies, Practices and Discourses* 5(1): 44–60.

Part I

Resilience as Discourse and Practice

Chapter 1

Setting the Scene of the 'Terror–Trauma–Resilience' Nexus in the 21st Century

This chapter begins by framing resilience discourse as a response to recent terror attacks, something Bean, Keränen and Durfy (2011) suggest has attempted to idealise and foster a sense of 'cosmopolitan nationalism' since the 2005 attacks in London. It then shows how resilience has also become a central feature of contemporary counterterrorism policy, critical incident recovery, and disaster management preparation. Cognisant of the volume of psychological 'resilience research', such as Bonanno's cited in the introduction to this book, the chapter subsequently considers how this research has positioned resilience in relation to the more established psychological lens of trauma. Doing so is not merely to contrast styles of reasoning inherent within each perspective, but rather to take seriously the notion that people frequently display a seemingly innate, natural ability to cope after adverse events or to withstand severe shocks to their lifeworlds. It considers this literature with the assumption that, notwithstanding undoubtedly important methodological discrepancies in the definition and measurement of resilience, such phenomena nevertheless surely exist. We see examples of such seemingly impossible, innate strength, whether in relation to illness, natural disasters or indeed high-profile terror attacks often enough for us to know this to be the case. Whether people should be implored to respond 'resiliently' (*qua* Furedi, 2008), or indeed whether resilience acts as an insidious neoliberal metaphor as has again been recently argued, for example, in relation to the international community's response towards Palestine (Browne, 2018), are important though well-trodden avenues of critique. Instead, the chapter finally considers the issue of temporality, which is frequently positioned within resilience literatures as characterised by an 'always-already' episteme (Aradau, 2014) and discourse of futurity (Schott, 2015). It also considers the suggestion that resilience has come to replace risk as the new governing rationality of public and private security. Taken together, these distinct 'angles' on resilience all contribute to a more complex, better informed, picture of this stretchy concept (Walklate, McGarry and Mythen, 2014: 410) than if we were to focus solely on one aspect of it, highlighting a series of questions and points of departure to explore in later chapters.

DOI: 10.4324/9781003154020-3

20 Resilience as Discourse and Practice

Declared Resilience in the Face of Terror and Trauma: An Ascendant Relationship?

> With your permission, Mr Speaker, I would like to make a statement on last Thursday's terrorist attacks in London. The number of confirmed dead currently stands at 52; the number still in hospital 56, some severely injured. The whole house, I know, will want to state our feelings strongly. We express our revulsion at this murderous carnage of the innocent. We send our deep and abiding sympathy and prayers to the victims and their families. We are united in our determination that our country will not be defeated by such terror but will defeat it and emerge from this horror with our values, our way of life, our tolerance and respect for others, undiminished. I would also like us to record our heartfelt thanks and admiration for our emergency services. Police, those working on our underground, buses and trains, paramedics, doctors and nurses, ambulance staff, firefighters and the disaster recover teams, all of them can be truly proud of the part they played in coming to the aid of London last Thursday and the part they continue to play. They are magnificent. As for Londoners themselves, their stoicism, resilience, and sheer undaunted spirit were an inspiration and an example. At the moment of terror striking, when the eyes of the world were upon them, they responded and continue to respond with a defiance and a strength that are universally admired.
>
> Tony Blair, House of Commons speech, 11th July
> 2005 (Blair, 2005)

Events such as 7/7 and the speeches that followed are often cited as important discursive moments, particularly by critical scholars working with constructivist methodologies broadly conceived (Jenkins, 2003; Jackson, 2005; Croft, 2006), where it is possible to witness and deconstruct narrative construction in action. There is obviously more to resilience than the claims of politicians, but speeches such as the one above by former Prime Minister Tony Blair provide a useful and intriguing point of departure. Holland and Jarvis (2014) emphasise the important temporal and commemorative function such narratives serve for the public at large. Speeches following events such as 9/11 and 7/7 continue to be cited by scholars framing a range of studies including temporality and the war on terror (WOT) (Jarvis, 2009) and the genealogy of resilience (Zebrowski, 2016). Despite their usefulness in this regard, we must be cautious when placing unique importance on these events. Ideals of 'Keeping Calm and Carrying On' or the infamous 'British stiff upper lip' cast our minds back to at least the First and Second World Wars and even earlier, although the extent to which such mantras reflect some innate sense of Britishness, or whether they were simply wartime propaganda, remains contested.

Political elites have long attempted to affix a sense of unbreakable spirit to nations in the aftermath of great traumas. Similarly, attempts at counternarrative

The Terror–Trauma–Resilience Nexus 21

have a long history, particularly from anti-war activists. Pat Mill's well-known comic strip *Charley's War*, published between the late 1970s and early 1980s, is an excellent example of this movement, which tried to portray the sobering realities of war and violence – the antithesis of elite discourse both during the World Wars and since. Whether resilience explicitly emerged as an elite alternative to 'Keep Calm and Carry On'-style rhetoric or not is a moot point. Focusing specifically on its discursive deployment in the immediate aftermath of terror attacks, however, 7/7 certainly marked a point at which resilience discourse coalesced with material shifts in the organisation of counterterror and security policy (Bean, Keränen and Durfy, 2011). The next section of this chapter looks more closely at these policies. First though, it is worth considering the deployment of resilience following 7/7 in more detail.

Bean, Keränen and Durfy (2011) argue that in the days, weeks, and months following 7/7:

> […] as an articulation that reveals peoples' anxieties, projections, and desires […] resilience became a site of struggle wherein national identity, historical memory, and the spectre of violence were marshalled, revisited, and revised in ways that cultivated particular responses to the attack. […] these responses, although not uniform, nevertheless encoded particular security predispositions that further enabled the broader adoption of resilience within official U.K. – and more recently, U.S. – security policy.

They go on to describe how 'a people' were activated in a time of great crisis. They identify Blair's use of resilience cited above, as well as reference to the resilience of Londoners by Prince Charles after he visited survivors in hospital. They also draw together a range of references to resilience or phraseology synonymous with resilience discourse in the media (see also McGreavy, 2016). These sources, for Bean, Keränen and Durfy (2011), evidence the presentation (whether real or imagined) of a collective subjectivity of Londoners, the activation of a British identity rooted in the Blitz spirit discussed above, and an illusory freedom granted to Londoners in which interruptions to economic life were minimalised by imbuing citizens with a proud sense of 'bouncing back'. They usefully highlight that fears and, in some cases, racist retaliation following the attacks were successfully marginalised, lest they complicate the prevalent discourse of Britain as a resilient nation in which ordinary, innocent people simply returned to 'business as usual' and 'got on with the job'.

Out of this collective wave of solidarity, Bean, Keränen and Durfy (2011) argue, came a range of security policy implications that rode the coattails of this 'resilient British identity'. This was mobilised, they argue, through the activation of a 'cosmopolitan nationalism' which they define as 'a political order that generally supports "universal", "progressive", or "cosmopolitan" values, yet translates those values into a distinctly nationalist vernacular to facilitate their codification into law or official state policy' (2011: 429). Older categories of

22 Resilience as Discourse and Practice

risk and security at local levels, such as physical borders, become less important than globally linked networks, necessary for neoliberalism to operate. The discourse of resilience, then, promotes not so much calls for human rights and protection as 'international market moving' (Bean, Keränen and Durfy, 2011: 454). Their thesis chimes with that of Naomi Klein (2007), whose *Shock Doctrine* shows how major policy upheavals often follow in the wake of great disasters or national crises when populations are too physically and emotionally distressed and distracted to effectively resist their introduction. This sense of rupture, in the case of terrorism, has also enabled the portrayal of exceptional threats which in turn warrant exceptional responses (Agamben, 2005). While their analysis of risk and globalisation neatly dovetails Beck's (1992) risk society, Bean, Keränen and Durfy (2011: 455) acknowledge the importance of Benedict Anderson's (2006) work on nationalism in *Imagined Communities*, providing a provocative and useful starting point for thinking through the policy legacies of 7/7.

Recourse to resilience was reiterated in similar ways more recently following the tragic Manchester Arena bombing and terror attacks in London in 2017. A review by Lord Kerslake into the response to the Manchester Arena attack refers to 'resilience' no fewer than 106 times (The Kerslake Report, 2018). During her Christmas Day speech, the Queen reflected on her hospital visit to meet with survivors of the attacks, describing the opportunity to meet with them 'as a "privilege" because the patients I met were an example to us all, showing extraordinary bravery and resilience' (Gripper, 2017). The Archbishop of Canterbury Justin Welby echoed these sentiments a week later in his New Year Day's message, with the threat and consequences of terrorism featuring centrally. The attacks in Borough Market, which left eight people dead, as well as the Manchester attack and other notable tragedies of 2017 including the Grenfell Tower fire, prompted the following reflections from the Archbishop (Welby, 2018):

> When things feel unrelentingly difficult, there are often questions which hang in the air: Is there any light at all? Does anyone care? Every Christmas, we hear from the Bible in the Gospel of John the extraordinary words, 'The light shone in the darkness and the darkness has not overcome it'. We see this light in the resilience of Borough Market. Today it is as crowded as ever and the people who work there are vibrant and welcoming.

Events of such magnitude repeatedly produce collective shows of solidarity. Community groups in Manchester and London were particularly active following the 2017 attacks, as were online 'communities'. They enacted resilience in the form of street clear ups, poetry readings and through symbolic imagery such as the widely recognised Manchester bumblebee which now appears on social media, merchandise, and frequently as a tattoo design. As we might expect, such activity is heightened in the short to medium term following

The Terror–Trauma–Resilience Nexus   23

such events, particularly among those who were present more than those who witnessed from afar via television, and is then intermittently reactivated over time through commemorative ceremonies (Collins, 2004).

How, then, do we reconcile the deployment of resilience within policy on an ongoing basis between such high-profile events during times of relative stability? Talk of resilience in this context requires an actual or envisaged state of harm, vulnerability, or, more likely, *trauma* to which we must respond. As Scheper-Hughes (2008: 37) argues, trauma and our recovery responses to it are inexorably linked within 'master narratives of late modernity as individuals, communities and entire nations struggle to overcome the legacies of mass violence' of all stripes. The trauma of individuals is sometimes said to mirror collective traumas (Neocleous, 2012: 196), as Scheper-Hughes (2008: 37) illustrates:

> The events of 9/11 turned the United States into a nation of trauma victims. The language of 'post-traumatic stress disorder' became part of a national discourse and the label was attached not only to the immediate victims and survivors of the world trade attack, but to those said to be 'traumatized' by televised images of the destruction. Similarly, in the wake of the Oklahoma bombing, victims came to include not only those who suffered the loss of a loved one, but those in the community and beyond who had no personal link to the event but felt that they were 'traumatized' by it in some uncertain way. An Oklahoma psychiatrist, cited by Linenthal (2001: 91) in his study of the memorialization of the bombing, said that trauma 'cases' multiplied in response to the grants funded to study PTSD among survivors. Like the folk syndrome, 'susto' in Mexico or 'nervoso' in Brazil, PTSD became a free-floating signifier of danger, harm, vulnerability and woundedness.

Trauma and our response to it, applied to a group or individual, carries inherently moral judgement (Fassin and Rechtman, 2009; Alexander, 2012). Resilience, with its ideals of self-sufficiency, innate strength, and quintessentially 'Keeping Calm and Carrying On', has come to be 'commonly understood as a resource for coping with trauma and adversity', particularly (within criminology) following terror attacks (Green and Pemberton, 2018: 84). As the discourse surrounding events such as 7/7 and the Manchester Arena bombing among others suggest, responding in this way has been publicly celebrated as the normative benchmark. Thus, recognising moments at which 'trauma narratives' (Walklate, 2016) are mobilised (such as in the aftermath of terror attacks) and that this links with how we frame resilience is an important analytical basis upon which to build, so heavily laden with political and moral judgement is our acceptance (or not) of what it is people should be resilient to and how they should express themselves. Grief is a complicated matter, as is coming to terms with opaque circumstances surrounding a death, making customs and norms for victims of different attacks inherently difficult to predict. Counterterrorism

24 Resilience as Discourse and Practice

policies and related discourses orienting themselves around 'resilience' often avoid this complexity trap altogether.

While it may be accurate to describe resilience as an ascendant concept, it is not necessarily used to describe new phenomena. The policy language associated with resilience has acquired a particularly securitised accent during the WOT, but we should guard against assuming novelty in things that have long histories. This includes actual strength and stoicism in the face of political violence, which has been observed since the Greeks and before. Contemporarily, resilience in the form of *group solidarity* is still widely evident among the collective consciousness of society in the wake of terror attacks irrespective of resilience discourse, as Collins' (2004) distinctly Durkheimian analysis convincingly suggests.

There is also the risk that resilience invites a post-9/11 focus which arguably perpetuates both 'mainstream' and 'critical' terrorism studies' preoccupation with the contemporary WOT (Toros, 2017). The focus here on the so-called Civil Contingencies Era assumes neither the absence of resilience prior to this period nor the homogeneity of historical conflicts. Rather, it was during this period that resilience became an explicit aim of counterterrorism and critical incident recovery. Partly because of this, many civil society organisations, such as the Warrington Peace Centre, have experienced greater demand over time as increasing emphasis was placed on the third sector – a relatively gradual rather than 'overnight' shift, though one nonetheless commensurate with ideals of a 'Big Society' promoted by the Conservative-Liberal Democrat and subsequent governments since 2010. Led by principals of libertarian paternalism, free market economics and voluntarism, resilience thinking flourished during this period (Mythen and McGowan, 2018: 373), in turn changing the accent placed upon security. It is to these developments the chapter now turns.

Securing Resilience: Building 'Bounce-back-ability' into Counterterrorism, Critical Incident Recovery, and Civil Society

The ideals underpinning 'resilience' are well established, having a long history in complex systems theory, ecology, and engineering fields long before it was recognised for becoming ubiquitous in the context of terrorism and security (Walker and Cooper, 2011; Joseph, 2013; Evans and Reid, 2014; Zebrowski, 2016; Michelsen, 2017; Bourbeau, 2018). Often, these fields utilised resilience 'quietly' as a means for experts to describe observable physical or environmental properties such as habitat or flood defence. Zebrowski (2016: 94) offers a useful analysis of the period when resilience began gaining a foothold in the world of national policy during the late-1990s to promote multi-agency responses to complex and opaque 'new security challenges' of the post-Cold War world. Part of this strategy involved the reorganisation of UK Civil Contingencies, which would draw heavily on military developments associated with the Revolution in Military Affairs (RMA). As Zebrowski (2016: 104) explains, former US

The Terror–Trauma–Resilience Nexus 25

Secretary of Defence Donald Rumsfeld was a major advocate of the RMA in the post-9/11 era for promoting virtues of adaptation and resilience alongside more material advances in weaponry, defence budgets, and traditional training (see also O'Malley, 2010).

7/7 provided a major opportunity to usher resilience into security policy, expanding some of the earlier military developments mentioned here into everyday urban landscapes (Coaffee, 2009). One major consequence was increased surveillance. While the Prevent legislation represents the most obvious policy example, the explicit and statutory linking of detection, prevention and recovery dates back further, implicating a panoply of government departments, agencies, local authorities, and employment sectors. The UK Cabinet Office's 2003 definition of resilience was totalising in pitch, emphasising 'the ability at every relevant level to detect, prevent, and, if necessary, to handle and recover from disruptive challenges' (Chappells and Medd, 2012: 307). Reflective of broader shifts in late 20th and early 21st-century governance characterised by preparedness, identification of potential crises, and 'an emphasis on more adaptive forms of demand-side management alongside supply development' (Chappells and Medd, 2012: 307), resilience quickly became a stock policy blueprint. Hence, although the 7/7 attacks in London quickly ushered in the widespread adoption of 'resilience to terrorism', creating 'constraints and possibilities for British national identity and security policy' (Bean, Keränen and Durfy, 2011: 427), the burgeoning policy discourse of resilience in the UK was firmly sandwiched between earlier legislative introductions such as the Civil Contingencies Act 2004 and subsequently the implementation of austerity from 2010 onwards which went even further in mobilising talk of resilience in the public and policy sphere (Mythen and McGowan, 2018: 373).

The elasticity of resilience (Walklate, McGarry and Mythen, 2014: 410) is particularly evident in CONTEST, the UK government's counterterrorism strategy. Within this overarching strategy sit its *Prepare* and *Prevent* strands. Hardy (2015) offers a thorough analysis of resilience within CONTEST, suggesting that it's meaning in each of these two major strands stand diametrically opposed. *Prevent* was the first counter-radicalisation strategy in Europe (or America), which aimed to foster 'community resilience'. Again, its introduction must be understood in relation to the 7/7 bombings (see Heath-Kelly, 2017: 299–300). Citizen awareness of potential sources of radicalisation are encouraged, and now mandated, as university, school, and healthcare system workers are legally required to report any suspicions they may have about students, pupils, patients, or co-workers. This form of 'soft security' sits alongside more typical acts of intelligence gathering and surveillance, military and police actions, and targeted counterterror operations prior to an attack taking place. *Prepare*, on the other hand, was introduced to 'mitigate the impact of a terrorist attack where that attack cannot be stopped' (Home Office cited in Hardy, 2015: 84). The maintenance of essential services, improvement of emergency services, and business continuity plans among private and third sector organisations in the immediate

26 Resilience as Discourse and Practice

aftermath of attacks underpin this strategy. This may be deemed the 'recovery phase', operating at several levels including national, local, and individual, and is geared towards 'maintaining core functions in the face of adversity' (Hardy, 2015: 84). Taking account of the theoretical literature on resilience, including criticisms of it, Hardy (2015) suggests that resilience, as it appears in *Prevent*, may tenuously resemble some characteristics described in the psychological literature. The pre-emptive focus, however, is on resistance to terrorist ideology rather than recovery from specific post-attack stressors. He rightly concludes that resilience within *Prevent* embodies the negative and dangerous forms of responsibilisation highlighted by so many of its critics (see, for example, Joseph, 2013; Neocleous, 2013; Diprose, 2015). Within *Prepare*, however, resilience closely resembles ecological conceptualisations (Holling, 1973) focusing on mitigation of impacts to systems and recovery for individuals and communities after an attack has occurred. In comparison, *Prepare* thus represents a sensible and important set of procedures, aimed at improving the speed and capacity of emergency responders to isolate hazardous materials and get endangered people to safety (Hardy, 2015: 86). Hence, we see resilience being deployed before and after terror attacks but with markedly different emphases and heterogeneous links to existing theory.

Several authors have traced the utilisation of resilience within military regimes and soldier fitness initiatives (O'Malley, 2010; McGarry, Walklate and Mythen, 2015). Bringing this analysis to bear upon the individual, O'Malley (2010: 501) argues that this psychologically driven approach creates a demand for 'warrior' like subjects who are flexible, adaptive, and entrepreneurial – traits commonly associated with neoliberalism (Brown, 2015) – and a replacement of mystifying human conditions by treatable disorders diagnosed by experts in therapeutically guided care settings. This medicalisation is said to have become central to the governance of the individual in contemporary social life (O'Malley, 2010: 491). Here, the authority of the 'psy' disciplines, theologians, and the military all contribute to an expectation of how adaption and recovery in the face of adversity should be valued in a moral sense (O'Malley, 2010; Rose, 1998). There are two key points to consider here in relation to both national resilience discourse and the work of psychologists who have positioned resilience firmly alongside trauma as a useful antonym. Critical theorist Mark Neocleous (2012: 196), who charts the inclusion of resilience in the Civil Contingencies Act 2004 and National Security Strategy 2008, argues:

> By pairing trauma with resilience, the subject's personal anxieties become bound up with the political dangers facing the nation; the trauma is individual and collective, and so the resilience training is the training in and of liberal subjects such that capitalist order might be properly secured.

The most interesting aspect of this claim is the suggestion that subjective, personal anxieties of individuals begin to mirror those of the nation at large. If this seems at first hyperbolic, there would appear to be no shortage of growth in industries providing strategies that not only legitimise these fears and anxieties but also actively promote and materialise their reality in order to prepare individuals for inevitable disaster.

At the intersection between stoic nationalism and declarations of collective resilience highlighted at the beginning of this chapter, and the kind of policy responses described here, the private and voluntary sectors have been proactive in providing (and profiting from) tailored 'resilience solutions'. 'Crisis Cast', for example, is a private limited company that employs role-play actors, film crews, and trained stunt artists to produce 'disaster dramas' for educational purposes. Their team includes a former counterterrorism security advisor from the Metropolitan Police, a Business Continuity lead with direct experience of terror attacks in London, and leading trauma counsellors. A somewhat foreboding strapline of theirs states: *It is our conviction that the near future will bring a requirement for greater realism in live training events.* Tapping into the colonisation of resilience expertise by psychology, their actors are 'specially trained by psychologists in criminal and victim behaviour for crisis management and disaster recovery'. Just as you might want to book tailored IT service training for your organisation or workplace, Crisis Cast 'rehearse and deliver highly credible, immersive crisis events which we can film and supply as interactive training tools'. They can reportedly provide 'up to 400 actors, fully trained and rehearsed along with professional teams that look after make-up, prosthetics, pyrotechnics, wardrobe, special effects, covert and aerial footage'. As they state enthusiastically on their website:

> Large cast or small, our mission is to deliver high adrenaline events to make sure your people are prepared, trained and ready to save lives, with battlefield civilians, foreign language speakers, tribal elders and all the elements of a conflict zone ready go.

In-line with their mantra – 'In a crisis revert to training …' – they offer 'Professionally Developed Crisis Management and Resilience Training for the Education Sector', taking their role play into schools and classrooms (see www.crisiscast.com). The Home Office, G4S, NHS, universities, and various police forces appear on their client list, indicating something of the political and material reach of such widespread 'resilience creep' (Walklate and Mythen, 2015) in recent years.

Irrespective of how paradigmatic particular shifts (to, or from, 'resilience') may or may not have been in recent years, resilience continues to figure in a range of security service protocols, including simulated terror attacks. In October 2017, for example, a three-day national security exercise designed to simulate an attack on the Royal Bank of Scotland's HQ in Edinburgh was performed by security services in consultation with the Home Secretary Amber Rudd. The exercise, aimed at testing 'cross-border' response between emergency services

28 Resilience as Discourse and Practice

in Scotland and England, was overseen by the Cobra emergency response committee in Whitehall and the Scottish government who updated ministers from their dedicated 'resilience room' (Travis, 2017). Similarly in 2016, Greater Manchester Police controversially simulated terror attacks, including in The Trafford Centre shopping precinct, where a team of actors posed as distressed shoppers while a mock suicide bomber shouted 'Allahu Akbar' before detonating an explosive (The Telegraph, 2016).

Despite claims of 'reality simulation', the efficacy of this crisis management logic (to say nothing of its ethics) is debatable. However, readiness, preparedness, and resilience have continued to serve both material and symbolic functions in settings across the public, private, and third sectors, particularly in the post-9/11 period (McConnell and Drennan, 2006). Given its reach, resilience has in turn set benchmarks for third sector organisations reliant on commission-based funding to meet. Organisations keen to secure funding are thus likely to mirror the kind of lexicons available within existing policy, particularly where an emphasis is placed on multi-agency work and collaboration between charities and businesses. As a final point of reflection on the expanse of resilience-based legislation and industry initiatives, what kind of emotional registers are being engaged through the likes of *Prevent* or the more visceral and performative ventures such as 'Crisis Cast'? While this asks how people are perhaps emotionally 'readied' for inevitable disasters, the chapter now turns to the literature focusing on people's responses in and to their aftermath.

Taking 'Resilience' Seriously

This chapter has so far charted some key ways in which discursive appeals to, or proclamations of, resilience have become codified ways in which State departments, non-governmental organisations, media producers, and civil society groups have framed our collective response to terror attacks in recent years. This framing can and does occur at a range of levels, emanating back and forth between the harm of individual victims (both real and imagined) and the locally, nationally, and globally constituted spheres of public life pertinent to questions of (bio)security and geopolitics more broadly (Walklate, McGarry and Mythen, 2014). Having argued that resilience has come to feature centrally within early 21st-century political and security discourse, representing the fulcrum of a range of public policy areas, this chapter now considers how it has been conceptualised and measured in studies of individuals said to be responding 'resiliently'. In order to better understand the substantive and phenomenological characteristics associated with 'resilience', as so-labelled within a plethora of academic research, it turns to just some of the studies which have explored or deployed the term with the serious intention of developing or fleshing it out conceptually and empirically.

Inverted commas around the word resilience and this somewhat cynical-sounding way of describing such studies ('as so-labelled'), many of which are

The Terror–Trauma–Resilience Nexus   29

unified by little more than the word 'resilience' itself, are not used to provocatively group an 'over there' set of studies, nor to encourage cynicism towards them in the reader. Following Hacking (1995, 2002, 2004), naming and classification are taken seriously here and this includes the use of 'resilience' within academic parlance. Due to the ubiquity of 'resilience' vis-à-vis terrorism and security in recent years already alluded to here, the empirical data analysed and discussed later in this book were purposefully gathered in such a way as to minimise the *a priori* naming of 'resilience' where possible. Instead, the data was gathered and analysed in order to see how far, if at all, practices and processes described therein resemble those identified as 'resilience' in policy and prior research. Hence, it matters a great deal how other scholars are deploying the term and what they report to be studying. These epistemological points are returned to in Chapter 2; for now, the use and grammatical presentation of 'resilience' simply denotes heterogeneity and disparate usage – as an exercise in 'taking seriously' existing research and not one of dismissive or obligatory 'ground clearing'.

With these matters clarified and set to one side for the time being, what do we think we know about resilience as empirical phenomena? While numerous disciplines have considered the concept of resilience in counterterrorism policy and discourse, the same trend noted by McGarry, Walklate and Mythen (2015: 355) in relation to military resilience research – namely, that it 'has almost exclusively been the "property" of psychological discourse' – applies to the resilience of political violence survivors. Why this should be the case cannot be adequately captured by bluntly contrasting the epistemological rationales of clinical psychology or psychiatry with that of other social sciences. However, remembering the undeniable twinning of resilience and trauma pointed to earlier (Scheper-Hughes, 2008; Howell, 2012; Green and Pemberton, 2018), the most obvious clue is to be found in clinical models of trauma, most notably the *Diagnostic and Statistical Manual of Mental Disorders* (DSM) which featured the first definition of post-traumatic stress disorder (PTSD) in 1980 and has continued to adapt subsequent classifications. While these classifications do not only change according to clinical factors (see Cooper, 2014 for how they are also shaped by political and financial ones), their measurement and deployment in clinical settings are predominantly guided in policy and practice by the '"psy" disciplines' (Rose, 1998).

In other respects, however, the picture is more mixed and out of the shadow cast by overarching, universal diagnoses of trauma have emerged two important developments concerning our capacity to respond positively to it. Broadly speaking, the first is an appreciation of geography, place, history, and culture in moulding resilience, highlighting more heterogeneous and unpredictable ways of coping and thriving than is suggested in the 'bounce-back-ability' emphases of the policies discussed earlier. For anthropologist Nancy Scheper-Hughes, human resilience means the 'relative immunity from personal and psychological collapse that we have come to associate with exposure to a variety of human

30 Resilience as Discourse and Practice

calamities' (2008: 25), characterised by 'sources of strength, toughness, hardiness, and relative invulnerability' (2008: 37). Importantly for Scheper-Hughes (2008: 36–7), understanding the relationship between 'trauma, vulnerability, and resilience' cannot be divorced from normative (and therefore time-place-culture-specific) exposure to violence and collective responses to it. Hence, she argues:

> For those living in the affluent first world [sic], *crisis is understood as a temporary abnormality linked to a particular event* – the loss of a parent, a sexual trauma, a physical assault, or a natural disaster [...]. In these cases, assuming they represent isolated events, the aftermath of the original trauma, re-lived as a 'traumatic memory', may be worse than the original experience. But for those living in constant crisis and subject to repetitive traumas, and where 'emergency is not the exception but the rule' (Walter Benjamin 1969) the conventional wisdom and understanding of human vulnerability and resilience, especially as codified within the clinical model of post-traumatic stress, is inadequate. (Emphasis added)

Perhaps the most important starting point for contextualising studies of human resilience, then, is at least a recognition that 'what is required to survive and even to thrive where terror and trauma are ordinary and usual events' (Scheper-Hughes, 2008: 37) may not be the same for all survivors of isolated critical incidents. This is an important point and one which is explored in relation to differences within the data between survivors from Northern Ireland and England (see, for example, Chapter 4). Although, contra Scheper-Hughes' juxtaposition of an 'affluent first world [sic]' with 'those living in constant crisis and subject to repetitive traumas', one need only contrast the experiences of children growing up in the 1970s/80s rural England and urban Belfast, for example, or the police officers walking their streets, to find examples of this 'exposure-isolation' distinction operating within much closer proximities. This too is important when contrasting the experiences of participants in this research, some of whom certainly fall into the category of having experienced emergency as the norm rather than the exception.

The second important development, both in academic and (to a lesser degree) clinical settings, has been a conceptual recalibration away from the medicalised pathology of trauma symptoms, instead towards an appreciation of coping and thriving as naturally and predominantly occurring human responses to adversity. As Walklate (2011: 185) argues, resilience exhibits both individual and social dimensions, which we may usefully think of as 'inherent resilience' and 'structural resilience', respectively. Taking account of personal and social dimensions, as Walklate does, is to say something profound about the human condition in a way that makes space for both vulnerability and agency. Others talk of injury (and agency) rather than vulnerability to underscore tangible, rather than potential, harms (Schott, 2013). In this vein, Green and Pemberton (2018: 84) unequivocally state: 'Resilience equals agency'. Expanding on this, they posit that 'Our capacity, or resources, to exercise some control over how we react to injury is our level of resilience'. This vulnerability–agency, or injury–agency, dynamic is reminiscent of Fromm (1995 [1957]: 38) who states:

> even as equals we are not always 'equal'; inasmuch as we are human, we are all in need of help. Today I, tomorrow you. But this need of help does not mean that the one is helpless, the other powerful. Helplessness is a transitory condition; the ability to stand and walk on one's own feet is the permanent and common one.

This idea of a persistent overriding need and the ability to overcome human hardship and achieve existential equilibrium carries connections with Greek Stoicism and the ability to detach ourselves from lasting suffering. Exploring this connection, Wong (2006: 216) observes: 'The notion of embracing the whole and its ceaseless chain of creation and destruction is the broader context within which we might come to understand the possibility of resilience even in the face of great loss'. Contemporarily, promoting resilience as a philosophical framework of ethics in an attempt to imbue individuals with greater personal strength and emotional control have proven popular among corporate sectors, with book titles such as Tom Morris' (2004) *The Stoic Art of Living: Inner Resilience and Outer Results* roundly capturing a profitable literary genre of self-help. While space does not permit a detour easily worthy of a separate book, this link to the self-help industry must be flagged with a reminder that to 'take resilience seriously' is not to assume its character, nor to buy uncritically into deterministic proclamations of what resilience is (as self-help therapies frequently do). The rise in 'resilience as self-help' genre says as much, if not more, about an apparently more esoteric topic: the emergence and place of self and self-help within modernity and its interactions with the individualised human soul (see Rimke, 2000; Illouz, 2008). To join the trauma–resilience dots more fully, such accounts of this interaction must also recognise the 21st-century soul as one itself already individualised in large part by the new 'psy' sciences of memory and trauma starting over a century earlier (Hacking, 1995). This historic link between trauma and resilience is often suggested implicitly, or only referred to contemporarily.

The potential beginnings of a movement away from trauma towards resilience (Howell, 2012) are nonetheless a significant shift. Where PTSD posits 'a hardwired bio-evolutionary script around the experience and aftermath of trauma [...] based on a conception of human nature and human life as fundamentally vulnerable, frail, and humans as endowed with few and faulty defense mechanisms' (Scheper-Hughes, 2008: 37), resilience suggests hardiness, resourcefulness, and strength to prevail and overcome adverse events. That human beings find within themselves the ability to overcome hardship and suffering, as suggested above by Fromm, has prompted a broad set of approaches within clinical and social psychology which place their focus not on harm, vulnerability, injury, or post-traumatic stress, for example, but on recovery, strength, healing, and post-traumatic growth (Almedom, 2005; Westphal and Bonanno, 2007; Levine et al., 2009; Hobfoll et al., 2011). A recent Special Issue of the journal *Traumatology*, for example, brings together 14 articles whose focus is

> on the strengths of people who experience trauma [in order to] document the extraordinary ways in which they meet their challenges and develop new and effective ways of coping. Within these processes of learning to cope there are many important lessons about hope, commitment to health, and thriving.
>
> (McLeary and Figley, 2017: 2–3)

These approaches shift an excessive focus on human frailty and vulnerability, instead studying 'the awesome ability of people […] to withstand, survive, and live with horrible events' – 'not only to survive, but to thrive, during and following states of emergency, extreme adversity, and everyday as well as extraordinary violence' (Scheper-Hughes, 2008: 42).

Similarly, in her study of Cambodian survivors of the Khmer Rouge, Overland (2013: 6) deploys Aaron Antonovsky's work on salutogenic models of health to ask 'not, "why are people sick?" but "why are they healthy"'. Her attempt to set up 'a line of questioning that is salutogenic (health-promoting) as opposed to pathogenic' (Overland, 2013: 6) is again pertinent to the earlier discussion of resilience vis-à-vis trauma and the proclaimed need to move beyond deficit models of human health. Overland's study is disciplinarily eclectic and identifies a range of 'resilience resources' (2013: 204), including individual strength, familial and communal ties, and religious and spiritual practices particular to Cambodian culture. Contra Antonovsky's health model, she found that many of these resources were not centred around 'money' or 'ego strength', and not even in an articulated sense of 'self-understanding' so typical of how we might imagine Western reflexivity to operate. Antonovsky's term 'sense of coherence' was confirmed, however, with Overland's (2013: 205) interpreters making connections between the sense of existential equilibrium hinted at in the long term and more familiar Cambodian understandings of karma. Notably, Overland suggests that 'it may be easier to say what the properties and resources found in this study were *not*, than what they were' (2013: 204, emphasis in original), but that her research 'found no confirmation of expectations that work, or family, or religion as *individual factors* would support resilient recovery' (2013: 206, emphasis in original). Instead, they all contributed in different, but interconnected, ways to produce a 'coherent system of meaning' (Overland, 2013: 206).

Importantly, this interconnection between otherwise isolated resources is reminiscent of both human and non-human strength and adaptability characteristics highlighted within engineering and ecological (Holling, 1973;

The Terror–Trauma–Resilience Nexus   33

Gunderson and Holling, 2002), social ecological (Adger, 2000; Ungar, 2008, 2011, 2013), psychological/social-psychological (Bouvier, 2003; Bonanno, 2004, 2005; Bonanno et al., 2007; Cacioppo, Reis and Zautra, 2011), urban planning (Coaffee, 2009; Coaffee, Wood and Rogers, 2009; Coaffee and Fussey, 2015) and complexity governance (Rosenow, 2012; Chandler, 2014a) research, as well as syntheses of resilience which have drawn on disparate literatures to bottom out some commonality across these diverse fields (Brand and Jax, 2007; Windle, 2011; Davoudi, 2012; Walklate, McGarry and Mythen, 2014). This is certainly apt when referring to communities or groups affected by critical incidents, and the relationship between affected individuals and their respective communities. Interestingly, it is also reminiscent of the mix identified by O'Malley (2010) between the authority of the 'psy' disciplines, spiritual/religious motivation, and the altruism advocated by military training, which all contribute to an expectation of what adaption and recovery in the face of adversity might look like. While some position resilience as opposed, though dialectically related, to trauma, harm, or vulnerability (see, for example, Aguirre, 2007), others argue for a more complex understanding, particularly in relation to clinically diagnosable trauma. As Pfefferbaum et al. (2008: 354) put it, resilience is not merely a collection of individuals with an ability to cope – 'the whole is more than the sum of the parts'. Similarly, Almedom and Glandon (2007) argue that 'resilience is not the absence of PTSD any more than health is the absence of disease'.

Bonanno and colleagues have looked extensively at resilience through large-scale empirical psychological studies, including a sample of people in or near the World Trade Center during the September 2001 terror attacks (Bonanno, Rennicke and Dekel, 2005; Bonanno et al., 2006). Others have analysed responses from injured survivors in Israel (Bleich et al., 2006; Hobfoll et al., 2009). Where all of these studies boast sample breadth, they arguably lack depth and detail; we learn little about how individuals have traversed psychological trauma and adversity, other than at the point of completing a survey where they have reported higher or lower levels of stress. This has enabled scholars to identify phases of symptom trajectories over time, including the 'resilience trajectory', 'chronic distress trajectory', and the 'delayed distress trajectory' (Hobfoll et al., 2009) but offers nothing by way of narrative description by its methodological nature. The generality of these studies is reflective of psychology's focus on quantitative survey methods with empirical data being hailed as the most important and even self-explanatory factor. The quotation from Bonanno discussed in the introduction of this book, stating that 'the word resilience is not really necessary, 'cos this is really an empirical finding' (Bonanno, 2012), is indicative of this attitude which can spill over into other areas of psychology's intellectual 'style'. The complexity of 'terrorism' or its political context is similarly demoted and interchangeable reference is made to adverse events, disaster, critical incidents, and trauma exposure. This can have the effect of rendering over event details in favour of sweeping statements about generally negative

34 Resilience as Discourse and Practice

life experiences, which is again potentially linked to broad survey parameters designed to boost sample sizes. These observations are made not to denigrate such studies or wholly dismiss their usefulness, but rather to more clearly situate them among a panoply of methodological approaches to studying resilience.

While most research measuring resilience empirically has been the preserve of psychology, it has not solely focused on the individual. Williams and Drury (2009: 294) argue that resilience can be fostered at both the individual and the collective level, with the latter referring to the ways in which 'people in crowds express and expect solidarity and cohesion, and thereby coordinate and draw upon collective sources of practical and emotional support adaptively to deal with an emergency or disaster'. Ironically, this resonates with Neocleous' (2012: 196) suggestion that the anxieties of individuals begin to mirror those of the nation at large, albeit without his fundamental political critique. Taking empirical studies of resilience seriously, it is a complex picture. As Walklate, McGarry and Mythen (2014: 419–20) suggest in proposing a typology of resilience: 'Individual resilience may be inherent, learned through experience, or socialized as an institutional process, but it is also critically shaped, mediated, sustained, and revived (when required) by family and community relations'. It is thus also contingent upon different forms of culture. As they also argue, whether one is able to respond favourably to adverse conditions is not only dependent on which of the sources indicated above are available to them (such as personal, familial, and communal support) but also at which level we expect to see people thrive and that can only be reflective of a prior starting point. On this basis, they rightly criticise the kinds of policy frameworks discussed above for assuming a 'resilience deficit' which in turn risks assuming fragile and even traumatised responses to adversity. 'It is this notion of deficit that underpins the desire to *build* resilience' (Walklate, McGarry and Mythen, 2014: 420, emphasis in original) and so the trauma–resilience nexus remains mutually constituted. Despite arguments for and against trauma and resilience respectively and constituently, they are interconnected rather than oppositional (Schott, 2013); Scheper-Hughes (2008: 42, emphasis in original) perhaps strikes the right balance when she writes: 'the construction of humans as resilient and hardy or fragile, passive and easily overwhelmed by events should not be viewed as an either/or opposition. Human nature is both resilient *and* frail'.

Shifts in Temporality: 'Resilience' as Always-Already

The conceptual elasticity of resilience (Walklate, McGarry and Mythen, 2014) presents considerable methodological challenges for researchers trying to determine definitional parameters in their own, and previous, work. As Windle (2011: 153) observes, much research around resilience comprise 'broad-brush' concept analyses, which despite seeking to synthesise and clarify meanings of resilience from a disparate array of literature, fail to adequately set out their inclusion/exclusion criteria. Beyond definitional ambiguity, this is a partial

The Terror–Trauma–Resilience Nexus   35

indicator of how unlimited in scope the concept is often perceived to be, adding weight to the view that resilience can encapsulate the ideals of policymakers in a vast range of sociolegal areas in ways which would have been previously much more difficult (Neocleous, 2013: 4). This arguably overstates the political 'uniqueness' of resilience. As a growing body of critical research attests, resilience is often cast as the most recent articulation in a longer line of neoliberal governance, decentralisation of regulatory powers, and development of 'anticipatory technologies' (O'Malley, 2010: 488), primarily geared towards encouraging individual preparedness in the face of ever increasing socio-economic adversity and uncertainty (Neocleous, 2012; de Lint and Chazal, 2013; Joseph, 2013; Evans and Reid, 2014; Diprose, 2015). This position remains distinctly affiliated to established Foucauldian perspectives around crime and security, posited as responsibilisation or 'social control at a distance' (*qua* Rose, 2000; Garland, 2001), as well as neo-Marxist critiques of capitalism. In both traditional and contemporary iterations of governmentality, the natural milieu occupied by humanity is assumed, implicitly and explicitly, to be the object of precise management by a complex and pervasive plethora of regulatory connections which target not only the population but also '"life" as a whole' (Rosenow, 2012: 541; Evans and Reid, 2014; Foucault, 1991 [1975]). This trend continues to vindicate Furedi's (2008: 646–8) earlier observations in some quarters, with resilience continuing to act primarily as a synonym for emergency planning and risk management – 'a cultural metaphor rather than an analytical concept' (2008: 648). In many ways, it would seem we have been here before – certainly where political rhetoric around counterterrorism, risk, and security are concerned.

Conceptual work around resilience has produced an abundance of speculative judgements concerning ontological and epistemological affect, with several such studies focusing on State governance and the governmental 'logic' underpinning resilience as a political metaphor for more sophisticated and insidious mechanisms of neoliberal social control from a range of critical perspectives (see *inter alia*, Neocleous, 2012; 2013; de Lint and Chazal, 2013; Evans and Reid, 2013; Joseph, 2013; Diprose, 2015; Chandler and Reid, 2016). This is an important body of work serving to remind us that the State should not, and cannot, hold some sort of monopoly over what resilience is or should be. However, to some extent it also assumes the inevitability that individual subjects will internalise discursive framings of vulnerability and succumb to governmental 'technologies of the self'. It also suggests that, taken at the level of policy, resilience is an inherently dangerous and undesirable characteristic. Resilience is deemed to represent an epistemic shift to the governance of 'unknowability' in an increasingly complex world, 'assert[ing] a flatter ontology of interactive emergence' (Chandler, 2014b: 47; Aradau, 2014), in which surprise is embraced and preparedness prescribed. Underscoring this tranche of philosophical thought more explicitly, Evans and Reid (2013: 84) argue that the ontology of resilience *is* vulnerability, stating that: 'To be able to become resilient, one must first accept that

36 Resilience as Discourse and Practice

one is fundamentally vulnerable'. Central to these epistemological and onto-logical arguments is the notion that unlike governance of earlier decades, resilience does not seek to minimise risk and uncertainty but to actively embrace it (O'Malley, 2010: 506). While scientific and political discourse around risk is said to rely on the modelling of a parallel world, one which we can map potential scenarios onto in an effort to calculate likelihoods of harm, resilience is said to present us with an altogether different epistemic regime.

As Aradau (2014) argues, the fact that resilience shifts its focus from problems to solutions means it is far from an astute solution but rather 'a solution to particular problematisations of future events' (2014: 4). The articulation of 'resilience as solution' assumes a taken-for-granted nature of the problem, thus beginning before the event has even occurred, predetermining answers to as-yet-unasked questions. Knowledge comes 'readymade' to borrow Latour's (1987: 4) phraseology. Resilience, for Aradau (2014), operates within an epistemic regime of 'surprise and novelty' which assumes the control of complex or contingent events by embracing their potentiality. She presents this alongside two other epistemic regimes said to represent earlier security discourses and practices. While the 'secrecy and ignorance' of earlier decades relied on the 'smoke and mirror' management of catastrophe (an epistemic regime of knowledge and non-knowledge, of surface and depth), 'risk and uncertainty' later came to present problems as knowable only through probability and statistical modelling, applying questions of knowledge to masses rather than individuals (Aradau, 2014). Again, within this second epistemic regime, surface and depth are replaced by parallel worlds: on the one hand a reality and on the other a model of that reality which assumes the unknowability of individual complexity and instead describes patterned behaviour of broad populations. Aradau's third epistemic regime, in which she places resilience, represents a promise of security by the liberal state which perpetually avails itself to the caveat: 'we may not be able to protect people' (2014: 10). In 2016, this was exemplified when Metropolitan Police Service Commissioner Sir Bernard Hogan-Howe addressed public concerns about the ongoing terror threat after attacks around Europe and the subsequent increase in firearms officers in London. Despite favourably appraising the UK's gun control laws, assuredly suggesting the difficulty of attaining firearms in the UK relative to continental Europe, and describing the relationship between UK police and intelligence agencies as a 'world-beater', Hogan-Howe conceded that a future terrorist attack was inevitable – 'a case of when, not if' (BBC, 2016). Resilience, then, is said to reflect an attempt to capture the world in all its complexity. Hence, epistemically, 'surface and depth' between knowers and non-knowers, and 'parallels' between actual and actuarial realities, give way to an ever-emergent 'flatness'. Within this regime, 'surprise [harm, vulnerability, catastrophe] is inevitable and novelty always already in the making' (Aradau, 2014: 77).

There exist obvious parallels between risk and resilience, not least of all in the shifting logic of security, broadly speaking; a shift which, as Mythen

The Terror–Trauma–Resilience Nexus   37

(2012: 412) suggests in relation to risk, emphasised futurity 'from *post hoc* regulation and towards *pre hoc* intervention' (emphasis in original). The logic of resilience strategies within national security has been understood as an extension of this shift in that catastrophic events are assumed to exist and continue to exist, but a departure from it insofar as promises of prevention are replaced by recommendations for preparation. Conversely, O'Malley's (2010: 505) suggestion that 'risk always calculates on the basis of a past projected into the future' renders the 'newness' of resilience vis-à-vis risk somewhat superficial. While risk and resilience may place greater emphases on prevention and preparation, respectively, placing differing importance on past events, their temporal qualities are not nearly so neatly distinguishable within everyday security practices. As Garland (2001: 168) reminds us in-line with Foucauldian genealogy, when we move from one epoch to the next and are faced with the concomitant shift in discursive paradigms (in this case from risk to resilience), we do not literally leave the past behind: 'History is not the replacement of the old by the new, but the more or less extensive modification of one by the other'. The extent to which resilience is coming to replace risk, as not 'merely' a discursive political tool in the 'war on terror', but as a primary driver behind security policy, remains a moot point. Counterterror and security responses still very much operate within, and continue to rely upon, risk-based logics of prevention and social control. Moreover, the two overlap in important ways. As Ulrich Beck commented in a 2013 interview about European politics:

> We have to make a distinction between a *risk* society and a *catastrophe* society. A catastrophe society would be one in which the motto is 'too late': where we give in to the panic of desperation. A risk society in contrast is about the anticipation of future catastrophes in order to prevent them from happening. But because these potential catastrophes are not supposed to happen – the financial system could collapse, or nuclear technology could be a threat to the whole world – we don't have the basis for experimentation. The rationality of calculating risk doesn't work anymore. We are trying to anticipate something that is not supposed to happen, which is an entirely new situation.
>
> (Beck, 2013)

Risk here signifies an attempt at prevention, whereas catastrophe signifies the need to prepare for inevitable suffering and struggle. It is within this so-called catastrophe society that most theorists locate the pervasive logic of resilience and its attendant temporal dimensions.

These temporal dimensions, discussed above, are interesting on their own terms. Contrasting them with the literature focusing on PTSD and trauma, particularly within psychology, this proclaimed shift in temporal emphasis becomes even more intriguing in relation to survivors of political violence and terrorism. As both a collective sense-making narrative of past events (Alexander, 2012),

38 Resilience as Discourse and Practice

and as a clinical way of individually understanding intrusive symptoms such as hyper-vigilance or flashbacks to a previous event (Herman, 2001), trauma often invokes an inherently retrospective way of narrating human suffering. In this vein, Schott (2015: 186, emphasis added) argues:

> Whereas post-Holocaust discourses have been oriented towards the past – the nature of past crimes, recovery after trauma, and the responsibility of the present for acknowledging past wrongs in order to prevent future atrocities – *the discourse of resilience is a discourse of futurity*.

It is perhaps too simplistic to talk of trauma as retrospective and resilience as prospective. Ian Hacking, who is drawn on in later chapters to make epistemic sense of narrative data, troubles this temporal dichotomy further by talking instead of 'retroactive' narration to describe old actions under new descriptions which 'may be reexperienced in memory' (Hacking, 1995: 249). More nuanced questions around temporality thus require further exploration. Exploring how critical incidents and harms from the past are implicated in the present, including survivors' projections of the future, is key to understanding narratives of managing trauma and the possibility that 'critical moments' or turning points in these narratives could prove significant in the strengthening or challenging of survivors' resilience.

Connecting the centrality of resilience as security discourse to its primacy in therapeutic settings, including at psychological and interpersonal levels, it would be easy to assume that resilience has gained an unchallenged foothold in a range of public and private settings at micro, meso, and macro levels. This is far from the case. Resilience has proven to be one of the most politically divisive concepts within contemporary social science research, receiving strong endorsements and sustained attention from some quarters while being strongly rejected by others. Heuristically, the poles of debate can be positioned as follows:

> By demonstrating that a society is resilient and well prepared for dislocations and shock, with intelligent design and disaster recovery procedures embedded into government and private sector behaviour, the target communities will also be reassured and confident of recovery.
>
> (Gearson, 2012: 191)

> Left unexplored, resilience risks becoming axiomatic and hides broader issues that critical criminology must address, such as how to maintain the dignity and worth of individuals, and how to examine the power and potential harm in social structures suffused with neoliberal ordering.
>
> (de Lint and Chazal, 2013: 172)

Both positions grant resilience an incredible and arguably inordinate amount of power. That certain discursive appeals to resilience from the State occur at the macro level is not in question (see Walklate, Mythen and McGarry, 2012), but current criminological and sociological research has largely failed to pursue the question of resilience empirically, thus overlooking the everyday, experiential 'fissures' of change which may occur within individuals following a traumatic incident(s). Furthermore, energetic as they are, critiques that attack neoliberal constellations of resilience without digging beyond its discourse or examining specific practices (as encouraged by Schott, 2015) risk reifying the very concept they seek to dismantle. The above claims make some interesting assumptions about where the individual may, or may not, appear and act in this envisaged milieu and it is important not to misread them. Most critical theorists drawing attention to the insidious, future-oriented nature of resilience are not claiming that it necessarily reflects the lived experiences of social actors at all times or in all places. Their work often represents a 'call to arms' to resist such logics through practical means, such as a refusal to propagate 'resilience' within the political economy of research publication and dissemination (see, for example, the lively exchange between Mark Neocleous (2013) and David Chandler (Chandler and Neocleous, 2013) in *Radical Philosophy*). Others speak somewhat more abstractly of injecting life back into an envisaged, potential, or actual landscape characterised in different ways by social death and compromised human autonomy (Chandler and Reid, 2016: 99–117).

Nevertheless, to characterise resilience as a strictly future-oriented discourse, encouraging as this does an always-already brace position in preparation to withstand inevitable and unavoidable shocks, is to offer a particular rendering of power and practice.

Conclusion

In making space for a specific empirical line of enquiry into the conditions of victimisation following political violence and terror attacks, this chapter has touched upon a range of related concepts, including trauma, security, and resilience. Focusing predominantly on the latter, it has sketched just some of the many sides to this pervasive concept that continue to provoke polarising endorsement and fierce contestation, particularly where it has been utilised in public policy. Taking a disparate range of these voices seriously, the general characteristics of 'resilience' have been outlined from the perspectives of both its advocates and its critics. However, if we are to arrive at more nuanced understandings of this 'stretchy concept' (Walklate, McGarry and Mythen, 2014: 410), it is important that this is understood merely as a heuristic exercise at this stage. Unlike trauma, the meaning of which has proliferated and morphed quite considerably over a longer period of time within therapeutic practice, resilience may seem to have remained close to its etymological roots, at least as it is used in everyday language. As Bean, Keränen and Durfy (2011: 431) remind us, 'the alluring idea of strength in the face of grave threat possesses deep roots'. Conversely, as this chapter has shown, utilisation of 'resilience rhetoric' within a diverse range of

40 Resilience as Discourse and Practice

academic and policy fields has been far from unified – at times displaying little, if any, shared understanding or deployment of the concept.

The importance of sketching out shifts in disaster management rhetoric and counterterrorism policy, despite focusing empirically on victims' experiences of violence, is twofold but broadly relates to the politically charged nature of terrorist attacks amid a powerful backdrop of representations and continually unfolding events/phenomena. As this chapter has made clear, a shift in recent years has been to incorporate resilience into counterterrorism policy alongside more established forms of security discourse. Whether the logics at play within such a shift reflect or accord with victims and survivors 'on the ground' remains oblique. Secondly, the way language is deployed by the state, the public, and civil society organisations can be critical in securing social consensus around terror prevention and response and is capable of shaping the way we interpret competing political and cultural meanings of terrorism (Jackson, 2005). Consequently, and something always to be borne in mind when interpreting data, victim's responses to terror attacks are likely to be framed to a greater or lesser extent by the structural and political contexts in which they are articulated *now*, as much as by those in which they historically occurred. This is what Hacking (1995) means when he talks of retroactive sense-making – or actions, including language, relating to historical phenomena committed under new descriptions.

Drawing on Foucault's three 'cardinal axes' of ethics, power and knowledge, Hacking (2002: 3, emphasis added) stresses that power is not necessarily causal or reducible to 'political, social, or armed clout', but rather: 'It is as much our own power as that of anyone else that preoccupied him [Foucault]: "power through which we constitute ourselves as subjects acting on others", *not ourselves as passive victim*'. This understanding of power provides as much mileage for making sense of 'the resilient terrorism survivor' discourse sketched out in this chapter as it does the direct phenomenological experiences of survivors of terrorism. While later chapters focus primarily on the latter (direct experiences), or what Hacking (1997) would deem the 'object' under study, it would be a mistake to wholly divorce this from the discourse or 'idea' (Hacking, 1997) of 'the resilient terrorism survivor' which pervades the present conjuncture and this is picked up again at the end of the book.

Orienting earlier insights around the temporal dimensions of resilience to survivors of political violence and critical incidents prompts a number of initial questions. To what extent is resilience characterised by linear processes? Conversely, are there critical moments at which resilience is fortified or challenged? Coupling these insights with earlier discussion of resilience as a somewhat abstract security discourse prompts yet more questions. Most obviously, how are these processes or moments articulated by survivors themselves? Taking seriously the existence of resilience as an object of academic, scientific and therapeutic study and remaining open-minded about its place and value for survivors of extreme violence adds yet more layers. How closely, if at all, do survivors' narratives cohere with or resemble resilience as it appears in these literatures? This can be posed the other way around too. What fundamental resources described within these literatures, said to constitute resilience, are actually harnessed by survivors in the aftermath of political violence and terrorism?

It is clear that a more nuanced framework for making sense of temporality than those often exhibited in current resilience research and policy is needed in order to tackle such questions. It is to this that Chapter 2 now turns.

References

Adger, W.N. (2000) Social and ecological resilience: Are they related? *Progress in Human Geography* 24(3): 347–64.

Agamben, G. (2005) *State of Exception*. Chicago: The University of Chicago Press.

Aguirre, B.E. (2007) Dialectics of vulnerability and Resilience. *Georgetown Journal on Poverty Law & Policy* 14 (1): 39–59.

Alexander, J.C. (2012) *Trauma: A Social Theory*. Cambridge: Polity Press.

Almedom, A.M. (2005) Resilience, hardiness, sense of coherence, and posttraumatic growth: All paths leading to "light at the end of the tunnel"? *Journal of Loss and Trauma* 10(3): 253–65.

Almedom, A.M. and Glandon, D. (2007) Resilience is not the absence of PTSD any more than health is the absence of disease. *Journal of loss and Trauma* 12(2): 127–43.

Anderson, B. (2006) *Imagined Communities: Reflections on the Origin and Spread of Nationalism*. London: Verso.

Aradau, C. (2014) The promise of security: Resilience, surprise and epistemic politics. *Resilience: International Policies, Practices and Discourses* 2(2): 73–87.

BBC (2016) Terror attack on UK 'when, not if' – Sir Bernard Hogan-Howe. *BBC News*, [online] 31 July. Available at: www.bbc.co.uk/news/uk-36935585 [Accessed 16 December 2018].

Bean, H., Keränen, L. and Durfy, M. (2011) 'This is London': Cosmopolitan nationalism and the discourse of resilience in the case of the 7/7 terrorist attacks. *Rhetoric & Public Affairs* 14(3): 427–64.

Beck, U. (1992) *Risk Society: Towards a New Modernity*. London: Sage.

Beck, U. (2013) Five minutes with Ulrich Beck: 'Germany has created an accidental empire'. *LSE Blogs*, [online] March 25. https://blogs.lse.ac.uk/europpblog/2013/03/25/five-minutes-with-ulrich-beck-germany-has-created-an-accidental-empire/ [Accessed 6/6/2018].

Blair, T. (2005) The prime minister's first Commons statement after the bomb attacks in London. *The Guardian*, 11 July. Available at: www.theguardian.com/politics/2005/jul/11/uksecurity.terrorism [Accessed 03/04/2019].

Bleich, A., Gelkopf, M., Melamed, Y. and Solomon, Z. (2006) Mental health and resiliency following 44 months of terrorism: A survey of an Israeli national representative sample. *BMC Medicine* 4(1): 21.

Bonanno, G.A. (2004). Loss, trauma, and human resilience: Have we underestimated the human capacity to thrive after extremely aversive events? *American Psychologist* 59(1): 20–8.

Bonanno, G.A. (2005). Resilience in the Face of Potential Trauma. *Current Directions in Psychological Science* 14(3): 135–8.

42 Resilience as Discourse and Practice

Bonanno, G.A. (2012) *George Bonanno: Measuring Human Resilience.* Available at: www.youtube.com/watch?v=M-W7wJlB6Y8 [Accessed 03/04/2019].

Bonanno, G.A., Galea, S., Bucciarelli, A. and Vlahov, D. (2006) Psychological resilience after disaster: New York City in the aftermath of the September 11th terrorist attack. *Psychological Science* 17(3): 181–6.

Bonanno, G.A., Galea, S., Bucciarelli, A. and Vlahov, D. (2007) What predicts psychological resilience after disaster? The role of demographics, resources, and life stress. *Journal of Consulting and Clinical Psychology* 75(5): 671–82.

Bonanno, G.A., Rennicke, C. and Dekel, S. (2005) Self-enhancement among high-exposure survivors of the September 11th terrorist attack: Resilience or social maladjustment? *Journal of Personality and Social Psychology* 88(6): 984–98.

Bourbeau, P. (2018) A genealogy of resilience. *International Political Sociology* 12(1): 19–35.

Bouvier, P. (2003) Child sexual abuse: Vicious circles of fate or paths to resilience? *The Lancet* 361: 446–7.

Brand, F.S. and Jax, K. (2007) Focusing the meaning(s) of resilience: Resilience as a descriptive concept and a boundary object. *Ecology and Society* 12(1): 23.

Brown, W. (2015) *Undoing the Demos: Neoliberalism's Stealth Revolution.* New York: Zone Books.

Browne, B.C. (2018) Stop telling Palestinians to be 'resilient' – the rest of the world has failed them. *The Conversation* May 14. Available at: https://theconversation.com/stop-telling-palestinians-to-be-resilient-the-rest-of-the-world-has-failed-them-96587 [Accessed 03/04/2019].

Cacioppo, J., Reis, H. and Zautra, A. (2011) Social resilience: The value of social fitness with an application to the military. *American Psychologist* 66(1): 43–51.

Chandler, D. (2014a) *Resilience: The Governance of Complexity.* London: Routledge.

Chandler, D. (2014b) Beyond neoliberalism: Resilience, the new art of governing complexity. *Resilience: International Policies, Practices and Discourses* 2(1): 47–63.

Chandler, D. and Neocleous, M. (2013) Pre-emptive strike: A response to 'resisting resilience'. *Radical Philosophy* 179(6): 58–9.

Chandler, D. and Reid, J. (2016) *The Neoliberal Subject: Resilience, Adaptation and Vulnerability.* London: Rowman & Littlefield International, Ltd.

Chappells, H. and Medd, W. (2012) Resilience in practice: The 2006 drought in southeast England. *Society and Natural Resources* 25(3): 302–16.

Coaffee, J. (2009) *Terrorism, Risk and the Global City: Towards Urban Resilience.* Farnham: Ashgate.

Coaffee, J. and Fussey, P. (2015) Constructing resilience through security and surveillance: The politics, practices and tensions of security-driven resilience. *Security Dialogue* 46(1): 86–105.

Coaffee, J., Wood, D. and Rogers, P. (2009) *The Everyday Resilience of the City.* London: Palgrave.

Collins, R. (2004) Rituals of solidarity and security in the wake of terrorist attack. *Sociological Theory* 22(1): 53–87.

Cooper, R. (2014) *Diagnosing the Diagnostic and Statistical Manual of Mental Disorders.* London: Karnac.

Croft, S. (2006) *Culture, Crisis and America's War on Terror.* Cambridge: Cambridge University Press.

Davoudi, S. (2012) Resilience: A bridging concept or a dead end? *Planning Theory and Practice* 13(2): 299–333.

The Terror–Trauma–Resilience Nexus   43

de Lint, W. and Chazal, N. (2013) Resilience and criminal justice: Unsafe at low altitude. *Critical Criminology* 21(2): 157–76.

Diprose, K. (2015) Resilience is futile. *Soundings: A Journal of Politics and Culture* 58: 44–56.

Evans, B. and Reid, J. (2013) Dangerously exposed: The life and death of the resilient subject. *Resilience: International Policies, Practices and Discourses* 1(2): 83–98.

Evans, B. and Reid, J. (2014) *Resilient Life: The Art of Living Dangerously*. Cambridge: Polity Press.

Fassin, D. and Rechtman, R. (2009) *The Empire of Trauma: An Inquiry into the Condition of Victimhood*. Oxford: Princeton University Press.

Foucault, M. (1991 [1975]) *Discipline and Punish: The Birth of the Prison*. Translated from French by Sheridan, A., 1977. London: Penguin Books.

Fromm, E. (1995[1957]) *The Art of Loving*. London: Thorsons.

Furedi, F. (2008) Fear and security: A vulnerability-led policy response. *Social Policy and Administration* 42(6): 645–61.

Garland, D. (2001) *The Culture of Control: Crime and Social Order in Contemporary Society*. Oxford: Oxford University Press.

Gearson, J. (2012) Deterring conventional terrorism: From punishment to denial and resilience. *Contemporary Security Policy* 33(1): 171–98.

Green, S. and Pemberton, A. (2018) The impact of crime: Victimisation, harm and resilience. In S. Walklate (Ed.) *Handbook of Victims and Victimology*, 2nd edition. London: Routledge. pp.77–101.

Gripper, A. (2017) Watch the Queen's Christmas speech 2017 and read full transcript of Her Majesty's message to the nation. *Mirror*, December 26. www.mirror.co.uk/news/uk-news/watch-queens-christmas-speech-2017-11750074 [Accessed 03/04/2019].

Gunderson, L.H. and C.S. Holling, (Eds.) (2002) *Panarchy: Understanding Transformations in Human and Natural Systems*. Washington, DC: Island Press.

Hacking, I. (1995) *Rewriting the Soul: Multiple Personality and the Sciences of Memory*. Princeton, NJ: Princeton University Press.

Hacking, I. (1997) Taking bad arguments seriously. *London Review of Books* 19(16): 14–16.

Hacking, I. (2002) *Historical Ontology*. Cambridge: Harvard University Press.

Hacking, I. (2004) Between Michel Foucault and Erving Goffman: Between discourse in the abstract and face-to-face interaction. *Economy and Society* 33(3): 277–302.

Hardy, K. (2015) Resilience in UK counter-terrorism. *Theoretical Criminology* 19(1): 77–94.

Heath-Kelly, C. (2017) The geography of pre-criminal space: Epidemiological imaginations of radicalisation risk in the UK Prevent Strategy, 2007–2017. *Critical Studies on Terrorism* 10(2): 297–319.

Herman, J.L. (2001) *Trauma and Recovery*. London: Pandora.

Hobfoll, S.E., Palmieri, P.A., Johnson, R.J., Canetti-Nisim, D., Hall, B.J. and Galea, S. (2009) Trajectories of resilience, resistance, and distress during ongoing terrorism: The case of Jews and Arabs in Israel. *Journal of Consulting and Clinical Psychology* 77(1): 138.

Hobfoll, S.E., Hall, B., Horsey, K.J. and Lamoureux, B.E. (2011) Resilience in the face of terrorism: Linking resource investment with engagement. In S.M. Southwick, B.T. Litz, D. Charney and M.J. Friedman (Eds.) *Resilience and Mental Health: Challenges Across the lifespan*. Cambridge: Cambridge University Press. p.253.

Holland, J. and Jarvis, L. (2014) 'Night fell on a different world': Experiencing, constructing and remembering 9/11. *Critical Studies on Terrorism* 7(2): 187–204.

44 Resilience as Discourse and Practice

Holling, C.S. (1973) Resilience and stability of ecological systems. *Annual Review of Ecology and Systematics* 4: 1–23.

Howell, A. (2012) The demise of PTSD: From governing through trauma to governing resilience. *Alternatives: Global, Local, Political* 37(3): 214–26.

Illouz, E. (2008) *Saving the Modern Soul: Therapy, Emotions, and the Culture of Self-Help.* Berkeley: University of California Press.

Jackson, R. (2005) *Writing the War on Terrorism: Language, Politics and Counter-terrorism.* Manchester: Manchester University Press.

Jarvis, L. (2009) *Times of Terror: Discourse, Temporality and the War on Terror.* Hampshire: Palgrave.

Jenkins, P. (2003) *Images of Terror: What We Can and Can't Know about Terrorism.* New York: Aldine de Gruyter.

Joseph, J. (2013) Resilience as embedded neoliberalism: A governmentality approach. *Resilience: International Policies, Practices and Discourses* 1(1): 38–52.

Klein, N. (2007) *The Shock Doctrine: The Rise of Disaster Capitalism.* London: Penguin Books.

Latour, B. (1987) *Science in Action: How to Follow Scientists and Engineers Through Society.* Cambridge, MA: Harvard University Press.

Levine, S.Z., Laufer, A., Stein, E., Hamama-Raz, Y. and Solomon, Z. (2009) Examining the relationship between resilience and posttraumatic growth. *Journal of Traumatic Stress* 22(4): 282–6.

McConnell, A. and Drennan, L. (2006) Mission impossible? Planning and preparing for crisis. *Journal of Contingencies and Crisis Management* 14(2): 59–70.

McGarry, R., Walklate, S. and Mythen, G. (2015) A sociological analysis of military resilience: Opening up the debate. *Armed Forces & Society* 41: 352–78.

McGreavy, B. (2016) Resilience as discourse. *Environmental Communication* 10(1): 104–21.

McLeary, J. and Figley, C. (2017) Resilience and trauma: Expanding definitions, uses, and contexts. *Traumatology* 23(1): 1–3.

Michelsen, N. (2017) On the genealogy of strategies: Resilience in the revolution. *Resilience: International Policies, Practices and Discourses* 5(1): 61–77.

Morris, T. (2004) *The Stoic Art of Living: Inner Resilience and Outer Results.* Chicago: Open Court.

Mythen, G. (2012) 'No one speaks for us': Security policy, suspected communities and the problem of voice. *Critical Studies on Terrorism* 5(3): 409–24.

Mythen, G. and McGowan, W. (2018) Cultural victimology revisited: Synergies of risk, fear and resilience. In S. Walklate (Ed.) *Handbook of Victims and Victimology*, 2nd edition. London: Routledge. pp.364–78.

Neocleous, M. (2012) 'Don't be scared, be prepared': Trauma-anxiety-resilience. *Alternatives: Global, Local, Political* 37(3): 188–98.

Neocleous, M. (2013) Resisting resilience. *Radical Philosophy* 178(6): 2–7.

O'Malley, P. (2010) Resilient subjects: Uncertainty, warfare and liberalism. *Economy and Society* 39(4): 488–509.

Overland, G. (2013) *Post Traumatic Survival: The Lessons of Cambodian Resilience.* Newcastle upon Tyne: Cambridge Scholars Publishing.

Pfefferbaum, B.J., Reissman, D.B., Pfefferbaum, R.L., Klomp, R.W. and Gurwitch, R.H. (2008) Building resilience to mass trauma events. In L.S. Doll, S.E. Bonzo, D.A. Sleet and J.A. Mercy (Eds.) *Handbook of Injury and Violence Prevention.* Boston: Springer. pp.347–58.

Rimke, H.M. (2000) Governing citizens through self-help literature. *Cultural Studies* 14(1): 61–78.

Rose, N. (1998) *Inventing Our Selves: Psychology, Power and Personhood.* Cambridge: Cambridge University Press.

Rose, N. (2000) Government and control. *British Journal of Criminology* 40(2): 321–39.

Rosenow, D. (2012) Dancing life into being: Genetics, resilience and the challenge of complexity theory. *Security Dialogue* 43(6): 531–47.

Scheper-Hughes, N. (2008) A talent for life: Reflections on human vulnerability and resilience. *Ethnos* 73(1): 25–56.

Schott, R.M. (2013) Resilience, normativity and vulnerability. *Resilience: International Policies, Practices and Discourses* 1(3): 210–18.

Schott, R.M. (2015) 'Not just victims … but': Toward a critical theory of the victim. In H. Marway and H. Widdows (Eds.) *Women and Violence: The Agency of Victims and Perpetrators.* Basingstoke: Palgrave Macmillan. pp.178–94.

The Kerslake Report (2018) *The Kerslake Report: An independent review into the preparedness for, and emergency response to, the Manchester Arena attack on 22nd May 2017.* Available at: www.kerslakearenareview.co.uk/media/1022/kerslake_arena_review_printed_final.pdf [Accessed 03/04/2019].

The Telegraph (2016) Police chief apologises after fake Muslim shouts 'Allahu Akbar' in simulated suicide bomb attack at Manchester's Trafford Centre. May 10. Available at: www.telegraph.co.uk/news/2016/05/10/police-simulate-dramatic-terror-attack-at-manchesters-trafford-c/ [Accessed 03/04/2019].

Toros, H. (2017) '9/11 is alive and well' or how critical terrorism studies has sustained the 9/11 narrative. *Critical Studies on Terrorism* 10(2): 203–19.

Travis, A. (2017) Counter-terror exercise simulates vehicle attack in Edinburgh. *The Guardian,* October 3. www.theguardian.com/uk-news/2017/oct/03/counter-terror-exercise-simulates-vehicle-attack-in-edinburgh [Accessed 03/04/2019].

Ungar, M. (2008) Resilience across cultures. *British Journal of Social Work* 38: 218–35.

Ungar, M. (2011) The social ecology of resilience: Addressing contextual and cultural ambiguity of a nascent construct. *American Journal of Orthopsychiatry* 81(1): 1–17.

Ungar, M. (2013) Social ecologies and their contribution to resilience. In M. Ungar (Ed.) *The Social Ecology of Resilience: A Handbook of Theory and Practice.* London: Springer. pp.13–32.

Walker, J. and Cooper, M. (2011) Genealogies of resilience: From systems ecology to the political economy of crisis adaptation. *Security Dialogue* 42(2): 143–60.

Walklate, S. (2011) Reframing criminal victimization: Finding a place for vulnerability and resilience. *Theoretical Criminology* 15(2): 179–94.

Walklate, S. (2016) The metamorphosis of the victim of crime: From crime to culture and the implications for justice. *International Journal for Crime, Justice and Social Democracy* 5(4): 4–16.

Walklate, S. and Mythen, G. (2015) *Contradictions of Terrorism: Security, Risk and Resilience.* London: Routledge.

Walklate, S., McGarry, R. and Mythen, G. (2014) Searching for resilience: A conceptual excavation. *Armed Forces & Society* 40(3): 408–27.

Walklate, S., Mythen, G. and McGarry, R. (2012) States of resilience and the resilient state. *Current Issues in Criminal Justice* 24(2): 185–204.

Welby, J. (2018) The Archbishop of Canterbury's New Year Message 2018. Available at: https://cms.archbishopofcanterbury.org/news/latest-news/archbishop-canterburys-new-year-message-2018 [Accessed 03/04/2019].

Westphal, M. and Bonanno, G.A. (2007) Posttraumatic growth and resilience to trauma: Different sides of the same coin or different coins? *Applied Psychology* 56(3): 417–27.

Williams, R. and Drury, J. (2009) Psychosocial resilience and its influence on managing mass emergencies and disasters. *Psychiatry* 8(8): 293–6.

Windle, G. (2011) What is resilience? A review and concept analysis. *Reviews in Clinical Gerontology* 21(2): 152–69.

Wong, D.B. (2006) The meaning of detachment in Daoism, Buddhism, and Stoicism. 5(2): 207–19.

Zebrowski, C. (2016) *The Value of Resilience: Securing Life in the 21st Century.* London: Routledge.

Chapter 2

To Survivors Themselves

Why, Where, and How to Study Survivors of Political Violence and Terrorism?

Chapter 1 unpacked the contested concept of 'resilience', alluding to the need for further empirical research with survivors themselves. But it was necessarily partial, being noticeably silent on tackling the more 'technical' and methodological issues of researching 'political violence and terrorism' (PVT) against this backdrop. For that reason, this chapter pursues three deceptively straightforward questions: why, where, and how might we study survivors of PVT?

Firstly, the chapter asks why we should preoccupy ourselves with attempting to elicit the experiential narratives of survivors themselves (*qua* Walklate et al. 2019). It does so in the belief that while such narratives are frequently ignored or omitted from mainstream political discourse (where, for example, such narratives may be unpalatable to the prevailing or aspirational worldview of relevant actors, including political elites), they suffer from a similar academic treatment within a range of critical approaches to the study of PVT with which this work more closely identifies. I have explored this 'double omission' at length elsewhere (McGowan, 2016). While that work is concerned primarily with a heterogeneous and interdisciplinary subfield of terrorism studies widely recognised as 'Critical Terrorism Studies' (see, *inter alia*, Gunning, 2007a, 2007b; Jackson, 2007; Breen Smyth et al., 2008; Jackson, Breen Smyth and Gunning, 2009), it draws on, and applies to, a much wider set of conceptual debates within critical criminology and victimology, political sociology, and social science philosophy informing this book. While there is great value in paying attention directly to narratives of survivors in order to explore a range of issues, the rationale underpinning a turn to survivor narratives here (itself not without its problems as alluded to in the introduction) bridges the gap identified in Chapter 1 between discourse in the abstract and specific practices (Hacking, 2004). In short, how closely, if at all, do survivors' narratives cohere with or resemble 'resilience' as it appears in social policy and cognate literatures? Conversely, what fundamental resources described within these literatures, said to constitute resilience, are actually harnessed by survivors in the aftermath of PVT?

Secondly, in posing the question of where we might look specifically to study such phenomena, this chapter provides an overview of the site at which

DOI: 10.4324/9781003154020-4

exploratory fieldwork and subsequent data collection took place during this project – The Tim Parry Johnathan Ball Foundation for Peace (FfP) in Warrington, UK. In addition to the Survivors Assistance Network (SAN), a strand of the organisation's work focused on here, the FfP as a whole has been a high-profile and relatively influential NGO among others in promoting peaceful dialogue between survivors and former perpetrators both pre and post-Good Friday Agreement (GFA) and in relation to a wide range of conflicts and incidents. It also continues to support survivors of contemporary and ongoing attacks and conflicts, pursuing a broader remit than more focused or single-issue NGOs and campaign groups. As the Foundation's founder Colin Parry explained during an interview, the organisation's remit does not include the pursuit of truth and justice, nor affiliate itself to other justice campaign groups. As Chapters 5 and 6 show, this focus has implications for the overall outlook of the charity and certainly for the way Colin personally envisages recovery and resilience. It also carries different temporal inflections to the precedent of justice campaigning. Looking beyond the organisation's mission and ethos in later chapters, it is clear that several participants align more closely with justice campaigning than the pursuit of peace and vice versa. In this chapter, the purpose is simply to provide some context and background information about the organisation before delving into these issues in more depth later.

Thirdly, it asks how we might traverse the vast and complex conceptual terrain of PVT, particularly the issue of definition. Rather than attempting to encapsulate book-length controversies about 'terrorists' versus 'freedom fighters', it argues that even among 'critical terrorism studies' literatures alluded to above, there are two chief ways in which PVT definitions are typically negotiated. The first employ predominantly *a priori* reasoning, while the second employ predominantly *a posteriori* reasoning. A third epistemological route, adopted here, is offered which utilises the work of philosopher Ian Hacking. Drawing briefly on aspects of Hacking's *oeuvre*, particularly his conception of what he variously refers to as 'dynamic nominalism' or 'dialectical realism', it is argued that only an appraisal of epistemology and ontology which takes seriously the perpetual 'to-ing and fro-ing' between *classification*, *action*, and related *interaction* suffices when listening to survivors from a range of critical incidents. This range of incidents is more or less readily assigned the labels 'terrorism' or 'political violence' by different actors at different times and in different spaces – including, for example, by survivors and FfP staff talking to different 'combinations' of survivors and FfP staff at different types of event in different spaces and places during fieldwork.

Taken together, these three deceptively straightforward questions – why, where, and how – enable me to work through the rationale for arriving at this particular research topic in this way, the places in which that topic was pursued, and the way I chose to negotiate inherent methodological controversies when trying to elicit and collect data in the process.

Why Turn to the Narratives of Survivors Themselves?

Speaking on 7 July 2015, in a speech reminiscent of President Bush's Address to the Nation on the evening of 11 September 2001, David Cameron (2015) insisted that 'ten years on this is one of those days where everybody remembers exactly where they were when they heard the news'. The prime minister spoke of the 'resolve and resolution' of Londoners and the UK in the aftermath of the London bombings, reminding us of 'the threat that we still face' – a pertinent moment in light of Chapter 1's discussion of 'declared resilience'. Linking the tragic reality of the past with the imminent and inevitable threat of the present and future, he went on to speak of the 'grace and the dignity of the victim's families for all they've been through', emphasising the need to 'honour the memory of those victims and all those that were lost ten years ago today'. Despite the focus on victims of the 7 July 2005 attacks and their families, there seemed to be a lot 'going on' in addition to paying tribute; a multiplicity of political agendas seemed to be at play. In another speech during the day, Cameron said:

> Ten years on from the 7/7 London attacks, the threat from terrorism continues to be as real as it is deadly – the murder of 30 innocent Britons while holidaying in Tunisia is a brutal reminder of that fact. But we will never be cowed by terrorism. We will keep on doing all that we can to keep the British public safe, protecting vulnerable young minds from others' extremist beliefs and promoting the shared values of tolerance, love and respect that make Britain so great.
>
> (Davies and Addley, 2015)

In this excerpt alone, the prime minister spoke of '7/7', the tragic 2015 attack in Sousse, Tunisia, Britain's refusal to be intimidated by terrorism, the government's 'anti-extremism' strategy, and provides an indirect nod to the Conservative Party's contested promotion of 'fundamental British values' (see Department for Education, 2014). As Chapter 1 suggested, the discursive significance of speeches such as this for the representation of terrorism and counterterrorism more broadly has been a staple analytical focus for critical terrorism studies (CTS) and constructivist approaches more broadly (Jenkins, 2003; Jackson, 2005; Croft, 2006), with recent work emphasising the important temporal and commemorative function such constructions serve (Holland and Jarvis, 2014). While speeches such as these ostensibly position victims of specific critical incidents at the centre of political discussion, we are unlikely to hear much about them for much of the time.

This is not an issue restricted to elite politicians. The direct engagement with victims of critical incidents deemed to be 'terrorist attacks' by the State has been noticeably absent in several important and prominent quarters, including the CTS subfield – a subfield appositely placed to further our understanding of such instances of victimisation and the dynamics it engenders (see McGowan, 2016). To clarify, there is no shortage of research into competing understandings of 'victimisation' (both explicitly and implicitly labelled as such), either from CTS or within cognate areas of sociology, criminology, or critical victimology. However, some general observations from these literatures point to important spaces for development.

Within CTS and cognate critical scholarship, attention to instances of victimisation largely revolves around three sets of interrelated phenomena. The first is the disproportionate, though legal, surveillance of 'suspect communities' (Hillyard, 1993; Pantazis and Pemberton, 2009; Mythen, 2012) and the routine, day-to-day manifestations of State power which have impacted particularly negatively upon the citizenship of ethnic minority groups (Mythen, Walklate and Khan, 2009, 2012; Jarvis and Lister, 2015). The second, intimately connected, issue relates to miscarriages of justice which have occurred in the pursuit of capturing and punishing alleged terrorists, such as wrongful convictions, torturous interrogation tactics, arrests and detentions without charge, and forms of immigration detention justified and deployed under the general auspices of security (see, *inter alia*, Roach and Trotter, 2005; Sands, 2009; Roach, 2011; Thornton, 2011). The third way that critical approaches to terrorism studies have furthered our understanding of victimisation is by making global suffering more visible, exploring the political and moral hegemony of the West and the impact of the war on terror for countries in the Global South (see Göl, 2010) (for a more nuanced discussion of these respective areas see McGowan, 2016: 14–17).

Within and across each of these areas of study has also been a disparate and varied focus on gendered violence, drawing on much longer lineages of feminist and feminist-inspired scholarship preceding contemporary terrorism studies. This work continues to highlight the disproportionate and gendered impact of war, insecurity, and terrorism, as well as exploring renewed understandings of gendered violence as, for example, 'terror of the everyday' (Innes and Steele, 2015) and 'intimate terrorism' (Sjoberg and Gentry, 2015; see also Walklate et al., 2017). Space does not permit a fuller historical account of how feminist research has engaged differential understandings of 'political violence' and 'terrorism'. However, reflecting on the so-called 'everyday', 'experiential', or 'narrative' turns within International Relations, Geography, Cultural Theory, and their influences on contemporary terrorism studies (see Heath-Kelly, Jarvis and Baker-Beall, 2014), it is possible to identify a range of links with feminist methodologies advocating for a direct engagement with survivors' ontological standpoint (*qua* Reinharz, 1992; Webb, 2000). These are only links and they are only partially related to feminist conceptions of standpoint, as theorised by Nancy Hartsock, Dorothy Smith, Donna Haraway, and Sandra Harding, among others, who explore the ways in which women's tacit and situated knowledges of the world produce not relative truths to be dismissed as unscientific and therefore invalid but a strong objectivity and authoritative account of social life.

Taking a further step back from 'terrorism', the study of victimisation more broadly has of course received long-standing attention from within cognate disciplines such as criminology, sociology, and critical victimology. At this more general level exist well-established conceptual questions around who we take victims to be, who might be most at risk of victimisation, who holds the power to define competing notions of victimhood, and to what ends such definitions are put (see, *inter alia*, Quinney, 1972; Rock, 2002; Spalek, 2006; Walklate, 2012; McGarry and Walklate, 2015).

In many instances, such approaches have advocated for a greater 'voice' from survivors through research. It is clear that victims and survivors of terrorist attacks represent a significant source of political capital for those in positions of power (McGowan, 2016). This is often used to advance policies 'in the name of the victims' (Ginsberg, 2014), yet silences or denies participation of dissenting victims whose vision of civil rights and social justice differs to that of prevailing political, economic, and military hegemony. Victims of terrorism, as in other contexts, become ordered hierarchically (McGarry, 2016). Taking these claims seriously requires taking 'the category of victim more seriously as a form of political and activist subjectivity' (Rentschler, 2011: 24). It also requires more critical analyses of victimhood capable of exploring vulnerability through discussions of both 'injurability' and agency (Schott, 2013; see also Walklate, 2011). Nevertheless, the synthesis between these literatures and critical terrorism scholarship more broadly remains patchy and incomplete, despite both being well placed to contest status quo thinking around victimisation and scrutinising the 'hierarchy of credibility' (Becker, 1967: 242) found within official discourse.

Notwithstanding the perpetually contested nature of what constitutes 'terrorism' (explored later in this chapter), Wilson's (2018: vii) comments ring true at least in terms of contemporary social science research: 'Genesis, and not aftermath, has tended to dominate the study of terrorism'. While this has led to a predominant focus on what motivates perpetrators of violence, as well as the prevention and security apparatuses operating to counterterrorism, a number of key epistemic claims encourage us to take seriously the views of 'those on the ground', including both perpetrators and victims. Despite overlooking the victim somewhat in their analyses (see McGowan. 2016), CTS' general outlook on standpoint offers an important ethos from which to start, asking 'whose voices are marginalised or silenced and whose are empowered in defining "terrorism" and responses to it in particular contexts' (McDonald, 2009: 114). CTS aims 'to engage in conversations with *actors who have important and interesting points of view on terrorism-related issues, but who might otherwise be marginalized in public debate*, including policy-makers and those designated as "terrorists"' (Breen Smyth et al., 2008: 3; emphasis added). Clearly, victims and survivors of PVT represent such a group of actors who are rendered hyper-visible in certain respects (as in David Cameron's commemorative and political speech above), and yet often remain experientially marginalised from public debate and policymaking in others. As we know, the scale of victimisation because of State-led counterterrorism policies at home and abroad since '9/11' far exceeds that of officially recognised terrorist violence. However, this does not wholly explain the relative paucity of research focusing on victims of such violence within critical subfields such as CTS which, despite providing an ideal forum for such discussions to flourish, rarely engages with such actors (McGowan, 2016). Speaking directly with survivors has the potential of drawing attention to 'moments of bias, selectivity, exclusion, aporia or inaccuracy within terrorism discourse' (Holland and Jarvis, 2014, 190), security policy, emergency response, and socio-economic arrangements more broadly in relation to a range of aggrieved and bereaved actors. This includes, among other things, holding resilience traits considered in Chapter 1 to closer empirical scrutiny.

Victims and survivors of PVT are key actors (both active and passive) in the (re)production of hegemonic framings of terrorism and counterterrorism, and therefore constitute an important 'group' to consider in relation to policy and practice. As Hickey et al. (2017: 272) argue: 'Victim voices are important, since victims are in a special epistemic situation: they have distinctive first-person experience in suffering grave wrongs'. This stands in contrast with Agamben's (1999: 34) more complex and controversial view of testimony which 'discharges the survivor of authority', a view not necessarily supported here but one carrying fascinating resonance with two participant's stories and thus considered more closely in Chapter 5. While victims or survivors should not occupy our sole purview, they represent an important point of critique for understanding both state and non-state violence, and state and non-state responses to it. Incorporating victims of terrorist attacks into critical studies of terrorism is not to view victims simply as a form of political capital to be exploited as they so often have been before (McGowan, 2016). Rather, the experiences of victims should be recognised as an important symbolic and material source of knowledge and meaning-making – 'as the privileged site of political agency and subjectivation' (Zulaika and Douglass, 1996: 192). As Jackson (2007: 248) emphasises, we must understand 'terrorism' as an instrumental use of political violence by actors operating within particular sets of circumstances, at particular times, in particular places, all of which point to the 'ontological instability of the terrorist label'.

Set against this, the physical injury and loss of life caused by both terrorism and counterterrorism provide us with a starkly rooted, irrefutable, and material 'trace' (Fassin, 2011; Walklate and McGarry, 2015) to the lived experiences of those touched by terror. In one of his best-known nonfictional works, Japanese writer Haruki Murakami (2003) presents an impressive and sensitive compilation of stories from survivors (and perpetrators) of the 1995 Tokyo gas attacks. The stories, many of which capture the mundane everyday life of the Tokyo commuter, reveal more of the scale and impact of victimisation than 'just' the numbers of injured passengers ever could and hand the power to describe this 'trace' back to those who were present at the time. To hear them describe the smell of sarin gas, or to reflect on their confusion as chaos ensued, is powerful and brings the reader somewhat closer to an appreciation of violence in a visceral sense. Murakami (2003: 213) wanted to 'feel what these people felt, think what they thought', as he puts it, 'not one clear viewpoint, but flesh-and-blood material from which to construct *multiple* viewpoints' (2003: 215). Bringing together a dynamic sensitivity to the language and definitions used by survivors and a diverse participant sample from a range of critical incidents, one aim of this book is to similarly include a multiplicity of viewpoints. In this spirit, the chapter now turns to a brief history of the site at which it was possible to canvass such an array of survivor narratives.

The Tim Parry Johnathan Ball Foundation for Peace (FfP): A Brief History

This project started life as an Economic and Social Research Council (ESRC) CASE studentship, the aim of which was to facilitate collaboration between the university and organisations operating in the public, private, or voluntary sectors. In this case, the collaboration involved the University of Liverpool and the Tim Parry Johnathan Ball Foundation for Peace charity (widely known as the 'Foundation for Peace' and abbreviated throughout to 'FfP') in Warrington, a large town in the North West of England located near to Cheshire's northernmost boundary. FfP's genesis begins with the tragic events of 20 March 1993 when two Irish Republican Army (IRA[1]) bombs exploded in Warrington town centre (hereafter 'the Warrington bombing'), killing 12-year-old Tim Parry and 3-year-old Johnathan Ball. Bronwen Vickers, a 32-year-old mother of two, was also severely injured and had to have her leg amputated. She died a year later from a skin cancer some specialists believed could have been triggered by her recent injuries. The charity was registered on 5 April 1995 by Tim's parents, Colin and Wendy Parry. As Colin recalled during an interview for this project, he and Wendy took part in making a BBC Panorama documentary in summer 1993 which was filmed in the UK, The Republic of Ireland, and America. During their visit to Northern Ireland, they visited a small charity based on a farm in Coleraine which aimed to promote peaceful dialogue between members of 'sectarian' communities. They would hold weekend-long gatherings between Catholics and Protestants of all ages and of different political persuasions, who, despite their differences, wanted to see an end to the ongoing conflict. Colin and Wendy sat in on some of these discussions. They met three young people who had lost family members in 'The Troubles' but who sought peace in place of revenge. Relating these views to their own circumstances, they were immediately impressed and inspired to champion a similar narrative and recognised the emotive power and potential such dialogue could have for conflict resolution.

At first, the charity had no physical building of its own and took the form of the 'Tim Parry Scholarship'. Colin and Wendy wanted teenagers from

Warrington, Northern Ireland, and the Republic of Ireland to meet, get to know each other, and discuss 'The Troubles' in a way that would help each side understand different perspectives on the conflict. Eight teenagers from Tim Parry's high school in Warrington visited the other two groups in Ireland and the visit was a huge success. The Parrys began looking for suitable premises to build a dedicated Peace Centre, continuing to work from Tim's bedroom in the meantime. Their ideas soon attracted support from a number of relatively high-profile dignitaries and politicians, including the then Secretary of State for Northern Ireland, Mo Mowlam, who encouraged the Parrys to go ahead with the plans and helped to fundraise the necessary amount. While they managed to raise a significant amount, including a donation of around £100,000 from a local business, they were still far short of the money needed for the physical premises they were looking for. Facing such a shortfall, Colin approached Atlantic Philanthropies, a private foundation in America founded by Irish-American businessman Chuck Feeney. Feeney, who pioneered duty-free shopping in the 1960s and went on to become a multi-millionaire, established Atlantic Philanthropies as a way of championing public policy causes around health, education, and social welfare. It has donated money all over the world, including in Ireland, where it has funded a number of human rights and civil society groups. By 2016, Feeney and Atlantic Philanthropies had given away the last of its $8 billion fortune and closed permanently in 2020. The foundation donated just under £1 million to the Parry's cause who were then able to build the centre with co-owners, the National Society for the Prevention of Cruelty to Children, and seven years on from the Warrington bombing on 20 March 2000 the Peace Centre was officially opened by the Duchess of Kent, former Irish Taoiseach Albert Reynolds, and former Prime Minister John Major who had been involved in initial peace process negotiations in 1993–94. High-profile visitors to the Peace Centre since then include former deputy First Minister of Northern Ireland Martin McGuiness, Irish President Michael D. Higgins, and war correspondent Jeremy Bowen, among others, who have delivered speeches and annual peace lectures to public audiences.

The Warrington bombings, the formation of the Tim Parry Johnathan Ball FfP, and later building of the Peace Centre were seismic events in the lives of the Parrys but were also significant for geopolitical reasons too. As Lelourec (2017) explains, the killing of two young children shocked the nation and while IRA murders often attracted significantly more media attention than the deaths of IRA members or even innocent Irish civilians at the hands of Loyalist groups or British Armed Forces, the Warrington victims received even more coverage for a more sustained period. Not only were English publics appalled by the level of depravity realised through the deaths of two children, some Irish republican communities also expressed their outrage and condemnation of the attack. In many ways, the attack only served to alienate potential supporters of the IRA, whose tolerance of civilian casualties had all but declined since the Proxy Bombs of the 1970s and early 1990s (most notably in 1990), Bloody Friday, and the deaths of innocents in Woolwich, Guildford, and the Harrods store bomb (Bloom and Horgan, 2008). The Irish community club in Warrington was targeted with stones and an outhouse set alight, causing fears that the attacks might provoke yet more retaliatory violence. Community leaders instead stepped in and denounced the retaliations which, along with the establishment of the FfP outlined above, began to set a precedent for what the Warrington bombings would come to stand for. For these reasons, along with sufficient public and political support for ongoing peace negotiations and ceasefires in the early-mid 1990s, Lelourec (2017) concludes that the Warrington bombing marked a significant turning point in the peace process and, therefore, 'The Troubles' themselves. Sandwiched between the establishment of the charity and the building of the centre came the GFA 1998, meaning the FfP had experienced both pre- and post-agreement conditions – a significant transition for many of the victims working with the organisation and engaging in dialogue in years to come with former political prisoners released under the agreement.

The FfP was also established at a time of burgeoning growth for 'the peace industry'. Many organisations around the UK and Ireland were starting up and providing proactive solutions to a whole range of issues which, linking back to Chapter 1, marked a shift to greater civil society responsibility. The philanthropic boost the FfP received to kick start it, while undoubtedly substantial, is typical of many victim support groups assisting victims of terrorism (Gilbert, 2017). Increases in the number of NGOs and eventually a shift from grant-based income to piecemeal funding for specifically commissioned projects (Simmonds, 2016) have characterised the 20 years since the GFA and has meant that the FfP is only atypical of many similar organisations in one sense – it is still in operation. While many charities were forced to close with the onset of austerity (of course, others came into being precisely because they serve(d) a purpose for the governance of an allegedly decentralised 'Big Society'), the FfP has always managed to secure funds (sometimes with only weeks to spare) before programmes are closed. In this sense, the organisation itself has had to embody the kind of resilience often associated with the 'Big Society' era, where it often became synonymous with financial cuts in the public sphere (Harrison, 2013). Early in the project, a staff member sensitively disclosed that had it not been for the attacks in London in 2005, the organisation's contemporary remit was beginning to look somewhat tenuous. Since then, a range of attacks around the UK, Europe, and beyond have ensured that the organisation has consistently been justified in its claims that conflict resolution and victim support for survivors of PVT should remain high on the political agenda. Despite this, it has had to diversify its work which now includes resilience education and radicalisation awareness programmes for delivery in schools alongside its victim support work. This fascinating insight alone provides compelling support for the kind of dialectical relationship between NGOs and their beneficiaries described by Krause (2014), who suggests that despite genuinely hoping to improve the lives of particular groups, NGOs are nonetheless practically motivated by the production and promotion of 'good projects'. Were we to see an extended hiatus in terror attacks in the UK, the FfP may once again be facing difficulties in securing long-term funding, as well as mounting pressure to evidence and quantify the impact of their programs; almost irrespective of financial supply and humanitarian demand, the latter now represents a pressing reality for the charity and its daily operation.

The FfP operates several strands. The participants and activities described here, in the main, form part of the SAN strand (formerly Survivors for Peace). Despite the scale and gravitas of the conflicts associated with the FfP, the premise of most SAN activities is, in essence, deceptively modest. Among its aims are the provision of 'free practical and emotional support to individuals and families affected by a terrorist incident' and to 'facilitate the sharing of experiences and dialogue where appropriate to the needs of survivors' (The Tim Parry Johnathan Ball Foundation for Peace, 2017). The charity runs a weekend-long residential event called 'Sharing Experiences', which is often the first-time new participants to the FfP get a chance to talk openly about their experiences to fellow survivors. It also provides educational 'Living with Trauma' weekends. As Chapter 4 shows, 'Sharing Experiences' is often the catalyst for a range of friendships, networks, and long-term relationships. The core tenet of the organisation over the years has revolved around conflict resolution, and a major strand of the organisation's work has been to provide survivors of PVT and former combatants a safe space in which they can share their experiences and personal stories of conflict. As an ongoing part of this research, regular field visits to the FfP provided an insight into some of these experience-sharing events and activities which helped to shape the project's research design. This fieldwork also provided fascinating insight into the working practices of the organisation and its interactions with its participants and these insights are interspersed throughout the book where relevant. In summary, the trajectory of the FfP outlined above, from its genesis to the present day, continues to be told and retold by beneficiaries and staff which serves as a powerful and emotive form of organisational storytelling (Gabriel, 2000), fortifying its identity among new and existing audiences.

Surviving What? How to (Not) Define Political Violence and Terrorism

There is widespread acceptance among academics, policymakers, and criminal justice practitioners that no singular definition of 'terrorism' exists (Martin, 2013: 35). Even the most systematic attempts to codify terrorism, such as Schmid's (1984) collation of over 100 definitions, ultimately concede to the perpetual diversity terrorism and terrorism studies furnish. While many definitional discussions of terrorism espouse the age-old 'terrorist' versus 'freedom fighter' relativist adage to convey the importance of standpoint, both acknowledging yet often bypassing political dispute, this chapter more securely (un)fixes terrorism and violence more broadly as a necessarily 'contested concept' (Lynch and Argomaniz, 2015: 3; de Haan, 2008) precisely so that methodological context remains at the forefront of discussion.

It is not the intention of this work to reproduce and compare multiple definitions of terrorism as many others have done before, but it is worth considering, for instance, how the UK government demarcates terrorism in the Terrorism Act 2000. It is perhaps telling that the government itself uses both 'definition' and 'interpretation' interchangeably to denote what they understand to be terrorism. Section 1 of that Act defines terrorism as the use or threat of action that is designed to influence a government or intimidate the public for the purpose of advancing a political, religious, racial, or ideological cause. That action or threat must include serious violence against the person, serious damage to property, endangerment of life, serious risk to the health and safety of the public, or seriously interfering with an electronic system. The action can be directed at the UK government and public or another government or public. If it is not directed at a government or public but involves the use of firearms or explosives, then it may still constitute terrorism if it fulfils the damages or risks listed above. These actions may be committed for the benefit, or on behalf, of an individual or a 'proscribed organisation'.

The first thing to note is the obvious fact that political, religious, racial, and ideological ideas are in perpetual flux and so by condemning actions or threats which aim to advance anything containing political, religious, racial, or ideological motives paradoxically includes almost everything the government itself does. Of course, the emphasis here is on the means by which those ends are met and Weber's (1948: 78) widely cited observation that states hold a monopoly over what is considered to be *legitimate* violence is still an illuminating one in relation to terrorism. Prior to modern state formation, violence was routinely exercised alongside non-state or semi-state institutions until such a time when this violence had served its purpose and the state emerged as the dominant institution; violence which was once central to the colonial project became untenable and thus, at once, had to be eliminated from view (Neocleous, 2003: 102–3). As Grozdanova (2014: 333) notes, there is existing legislation in place that directly prohibits serious violence against the person, serious damage to property, and so on, meaning that 'terrorism' is used to signify something else, something 'special'. The fact that political or ideological ends and violent means together may constitute terrorism suggests the demarcation of something or someone particularly menacing, exceptional in their threat to the status quo, to law and order. From a legal perspective, it would seem that defining terrorism is ostensibly superfluous. The government's definition explicitly emphasises that violence must be politically or ideologically motivated. It may be adequate for describing violence that victims may deem to be terrorism, it may not. In-line with adversarial legal procedure, the definition was not constructed with victims chiefly in mind and certainly its sweeping nature has more often been

58 Resilience as Discourse and Practice

mobilised to encompass the actions of perpetrators or suspected perpetrators rather than to truly reflect the lived experiences of terrorism survivors.

Of course, official designations of terrorism not only deviate along national-sub-national lines but, more specifically, they also operate according to race too. The selective use of policing and security measures not only operates in the name of prevention, as is now widely accepted, but also following acts of terror that have been successfully carried out. Even acts committed by subnational groups or individuals, in-line with officially defined notions of terrorism, can fail to attract the ubiquity that they would otherwise have if they were committed by persons of a different race. Attention was widely and tragically drawn to this paradox in Charleston, South Carolina, in June 2015 when Dylann Roof entered the Emmanuel African Methodist Episcopal Church and opened fire, killing nine African American churchgoers. Much of the media and criminal justice response positioned this as a 'hate crime' – the isolated actions of an insane individual. This was despite strong evidence that Roof acted according to ideologically motivated prejudice that had led to the targeting of African Americans at this church on other occasions against a historical backdrop of systemic racism. Meanwhile, ideology is routinely targeted as a key driver in the 'radicalisation' of young Muslims, even before they have committed an offence. In 2011, reactions from officials, the media, and the public following the killing of 77 people in Norway by far-right terrorist Anders Breivik also stood in stark contrast to comparable instances of Islamist extremism. Although Breivik was charged with terrorism offences, he was given an open trial and a concerted effort was made to understand his motives (Lewis, 2015). Compare this due process to the detention of terror *suspects* at Guantanamo Bay (see Sands, 2009). Compare it also to the lack of serious attention given to the verbalised and self-proclaimed motives of London 7/7 bomber Mohammed Sidique Khan (Walklate and Mythen, 2015: 76–7), or Woolwich attackers Michael Adebowale and Michael Adebolajo (McGarry, 2013), all of whom cited British foreign policy as motivating them to commit the violence they did. These discrepancies cannot be reduced to questions of race and ethnicity, but it is clear that race, ethnicity, and particularly religion continue to represent a common denominator among instances of over-policing, criminal profiling, targeted surveillance, and media coverage.

What is clear about terrorism is the importance of language and how it is used in the political-public sphere. In this arena, language is mobilised to reflect, and affect, the views of protagonists and audiences. As Gearty (2002) argues, counterterrorism involves both linguistic distortion and moral contradiction. This contradiction is palpable in a 2007 report by the Independent Reviewer of Terrorism Legislation, Lord Carlile, into the definition of terrorism in which he emphasises the dangers and capabilities of ideologically driven Islamists specifically, dedicated to supporting 'violent and lethal jihad' (2007: 24). This is followed by suggesting that there are also groups and individuals unconnected with 'violent jihad' with 'broadly terrorist purposes and means' (2007: 25) but who, for several vague and unsupported reasons, should be dealt with under criminal law without the use of terrorism legislation. 'Put simply', he states, 'what I mean by this is that the authorities should always treat suspects within the normal rather than special criminal laws unless their threat and structure requires operationally that they should be regarded formally as terrorists' (2007: 25). As well as 'extreme animal rights activists', individuals acting alone fall into Lord Carlile's class of criminals whose threat and structure fail to qualify as genuine terrorism. Examples he gave of this kind of non-terrorist include neo-Nazi militant David Copeland who targeted London's ethnic minorities and gay population with nail bombs in 1999, killing three people and injuring over one hundred more. In what must be a confusing and insulting linguistic sleight for both the victims of such attacks and Muslim communities, he goes so far as to brand such non-Islamist groups and individuals as 'imitators'. Furthermore, despite several isolated attacks in recent years, he also dismisses the contemporary IRA threat as effectively the predecessors of today's 'real' terrorists. Without downplaying the seriousness of recent terrorist attacks in large areas of the Middle East, Africa, and (less commonly) parts of Europe, it is fair to say that the threat of Muslim extremism has been cast pervasively by many actors, fixing its status as a contemporary 'moral panic' (Cohen, 1972; Hall et al., 1978). Terrorism is thus a highly fluid, historically contingent term likely to describe a category of person rather than a specific technique of violence with that category referring to a subversive group or individual opposed to the established order (Gearty, 2002).

As Mythen and Walklate (2012: 328) argue, '[t]here is now a palpable need to factor the role of the state more firmly into discussions about the production and escalation of terrorism', urging us to recognise 'terroristic' violence committed by states. The adjective 'terroristic' is important, since it encourages broader connotations of violence than are often implied when we use only the nouns 'terrorism' or 'terrorist'. Morally, it encourages us to think about the nature of violent acts in and of themselves, independently of who commits them (Gearty, 2002). Once again, in a UK context, Lord Carlile's 2007 report into the definition of terrorism is insightful. In addressing calls for state definitions to include explicitly that state actors too are capable of carrying out terrorism, he acknowledges the 'attraction of the argument' (2007: 46) but goes on to dismiss this as a definitional issue. Instead, according to Lord Carlile, it is an issue of jurisdiction. In essence, his report advances the notion that nobody should be above the law but that the law should perhaps be looking in particular places and at particular groups. Subsequent legislation, such as the Counter-Terrorism Act 2008, enshrines this ambiguity further by stating that offences, including murder, may have 'terrorist connections' and, of course, the importance placed on far-right perpetrators as well as 'Islamic' extremists and left-wing activists has shifted in recent years following a range of high-profile attacks, such as the murders of Labour MP Jo Cox in 2016 and Conservative MP David Amess in 2021. Yet terrorism legislation remains characterised by its moral contradictions and deliberate ambiguity.

60 Resilience as Discourse and Practice

Seeking a much wider understanding of terrorism than mere enemies of the state, this book recognises the consequences of political violence perpetrated at all levels, from non-state individuals to systematic abuses committed by state regimes. Contrary to the overt focus on terrorists so widely accepted in mainstream political debate and policy, this research takes seriously the need to refocus scholarly attention on the immoral use of violence where it occurs, independently of who perpetrates it (Gearty, 2002). However, this still does not resolve the problem of how to define or at least classify violence. In order to shed some light on this methodological issue, it may be useful to consider the fact that many scholars tend to fix the point at which they classify violence. This chapter focuses on the *point* at which the fixing of definitions occur, rather than delving into what exactly constitutes violence (e.g. physical force, psychological intimidation, use of threats, and so on). For an erudite and useful discussion of how to classify violence according to either physical force or violation, see both Bufacchi's (2005) paper and his anthology of violence (Bufacchi, 2009), respectively. Even among 'critical terrorism studies' literatures, there are two chief ways in which PVT definitions are typically negotiated. The first employ predominantly *a priori* reasoning, while the second employ predominantly *a posteriori* reasoning. This chapter briefly considers examples of each approach now, before offering a more promising, dynamic way of negotiating the definitional morass inherent in the field.

Pre-Defining and A Priori Reasoning

The use of *a priori* logic and definition to set out terms of reference and objects of analysis prior to fieldwork may seem synonymous with 'mainstream' terrorism studies. Traditionally, the drive for definitional clarity could be seen as the preserve of Coxian problem-solving experts whose rationale included the preservation of order and smoothing out sources of trouble, identifying risks, and managing terror threats (Jarvis, 2009: 13). What we frequently see from lawmakers, however, as the UK Terrorism Act 2000 showed above, are definitions that are purposefully broad, stretchy, and open to considerable interpretation. Pre-definition is not limited to policymakers and security experts either, but is also used by critical scholars alike. Frequently we see the deconstruction of 'terrorism' as it is presented by the likes of governments, think tanks, and experts, followed by the proposal of a carefully considered and more inclusive definition. Taking seriously as many potential exceptions and inclusions as possible, Ruggiero (2006) is acutely aware of the difficulty of definition, only reluctantly offering a definition based on what he calls 'pure violence':

> The concept of 'pure' violence provides, in this respect, invaluable help: we have pure violence when organized forces, overtly or covertly, inflict mass violence on civilians. Terrorism, therefore, is defined as pure, random violence, incorporating a notion of collective liability. The targets of terrorism,

in other words, are not precisely identifiable actors whose conduct is regarded as wrongful, but general populations, which are hit because of their nationality, ethnicity, religious or political creed. This definition brings to mind not only international terrorism but also, and perhaps even more immediately, the characteristics of contemporary wars. [...] Contemporary international terrorists, in this perspective, appear as 'clones' of those who wage war against them, namely of those who utilize 'pure', random violence against non-combatants.

(Ruggiero, 2006: 6)

Taking such a wide conception of violence, the characteristics of which are set out independently of who commits it, makes Ruggiero's definition suitable for studying both state and non-state violence. Rather than using this language, he refers to 'institutional' and 'anti-institutional' violence, which he usefully demarcates in the following way:

Authorized force amounts to law-making violence, and may be foundational, when it establishes new systems and designates a new authority. But it may also amount to law-conserving violence, when it protects the stability of systems and reinforces authority. I call both these types of violence *institutional violence* (or violence from below). I use the term *anti-institutional violence* (or violence from below) to designate unauthorized force addressed against the authority.

(Ruggiero, 2006: 1)

Similarly, in an attempt to widen our consideration of what constitutes terrorism, Webel (2004: 9) states: 'Terrorism is a premeditated, usually politically motivated, use, or threatened use, of violence, in order to induce a state of terror in its immediate victims, usually for the purposes of influencing another, less reachable audience, such as a government'. As is clear from his definition, acts of terror are often committed against states or in order to influence them. Importantly though, this definition makes space for us to consider political violence committed by both nation-state and subnational individuals and groups alike, unlike the majority of official definitions. Emphasising this point further, he adds that if we consider violence primarily through a moral lens, state terror ('terrorism from above') is even more morally reprehensible than other forms of terrorism due to its sheer scale, resources, and privileged positions of responsibility occupied by the perpetrators (2004: 103).

Despite exhibiting a large degree of moral integrity by not avoiding the issue of state violence, critical pre-definitions such as these still run into difficulty. What we mean by 'mass violence' or even 'random violence', as used in Ruggiero's definition above, remain contestable. They also fail to take into account the often-blurred lines between state and non-state groups, including state-backed militias and paramilitary organisations in receipt of covert state

62 Resilience as Discourse and Practice

backing. Finally, and most importantly, as definitions they are offered as a means of fixing meaning, if only temporarily, independently of the language used by the actors involved. Sartre (1968: 37) summarises this critique of *a priori* reasoning well:

> It [an a priori method] does not derive its concepts from experience – or at least not from the new experiences which it seeks to interpret. It has already formed its concepts; it is already certain of their truth; it will assign to them the role of constitutive schema. Its sole purpose is to force the events, the persons, or the acts considered into prefabricated moulds.

As this chapter will argue, one of the most important aspects of PVT is not only contested language, as alluded to above, but also the way this language intersects with and moulds existing official discourse, established terminologies, and survivor lexicons.

Post-Defining and A Posteriori Reasoning

In order to overcome such difficulties, the second approach commonly used is to leave the problem of definition until after empirical observation and analysis. Interestingly religion, which features in the UK definition and currently occupies perhaps the most scrutinised position in the global war on terror and the search for radicalisation 'drivers', shares many of the same definitional difficulties as terrorism itself. In this vein, as a question of empirical inquiry, Weber (1965 [1922]: 1, emphasis in original) famously advocated *a posteriori* definition, stating that: 'To define "religion", to say what it *is*, is not possible at the start of a presentation such as this. Definition can be attempted, if at all, only at the conclusion of the study' (see also Turner, 2011: 4). Similarly, in recapitulating the challenge of definition, Wieviorka (1995: 598–9) asserts:

> Although we agree that the commonsense notion of terrorism has to be deconstructed, we do not have to begin research by redefining it. Instead, its definition should be the outcome rather than the starting point of our analyses, the conclusion rather than a postulate.

Driving this point further, de Haan (2008: 38) concludes that 'a proper definition of "violence" should not *a priori* be seen as a starting point for empirical research but as a temporary outcome, which may or may not prove to be useful in future research'.

This approach avoids some of the difficulties of the first. In many ways, its most distinguishing feature is a purely inductive approach to analyses rather than a deductive one which sets out terms of reference in advance and seeks to find examples of them. Here, violence simply represents what one finds through the course of doing research. Part of the problem with

To Survivors Themselves 63

this approach, however, is that such a 'blank page' is hard to achieve, particularly with a concept as ubiquitous as 'terrorism'. Furthermore, as the rest of this chapter will argue, such prior knowledge, language, and classifications may be an important point of departure and one we should be paying close attention to. With this in mind, only an approach that can negotiate both *a priori*, *a posteriori* and both deductive and inductive reasoning (*qua* Tavory and Timmermans, 2014) is capable of exploring violence and its aftermaths as a set of ever-moving parts.

Dynamically 'Defining': Violence as Necessarily Contested

The third approach, adopted here, is not to define 'terrorism' at all, partly 'because the concept of terrorism arrived at by the definitional debate obfuscates rather than clarifies its meaning in the situations in which it is actually put to use' (see Ramsay, 2015: 212). Clearly, this is pertinent for a situated study of both organisational framing and participant interview data from a range of diverse events and incidents. Deconstructing terrorism definitions is important, but we must also remain alert to the potential work that both new and existing definitions do. If we take seriously Jackson's (2005: 8) assertion that '[t]he "WAR ON TERRORISM" is the most extensive counterterrorist campaign in history and the most important conflict since the fall of the Berlin Wall', then the way survivors and organisations experience terrorism and its aftermath may be at least partly affected and shaped by this political and historical context. This remains the case for survivors of events preceding the 'war on terror' era and all the ubiquity it represents, whose past experiences are narrated in the context of both the past and present. Pointing to the use of new descriptions to redescribe old actions, Hacking (1995: 6) argues:

> New meanings change the past. It is reinterpreted, yes, but more than that, it is reorganized, repopulated. It becomes filled with new actions, new intentions, new events that caused us to be as we are. I have to discuss not only making up people but making up ourselves by reworking our memories.
>
> (Hacking, 1995: 6)

The world operates through an ongoing and iteratively constituted system of classification moulded by language and action, which changes over time. Despite the apparently sound rationale of Weber and Wieviorka considered above, the idea that definitions, whether posed before or after empirical observation, can fix future activity or even describe it particularly well is unrealistic. As Sacks (1989: 256) says of definitions more generally:

> What has definition got to do with anything? Let's consider what a definition can do. A definition could be an epitaph to be put on a headstone: 'That's

what this was'. The notion that it's a control of activity: that is, if you don't define what you're saying you can't do anything, is an absurdity.

Consistent with Hacking's work, considered in more detail below, and his utilisation of Wittgensteinian language analysis, words are instead more akin to tools, which are adaptable and able to function for multiple purposes. That is, they become useful for the tasks to which they are put. Words, for Wittgenstein, are less like pictures of meaning – that is, that they picture what they are about, than tools of meaning – that is, what they mean is what you can do with them (Wittgenstein, 1958). This furnishes a huge array of meaning without, as Sacks points out above, controlling activity. Of course, where violence is concerned, this huge array of meaning inevitably leads to contestation which changes across time.

Even within the organisation at which fieldwork was conducted, this contestation became quickly apparent. The FfP describe their SAN as follows: 'The "Survivors Assistance Network", run by the Peace Foundation, provides free practical and emotional support to individuals and families affected by a terrorist incident' (The Tim Parry Johnathan Ball Foundation for Peace, 2017). At a later event with several SAN members present, a former member of the Ulster Defence Association gave an invited talk to a group of survivors. Reflecting on his experiences of talking to people about his past, he expressed dismay to learn that following a meeting with a group of American politics students and a fellow former combatant, the students returned, excitedly telling their peers: 'oh we've just been talking to two terrorists!' (Field note, 17 May 2015). The contradiction between the two standpoints is obvious, though no direct conflict arose as a result; again, tying down definitions in advance is guaranteed neither to control activity nor predict it, even when actors in question hold opposing viewpoints. Naming phenomena thus becomes less important than simply describing it.

Resorting to the continued use and abbreviation of 'political violence and terrorism' (PVT) throughout this book came about as a result of such fieldwork observations, so contested and variable was their use by staff and survivors from all manner of conflicts. This posed a methodological problem. Based on sustained (though, crucially, desk-based) research and reading, pre-fieldwork plans included referring to all violence discussed during the project as 'political violence'. However, upon hearing extensive use of other labels (including 'terrorism') by participants, and in light of the preceding discussions around the politicisation of victimhood and the importance of classification, it seemed disingenuous and epistemologically suspect to cast aside the terms of use deployed (consciously or otherwise) by the very actors whose viewpoints the project had purported to be interested in. Thus, a more encompassing shorthand seemed to more faithfully reflect the observations of, and interviews with, the study's participants 'as a whole'. In some respects, this is still an unsatisfactory 'resolution', not least of all because PVT is an unfortunate acronym with unwanted associations with 'mainstream' terrorism studies and the military-industrial complex linking 'terrorism experts', right-wing political think tanks, and strategic/weapons research where 'political violence' and 'terrorism' are often used and abbreviated in tandem to facilitate vague description and thinly veiled diplomacy. A prominent example is the 'Centre for the Study of Terrorism and Political Violence' at St Andrews University, founded by 'terrorism expert' Paul Wilkinson in 1994 and synonymous with UK counterterrorism policymaking (Miller and Mills, 2009: 426; see also Burnett and Whyte, 2005). Furthermore, within the global insurance industry 'PVT' policies, described in purposefully vague terms for obvious reasons, are now commonplace in relation to a panoply of mitigation and risk management. In other respects, this wider-ranging, dynamic and language-led (decidedly un-definitional) 'definition' not only stems from first-hand fieldwork observations but aptly reflects the broader historical journey of the charity organisation that kindly facilitated access and collaboration in this project.

A final note on terminology, which straddles the first two sections of this chapter, is important. 'Victim' and 'survivor' are also deeply politicised terms. Debates about their respective origins, characteristics, and connotations have occurred in a range of intellectual spaces, from feminist literatures around sexual violence (Kelly, Burton and Regan, 1996) to political violence rooted in specific geopolitical conflicts (Dillenburger, Fargas and Akhonzada, 2006), among others. These debates are acknowledged but not embellished here. As with several labels used throughout this work to denote contested phenomena (including fraught classifications of both violent acts and the social actors involved), there is a need to represent this tension as it presents itself empirically while doing so within practicable limits. To reiterate a point made in the last paragraph, at times these practicable limits might seem unsatisfactory. However, they reflect the language predominantly used by the organisation and participants who were studied, in a bid to stay 'close' to the context in which empirical data was gathered and the messy moral considerations around violence implicated in this book were forged. The words 'victim' and 'survivor' are both used but the latter preferred. All participants interviewed can be considered survivors for different reasons. 'Survivor' refers to both individuals who have personally survived acts of PVT, or to family and friends of victims killed in such acts who they literally 'survive'. It is for these reasons that the FfP's SAN is named as such. As the start of Chapter 4 explores, the term 'survivor' elicited different responses and resonated disparately among participants.

PVT and understandings of it presented in this study are informed primarily through empirical investigation and discussion with survivors; with this insight it may be possible to suggest groupings of shared experiences or incidents which seem to commonly reflect what survivors understand to be terrorism. It has been justifiably argued that we should not attempt to define terrorism precisely because it is not the act(s) itself that denotes terrorism but our subsequent debates around morality, legitimacy, and violence prompted by these acts (Ramsay, 2015). Whilst this may share some ties with state definitions of terrorism (as politically motivated), it goes further in insisting that it is only our responses to it that fix notions of terror, rejecting the notion that terrorism's political effectiveness is preordained.

Acknowledging the imprecision of words such as 'terrorism' and, indeed, 'political violence' and the rendering effect they can have over victim experiences of diverse histories (Lynch and Argomaniz, 2015: 3–4), on what basis were participants identified then? Despite the preceding discussion, surely some parameters were necessary for identifying and recruiting survivors? I relied on three key features of PVT, adopted from Lynch and Argomaniz (2015).

Firstly, the violence or threat of violence in question was politically motivated. Secondly, who the perpetrators of such violence or threats of violence were was immaterial vis-à-vis whether we understand that violence as 'terrorism'. Lastly, and most importantly, rather than using a definition to artificially encapsulate the experiences of a group of survivors as diverse as those involved in this study, PVT will be described in its effects as they were described by those individuals. As an 'organizing concept' (Crenshaw, 1995: 9), terrorism denotes a disparate contextual array of time-place and political conflicts. Like all social change, its causes, effects, and cultural repercussions cannot be divorced from the contested history that preceded it. Like all forms of violence, for a range of technical, ethical, political, and moral reasons, terrorism must remain an 'essentially contested concept' (de Haan, 2008; Lynch and Argomaniz, 2015: 3).

While naming in the form of definitions is less important than naming according to what survivors say, naming remains powerful. As Hacking (2004: 279–80) emphasises, descriptions used by people inform classifications which in turn have the ability of influencing behaviour; subsequent changes in behaviour often force changes in descriptions and thus classifications, producing what he calls 'looping effect of human kinds'. This forms the basis of his dialectical realism, not as a way of deconstructing political violence but rather partially reconstructing it in relation to the lived experiences of civilians whose lives have been affected by it while taking account of their relationship to the FfP. Treating language dynamically in this way avoids some of the impasses of pre or post-definitions. Given the importance of this body of work for my analysis, it is to Ian Hacking's work that the final section of this chapter now turns.

Making Sense of the Past in the Present: Making Up People

This book takes elements from analytic philosopher Ian Hacking's work as a critical point of departure and return for thinking through the epistemological problems posed by researching first-hand narratives of PVT survivors. More specifically, it draws upon his critiques of 'social construction' (Hacking, 1999) as a way of sceptically, yet positively, asking how we might say something tangible about the discursive *idea* of 'resilience' without losing sight of survivors' reported experiences through their narratives as the phenomeno-logical *object* of analysis – whether the latter necessarily coheres with the former or not (Hacking, 1997). Importantly, discursive ideas are brought into being and shaped as much by academics and 'experts' as they are by policymakers, politicians, civil society groups, and the media. Hence, such an approach allows for (and encourages) a reflexive questioning of academic knowledge while concomitantly paying attention to changes in apparently more 'natural' phe-nomena. Keeping this principle in mind, while remembering the historical ascendency of 'resilience' within both policy and academic research in recent decades, Hacking's introductory remarks about his novel conception of a 'his-torical ontology' provoke curiosity if we think about the discursive emergence of 'resilient survivors', 'resilient communities', and indeed the 'resilient nation', particularly since the London tube attacks of 2005, as explored in Chapter 1:

> [S]ome of the old connotations of 'ontology' serve me well, for I want to talk about objects in general. Not just things, but whatever we indi-viduate and allow ourselves to talk about. That includes not only 'material' objects but also classes, kinds of people, *and, indeed, ideas*. Finally, if we are concerned with the coming into being of the very possibility of some objects, what is that if not historical?
>
> (Hacking, 2002: 2, emphasis added)

The influence of interactionist sociology and Wittgensteinian language ana-lysis in Hacking's work, along with the fluid understandings of power derived from Foucault, is evident in his interest in how individuals are constituted and constitute themselves as subjects and not merely pushed in certain directions according to the abstract flows of social systems. 'In thinking of constituting ourselves', he writes, 'we should think of constituting *as* so and so; we are concerned, in the end, with possible ways to be a person' (Hacking, 2002: 2, emphasis in original).

This kind of focus on the individual also chimes with earlier sociological approaches. Max Weber asserted that our endeavours to understand the social world must fundamentally begin with the individual which he saw as the only 'unit of investigation' capable of meaningful social action (Parkin, 1982: 17). In suggesting this, Weber did not believe that only individuals matter or that we can make no broader generalisations beyond the level of the individual, but rather that our attempts to understand how society works must acknowledge that the worldviews of the social actors involved in it (not necessarily the quality or veracity of such worldviews, simply their existence) are integral factors in its (i.e. society's) (re)production. This central principle forms the basis of his classic Verstehen sociology (see Hughes, Martin and Sharrock, 1995: 137) and funda-mentally underpins the endeavours of this project. This work aims to explore the worldview of the PVT survivor. Temporarily leaving aside considerations of how logics of social control may operate, how do survivors who have direct

68   Resilience as Discourse and Practice

experience of PVT understand resilience? Alternatively, how closely do their experiences appear to cohere with theoretical and policy frameworks of resilience? Epistemologically then, the task at hand requires a return to one of the oldest rationales in the interpretive sociological tradition, broadly speaking: to understand glimpses of a worldview other than our own; in this case, from the standpoint of survivors of PVT.

However, discursive projections of what individuals, communities, and nations affected by political violence look like and how they should behave cannot be ignored. As an organising metaphor, resilience displays unprecedented reach in contemporary governance as shown through both governmentality and genealogical analyses (see, for example, Joseph, 2013 and Walker and Cooper, 2011, respectively). Both directly and indirectly, work such as this stands on the shoulders of Foucault (Michelsen, 2017) and shares his concern with documenting the diffuse techniques of discipline that are at work when, in this case, we naturalise, and aspire to become, 'resilient subjects'. Interestingly, while the historical work and political ethics of Weber and Foucault 'lie worlds apart', it is this concern with questions of rationalisation that unite them (Gane, 2004: 129–30). Returning to Weber's prioritisation of the individual as capable of meaningful social action, a move later extended radically by Erving Goffman, without abandoning Foucault's overriding interest in discursive practice, we may usefully draw on Hacking's dynamic nominalism (which he also refers to as dialectical realism (Hacking, 2004: 279–80)). Hacking (2004) draws on both Foucault and various contributors from the existentialist and interactionist traditions, including Goffman and Sartre, to explore the ways in which people are classified and react to such classifications. Despite the aims of this research being to look beyond the ways in which survivors of political violence are imagined in public policy and media framings, it would be unrealistic to think that such framings have had no bearing on the way NGOs such as the FfP come to define survivors. There is also the possibility that survivors themselves have considered their relation to such framings, which may in turn influence the way they perceive and cope with their experiences. As Hacking (2004: 279–80) puts it:

> The traditional extreme nominalist is supposed to hold that stars, or algae, or justice, have nothing in common except for their names, that is, the usage of the words 'star' or 'algae' or 'justice'. [...] I am not sure there has ever been such a paradoxical nominalist. Dynamic nominalism is a nominalism in action, directed at new or changing classifications of people. In some cases, it suggests that there was not a kind of person who increasingly came to be recognized, and to which a new name was given. Rather a kind of person came into being at the same time that the name (or a special sense of that name) became current. In some cases our classifications and the classified emerge hand-in-hand, each egging the other on. [...] I could equally call this philosophy *dialectical realism*. I like this alternative, for the

classes of individuals that come into being are real enough, in any plausible sense of the word. They come into being by a dialectic between classification and who is classified. *Naming has real effects on people, and changes in people have real effects on subsequent classifications* (emphasis added). In any event, we are not concerned with an arid logical nominalism or a dogmatic realism. Above all, this philosophy is both dynamic and dialectical.

This 'special sense of a name' alluded to by Hacking usefully hints at historical points of changed emphasis or rupture in the way language is deployed, for example, in the shift to exhortations of citizen resilience in the face of terror and trauma. Hacking's epistemology also offers a useful framework for negotiating analytical issues associated with testimony, memory, and the recounting of historical events. As Marxist anthropologist Michael Taussig similarly argues, neither events nor the influence of time on our abilities or proclivities to interpret them stand still, furnishing ever-changing ways of making sense of ourselves, our pasts, and our desired futures:

> It is not just that our perception is historically conditioned, that the eye becomes here an organ of history, that sensations are a form of activity and not passive carbon copies of externals, but that the history that informs this activity also informs our understanding of seeing and of history itself.
> (Taussig, 2010 [1980]: 8)

The time span between critical incidents affecting participants and the interviews used in this book (which were all conducted between March and November 2016) varied from just over a year to just under 45 years. Methodologically, how might we negotiate the issue of interviewing people about events from such a wide time range? While several questions may spin-off this, one that I was frequently asked during conference discussions specifically concerned questions of historical accuracy and the fallibility of human memory, inevitably returning to debates about account authenticity. While this is an age-old epistemological question around how we (think we) know what we know and what we understand to represent 'truth', an individual's cognitive or neurological reliability of memory need not be established in order to say something meaningful about how violence has affected their outlook on life. Whether the labelling of phenomena (e.g. as 'victimhood', 'terrorism', 'traumatic', or 'resilient') are even clear when such events occur, and how descriptions of those historical phenomena may reflect subsequent available lexicons, are both implicated in this question of memory. Hacking remains alert to this contingency, while being unequivocal in his stance towards memory recall:

> I am not here preoccupied by the customary question, [...] of whether a memory accurately represents the past. I am concerned with the phenomenon of indeterminacy of human action in the past. In various ways it may

not have been determinate, then, that an action fell under certain present-day descriptions. Thus the question of accuracy may not arise, at least not in any direct or simplistic version.

(Hacking, 1995: 254)

Unless one's memory recall around an event no longer exists at all, the way people describe how routine life events since a violent incident *are said* to relate to '*that*' event is important precisely because of how people choose to relay their story. From a dialectical realist perspective (*qua* Hacking, 2004), the literal accuracy of testimony is less important than the practical work that testimony does and has done to it (or is done because of it).

Another important point is that while being cautious or even sceptical towards the accuracy of historical testimony might be prudent in some contexts, it runs the risk of assuming ignorance on the part of the actors involved. It was clear during the research that survivors are acutely aware of their ability or tendency to express themselves differently each time they tell and retell their stories. Many participants pointed out that there were bound to be parts of the story that they had forgotten to describe on that particular occasion, and others knew that they told different versions of the same story. Several participants acknowledged that certain ways of describing the past simply were not available to them before, either because they literally did not exist (see Paul's explanation in Chapter 3, that PTSD 'didn't exist back then' [in 1972], having not been invented for another eight years), or because they had not been 'educated' towards these descriptions and lexicons yet by therapists, counsellors, or FfP staff (see Chapters 4 and 6 in particular). Why this should be the case is, in and of itself, fascinating and points both to vast connections such events may hold across survivors' lives (including people, places, and little anecdotes that these spark), but also to changing life circumstances in which past events are framed anew. It was always possible, due to the high-profile nature of the events being described, to read and watch other information sources to help to corroborate aspects of accounts being offered. Corroboration, however, was only ever meant to clarify factual time/place details for the researcher's benefit and not to verify survivors' reliability at relaying events. Writing from a novelist's perspective, Murakami (2003: 214) captures this perfectly when reflecting on his experiences of interviewing survivors and perpetrators of the 1995 Tokyo gas attacks:

Generally few attempts were made to check whether the statements made in the interviews were factually correct or not, other than when they obviously contradicted known facts. Some people might object to this, but my job was to listen to what people had to say and to record this as clearly as possible. Even if there are some details inconsistent with reality, the collective narrative of these personal stories has a powerful reality of its own.

Simply listening to what people had to say, articulated in their terms, and attempting at all times to convey this as faithfully as possible, thus upholds a certain moral and compassionate precedent evident in calls to 'bear witness' to suffering through social research (*qua* Quinney, 1998, 2000; Spencer, 2010; McGarry and Walklate, 2015).

In sum, Hacking's (1995, 1997, 1999, 2002, 2004) long-standing scepticism towards declarations of 'socially constructed' phenomena does not assert universal scientific objectivity, but rather guards against the glossing over of concrete and documentable observations of the social world with vacuous truisms that often lack either empirical evidence or sufficient analytical depth. Hacking's interests span a wide-array of topics including mathematics, science and technology studies, and mental illness, among many others. Some of these topics entail a greater focus on human (over non-human) subjects than others and many demand recognition of scientifically objective facts. Taking seriously both constructionist arguments and biological facts when thinking through the dynamics of classification, Hacking (1997) proposed the notion of 'interactive kinds' and 'indifferent kinds' in his analysis of people in the human/social sciences and unaware 'things' in the natural sciences, respectively.

Documentable observations might include historical practices, attitudes and beliefs, or new ways of talking, describing, or classifying things (including through academic parlance) – in short, things that are not fixed or inevitable. In at least this respect, Hacking's epistemology shares with Weber (1949: 72, emphasis in original) a wish 'to understand on the one hand the relationships and the cultural significance of individual events in their contemporary manifestations and on the other the causes of their being historically *so* and not *otherwise*'. Beside this incidental link with classic historical sociology, his deliberate and explicit connection between Wittgensteinian language analyses, aspects of Sartrean and Goffmanian social interactionism, and Foucault's archaeological method combine to produce an account of time and change that sits comfortably alongside social representation theorists across the social science spectrum. His life's work on the history of scientific ideas, science and technology studies, and classificatory practices that give rise to new ways of new kinds of things (including people) to 'come into being', stimulated in large part by the work of philosopher Elizabeth Anscombe, come together to form what he describes as a dialectical or dynamic relationship (variously termed *dialectical realism* or *dynamic nominalism*). This relationship comprises three interrelated stages of social action: (i) macro-level discourse; (ii) the everyday practices which are prevented, changed, or made possible by such discourse; (iii) subsequent shifts in discursive practices to accommodate new ways of being that have outgrown old ways of talking, labelling, or describing.

Hacking's work is flagged up in some of the following chapters where his insights bring clarity to discussions of the data. Beyond these discussions, his work informed the iterative way in which data was read and analysed, operationalised through Tavory and Timmermans' (2014) abductive analysis to both look

72 Resilience as Discourse and Practice

deductively for characteristics of so-called resilience found in Chapter 1 and to read inductively for surprising or apparently unconnected themes in survivors' narratives. To reiterate the note on theory and method in the introduction, this analysis was not done in order to generate a 'theory of resilience', nor to generalise beyond the specific cases found here. While Hacking (2002: 114) terms his approach to studying classificatory knowledge and our shifting relations to such knowledge, 'making up people', he also concludes: 'I see no reason to suppose that we shall ever tell two identical stories of two different instances of making up people'. In asking readers to think about the 'making up' of 'resilient survivors', it is hoped that they will perhaps be given pause to reflect on their own lives, their own experiences, and their own research topics – what mixture of things, be they psychological, interpersonal, historical, contemporary, political, or discursive, come together to constitute, or 'make up', you and the world around you?

Conclusion

This chapter has outlined a framework for thinking through contested definitions of 'terrorism' and 'political violence' which rely on neither *a priori* nor *a posteriori* reasoning but that remain alert to society's changing interactions with sociolegal classifications on a case-by-case basis. As the chapter explained, activities associated with 'terrorism' are already prohibited under existing laws (Grozdanova, 2014: 333), yet history has repeatedly shown that the designation of an act as 'terrorism' allows for an extension of legal powers, or 'special measures', and emphasises an enhanced role for discretionary deployment of those powers in the pursuit of countering 'terrorism' once defined (see, *inter alia*, Agamben, 2005; Chomsky, 2015; Shehadeh, 2015). In short, debates and disputes around what constitutes terrorism are fought in sociopolitical, rather than strictly legal, realms. Fuelled by high-profile attacks on Western States and their citizenry in recent years, appeals to victimhood at individual, local, national, and international levels continue to represent discursive keystones within anti-terror rhetoric and policy. Connecting this point to Chapter 1, this has been partly characterised by an increased emphasis on victims' resilience in the face of always-already-present catastrophe.

Despite some evidence pointing to the pertinence of resilience for survivors reviewed in Chapter 1, it remains an intensely contested concept. Subjecting some of the assumptions made around resilience and victimhood within policy and academic fields to grounded empirical scrutiny, this book explores a standpoint largely neglected in the sociological and criminological literature – that of the PVT survivor. Drawing together several conclusions from Chapter 1, it is clear that resilience is a complex, subjective, and multifaceted everyday reality for individuals which is exercised both outside, and in spite of, 'big policy' and global capitalist developments (Walklate, McGarry and Mythen, 2014; Cavelty, Kaufmann, and Kristensen, 2015; Brassett and Vaughan-Williams,

2015). Consequently, more critical analyses of victimhood capable of exploring vulnerability through discussions of both 'injurability' and agency are needed (Schott, 2013; see also Walklate, 2011; McGowan, 2016).

The eclectic sample of survivors interviewed during this project reflects a range of PVT perpetrated at various levels, from individuals to violence committed by state or state-backed groups, taking seriously the need to refocus scholarly attention on the immoral use of violence where it occurs, independently of who perpetrates it (Gearty, 2002). What links them is not necessarily their experienced event but rather the FfP as a site at which they were almost all variously engaged in acts of storytelling. These survivors have experienced events spanning more than forty years between them – including events that occurred long before, and well into, the 21st-century WOT. This is important, offering a holistic viewpoint from which to analyse the messy and necessarily contested understandings of PVT discussed earlier in this chapter. The focus on terrorism as a post-9/11 tranche of study to some extent reifies already rigid conceptions of what terrorism is, potentially diverting our attentions from the many conflicts that punctuated the 20th century and continue today (see Toros, 2017). This book takes a broader view of PVT and whom it affects, thus offering a study informed by historical comparison and temporal inflection. A recurring effort has been made in this chapter to stress the importance of power, narrative, and legitimacy. Ultimately, those with greatest power often dictate the narrative structure terrorist violence ostensibly takes in an effort to establish their own legitimacy and undermine that of the enemy, be that domestic, international, military, or paramilitary. This has profound implications for the way we view, hear, and represent the PVT survivor. The following three chapters focus exclusively on the voices of survivors in the data collected, before picking back up and revisiting such implications towards the end of the book.

Note

1 The history of the IRA as a political movement, including contested understandings of its visions, causes, membership criteria, name and organisational ethos is a complex one beyond the scope of this book (though see, for example, Coogan, 2002 and English, 2003). Reference to the IRA at various points throughout the book, reflective of different parts of their history both pre and post-Good Friday Agreement (GFA) 1998, is not intended to cast the movement in monolithic terms but rather proceeds with a cognisance of this complexity.

References

Agamben, G. (1999) *Remnants of Auschwitz: The Witness and the Archive*. New York: Zone Books.

Agamben, G. (2005) *State of Exception*. Chicago: The University of Chicago Press.

Becker, H.S. (1967) Whose side are we on? *Social Problems* 14(3): 239–47.

74 Resilience as Discourse and Practice

Bloom, M. and Horgan, J. (2008) Missing their mark: The IRA's proxy bomb campaign. *Social Research* 75(2): 579–614.

Brassett, J. and Vaughan-Williams, N. (2015) Security and the performative politics of resilience: Critical infrastructure protection and humanitarian emergency preparedness. *Security Dialogue* 46(1): 32–50.

Breen Smyth, M., Gunning, J., Jackson, R., Kassimeris, G. and Robinson, P. (2008) Critical terrorism studies – An introduction. *Critical Studies on Terrorism* 1(1): 1–4.

Bufacchi, V. (2005) Two concepts of violence. *Political Studies Review* 3: 193–204.

Bufacchi, V. (Ed.) (2009) *Violence: A Philosophical Anthology*. Hampshire: Palgrave Macmillan.

Burnett, J. and Whyte, D. (2005) Embedded expertise and the new terrorism. *Journal for Crime, Conflict and the Media* 1(4): 1–18.

Cameron, D. (2015) 7/7 Bombings: David Cameron honours victims. *The Guardian*, July 7. www.theguardian.com/uk-news/video/2015/jul/07/77-july-london-bombings-david-cameronhonours-victims-video [Accessed 09/02/2017].

Cavelty, M.D., Kaufmann, M. and Kristensen, K.S. (2015) Resilience and (in)security: Practices, subjects, temporalities. *Security Dialogue* 46(1): 3–14.

Chomsky, N. (2015) *Culture of Terrorism*. 2nd edition. London: Pluto Press.

Cohen, S. (1972) *Folk Devils and Moral Panics: The Creation of the Mods and Rockers*. London: MacGibbon and Kee Ltd.

Coogan, T.P. (2002) *The IRA* (revised and updated). New York: St Martin's Press.

Crenshaw, M. (1995) Thoughts on relating terrorism to historical contexts. In M. Crenshaw (Ed.) *Terrorism in Context*. University Park, PA: The Pennsylvania State University Press. pp.3–26.

Croft, S. (2006) *Culture, Crisis and America's War on Terror*. Cambridge: Cambridge University Press.

Davies, C. and Addley, E. (2015) 7/7: London comes together to remember and reflect 10 years on. *The Guardian*, July 7. www.theguardian.com/uk-news/2015/jul/07/77-bombslondonmemorial-10-years [Accessed 09/02/2017].

de Haan, W. (2008) Violence as an essentially contested concept. In S. Body-Gendrot and P. Spierenburg (Eds.) *Violence in Europe: Historical and Contemporary Perspectives*. New York: Springer. pp.27–40.

Department for Education (2014) *Promoting Fundamental British Values as part of SMSC in Schools: Departmental Advice for Maintained Schools*. London: Crown copyright.

Dillenburger, K., Fargas, M. and Akhonzada, R. (2006) Victims or survivors? Debate about victimhood in Northern Ireland. *The International Journal of the Humanities* 3: 222–31.

English, R. (2003) *Armed Struggle: The History of the IRA*. Oxford: Oxford University Press.

Fassin, D. (2011) The trace: Violence, truth and the politics of the body. *Social Research* 78(2): 281–98.

Gabriel, Y. (2000) *Storytelling in Organizations: Facts, Fictions, and Fantasies*. Oxford: Oxford University Press.

Gane, N. (2004) *Max Weber and Postmodern Theory: Rationalization versus Re-enchantment*. Hampshire: Palgrave Macmillan.

Gearty, C. (2002) Terrorism and morality. *European Human Rights Law Review* 4: 377–83.

Gilbert, E. (2017) Victim compensation for acts of terrorism and the limits of the state. *Critical Studies on Terrorism* DOI: https://doi.org/10.1080/17539153.2017.1411234.

Ginsberg, R. (2014) Mighty crime victims: Victims' rights and neoliberalism in the American conjuncture. *Cultural Studies* 28(5/6): 911–46.

Göl, A. (2010) Editors' introduction: Views from the 'Others' of the war on terror. *Critical Studies on Terrorism* 3(1): 1–5.

Grozdanova, R. (2014) 'Terrorism' – too elusive a term for an international legal definition? *Netherlands International Law Review* 61(3): 305–34.

Gunning, J. (2007a) A case for critical terrorism studies? *Government and Opposition* 42(3): 363–93.

Gunning, J. (2007b) Babies and bathwaters: Reflecting on the pitfalls of critical terrorism studies. *European Political Science* 6(3): 236–43.

Hacking, I. (1995) *Rewriting the Soul: Multiple Personality and the Sciences of Memory.* Princeton, NJ: Princeton University Press.

Hacking, I. (1997) Taking bad arguments seriously. *London Review of Books* 19(16): 14–16.

Hacking, I. (1999) *The Social Construction of What?* Cambridge: Harvard University Press.

Hacking, I. (2002) *Historical Ontology.* Cambridge: Harvard University Press.

Hacking, I. (2004) Between Michel Foucault and Erving Goffman: Between discourse in the abstract and face-to-face interaction. *Economy and Society* 33(3): 277–302.

Hall, S., Critcher, C., Jefferson, T., Clarke, J. and Roberts, B. (1978) *Policing The Crisis: Mugging, the State, and Law and Order.* London: The MacMillan Press Ltd.

Harrison, E. (2013) Bouncing back? Recession, resilience and everyday lives. *Critical Social Policy* 33(1): 97–113.

Heath-Kelly, C., Jarvis, L. and Baker-Beall, C. (2014) Editors' introduction: Critical terrorism studies: Practice, limits and experience. *Critical Studies on Terrorism* 7(1): 1–10.

Hickey, D., Li, S.S., Morrison, C., Schulz, R., Thiry, M. and Sorensen, K. (2017) Unit 731 and moral repair. *Journal of Medical Ethics* 43(4): 270–6.

Hillyard, P. (1993) *Suspect Community: People's Experiences of the Prevention of Terrorism Acts in Britain.* London: Pluto Press.

Holland, J. and Jarvis, L. (2014) 'Night fell on a different world': Experiencing, constructing and remembering 9/11. *Critical Studies on Terrorism* 7(2): 187–204.

Hughes, J.A., Martin, P.J. and Sharrock, W.W. (1995) *Understanding Classical Sociology: Marx, Weber, Durkheim.* London: Sage Publications Ltd.

Innes, A.J. and Steele, B.J. (2015) Spousal visa law and structural violence: Fear, anxiety and terror of the everyday. *Critical Terrorism Studies* 8(3): 401–15.

Jackson, R. (2005) *Writing the War on Terrorism: Language, Politics and Counter-terrorism.* Manchester: Manchester University Press.

Jackson, R. (2007) The core commitments of critical terrorism studies. *European Political Science* 6(3): 244–51.

Jackson, R., M. Breen Smyth, and J. Gunning (2009) (Eds.) *Critical Terrorism Studies: A New Research Agenda.* London: Routledge.

Jarvis, L. (2009) *Times of Terror: Discourse, Temporality and the War on Terror.* Hampshire: Palgrave.

Jarvis, L. and Lister, M. (2015) *Anti-Terrorism, Citizenship and Security.* Manchester: Manchester University Press.

Jenkins, P. (2003) *Images of Terror: What We Can and Can't Know about Terrorism.* New York: Aldine de Gruyter.

Joseph, J. (2013) Resilience as embedded neoliberalism: A governmentality approach. *Resilience: International Policies, Practices and Discourses* 1(1): 38–52.

76 Resilience as Discourse and Practice

Kelly, L., Burton, S. and Regan, L. (1996) Beyond victim or survivor: Sexual violence, identity and feminist theory and practice. In L. Adkins and V. Merchant (Eds.) *Sexualizing the Social: Power and the Organization of Sexuality*. London: Palgrave. pp.77–101.

Krause, M. (2014) *The Good Project: Humanitarian Relief NGOs and the Fragmentation of Reason*. Chicago: The University of Chicago Press.

Lelourec, L. (2017) Responding to the IRA bombing campaign in mainland Britain: The case of Warrington. In G. Dawson, J. Dover and S. Hopkins (Eds.) *The Northern Ireland Troubles in Britain: Impacts, Engagements, Legacies and Memories*. Manchester: Manchester University Press. pp.263–78.

Lewis, H. (2015) When is a terrorist not a terrorist? When he's a white man with a gun. *New Statesman*, [online] 2 July 2015. Available at: www.newstatesman.com/politics/2015/07/when-terrorist-not-terrorist-when-he-s-white-man-gun [Accessed 07/07/2015].

Lord Carlile of Berriew (2007) *The Definition of Terrorism: A Report by Lord Carlile of Berriew Q. C, Independent Reviewer of Terrorism Legislation*. Home Office. London: Stationary Office.

Lynch, O. and Argomaniz, J. (2015) Victims of terrorism: An introduction. In O. Lynch and J. Argomaniz (Eds.) *Victims of Terrorism: A Comparative and Interdisciplinary Study*. London: Routledge. pp.1–9.

Martin, G. (2013) *Understanding Terrorism: Challenges, Perspectives and Issues*. 4th edition. Thousand Oaks: Sage Publications, Inc.

McDonald, M. (2009) Emancipation and critical terrorism studies. In R. Jackson, M. Breen Smyth and J. Gunning (Eds.) *Critical Terrorism Studies: A New Research Agenda*. London: Routledge. pp.109–23.

McGarry, R. (2013) Dismantling Woolwich: Terrorism 'pure and simple'? *Criminal Justice Matters* 95(1): 28–9.

McGarry, R. (2016) Hierarchical victims of terrorism and war. In D.C. Spencer and S. Walklate (Eds.) *Reconceptualizing Critical Victimology*. London: Lexington Books. pp.155–72.

McGarry, R., and S. Walklate. (2015) *Victims: Trauma, Testimony and Justice*. London: Routledge.

McGowan, W. (2016) Critical terrorism studies, victimisation, and policy relevance: Compromising politics or challenging hegemony? *Critical Studies on Terrorism* 9(1): 12–32.

Michelsen, N. (2017) On the genealogy of strategies: Resilience in the revolution. *Resilience: International Policies, Practices and Discourses* 5(1): 61–77.

Miller, D. and Mills, T. (2009) The terror experts and the mainstream media: The expert nexus and its dominance in the news media. *Critical Studies on Terrorism* 2(3): 414–37.

Murakami, H. (2003) *Underground: The Tokyo Gas Attack and the Japanese Psyche*. Translated from Japanese by Birnbaum, A. and Gabriel, P. London: Vintage.

Mythen, G. (2012) 'No one speaks for us': Security policy, suspected communities and the problem of voice. *Critical Studies on Terrorism* 5(3): 409–24.

Mythen, G. and Walklate, S. (2012) Global terrorism, risk and the state. In S. Hall and S. Winlow (Eds.) *New Directions in Criminological Theory*. London: Routledge. pp.317–32.

Mythen, G., Walklate, S. and Khan, F. (2009) 'I'm a Muslim but I'm not a terrorist': Victimization, risky identities and the performance of safety. *British Journal of Criminology* 49(6): 736–54.

Mythen, G., Walklate, S. and Khan, F. (2012) 'Why should we have to prove we're alright?': Counter-terrorism, risk and partial securities. *Sociology* 47(2): 383–98.

Neocleous, M. (2003) *Imagining the State*. Maidenhead: Open University Press.

Pantazis, C. and Pemberton, S. (2009) From the 'old' to the 'new' suspect community: Examining the impacts of recent UK counter-terrorist legislation. *British Journal of Criminology* 49(5): 646–66.

Parkin, F. (1982) *Max Weber*. Chichester: Ellis Horwood Limited.

Quinney, R. (1972) Who is the victim? Criminology November: 309–29.

Quinney, R. (1998) Criminology as moral philosophy, criminologist as witness. *Contemporary Justice Review* 1: 347–64.

Quinney, R. (2000). *Bearing Witness to Crime and Social Justice*. Albany: State University of New York Press.

Ramsay, G. (2015) Why terrorism can, but should not be defined. *Critical Studies on Terrorism* 8(2): 211–28.

Reinharz, S. (1992) *Feminist Methods in Social Research*. Oxford: Oxford University Press.

Rentschler, C.A. (2011) *Second Wounds: Victims' Rights and the Media in the U.S.* Durham, NC: Duke University Press.

Roach, K. (2011) *The 9/11 Effect: Comparative Counter-Terrorism*. New York: Cambridge University Press.

Roach, K. and Trotter, G. (2005) Miscarriages of justice in the war against terrorism. *Penn State Law Review* 109(4): 967.

Rock, P. (2002) On becoming a victim. In C. Hoyle and R. Young (Eds.) *New Visions of Crime Victims*. Oxford: Hart Publishing. pp.1–22.

Ruggiero, V. (2006) *Understanding Political Violence: A Criminological Analysis*. Maidenhead: Open University Press.

Sacks, H. (1989) Lecture four: An impromptu survey of the literature. *Human Studies* 12(3/4): 253–9.

Sands, P. (2009) *Torture Team: Uncovering War Crimes in the Land of the Free*. London: Penguin Books Ltd.

Sartre, J.P. (1968) *Search for a Method*. New York: Vintage Books.

Schmid, A.P. (1984) *Political Terrorism: A Research Guide to Concepts, Theories, Databases and Literature*. New Brunswick, NJ: Transaction Books.

Schott, R.M. (2013) Resilience, normativity and vulnerability. *Resilience: International Policies, Practices and Discourses* 1(3): 210–18.

Shehadeh, R. (2015) *Language of War, Language of Peace: Palestine, Israel and the search for justice*. London: Profile Books Ltd.

Simmonds, L. (2016) The potential impact of local commissioning on victim services in England and Wales. *International Review of Victimology* 22(3): 223–37.

Sjoberg, L. and Gentry, C.E. (2015) Introduction: Gender and everyday/intimate terrorism. *Critical Studies on Terrorism* 8(3): 358–61.

Spalek, B. (2006) *Crime Victims: Theory, Policy and Practice*. Hampshire: Palgrave Macmillan.

Spencer, D. (2010). Event and victimisation. *Criminal Law and Philosophy* 5(1): 39–52.

Taussig, M.T. (2010[1980]) *The Devil and Commodity Fetishism in South America*. Chapel Hill: The University of North Carolina Press.

Tavory, I. and Timmermans, S. (2014) *Abductive Analysis: Theorizing Qualitative Research*. Chicago: The University of Chicago Press.

The Tim Parry Johnathan Ball Foundation for Peace (2017) Survivors Assistance Network: Have you or someone you know been affected by an act of terrorism at

78 Resilience as Discourse and Practice

home or abroad? [online] Available at: http://foundation4peace.org/survivors-assista nce-network-we-can-help/ [Accessed 16/01/2017].

Thornton, R. (2011) Counterterrorism and the Neoliberal University: Providing a check and balance? *Critical Studies on Terrorism* 4(3): 421–9.

Toros, H. (2017) '9/11 is alive and well' or how critical terrorism studies has sustained the 9/11 narrative. *Critical Studies on Terrorism* 10(2): 203–19.

Turner, B.S. (2011) *Religion and Modern Society: Citizenship, Secularisation and the State.* Cambridge: Cambridge University Press.

Walker, J. and Cooper, M. (2011) Genealogies of resilience: From systems ecology to the political economy of crisis adaptation. *Security Dialogue* 42(2): 143–60.

Walklate, S. (2011) Reframing criminal victimization: Finding a place for vulnerability and resilience. *Theoretical Criminology* 15(2): 179–94.

Walklate, S. (2012) Who is the victim of crime? Paying homage to the work of Richard Quinney. *Crime Media Culture* 8(2): 173–84.

Walklate, S. and Mythen, G. (2015) *Contradictions of Terrorism: Security, Risk and Resilience.* London: Routledge.

Walklate, S., Maher, J., McCulloch, J., Fitz-Gibbon, K. and Beavis, K. (2019) Victim stories and victim policy: Is there a case for a narrative victimology? *Crime, Media, Culture* 15(2): 199–215.

Walklate, S., McCulloch, J., Fitz-Gibbon, K. and Maher, J. (2017) Criminology, gender and security in the Australian context: Making women's lives matter. *Theoretical Criminology* Online Advanced Access: https://doi.org/10.1177%2F1362480617719 449 [Accessed 26/02/2018].

Walklate, S., McGarry, R. and Mythen, G. (2014) Searching for resilience: A conceptual excavation. *Armed Forces & Society* 40(3): 408–27.

Webb, S. (2000) Feminist methodologies for social researching. In D. Burton (Ed.) *Research Training for Social Scientists: A Handbook for Postgraduate Researchers.* London: Sage Publications Ltd.

Webel, C.P. (2004) *Terror, Terrorism, and the Human Condition.* Hampshire: Palgrave Macmillan.

Weber, M. (1948) *From Max Weber: Essays in Sociology.* Translated and Edited by H.H. Gerth and C.W. Mills. London: Routledge.

Weber, M. (1949) *The Methodology of the Social Sciences.* Translated and Edited by E.A. Shils and H.A. Finch. New York: The Free Press.

Weber, M. (1965 [1922]) *The Sociology of Religion.* Translated by Fischoff, E. London: Methuen & Co Ltd.

Wieviorka, M. (1995) Terrorism in the context of academic research. In M. Crenshaw (Ed.) *Terrorism in Context.* University Park, PA: The Pennsylvania State University Press. pp.597–606.

Wilson, T. (2018) Preface. In O. Lynch and J. Argomaniz (Eds.) *Victims and Perpetrators of Terrorism: Exploring Identities, Roles and Narratives.* London: Routledge. pp.vii–viii.

Wittgenstein, L. (1958) *Philosophical Investigations.* Oxford: Basil Blackwell.

Zulaika, J. and Douglass, W.A. (1996) *Terror and Taboo.* New York: Routledge.

Part II

Turning Points and Processes of Resilience

Chapter 3

'Resilient' to What?

Mapping the Impacts of Political Violence and Terrorism

This chapter provides an overview of the impacts that political violence and terrorism (PVT) has had on the lives of survivors and bereaved family members interviewed during this project. In doing so, it offers both a context and point of departure for Chapters 4 and 5 where several areas introduced here are developed. While Chapter 4 lays out the various sources of support participants utilise in order to cope with injury and bereavement, and Chapter 5 considers the intersection between participant's ontological security and time, such aspects of their narratives are always articulated in relation to material events and their consequences. This chapter, then, is a distillation of those consequences.

Despite this practical separation of data presentation, neither participants' spoken testimonies nor analysis of their typed transcripts exhibit such neat boundaries. Consequently, many of the observations and themes put forward in this chapter resonate with those discussed in later ones and vice versa. In speaking of some of the knock-on effects of, for example, physical injuries or emotional suffering, participants often described their hardships as part of a broader desire to cope as best they could with adversity facing them. This allows us to glimpse, in part, what survivors themselves understand to constitute both impacts associated with a range of critical incidents (this chapter) and their experiences of dealing with them (the chief focus of Chapter 4). Equally, by virtue of all testimony being retrospective at some level – a more complex picture which is explored further in Chapters 5 and 6 – many segments of analysis and quotations presented here speak strongly to the temporal dimensions of resilience explored in Chapter 5.

The chapter begins by outlining the direct impacts of PVT for survivors, including physical injuries, bereavement, and short-term emotional reactions. It then presents a range of indirect consequences including the negotiation of media attention and knock-on effects for personal relationships. It also flags up emotional responses which typically played out across the longer-term for survivors such as fear, anxiety, and hypervigilance. As this makes clear, within and across some of these dominant themes there is already a temporal dimension we can discern, with some impacts being felt in a more immediate, visceral way and others playing out across longer periods less directly.

DOI: 10.4324/9781003154020-6

Direct Impacts on Individual Survivors

Physical Injuries Over Time

As Table A.1 in the 'Methodological Appendix' at the end of the book shows, most participants interviewed during this research lost a member of their family in a violent attack, almost exclusively explosions or gunshots, which proved to be fatal. Five were directly physically injured at the incident scene. Some of these injuries carried significant impacts for these individuals which were not immediately apparent at the time of the attack but which manifested over time. Not all physical injury experienced by participants was incurred due to physical exposure to a critical incident such as gunfire or a bomb but was psychosomatically triggered, an example of which will be considered in the next section. These injuries also developed over time which complicates their impacts further. Highlighting the physical impacts of PVT, this section draws attention to themes emerging from the data which show how serious and complex such injuries can be. Despite this, it must also be noted physical injuries represented the least emphasised impact of violence by most survivors. They were spoken about far less than non-physical harms and where they were discussed it was often in passing to contextualise the scale of the attack or describe the survivors' exact position in relation to perpetrators and explosions.

This passing reference to physical injury was exemplified by Paul who was shot by a British soldier in a civil rights march in Derry, Northern Ireland, in 1972. He mentioned the fact that he had been shot a couple of times during our interview but almost exclusively focused on other aspects of the event. It is possible that due to the amount of time that has elapsed since this incident it no longer seems as important or vivid as perhaps it once did. However, during our interview Paul emphasised the harm done to others during that attack and seemed quite reserved, even aloof, when it came to talking about his own injury. Although I refrained from asking Paul directly about his willingness to talk in more depth about this and the impact it has had on him, it seemed that both the language available to people in the early 1970s to describe traumatic events and his own performance of a particularly stoic masculinity underpinned this reticence to elaborate. Another participant whose brother was killed in this same incident and who was interviewed with Paul commented on the extent of PTSD among fellow survivors, to which Paul replied, 'Well like I said earlier, people didn't talk about that in 1972'. This comment signalled the end of any discussion around Paul himself being shot. Indeed, his injury was palpably absent from discussion. It is possible that his injury simply healed relatively quickly and caused no further problems, but this did not seem something we could discuss during our interview. Again, the point of highlighting Paul's response is to underscore the importance of time as a mediating variable rather than to suggest uniqueness in his relative stoicism.

For some participants, physical injuries which were not immediately apparent or which were perhaps not seen as severe caused serious problems months and

'Resilient' to What?   83

years later. Ganesh, for example, was travelling to work on one of the tube trains in London that was targeted by suicide bombers in 2005. Although he was only around 15 or 20 feet away from one of the bombers and was knocked to the ground, he could see fellow passengers with far worse injuries and 'did not want to burden local hospitals in London'. Consequently, he only sought medical help from his local hospital later that day and was discharged with only minor injuries. Some years later, however, as growing back pain began to curtail pastimes and make travel more difficult he again sought medical assistance and in 2013 he underwent spinal surgery which resulted in two discs being removed from his neck which were replaced with prosthetic ones. It transpired that Ganesh had been suffering from spinal cord compression which initially seemed minor but which became degenerative. Despite being very fortunate to have survived the attack, this example points to just one of the ways Ganesh's injury has continued to affect him 15 years after the event. Chandani similarly incurred long-term back pain which materialised only years after the 1983 Harrods bomb in which she was injured. Her injuries are documented in more detail in Chapter 5, where, it is shown, they created a whole host of knock-on effects for her including problems at work, her eventual withdrawal from work altogether, and subsequently a range of difficulties accessing adequate disability benefits and housing.

Some participants (Jane and Kelly, for example) suffered comparatively minor physical injuries including damaged eardrums from their proximity to explosions as well as minor cuts and bruises from being knocked to the ground or being showered with glass and shrapnel. One participant in particular (Lynn) developed a physical ailment as a result of non-physical harm and stress. This example is considered in more detail in the next section but importantly highlights the potential complexity of pinpointing long-term injuries and harms caused by this kind of violence. Indeed, the very language involving 'injuries' proved ambiguous and even quite alienating for some survivors, particularly those who had not experienced physical injury but who still felt they deserved some claim to the status of 'injured'. Karen narrowly escaped being shot by gunmen at a beach resort in Tunisia in 2015 where she was staying on holiday and spoke explicitly about a division between 'the injured' and 'the non-injured survivors'. This was particularly evident when discussing her ineligibility to claim financial compensation following the attack:

> In the forms to fill out for any compensation, if you were non-injured, as in being shot, you're not gonna get anything. So, um … which I think – and everybody else said the same – psychologically we've been injured. But they're not taking that into account. […] Even if they just financially paid us what we lost from work. I'm not talking about people that were injured, I'm talking about just people that survived it like myself.
>
> (Karen)

Clarifying this a little later in the interview and resigning herself to the unlikelihood of securing compensation, she stressed the importance of injury recognition associated with receiving compensation over and above any stand-alone monetary value: 'But yeah, we're not gonna get any. Not that I'm looking for compensation really. But it would've been nice of them to acknowledge the fact that we've also got an injury'. Victim compensation was an issue discussed repeatedly and is returned to specifically in Chapter 4.

It is clear from these extracts that issues around injury arise not only in relation to direct physical injury, their lasting implications, and participants' readiness to discuss them, but also the way they potentially function to taxonomise and order seemingly nominal instances of victimisation; that is, different and even discrete cases but which nonetheless carry no intrinsic value over and above each other. Where compensation is concerned, it clearly is possible to produce ordinal, or 'ordered', cases pertaining to whether, and how, physical injury took place and the extent to which it inflicted damage on individuals. Participants that touched upon this notion of an ordering, or 'hierarchy', of victimhood (Carrabine et al., 2004; Breen-Smyth, 2009; McEvoy and McConnachie, 2012) understandably emphasised a lack of enthusiasm and even disdain for this way of grouping survivors. A detailed historical discussion of the classificatory processes of victim compensation and their legal development are beyond the remit of this work, though have been thoroughly excavated elsewhere (see Miers, 2007, 2014). Suffice it to say that perceptions of injustice, both emotionally raw for survivors such as Karen and firmly underpinned by this broader political economy of deservedness, emerge in intimate and yet complex tandem with both realised and potential physical injuries to the body.

Short-term Emotional Responses: Anger

Of all emotional responses described during the interviews, anger was among the most prevalent. It was writ large in how many participants described how they *felt* but did not reflect how most (though not all) were necessarily feeling now, adding some weight to Han's (2017) insistence that we distinguish between emotion and feeling. Crucially then, this was another response heavily mediated by time.

The fact that anger was described so extensively raises interesting issues in relation to resilience-based 'recovery' models, often associated with PTSD or other therapeutically diagnosed 'problems' to overcome. As a natural response to something as unexpected and shocking as falling victim to a violent attack or losing a loved one in such circumstances, anger provides an expressive conduit through which a surge of confused emotion can flow, positing more clearly 'not only the angry subject but also the object against which the anger is directed. It energetically tears ambiguities apart to create the dualisms of subject and object, this and not-this, us and not-us' (Rock, 1998: 101–2). Participants' views towards their own anger largely reflected that of the Foundation for Peace (FfP); anger was described as both natural and expected yet something individuals should nonetheless overcome and move beyond if they were to successfully cope in the longer term. In that sense, dealing with anger was not necessarily something survivors felt they needed to be 'resilient' to, at least not in the short term, and yet it could easily become a hurdle to recovery in and of itself.

An example of how anger may play out if left to spiral and grow was evident when speaking to Lynn, whose husband Jim was killed during the IRA's proxy bomb campaign in the early 1990s in Northern Ireland (see Bloom and Horgan, 2008). For several years after his death Lynn would reflect on how merciless her husband's assailants had been, how they had calmly sat around a table planning his abduction – 'meticulously planning every minute, from occupation of this house to the minute the bomb exploded. I just couldn't understand how human beings could do that' (Lynn). She had long considered how much she wanted to 'hurt them back' and hoped that they were somehow suffering for what they had done, 'unable to sleep in their beds at night'. Anger at the injustice of what had happened turned to more calculated and vengeful thoughts about what she would do to cause pain to the perpetrators. At first, Lynn explained, she just wanted to 'go out and stab them all'. She describes then constructing more elaborate plans about how she would have them all tied up in the room where she and her family had been taken hostage. Once secured she would inflict as much pain to them as possible, cutting off parts of their bodies one at a time. Finally, after considerable reflection, she imagined ways of inflicting maximum punishment on them for what they had done:

> I changed my mind. I thought no, they're trained to suffer pain, but what if I hurt one of their children? Or maybe one of their wives or something? Then they would understand how I feel, how they made me feel.
>
> (Lynn)

The way Lynn described these thoughts indicated that she could still quite readily and vividly envisage the emotional 'visions' associated with that period. However, there was what she describes as 'a major turning point' in her life. She began to develop quite large and noticeable brown rash-like blotches all over the core of her body, her back, stomach, and chest. During an appointment about an unrelated medical issue, her doctor noticed these blotches which would come and go seemingly at random. According to Lynn, he instantly asked about them because he had seen similar symptoms before in patients suffering from abnormal degrees of stress. He warned her:

> you are under severe stress, that's what that on your body is telling you. If you don't find a way of dealing with that stress and getting it out of your system you'll be in a wheelchair in five years' time, you'll be dead in ten.
>
> (Lynn)

Lynn's impassioned anecdote is supported by medical research which has found some evidence of stress-induced dermatological complaints (see Koblenzer,

1988; Kimyai-Asadi and Usman, 2001). This warning served as a stark 'wake-up call' of sorts and in many ways sounds like it had quite an emancipating effect on Lynn. She describes how from that moment on, she was somehow able to 'pass on' her anger, working around it and not devoting the emotional energy she once did to prolonged periods of rage and vengefulness. Her family picked up on this change immediately, noticing how much calmer and more laid back Lynn had become and, using this positivity as momentum, she managed to build on those early gains and now seems to have less problems negotiating feelings associated with that anger. While it surfaces again from time to time, it is never as visceral or forceful as it once was prior to that fateful meeting with her doctor.

Anger was described by many participants. However, in contrast to Lynn's experiences, Karen, John, Chandani, Stephen, George, and Kelly's accounts suggested more a kind of irritability and short temper which seemed to emerge after the event in question rather than a sustained anger. John, for example, describes getting angry at the slightest, least consequential thing, such as making a cup of tea and then needing to get back up from the sofa to walk to the kitchen to get a teaspoon. Chandani also described how she developed an uncharacteristic irritability that would manifest at unpredictable times for unimportant reasons. Participants describing this kind of low-level and sporadic anger certainly did not point to instances where their anger became so forceful that they were thinking vengefully or even directing that anger at the perpetrators. Several participants actively stressed that they never really felt anger towards the perpetrators themselves – 'I never felt vengeful. I actually feel quite sorry that the guys were young men, you know, blew themselves to bits … for an idea' (John); 'I never really felt anger towards the people who actually did it' (Ganesh); 'I wasn't angry. Not at the perpetrators' (Anne) – but rather felt frustrated, let down by security services or otherwise generally confused at the absence of an objective, tangible source to direct their irritability towards.

For victims of institutional violence, anger was also not typically directed at individual perpetrators but more generally at the system responsible for issuing the orders. Barry typifies this stance when referring to the justice campaign he is involved with: 'What we would look for is more political culpability, not so much the person who made or planted the bomb. We're more interested in the people who pulled the strings at different levels' (Barry). Barry, Liz, Kathy, Claire, and Paul all shared this stance and have tried, as much as possible, to direct their anger via their political campaigning and activism. In some cases, they emphasised the productivity of anger when it is directed in positive ways or at making change. In others, the dangers of letting anger take over were acknowledged while justifying that anger and explaining its place in driving forward activist activities:

> What drives us is a good bit of rage! A good bit of rage in there, honestly speaking, it's a good bit of rage, that's what drives us isn't it Paul? The

injustice of it just, the fact that there are people that are still waiting there, you know, for the people who done it to go to court 45 years later, there's a police service here that has no idea, the law's been turned on its head in this country, Jesus, people can't stand it. Do you see, most of the people in this city walk about in a rage, do you know what I mean? Yes I do suffer with blood pressure, I do pay the price for that rage.

(Liz)

Liz is referring to Bloody Sunday, a civil rights march in 1972 in Northern Ireland in which 14 civilians were shot dead by the British Army. She now volunteers with the Bloody Sunday Justice Campaign and helps to organise the annual march for justice in Derry. In a similar way, Claire still speaks of how angry she used to get when she thought about the shooting of her brother Ryan in 1976 by a British Army marksman on a bus in Derry but she is constantly trying to turn that anger to positive ends. Her anger has subsided somewhat with the passing of time but this is largely helped by her own desire to quell the negativity she associates with how she felt when she was younger:

I got so angry because of what happened to him, how he was treated and, you know, the fact that his life was cut short. [...] All right you're angry and you're enraged but don't go there [committing violence], have your feelings, you will feel them, you will work them out and I do think that's a point I've got to now. I've not got a place for everything, there's still sometimes where I, I can feel it just going up in the air again, as I mentioned last year [at an event at the FfP in Warrington] I felt anger and I didn't know why. It actually annoyed me that I felt anger because I'd felt it for so long when I was younger, it was something I wanted to leave behind, it was a destructive anger, it wasn't a constructive anger. And you see, I have a mix of emotions, I feel every emotion because we're human, you really can't, you can't control how an emotion will affect you when it comes along, but the one thing that I want to do if I do feel anger, I want it to be constructive now.

(Claire)

In a minority of instances, anger seems to last a lifetime. One participant affected by Bloody Sunday is Bridget, whose brother Sean was killed on that day. In contrast to Liz, Cathy, Paul, and her daughter Louise, she is far less involved in activist activities or campaigning, failing to see the relevance or efficacy of much of these causes in the face of continuing state violence. Of everyone interviewed, her anger was the most palpably felt during our interview and does not appear to have subsided considerably with the passing of time. If anything, she got understandably angrier the more she talked about Bloody Sunday and British state power in Northern Ireland.

It is clear that anger has a somewhat ambiguous relationship to resilience and here again it is worth considering Schott's (2015: 187) reservations. As she appositely asks: 'should people be able to adapt to anything?' (Schott, 2015: 187), to which we should add, should people *be expected* to adapt to anything? Are there occasions or periods when anger is fully justified? Should we remove anger from causal explanations of why it manifests? Why are anger and resilience implicitly seen as incompatible within academic and policy literatures? Would resilience necessarily seem desirable or necessary for someone whose loved one has been murdered? These questions are returned to in Chapter 6. It is possible to see how questions such as this might disappear beneath something of a 'resilience gloss' in terms of how policy imaginings often grate with the lived experiences of survivors, in turn producing and exacerbating further anger and resentment. In this context, particularly in the short term, resilience rhetoric among practitioners may appear insensitive and even unnatural rather than helpful. The data analysed here suggests that for most survivors and their families, anger is part of a process that gradually changes over time and naturally gives way to other coping mechanisms and emotions. Emotions generally become more manageable, providing they do not develop into prolonged periods of incessant anger, stress, or depression. While there was some space typically afforded to discussions of anger within the workshops and dialogue sessions attended at the FfP during the course of this research, it was routinely positioned as an unhelpful and potentially harmful emotion that can easily take hold of people's lives. While there is some evidence of such dangers being realised here, the majority of respondents exhibited what may be normatively termed a 'healthy' degree of anger to what is an exceptionally upsetting and stressful set of events. In that sense, there may be a useful space opened up for greater acknowledgement and discussion of anger as survivors traverse the adversities such events produce. These questions are picked up again and developed in Chapter 6.

Bereavement and Grief

Having acknowledged the disparate ways in which survivors traverse anger, it is important that we understand this negotiation more broadly as part and parcel of bereavement and grief which, again, are normatively considered natural processes following the death of a loved one. However, there were some aspects of grieving for loved ones highlighted in the data which set political violence apart as exceptional and unlike more natural deaths. This often made the grieving process more complex, part of a broader set of ongoing issues, or difficult to fully come to terms with due to the actual nature of how loved ones lost their lives. Rather than focusing on aspects of coping with a bereavement shared with natural or expected deaths, this section details the more exceptional circumstances or barriers emphasised by participants as aggravating an already upsetting and stressful period of time to negotiate.

The first of these concerns uncertainty over the remains of victims killed in explosions. Anne and Kevin, whose daughter Lauren was killed in the London underground tube attacks in 2005, described how this uncertainty was a factor that made the police investigation and their sense of 'completeness' of knowledge about the incident exceptionally fraught. They were prevented from viewing Lauren's body following the attack, both due to the severity of the injuries she sustained and because of the amount of time that had elapsed between her death and her body being recovered. While some of the bodies from other incident sites had been recovered relatively quickly, those on this particular tube train had been underground in excessive heat from the Thursday when the bombing took place until the Saturday of that week. Consequently, they had begun to badly decompose and officers strongly advised them not to view the body. Despite desperately wanting to prove beyond doubt that it was her daughter and not somebody else, Anne was afraid that if she saw Lauren like that she may never be able to unsee this image of her and that is not how she, or Lauren, would have wanted her to be remembered and so they refrained from doing so. Anne and Kevin both described this as a seminal aspect of their grief which took time to pass.

Similar difficulties were spoken about by other participants and in several cases were exacerbated by religious considerations. Lynn and Barry, for example, were forced to have closed coffin funerals with no option of an open casket wake. In Barry's case, his grandfather had been killed by a bomb in a pub in Belfast and was only identifiable by possessions found on his person. The fact that he and his family had to have a closed coffin – that they 'didn't have the luxury of grieving or looking and kissing and saying goodbye' (Barry) – continues to be an enduring memory for him. Again, the uncertainty over a loved one's remains played on Lynn's mind and took several years for her to reach 'closure' over. As the last section described, her husband was killed along with five soldiers in one of the IRA's proxy bombs during the early 1990s. She describes being 'unsure' about whether the remains contained within the closed coffin all belonged to her husband, whether it had been possible for police on the scene to ensure that his remains were not contaminated or mixed up with those of the soldiers. It was not until over a decade later when she eventually met one of the police officers from the incident scene that she was able to ask him about this. A devout Catholic, Lynn, had prayed for both her husband and the soldiers who died that day; 'It didn't matter one way or the other' (Lynn), she just needed to know for her own sense of closure or 'completeness' of knowledge.

Perhaps unsurprisingly, one of the most emotionally testing times was anniversaries such as the anniversary of the incident, relationship anniversaries, birthdays, or Christmases. While anniversaries were not described as being exceptionally difficult by all participants, everyone acknowledged them as carrying particular emotional resonance which would often affect family members differently. This is particularly true during the early years following the loss of a loved one, as family members come to terms with the passing of time and have to cope with their first anniversaries. As Amanda notes, 'It's still going to be the first, whatever, the first "x" years, you know, it's a year on, that kind of thing … every day is another anniversary of some sort for somebody in the family' (Amanda). Even when a long period of time has elapsed, anniversaries continue to be a reminder of the loss suffered, returning family members, if only temporarily, to a life they once shared with a loved one:

> The 24th October is the biggest anniversary which is also my eldest son's birthday so it's not a very [sighs] happy day to think of his birthday but, you know, it's 26 years now in a couple of weeks' time and 26 years is a long time. That might sound callous but it's not. If you had said to me 26 years ago that I would be doing what I'm doing now and Jim would have been dead that length of time I'd have said 'aye right', [melancholic laugh] you know. There's times when I look back and think how have I lived 26 years without him? You know, I'm not putting Jim on a pedestal or anything – he had his faults like the rest of us have faults – but he was a good family man and he loved me too, I know he really loved me and I loved him and that was the main thing that got us through our lives. That picture there [points across to a picture of Jim and the family on a table next to me] shows all I ever wanted in life was a husband and a family and my own home.
>
> (Lynn)

Participants who experienced the death of a child or a sibling found that grieving was also mediated by their partner, and they would often compare and contrast ways they dealt with bereavement with the way their partner did. Sometimes differences in the way partners behaved around each other or dealt with their grief became irreconcilable for couples, forcing them to separate (this is explored more fully towards the end of the chapter). For others, differences in the way they dealt with grief did not cause lasting damage to relationships but were nonetheless difficult to negotiate. FfP founder, Colin Parry, describes this difficulty for him:

> It [not talking about the deceased] adds to the sense of solitude – 'nobody understands, nobody talks to me because nobody understands what I've gone through therefore I am on my own'. Even if you're not on your own you can feel like you are. I can evidence that by saying Wendy and I grieved in different ways, grieved at different times. There were times when I thought she wasn't grieving and I'm sure times when she felt I wasn't so it can happen between a married couple, it can happen between parents. I can speak from personal experience. It's almost like a locked-in syndrome thing where you, you could go mad, whether mad's the proper term, but some people I'm sure do have their mind and their behaviour altered so much by this they never really are able to cope anymore.
>
> (Colin)

Anne and Kevin similarly noted differences in the way they grieved and the way they behaved around each other. They cited several factors which helped them to make sense of their grief and negotiate a way through for their relationship. They attended bereavement counselling so as not to 'overload' each other. Anne also expressed an interesting perspective on gender within their relationship, describing Kevin as emotionally sensitive – a trait which she explicitly associates with femininity but which, she says, she cannot associate with. The two of them described a sort of 'balancing out' between Kevin's emotional sensitivity and Anne's more stoic, often 'harder' emotional nature, making their natures perfectly suited to negotiating the bereavement together. They both also share a strong Christian faith which was strengthened by Lauren's death, as they found comfort in drawing on their faith when all else seemed so bleak. The fact that Kevin was Lauren's stepfather rather than biological father was also cited as one among many factors that unconsciously enabled Kevin to move on in more positive ways than Anne at a much earlier stage.

Participants from Northern Ireland with direct experience of The Troubles had a particular way of talking about grief and bereavement which was distinguished from other more isolated attacks. Several people whose family members had been killed during that period described 'not being able to grieve', 'not having space to grieve' or talked about the 'madness' of The Troubles which made it harder to identify a specific time period where they had the time or space to themselves in which to grieve privately. Every interviewee from Northern Ireland described a similar image of community life, one in which deaths in the family were met with enormous public shows of support and solidarity. While this was an overwhelming source of support, it also meant there was little time where they would be left alone in solitude because people in their wider family and community would rally around to ensure nobody was left on their own during a bereavement. Bridget remembers her mother's kitchen, living room, and hallway constantly occupied by everyone from the local priests to shopkeepers, friends, family, and passers-by expressing their sorrow at the family's loss. Consequently, if we bear in mind the potential struggles faced by couples outlined above, and place these struggles within a context such as this, we can imagine how such overwhelming communal support could both help and hinder the processes associated with bereavement and grief within families and within relationships.

Indirect Impacts on Survivors and Their Families

Long-term Emotional Responses: Fear, Anxiety, and Hypervigilance

In addition to short-term emotions such as anger as survivors come to terms with recent injuries or bereavements, there are also several clear long-term emotional impacts that continue to affect their lives and influence the decisions they make on a day-to-day basis. Chief among these emotional impacts are fear, anxiety, and hypervigilance, particularly in relation to travel. For some participants safety while travelling, such as while using public transport, was not an issue they seemed concerned by. These individuals had not typically experienced an attack involving public transport or known someone who had. They were also often reflecting on experiences from more than 20 years ago. For those who talked at length about facing the fear and anxiety of using public transport, not only had their experiences of political violence involved the use of public transport (e.g. the 2005 London bombings) or something associated with travel (e.g. the 2015 beach shooting in Sousse, Tunisia, which occurred on a holiday resort), but they also expressed a strong desire to overcome these feelings as part of their long-term recovery. Those with more recent experience of an attack, unsurprisingly, talked more explicitly of feeling anxious or fearful at the time of interview.

Jane, who was injured in Tavistock Square in July 2005, spoke at considerable length about her abject fear of trains and buses for years after the event. The sight of buses would immediately conjure up images of maimed wreckage and she described them as looking like 'coffins on wheels' (Jane). When she was injured, she had been travelling down to London for a rare business trip and never normally had occasion to use public transport. After 7/7, she became anxious thinking about travelling on public transport again even though this would be infrequent and she actively set herself the target of getting buses and trains again. Describing several failed attempts at this, including experiencing panic attacks, she has since been able to attend some of the annual memorial services held in London and travelled by public transport. These occasions are always difficult and serve as a reminder that while her physical injuries have healed as much as they are going to, 'I'm never gonna be the same person I was on 6th July 2005' (Jane).

Most participants, even those who would not describe themselves as actively fearful, told stories of interactions or episodes that shook them up a little and linked this passing fear or anxiety to their victimisation. Kelly, for example, who witnessed the Warrington bombing in 1993, did not consciously express fears around public transport or crowds but recalled a couple of incidents where she spotted lone individuals in shops or around town and found their behaviour suspicious which she would not normally have done. While Kelly described her anxieties as transitory and random, she also described finding it difficult to walk down Bridge Street again in the months following the attack. Understandably, participants with greater degrees of control over their anxieties seemed more likely to report fewer recent issues than those who have to rely on transport by rail or air where control is effectively handed over to someone else for the duration of the journey. Despite this, the majority of survivors do seem to take their anxieties in their stride and press on with intended journeys regardless. Karen, who narrowly escaped gunfire while on holiday in Sousse, Tunisia, in 2015, expressed suffering from great anxiety and hypervigilance around crowded places and travel of all kinds but negotiates this with extensive planning in advance. This seemed to have improved exponentially in a relatively

'Resilient' to What? 93

short space of time. After returning from Tunisia, Karen was signed off work and put on a form of antidepressants after suffering panic attacks and acute anxiety on buses and travelling to and from work. Despite being a relatively recent experience, she had travelled by tube and train on the day of our interview at her suggestion and had been away on holiday since as well. She still experiences episodic panic in transport settings such as airports or train stations, and her anxiety has reportedly contributed to other side effects such as poorer short-term memory recall, but overall she had continued to make improvements by the time we last spoke and she seemed quietly determined to go about her life as before without cancelling plans or trips.

Of course, these fears and anxieties are not felt in isolation; in addition to survivors' personal histories, they are also not immune from the anxiety felt by the general population towards terrorism. The contemporary terror threat is one way that both ongoing risks are conveyed by the state and that public fears and anxieties are shaped and influenced. During the fieldwork phase of this research when the interviews were conducted, there were several high-profile attacks around Europe including critical incidents in Paris, Nice, Normandy, Berlin, Brussels, among others, in addition to many more deadly attacks across Africa and the Middle East. Many of these incidents were cited by participants during their interviews as stark reminders of the grave danger such events continue to pose. In July 2016, the Metropolitan police commissioner Bernard Hogan-Howe stated that another terror attack on the UK was inevitable and that while the public wanted him to assuage their fears he was unable to do so, describing the risk of an attacks as a case of 'when' not 'if' the UK is targeted (BBC, 2016). Ultimately, he was proven tragically correct by subsequent attacks in Westminster, Manchester, London Bridge, and Finsbury Park. Hogan-Howe's comments were followed by the unveiling of Operation Hercules, a strategic increase in the number of firearms officers in London by 600 (Metropolitan Police, 2016). Reflecting on this recent announcement, John commented:

I saw that on the news and I thought my God they look like Stormtroopers don't they. That was a scary image to be fair and it does make you a little bit worried because you think, what are they, why, you know, why show people that because they're trained like the special forces aren't they, I was just like hmm. Scary.

(John)

As we discussed John's use of public transport, which was inevitably infrequent due to him having a job requiring lots of driving, he qualified his earlier statement by saying that what concerned him most was the way security threats are conveyed to the public:

I wouldn't describe myself as fearful actually. I'm more aware of it, if you know what I mean. I was always aware because I was a Warrant Officer in the Air Cadets for like 23 years and so I was always aware of the alert state cos you have to, you get reports every week because if you're gonna take cadets away and stuff like that, at certain alert states you can't have them travelling in uniform and that sort of thing. So I was always aware of the alert state and so that kind of helped me with, you know, that impending attack or whatever feelings. But yeah I kind of just took that route really, I was never fearful but I was more vigilant about it. I always used to read the alert state and … it's blue, green, red, whatever … or … red [laughs] you know what I mean. Before it was a sentence on a paper and I was just like oh as long as it's still black it's fine, you know, but after [7/7] I was more aware of what it should be and then, you know. […] If you knew what the security services knew about terrorism and stuff you wouldn't leave your house because there's always something going on, there's always people being investigated. So I think the state of alertness shouldn't always be just broadcast, it should be for people like myself who, you know, involved with the Air Cadets you need to know that sort of information because you don't want to sort of invite it so you've got to be vigilant for the wellbeing of everyone else but I think, like I say, it'd cause more problems to the general public if they're being constantly reminded of the alert state. I think it'd make life difficult in London. For him [Bernard Hogan-Howe] to say that was a bit irresponsible to be honest.

(John)

The most salient factors influencing survivors' propensity to express fear were the mode that their attack had taken, the length of time to have elapsed since the attack, and the strength of their desire to overcome a particular fear. Often this led them to make unnecessary journeys just to prove to themselves that they could make them should they choose to. Beyond these observations, it is difficult to assess individual survivors' 'resilience' to fears, anxieties, and hypervigilance because some of them are so complexly related to physiological reactions. Survivors who express an intention to travel and appear relatively calm may still be susceptible to debilitating physical reactions such as panic attacks or flashbacks. Some reactions may require medical treatments which, independent of psychological perceptions, are needed to literally quell bodily shock or tension from taking over. People expressing acute anxiety or fears were usually survivors from an incident within the last 15 years. While more research would be needed, it seemed that rather than time itself being the overriding factor influencing this, the culture of fear that has undoubtedly pervaded contemporary life since 9/11 may have rendered the terror threat so ubiquitous in settings such as airports, train stations, and crowded places that episodic spikes in anxiety or panic are almost inescapable for many survivors and 'ordinary' citizens alike.

Negotiating Media Attention

Perhaps it is inevitable that instances of PVT attract extensive and high-profile press coverage. Media attention represents a relatively enduring feature of such violent acts, both before and since the attacks on the World Trade Centre in 2001, challenging the notion of 'new terrorism' in at least one respect. Criticism of the media in recent years has emphasised the propensity for extensive and sensationalist coverage to encourage further attacks, with several commentators urging calmer, more proportionate reporting in a bid to reduce public fear (see Doward, 2015; English, 2017; Jenkins, 2017). Media attention described negatively was an overwhelmingly common theme to emerge from the data; regardless of whether participants were victims of institutional violence, anti-institutional violence, or whether their 'stories' were being represented sympathetically or not by the press, everyone interviewed seemed to hold 'the media' in a dim light.

Despite there being a fascinating set of debates surrounding social media in recent years, such as the creation of Facebook's 'safety check' feature whereby civilians can instantly report themselves to be safe during or following terror attacks, participants referred almost exclusively to media in traditional terms as meaning the newspapers and television news channels. The exception of this was a couple of participants coming across distressing news items via social media profiles during breaking news or after recent terror attacks which they were actively encouraged to avoid by FfP staff, who would often advise participants to 'be kind to yourself', a phrase which came to be recognised by them as meaning staying away from news coverage for a few days following a terror attack 'while things quietened down'. This advice was recently echoed by NHS England that drew up new guidance for victims of terrorism following attacks in Manchester and London, advising them to avoid social media in case they are 'trolled' or persuaded to tell their story to journalists. The guidance states:

> After an upsetting event try to stay off social media in case you say more than you intend because of what you experienced; messaging your story can keep you in the trauma; retelling your story can also bring back bad memories and you can even relive the trauma.
>
> (Donnelly, 2017)

For most, the media represented yet another hurdle to negotiate in the aftermath of losing a loved one or trying to come to terms with surviving a violent attack. Within this interview data, negativity towards media attention falls into three sub-themes.

Firstly, the issue of harassment and the intrusion of privacy for survivors featured extensively. The most extreme instances of this were reported by Anne and Kevin who eventually moved house to escape the harassment. This period of their lives was hugely influential in shaping Anne and Kevin's outlook on how and why they wanted to try and move on from Lauren's death. Rather than removing this experience from an equally important context, the details of their story are considered at greater length in Chapter 5. Importantly, they avoid memorial services held in London and exercise caution around anniversaries as a result of their experiences for fear that reporters may find them and print more untrue stories or take their quotations out of context. George, whose brother Peter was killed in Syria by ISIS, explained that it took just six minutes from the video of a hostage scene being released to the press turning up on his mother's doorstep. Stephen, a participant whose son Nick was killed in the 2005 London bombings, now shares a similar view of the media after he found out about a journalist who had quoted him in a book without seeking prior approval. That, he said, angered him more than anything else, including his contempt for the Blair government. Anne, Kevin, George, and Stephen shared a particular criticism of the media which centred on their responsibility to report on events factually and not stoke divisions between groups within society. In particular, the tensions between Muslims and non-Muslims heightened as a result, they believe, of media reporting following terror attacks is something to hold the press to account over. Again, bearing similarities to the experiences of 7/7 survivor John Tulloch (see Tulloch, 2008; McGarry and Walklate, 2015: 91–2), they identified ways in which victims of terrorist atrocities are mobilised in the media to set up a form of 'us' and 'them' division which, in reality, does not necessarily exist – at least not prior to such reporting.

Secondly, the more indirect problem of participants unwittingly viewing media coverage of violent incidents or atrocities, including those they were involved in, featured in much of the interview data. Closely linking this sub-theme and the first was the issue of anniversaries, which would always attract renewed media attention for participants. On top of the private anguish and emotional toil of dealing with anniversaries, the problem of such milestone dates is twofold with regard to the media. Participants reported how they would be on high alert before and during significant anniversaries (such as the ten-year anniversary of the 2005 London bombings or recent commemorations marking attacks in Paris, London, and Manchester) as journalists would often pursue them for interviews. In addition, television and radio broadcasts typically focus on anniversaries making sure to recap on the incident in their headline news. Often this involves replaying original video footage of events as they happened on television or airing original interviews over the radio. Every participant to speak about this issue described ways of coping with it in advance, clearly suggesting that they are all too aware of the media's penchant for reporting on such occasions.

> Every time there's an anniversary I always give myself a couple of weeks beforehand to build myself up because obviously it's in the [Warrington]

'Resilient' to What?   97

Guardian, it's on the news and everything and it's on the internet – so you can't get away from it. So I find the best way is looking at the photos and everything and I think well I was there and, yes, it messes with your head but it gets you prepared as well. When it comes to the day as you're seeing photos of what's happened the day's not too bad to deal with. You're not turning up on the day and everything is hitting you. You're seeing the photographs but you've been looking at them anyway.

(Kelly)

In contrast with situations like the one described by Kelly, there is always the chance survivors will stumble across traumatic scenes on the television as new incidents get reported. As one participant described:

I find it really hard. [A member of FfP staff] always rings us – 'don't watch the news, don't watch the news if you can help it' – but you know, cos I've been off sick anyway you've got the TV on and then you'll get a news flash and then, of course, you're drawn to it. So, it is very upsetting.

(Karen)

Not only was avoiding such coverage said to be difficult, some survivors also suggested that until they were able to watch the news without feeling anxious, upset, or angry, they did not consider themselves to be coping sufficiently. As Kelly's comments above attest, for some survivors the only way to fully make sense of, prepare for, or take control of such situations is to confront them head on. While staff at FfP would typically advise participants against watching the news if they could avoid it, this clearly highlights the complexity of media coverage as an issue faced by survivors – one which is perhaps not as easy to negotiate as simply avoiding the news altogether.

Finally, a common complaint among survivors of institutional violence was the power of the press in determining the master narrative surrounding events. Not only could the media be extremely intrusive, as other participants have highlighted, but they would often be presenting the victims' plight in an unsympathetic and even hostile way. This is highlighted most explicitly by Barry in relation to the McGurk's Bar justice campaign he helps to organise:

Who fed the stories to the media and why? […] How you do all that stuff, without any help from the State, in fact the State stops you? When we were holding our original press conference and all, they [the media] were like 'you're an Irish propagandist, you're telling us that the police told lies and the British army told lies, that the Unionist government told lies and the British government told lies?' And this is the BBC, the British Broadcasting Corporation, almost rubbishing our … getting up and walking away and, you know lifting their cameras and walking out, you know – 'Yous are just doing the IRA's work for them, I mean yous call yourselves families I mean you're only apologists for terrorists.' And this is the BBC presenter, being that hostile, you know what I mean. You just felt humiliated at some of these press conferences. But then as years went on this whole idea of collusion and this whole idea of State involvement in a lot of these atrocities becomes almost, [unclear] almost a few bad apples, but now it's almost acceptable. 'Oh maybe the McGurk's Bar families maybe have a point, maybe there's something in it.'

(Barry)

Among all of the interviews in which hostility or negativity towards the media was overwhelming, there was one significant exception. This came from Colin who describes quite enjoying speaking to the media because it gave him a chance to talk about his son Tim when it may have otherwise been difficult to do so amongst family. It gave a clear opportunity to talk about his death which everyday family life did not always afford. He also felt grateful in some ways that they were showing a genuine and compassionate interest in his feelings and family's well-being. His experience in this regard, however, is unique among everybody interviewed.

Effects on Personal Relationships

It is clear from the data that personal and familial relationships are one of the most important resources survivors rely on in order to cope with the impacts of trauma and loss. In some cases, however, the strain relationships can be put under proves too much to bear. Although the challenges victimisation from political violence may pose for personal relationships has been termed an indirect impact here, the knock-on effects of breaking up from long-term partners or experiencing prolonged relationship difficulties can become all too direct in time. As Chapter 5 highlights, more ordinary or everyday hardships including relationship difficulties often become bound up with events from the past which sometimes serve to periodically return survivors to those events. While that chapter focuses more explicitly on the temporal aspect of such adversity, two main impacts to emerge in relation to personal relationships from the data are considered here.

Firstly, the fact that extraordinary events such as terrorist attacks were followed, in many cases, by couples experiencing strain to their relationships and even separating was reported by over half of the interview sample. Whether people always felt that critical incidents such as this directly led to these difficulties and break-ups was not always clear, that is, whether they directly caused break-ups, but for many participants there was a correlation. Ganesh, for example, mentioned other survivors he had met at the FfP who had also negotiated relationship difficulties or break-ups after the physical wounds had healed. As his following quotation shows, these kinds of hardships often become entangled in ways of explaining new or changed forms of behaviour on the part of the survivor:

> It, it's hard to see a future ... it's hard to see a happy future but other people who've been through divorce they've, er, you know they've said, you know you come through it. I don't know anybody, erm, yeah other people who have been through divorce will say well you know eventually you realise it's probably the best thing that ever happened and I'm sure I will and then I'll start to see some future but, erm, when you've, I dunno how many survivors of terrorist attacks end up being divorced but ... on the one hand you'd expect there'd be quite a few because PTSD does get in the way of relationships and I, I, I don't mean to label myself with PTSD continuously but ... it's just an easy way of saying what it is.
>
> (Ganesh)

Ganesh and his wife began divorce proceedings after he learned that she had left him for another partner and while there may be several factors involved beyond the critical incident behind his PTSD he was quite clear in associating the end of his relationship with a changed form of self-identity linked directly to the 7/7 bombings in which he was severely injured. There was no mention of his relationship aside from its demise, no reference made to previous difficulties or changes in his family life, and no suggestion that he had any agency over the situation. Later in the interview he suggests that while PTSD may be partially responsible and may have made him 'a little dysfunctional' and less likely to 'connect to people' it is mainly other factors at play, namely his wife 'going through a midlife crisis or whatever it is'. In contrast, John described his divorce as something which may well have sprung from other sources, such as his relationship becoming somewhat platonic and even 'stale'. As the following extract from his interview shows, while he clearly attributes his divorce to the London bombings he does not shy away from acknowledging his role in the relationship breakdown. Indeed, it is spoken about as a source of regret for him:

> I just thought it was that, that sort of deterioration of, you know, our sort of personal life, you know, and just growing apart and that's what I thought and I didn't really associate it with me, or, or 7/7, I didn't think it was too much to do with me cos I was busy and, you know what I mean, you know and I'd, I ignored her a fair bit to be fair. You know and that's, you know, it'll always be a kind of regret with me because ... and ... yeah you just, I dunno it, it does go back to that, that incident and after that incident you can sort of pinpoint dates where things, things went downhill. Looking back on it it's like I can say well it was kind of me that ... cos I threw myself into other things, cos I didn't want to feel angry, frustrated, scared or whatever, you know. So, yeah.
>
> (John)

100 Turning Points and Processes of Resilience

Earlier in the interview John describes how following the attack he began to get angry at the slightest, least consequential things in work or around the house. This anger, he suggests, was mostly not directed towards anyone but often his wife would have to endure days of mood swings and a lack of communication. The two interview extracts considered above are interesting because they evince that while survivors of political violence who experience relationship difficulties often attribute those difficulties directly to the critical incidents in question, the ways participants described their own role or behaviour in this can differ markedly. While both John and Ganesh, for example, had been diagnosed with PTSD, John seemed far less defined by '7/7' than Ganesh, perhaps partly because he was not physically injured. Perhaps this is a moot point, since both men spent considerable amounts of time seeking out and associating with dedicated 7/7 survivor groups in and around London and, of course, Warrington's FfP. However, in another section of Ganesh's interview, he attributes not getting past a particular job interview to his PTSD and 7/7. Surviving 7/7 has become, at least to some extent, part of his overriding or 'master status' (Hughes, 1945; Kenney, 2002: 262) which he seems to have internalised to a large degree and around which he situates other life events.

Finally, linking a number of themes already discussed including the uniqueness of this kind of bereavement, a small number of interviewees talked about adjusting to life after losing a loved one being made more difficult because of having to explain it to new partners, new members of their family, or children as they grow older. An interesting example of this was spoken about by Danielle who was actually present at the event in question as a baby with no recollection of it. Her mother died a year after being injured in the Warrington bomb through injuries directly caused by that event. Many years later, Danielle's father remarried and here she describes her own self-awareness when talking about her mother around her stepmother:

> I don't like to force things on people, if my dad wants to talk about it, absolutely fine, I will happily engage. Same with my sister. But equally I don't wanna force it upon them, I would always want it to come naturally, and it does sometimes through say talking about, if we were talking about my mum's humour, like right after the bomb when she woke up from the anaesthetic and stuff, erm, you know, she was cracking jokes and stuff like that and so it's talked about in a roundabout way but I would never just be like right let's have a talk [...] that's just not ... and also the fact that my dad remarried ... I feel like, not guilty, God not guilty, I'm not gonna not talk about it cos like, my dad chose to remarry and it's not my, it's not my step mum's fault that that happened to my dad and to me and my sister and everything like that so equally I wouldn't force her to have to talk about it cos sometimes I get the feeling that she, not, she doesn't feel second best but it must be such a hard thing to, you know, realise that you weren't the first choice ... Does that make sense? [...] If you started banging on about

how great my mum was, I mean, you know, I would be the first to say that but I […] I just temper it a little bit because, you know, it's kind of … yeah, it's just respectful. I mean she doesn't stop us from talking about it, if it ever comes up she's absolutely fine about it and my little sister actually is inquisitive about it and I'll happily, you know, talk to her about it […] there's just kind of a … a peace with it. I think, I mean, arguably I think it is quite a personal thing that you all have to deal with so … so yeah.

(Danielle)

Again, here we see evidence of enduring legacies. They are not, however, in this case, the typically spectacular or overtly manifest legacies of historical violence some might associate with trauma or injury but rather subtle and mundane. Partners and children, in this case, are the living legacy of a person whose life was taken but whose memory lives on with and through them. As Danielle explains, there are times when 'new' relationships require sensitive negotiation. Rather than seeing this as a bad thing or as an obstacle, it was clear from the rest of our interview that Danielle's relationship with her stepmother is a close one. While we did not discuss her father's experiences very much, it is possible to see how his decision to remarry and his daughter's subsequent relationship with a stepparent have been positive in the long term. In contrast with survivors who have experienced relationships breaking down, effectively 'losing' or leaving loved ones, this shows that the opposite may equally be true – that people gain friends and family through the creation of new relationships and even new communities. This practical element to 'making up' (Hacking, 2002; 2004) resilient survivor communities is returned to and considered explicitly in Chapter 6.

Conclusion

This chapter has mapped some of the most significant and recurring impacts of PVT as raised in the interview data by participants themselves, revealing a range of impacts on survivors that can be loosely grouped along continuums from short to long term and from direct to indirect. Time and physical proximity were both common ways in which participants referred to, and made sense of, the experiences they were trying to explain. In parts, it suggests there may be processes resembling 'resilience' at play and, similarly, reveals both overlaps and disconnections between the direct and indirect impacts of political violence reported here and dominant framings of critical incident harms as 'trauma/traumatic'. However, attaching such labels to these stories remains problematic for a number of reasons (some of which are addressed in Chapters 4 and 5 and some which are reflected on in Chapter 6). While the interviews and their analyses were not conducted using PTSD symptoms as markers or codes in any systematic way, many of the impacts described here seemed to cohere quite closely with such symptoms. As Pinchevski (2016: 56) notes, successive PTSD entries in the *Diagnostic and Statistical Manual of Mental Disorders* have become increasingly expansive in their description of trauma impacts. Exposure to events that result in, or threaten, death or serious injury continue to underpin the manual's definitions of traumatic events, while more recent editions emphasise both personal and secondary, or direct and indirect, experiences and impacts. Consequently, many of the impacts described by injured survivors as well as eyewitnesses were framed in terms of ongoing 'symptoms' rather than past experiences and several participants used language explicitly fixed around varying forms of therapeutic or medicalised discourse. It was not always clear whether each individual had been formally diagnosed with PTSD, whether they had sought support in the form of therapy or counselling, or whether their knowledge of PTSD and its symptoms stemmed largely from the FfP itself, who sometimes provide 'Living with Trauma' awareness day workshops designed to make trauma symptoms known and recognisable to their participants (something explored several times throughout the rest of the book). This is perhaps one clue pointing to the recognition, categorisation, and labelling of trauma, on the one hand, and the feedback loop between these processes and individuals reacting to them and interacting with them, on the other (Hacking, 2004: 280; 1995, 2002).

In situating these impacts as 'direct' and 'indirect', the intention is not to suggest neatness or even necessarily order to the ways in which these impacts can play out. Indeed, every participant experienced a combination of harms over time which carried both direct and indirect, as well as short- and long-term consequences. This data also supports extant theoretical work acknowledging the overlap between physical, mental, and social suffering (Wilkinson, 2005), as well as between individual trauma and collective ways of making sense of those events (Alexander, 2012). This may complicate the ways in which we frame and interpret such lived experiences. The infamy of events such as 'Bloody Sunday' or '7/7' ostensibly add to their exceptional nature; their physical wounds may have mostly healed but the psychological impacts at an individual level and the memory of those events in the 'collective psyche' continue to be stoked by the media's fascination with sensational violence. However, as Butler (2004: 20) reminds us, despite the prominence or visibility of such events which may seem to elevate the 'grievability' of certain lives over others, loss makes a 'we' of us all, constituting a collective by virtue of our being human. Our histories and geopolitical locations surely differ but fundamentally we find in death and loss a commonality. While this chapter has highlighted several contextual factors marking political violence out as exceptional or unique, these events may share this greater commonality with other forms of bereavement insofar as 'each of us is constituted politically in part by virtue of the social vulnerability of our bodies' (Butler, 2004: 20).

Within each of the sections discussed above, there are a range of multilayered, nuanced, and complex factors at play that make it difficult to always isolate what it is that must be negotiated or overcome to restore a sense of ontological security for survivors. For example, the issue of physical injury cannot be reduced to harm caused by bombs or bullets but may manifest psychosomatically. The language of 'injury' also sets up dichotomies and potential hierarchies among some survivors. Elsewhere there are seemingly confusing and ostensibly counterintuitive responses pertaining to, for example, media coverage and the desire from some participants to almost force themselves to endure distressing news items on TV or online, or to unnecessarily using public transport in order to reclaim a sense of autonomy over it. While this might be difficult for people who have not experienced such violence to conceive or comprehend, it also carries a sense of internal logic, if a somewhat self-flagellating one. There is also evidence to suggest that where problems such as relationship difficulties or break-ups are attributed to suffering critical incidents such as those represented in this data, the degree to which survivors claim to be exercising agency over such adversities can vary greatly. There are also interesting questions to ask in relation to emotion and, as the discussion around anger highlights, attempts among FfP staff, counsellors, and therapists to build and mobilise resilience among survivors must be cognisant of the natural responses to bereavement which may not always appear to cohere with theoretical projections of what coping should look and feel like. Unpacking these questions in greater detail, Chapter 4 turns to how participants have traversed injury and bereavement. In doing so, it identifies a range of potential sources of resilience. Their potentiality, rather than their immanence, rests with the fact that many remain so heavily mediated by social factors and time.

References

Alexander, J.C. (2012) *Trauma: A Social Theory*. Cambridge: Polity Press.

BBC (2016) Terror attack on UK 'when, not if' – Sir Bernard Hogan-Howe. *BBC News*, [online] 31 July. Available at: www.bbc.co.uk/news/uk-36935585 [Accessed 16 December 2018].

Bloom, M. and Horgan, J. (2008) Missing their mark: The IRA's proxy bomb campaign. *Social Research* 75(2): 579–614.

Breen-Smyth, M. (2009) Hierarchies of pain and responsibility: Victims and war by other means in Northern Ireland. *Trípodos. Facultat de Comunicació i Relacions Internacionals Blanquerna* 25: 27–40.

Butler, J. (2004) *Precarious Life: The Powers of Mourning and Violence*. London: Verso.

Carrabine, E., Iganski, P., Lee, M., Plummer, K. and South, N. (2004) *Criminology: A Sociological Introduction*. London: Routledge.

Donnelly, L. (2017) Terror victims 'should steer clear' of Twitter in aftermath of trauma. *The Telegraph*, [online] September 9. www.telegraph.co.uk/news/2017/09/09/terror-victims-should-steer-clear-twitter-aftermath-trauma/amp/ [Accessed 22/09/2017].

Doward, J. (2015) Media coverage of terrorism 'leads to further violence'. *The Guardian*, [online] August 1. www.theguardian.com/media/2015/aug/01/media-coverage-terrorism-further-violence [Accessed 29/04/2017].

English, R. (2017) The media must respond more responsibly to terrorist attacks – here's how. *The Conversation*, [online] April 4. https://theconversation.com/the-media-must-respond-more-responsibly-to-terrorist-attacks-heres-how-75490 [Accessed 29/04/2017].

Hacking, I. (1995) *Rewriting the Soul: Multiple Personality and the Sciences of Memory.* Princeton, NJ: Princeton University Press.

Hacking, I. (2002) *Historical Ontology.* Cambridge: Harvard University Press.

Hacking, I. (2004) Between Michel Foucault and Erving Goffman: Between discourse in the abstract and face-to-face interaction. *Economy and Society* 33(3): 277–302.

Han, B.C. (2017) *Psychopolitics: Neoliberalism and New Technologies of Power.* London:Verso.

Hughes, E.C. (1945) Dilemmas and contradictions of status. *American Journal of Sociology* 50(5): 353–9.

Jenkins, S. (2017) Media hype about the Westminster attack will only encourage others. *The Guardian*, [online] March 24. www.theguardian.com/commentisfree/2017/mar/24/coverage-westminster-attack-media-politicians [Accessed 29/04/2017].

Kenney, J.S. (2002) Victims of crime and labelling theory: A parallel process? *Deviant Behaviour: An Interdisciplinary Journal* 23(3): 235–65.

Kimyai-Asadi, A. and Usman, A. (2001) The role of psychological stress in skin disease. *Journal of Cutaneous Medicine and Surgery* 5(2): 140–5.

Koblenzer, C.S. (1988) Stress and the skin: Significance of emotional factors in dermatology. *Stress Medicine* 4(1): 21–6.

McEvoy, K. and McConnachie, K. (2012) Victimology in transitional justice: Victimhood, innocence and hierarchy. *European Journal of Criminology* 9(5): 527–38.

McGarry, R., and S. Walklate. (2015) *Victims: Trauma, Testimony and Justice.* London: Routledge.

Metropolitan Police (2016) Armed officers increased to protect London. *Metropolitan Police* [online], 03 August. Available at: http://news.met.police.uk/news/armed-offic ers-increased-to-protect-london-177226 [Accessed 21/06/2017].

Miers, D. (2007) Looking beyond Great Britain: The development of criminal injuries compensation. In S. Walklate (Ed.) *Handbook of Victims and Victimology.* London: Routledge. pp.337–62.

Miers, D. (2014) Compensating deserving victims of violent crime: The Criminal Injuries Compensation Scheme 2012. *Legal Studies* 34(2): 242–78.

Pinchevski, A. (2016) Screen trauma: Visual media and post-traumatic stress disorder. *Theory, Culture & Society* 33(4): 51–75.

Rock, P. (1998) *After Homicide: Practical and Political Responses to Bereavement.* Oxford: Oxford University Press.

Schott, R.M. (2015) 'Not just victims … but': Toward a critical theory of the victim. In H. Marway and H. Widdows (Eds.) *Women and Violence: The Agency of Victims and Perpetrators.* Basingstoke: Palgrave Macmillan. pp.178–94.

Tulloch, J. (2008) Becoming iconic. *Criminal Justice Matters* 73(1): 33–4.

Wilkinson, I. (2005) *Suffering: A Sociological Introduction.* Cambridge: Polity Press.

Chapter 4

Sources of Resilience for Survivors

Having mapped out the most significant impacts of political violence and terrorism (PVT) for survivors interviewed here, this chapter reveals a range of coping mechanisms and sources of support they variously draw upon in order to traverse these impacts. Each section of the chapter represents evidence of resilience at different levels, supporting the claim that 'resilience is multi-layered and multifaceted' (Walklate, McGarry and Mythen, 2014: 419). In curating these various sources of support identified by participants, the chapter provides an analysis of what Overland (2013: 204) terms 'resilience resources'. They are explained along a spectrum from the individual, through the economic, the communal, and practice-oriented support systems. This ordering of the data is designed to explicitly exhibit the different layers of support rather than place corresponding importance on them. In short, they are not ranked but arranged to sequentially build a picture of the kinds of support accessed by individuals and the varied phenomena they described. While many of these sections map onto the impacts highlighted in Chapter 3, other aspects of survivors' experiences are emphasised here which stand-alone as seminal moments or processes distinct from clearly tangible impacts.

Within the chapter are a number of themes touched on but more fully explored in Chapter 5. Similarly, the findings included in this chapter carry some potential implications for policy and practice. However, rather than trying to summarise these throughout the chapter, they are instead revisited towards the end of the book where they are listed more succinctly. The fact that many of the kinds of support survivors routinely draw on already form part of their everyday lives, and would be likely to occur for people facing ostensibly less 'spectacular' forms of adversity, provides further justification for stepping back from the data before immediately translating it into policy-relevant findings. This takes seriously the call to recognise that often people respond positively to adversity in ways which make policy interference either unnecessary (Furedi, 2008), or in some cases even morally oppressive, while leaving open the possibility that some experiences could be made more manageable for survivors by recognising avoidable or recurring issues, precisely through better informed

DOI: 10.4324/9781003154020-7

106 Turning Points and Processes of Resilience

policy. The chapter concludes with a brief reflection on existing arguments around survivors' capacity to cope with adversity and trauma, bringing together several arguments alluded to throughout the book around intersecting resilience(s).

Narrating Responses to Adversity: Inherent Resilience

The first level at which it was possible to observe and hear of survivors' resilient capacities as they responded to their experiences, some of which are still painfully vivid, was at an individual or personal one. This has been categorised as 'inherent resilience' (Walklate, 2011: 185), meaning individual attributes with which people are equipped and thus better able to cope with adversity. Focusing more closely on this individual level of resilience, Siapno (2009: 59) discusses the apparent quandary of categorising individuals facing adversity as either traumatised victims or resilient survivors and the implications of this decision. Some participants explicitly rejected identification as 'victims' while openly acknowledging the harm done to them. In such cases, the enmeshment of language, thought, and action was clearly evident. Participants who spoke of the 'victim'/'survivor' distinction did not accidently drift onto the topic but rather asserted their preferred 'status' in often quite defensive and forceful ways. At one point, Jane interrupted a question during her interview after hearing the word 'victim' in passing: 'Oh you can't use that "V" word in front of me! Oh my God'. For Chandani, it was not until she arrived at the Peace Centre for the first time and took home a SAN information leaflet that she started to think through the implications of language and it's potential for categorising people. It is here, as this potential became apparent to Chandani, that we clearly see the links between language, thought, and action within this context:

> That got me thinking. I thought, do you know what? I don't like the word victim. OK, in reality, I am [a victim], no getting away from that, but I survived it, you know. Maybe I would say a victim is somebody whose life maybe ended in that incident, that's a victim, you know, but if you've survived it and you're trying to make the best of stuff and, erm, being optimistic about your future and whatever then you are a survivor. So I do prefer that term.
>
> (Chandani)

Danielle echoed these sentiments, suggesting that both 'victim' and 'survivor' capture something of what participants at the Foundation for Peace (FfP) have been through, but that ultimately people have legitimate motivations for choosing one term over the other and should be respected for trying to adopt positivity in any way they choose. Similarly, Ganesh had never considered the distinction until attending a conference with an FfP staff member. The conference title contained the word 'victims' and, after being asked about this language by the staff member accompanying him, it was at that moment when it explicitly dawned on him that other people, at least, perceived him to be a victim. In the same way that Chandani associated the language of 'survivors' with optimism, Ganesh spoke of positive and negative connotations attached to 'survivor' and 'victim' labels:

> The way I see it is if the word victim comes to mind then the association with victims is something bad, maybe a burglary, rape, a victim of some crime or another, that's all that stays in your head, the bad thing that's happened that's led you to be a victim, whereas with survivor the association is different, you know, we survived that and aren't we good, there's more of a positive connotation with the word survivor than with victim. So that does affect your mentality and your mode of thinking and it affects what your thoughts dwell on – whether they dwell on the positive or negative.
>
> (Ganesh)

He subsequently described how his embrace of either term had been in flux in recent years, with the stress of going through relationship difficulties making it difficult for him to channel his thoughts in a positive direction. While not solely or directly related to his experience of surviving the 2005 London bomb attack, subsequent hardships in his life have proven to affect the way he feels and responds to instances of past suffering. While this was explored in Chapter 3, it is worth reiterating this facet of coping as something in constant flux over time. There is some consensus that resilience is clearly manifest in multiple, multifaceted and heterogeneous phenomena (Walklate, McGarry and Mythen, 2014; Walsh-Dilley and Wolford, 2015), to which, based on this data, we should also add and emphasise its temporal fluidity (Cavelty, Kaufmann and Kristensen, 2015) and, in some ways, its impermanence or even fragility. Although Cavelty, Kaufmann and Kristensen (2015: 9) rightly highlight the temporal fluidity of resilience beyond a sole focus on futurity, they mistakenly suggest that 'resilience emerges as a chimera that relates to the past and the future, but never exists in the present'. The data analysed here suggests infinite possibilities where resilience and time are concerned; this debate will be engaged with in Chapter 5. Equally important is the role played by organisational language which, as later sections explore, can clearly shape participants' outlooks in ways they may not have previously considered.

Other participants were more critical of dismissing the language of victimisation altogether. Danielle, for example, reiterated that even survivors with a positive outlook were still victims of violence. As the following discussion from Claire makes clear, the binary between 'victim' and 'survivor', including whether people chose to associate themselves with either label, does not dictate their outlook entirely:

108 Turning Points and Processes of Resilience

I find sometimes when people say, 'oh but you're a victim', you know, they're kind of being condescending, maybe, and saying, 'God love you', you know, 'you're a victim'. Well, what the fuck is wrong with being a victim, actually? What's wrong with it? You don't have to remain victimised, what you can do is say, right, I was a victim of those circumstances and I was, um, but am I now? Not really, not really, I've moved myself on a wee bit. Have you remained a victim? Do you want to be a victim? The choice is yours. But then I feel that I've moved on. I would say I've been victimised, I was made a victim, but that doesn't necessarily mean now. I was [a victim] at that one point but I've travelled on a wee bit. I'm at a point now where I'm healing, I'm coping, I'm surviving – there's a whole lot of words that I could use and I, ah, can look on the series of events that have happened to me in my life, and especially around that time of, ah, my brother's murder and onward, and I can either use the knowledge I have now and the learning that I've got from so many different people, and the healing, and I can use that to move forward or I can just stay stuck. If I want to stay stuck why would I be going around and talking if it's going to be all about me, myself, poor me? I'm no wallower, I don't need anybody's pity, um, empathy is a different thing, and to feel empathy and to give empathy is important to me. But, ah, I would not, I wouldn't keep going around [speaking about her experience] just to re-victimise myself, no, definitely not.

(Claire)

Claire has been much less involved in the SAN than, for example, Jane, Chandani, and Ganesh. Not only does she emphasise that she feels she is 'coping' and 'healing', but she is also explicit in suggesting that victims have a choice to make about whether they 'move themselves on' from their experiences or wallow in the past, a point also alluded to by Rock (2002). While this viewpoint does not contradict the ethos of the SAN, the language and rhetoric used expresses resilience in a way quite distinct from therapeutic or organisational promotion. Importantly, Claire's reference to giving and feeling empathy (from others) makes clear that she is not suggesting that she, or anyone else, can cope on their own without friends or family. Instead, her comments suggest that while those things are certainly important, she places the ultimate power of resilience within individuals themselves. From the rest of her interview, it is clear that communal and social support systems were almost as necessary for Claire as her own inner-strength but that without the latter, she would not be able to exercise the kind of agency required to cope or engage meaningfully again in social activities.

As this discussion alludes to, the language used by participants was an obvious signifier of how they intended to convey and situate themselves during their interviews. In addition to the distinction between 'victims' and 'survivors', some participants spoke of being on a journey, of healing, or of growing which connoted a sense of forward movement, of positive resolution, and even

Sources of Resilience for Survivors   109

transformation. While these terms were used to describe different phenomena, they always functioned to render challenging life experiences in a positive light, as a series of events people had learned a great deal about themselves from. Barry, for example, made repeated reference to being taken on a journey from 1971 when his grandfather was killed in a pub bombing in Belfast. He described being so angry at first which prompted him to become 'politically conscious' and later to volunteer with the IRA. He learned more about Irish history as well as the Irish language. Eventually, after being arrested in 1976 and serving a 12-year prison sentence, he became involved in the peace process and still advocates publicly for peaceful political negotiations in Northern Ireland. At every twist and turn of his life story, he emphasised that the hardships and adversities he encountered as part of the journey have all taught him so much and given him the experience and strength to overcome future hurdles. As Chapter 3 shows, traumatic incidents from the past can intersect with and influence contemporary events and how individuals manage them in a negative or stressful way. However, learning from past experiences and bringing them to bear on the present was something spoken about by around half of the participants, particularly in relation to managing emotions, as exemplified here by Claire:

> This is a very personal journey, you know, this really is about me understanding my thoughts and feelings a bit better from the past. I don't want to be in the past because that's a place that's, that's gone dark now, you know? Um, as I was saying, I don't even kind of project too far into the future, right now is all that I'm guaranteed, I can have hopes and aspirations for the future and I always want to be able to continue growing. You know, I feel much more of a sense of peace and tranquillity in myself. I was always a very impulsive person not knowing what to do with these emotions or this energy, whereas now just being able to connect with the past itself and see how far I've come and I know that I'm sort of near a completion of that, that's how I feel. I don't feel like I'm still kind of floundering.
>
> (Claire)

Understanding resilience phenomenologically, Ungar (2004: 352) suggests that 'resilience is the outcome of negotiations between individuals and their environments to maintain a self-definition as healthy'. Both 'self-definition' and reference to health resonate strongly with the mental well-being of survivors interviewed in this research. Ungar also refers simply to the 'positive outcomes' attained because of negotiating adversity. Clearly, the ways in which survivors position themselves are always relational; individuals' emotions are made sense of, ordered and negotiated according to social, as well as individual, influences and norms. As subsequent sections show, individual coping and well-being is facilitated and promoted at several levels by a whole host of collective interactions (Walklate, McGarry and Mythen, 2014). The cathartic process of speaking

110 Turning Points and Processes of Resilience

to fellow survivors is one example of how participants speak concomitantly about their personal and emotional strength and the fact that this is profoundly affected by others. However, as these extracts have shown, several participants in this research articulated their will, desire, and capacity to overcome present and future adversities by speaking strongly about how past experiences have not weakened, but ultimately fortified them at an individual level.

Economic Factors

Victim Compensation

In Chapter 3, the link between physical injuries and victim compensation was touched upon, particularly because of its taxonomising function in relation to injured and non-injured survivors. Karen was especially frustrated by this process and, as her account presented earlier showed, saw it as an obvious barrier to injury recognition by the state. The fact that struggles around victim recognition can arise as a result of this bureaucratic process, in various ways hindering or aggravating an already stressful period, might suggest that the obverse is also true. For example, might survivors who are readily awarded compensation find comfort in this apparent act of recognition? Or at a more practical level, does the money awarded to victims of such attacks provide an immediate level of support by enabling them to have more time off work or else ease financial burdens? Perhaps surprisingly this does not appear to be the case, although it still appears to be important to victims of violence. Just over a third of those interviewed spoke of compensation and, with the exception of Karen and Barry, these participants had been eligible for some form of financial compensation. Overwhelmingly, however, the claiming of compensation seemed to cause more grief, anger, and often bitterness towards the authorities – emotions which clearly overrode any significant material or supportive function.

The reasons for this are varied and context specific but fall into three categories. The first of these concerns the perceived crassness of compensating for the loss of a human life. As Stephen, who refused to accept a compensation award of £11,500 for the death of his son Nick in the London 2005 bombings after his family liaison officer applied to the Criminal Injuries Compensation Board (CICA) without his knowledge, simply put it: 'No amount of money can compensate for a son being killed'. In principal, Stephen felt that compensation should be afforded to those who have a reduced quality of life because of deliberate harm caused by somebody else. For example, he said that loss of work and therefore income, or the inability to perform the same leisure activities or hobbies as before, should theoretically be compensated for. However, in the case of losing his son, he feels that such an act does not fall into either category – 'it's just different' (Stephen). Interestingly, this discussion raised other issues shaped by financial considerations which point to tangible ways in which economic capital can be an important part of the grieving process. Stephen and his wife attended every meeting they were invited to by the government in London following the attack, including multiple trips from their home in the North West of England to attend the inquest hearings. The cost of these visits, which included train travel, hotel accommodation, and food expenses, ran into tens of thousands of pounds which Stephen could afford. In contrast, Stephen knew of another bereaved family who were only able to attend a single day of the inquest due to work constraints, lack of holidays or leave, and the cost of travelling there and back. Rather than paying compensation, Stephen argued, the state should at least ensure that every family member's expenses are paid which would enable them to attend such inquests if they wished. This more purposeful gesture, it seemed, would provide far greater support to families than seemingly abstract compensation awards.

Other reasons concern the differential amounts of compensation awarded to victims and that, particularly in Northern Ireland, taking compensation meant foregoing a degree of political agency. As suggested in Chapter 3, compensation was seen by some participants primarily as recognition of harms done to them. This included victims of the Bloody Sunday shootings as well as more recent attacks, such as the beach resort attack in Sousse, Tunisia. However, the different amounts awarded to victims and the varied speed with which victims received their compensation both appeared to mitigate, somewhat, the positive potential compensation had. Ironically, the only person who did not speak negatively about the compensation they received was Lynn who had no financial concerns by then anyway. She described spending her compensation money on taking her friends away with her or, in another instance, using it to build a garage conversion at her home which her son lived in for several years. She also gave a large proportion of it to her church and would sometimes deliver anonymous envelopes of cash through their door when she knew that the priest was trying to raise funds, for example, to buy new vestments. Her daughter, who was still in school, would sometimes ask for new shoes that she now bought without having to take the money from a household budget. These are some of the examples of how Lynn spent her money on other people. Throughout our interview, she reiterated that her family meant everything to her. To be able to treat them, and her friends, brought her a sense of pleasure. However, she also stated that 'the money meant nothing to me' (Lynn), clearly suggesting that the activities and experiences it enabled her to do with friends and family without thinking twice about the financial cost meant far more than the sum in, and of, itself. Her son had expected her to save or invest it but, as she saw it, 'there shouldn't have been any reason to have it in the first place' (Lynn). Bridget also recalls how her mother, who was awarded £250 following the death of her son during the Bloody Sunday shootings in 1972, gave all her compensation away to the church to either spend or pass on to charities. Unlike Lynn, this was because many Catholic families at the time were told that they should not pursue evidence against the British army now that they had received their compensation. However, Lynn also recalled that there was ambiguity around whether recipients of compensation could offer evidence to the Historical Enquiries Team. In addition to the issue of political agency, Bridget's mother was also verbally abused with sectarian insults by the local bank manager who awarded her the money. This, coupled with the fact that she perceived it to be British money being used to protect British interests, shaped her decision to give it away – 'She couldn't keep it, it was blood money' (Bridget). The amounts of money awarded to Catholic and/or Republican victims of British State violence in the 1970s were meagre, inconsistent, and inappropriately distributed compared to, for example, the amount awarded to Lynn and other victims of non-state violence, and certainly compared with contemporary compensation schemes.

At a time when compensation occupies an increasingly visible political space, including in relation to terrorism specifically with the establishment of a compensation scheme for victims of overseas terrorist attacks (see Ministry of Justice, 2012) and schemes such as the controversial Justice Against Sponsors of Terrorism Act (JASTA) in the US, greater scrutiny is needed around the function such compensation serves. It continues to be cited as an important, yet divisive, gesture by the authorities which appears to be fraught with difficulties and often used as a manipulative geopolitical instrument (see Gilbert, 2017). For this reason, it deserves further scrutiny and remains an area for future research to potentially explore.

Communal Support Systems

Beyond the individual, economic, or familial coping mechanisms are what we might most obviously term community-based sources of support. Viewing the data as a set of individual transcripts, it is possible to extrapolate a highly diverse set of coping mechanisms which either originate within, or are facilitated by, strong community ties. However, upon reflection, what was striking about community as a source of support after the interviews had been completed was the distinctions between survivors interviewed from England compared with Northern Ireland. Three main sub-themes emerged here which include class distinctions, religious cohesion, and friendship (including solidarity among fellow survivors), all of which were observed during the preliminary fieldwork stage of this research and which were reiterated, at times only implicitly, within the interviews.

The fieldwork sites in Northern Ireland from which participants were identified were Belfast and Derry, both of which are predominantly working-class cities that saw the majority of sectarian violence during The Troubles. When conducting interviews in these areas, particularly Derry, it was not unusual for interviews to be interrupted by friends or neighbours walking into the living room or kitchen for their daily 'catch up'. On several occasions, participants would offer to introduce their friends or neighbours who also had experienced political violence directly in the past, suggesting that they take part in the

Sources of Resilience for Survivors 113

research too. It would have been possible to interview two or three times as many people during this part of the fieldwork. However, as part of the project's ethical protocols, it was agreed that nobody who was totally unknown to the FfP's staff would be interviewed on safeguarding grounds. It would often take a long time before we got around to the interview questions as people were so keen to discuss aspects of their community and the history of their city.

In contrast, interviews conducted in England were more extensively planned and contingent upon making contact with specific individuals in advance. We would typically meet either at the FfP or, in several cases, at the participant's home. Once there, we would discuss the events that brought them to Warrington and the interviews would begin in similar, conventional ways. Participants in England typically talked about either religious cohesion or, more frequently, friendship and solidarity among fellow survivors, while Northern Irish participants made repeated reference to their geographical, as well as religious, communities.

A conversation occurred one evening in-between interviews while in Northern Ireland between several people, including two participants, in which they discussed and compared life in Northern Ireland with how they perceived life to be in London during The Troubles and into the present. It was a fascinating conversation that prompted me to ask Louise, one of the interlocutors, more about how and why she sometimes compared her experiences to that of survivors from outside Northern Ireland. This extract is taken from her interview which was conducted the day after overhearing this conversation:

Louise: If I had a normal life would I understand what I do now? Would I have made it down all the twists and turns of my life, that first relationship, the bad marriage, the drugs, the Troubles and all the rest? If I hadn't had all those would I be a wee housewife with the fake eyelashes and the perfect figure and conscious of what I looked like when I went out the door? Would I understand how to talk to people the way I do now and how to try and understand them? So, if I hadn't have gone through all that I wouldn't have been this version of me that I am. Right. So how do you get that across to, I don't wanna say 'normal' – but 'normal people'. How do you get that across to normal people if they don't know? And that's why I worry about people that have never had it tough, or people that have never had those experiences, whenever life suddenly hits them really hard. How the hell are they supposed to be able to cope? So whenever I think of Jane and Ganesh [both of whom were also interviewed for this research] and they're going around their lives, they have a good upbringing, they've gone through some tough times right but … and loss and stuff. But they're going to their work, their nine to fives, they're going home, they're hanging out with their mates, they're going clubbing, they're going back to the house watching Coronation Street, having their tea, getting a good night's sleep and then all of a sudden, in the blink of an eye, everything changes. So obviously they, when that happens to people they haven't had the massive build up that I have had.

Will: Which prepares you, is what you're saying?

Louise: Yeah, yeah

Will: So you're a stronger person ...

Louise: BECAUSE of my experiences

This way of contrasting the stressful, hectic and all too often tragic punctuations characteristic of growing up in a working-class city besieged by violent conflict with the perceived calm mundanity of suburban life in England tied in closely with competing notions of community life discussed the previous evening. With obvious significance for the temporal aspects of resilience explored in Chapter 5, Louise was perplexed at how people like Ganesh and Jane coped against this perceived historical backdrop of relative calm. Her comments about being so well equipped to deal with the impacts of violence because of not leading a 'normal' life point to a dialectic dynamics of resilience and harm which is touched upon in Chapter 5. While it would be tempting to simply contrast the cohesiveness of Catholic working-class community life with the relative atomisation of individualised middle-class suburbia, the reality is that close-knit community life also presents challenges and frustrations. Both Louise and her mother Bridget talked about community in positive ways but also recalled experiencing a sense of claustrophobia surrounding Bloody Sunday. Their family could not walk down the street without being recognised, their kitchen and living room were permanently occupied by friends and neighbours, and while this was a tremendous source of support it could also become overbearing and tiring at times.

Religion and Faith

A small number of participants explained that religion or faith had been a major source of support for them, often providing a comforting or guiding influence on them when almost all other areas of their lives seemed chaotic, lonely, or stressful. Although only a small number of interviewees discussed this, it was of paramount importance for those who did. Religious faith was often said to have been forged by the experience of losing a loved one. George, for example, whose brother Peter was killed in Syria by ISIS, described losing his Christian faith in his early 30s after a close friend of his lost his life. Paradoxically, it took another major bereavement in his life to bring him back to bible readings and to the church, although much of his faith-based community support now also come from mosques and from his many Muslim friends. Religious or faith-based support such as this cuts across both individual, personal characteristics, and community dynamics – both serve to mould, and are moulded by, religious conviction. Kevin and Anne, albeit who had a more sustained engagement with

Sources of Resilience for Survivors 115

their faith, similarly suggest circumstances where they have relied on and lent more heavily towards Christianity:

Kevin: Strength, comfort and rediscovering our faith was a very important part of that because, if we're gonna be honest, faith hadn't played possibly so big a part of our lives for many years. We'd both of us sort of wandered.

Anne: Yes, it's difficult when, in, it's most difficult to sustain your faith in middle years with a family, a job and just the everyday things of life. What losing Lauren did was strip away everything extraneous and left you with the absolute basics of survival, as it were, to survive, to survive that bereavement together and when there was no comfort, no joy left in life, the only comfort and joy we found was in our Christian faith. It WAS the love of God that kept us going really wasn't it and He, He has used that to bring us to where we are now. He's definitely brought us to this place [referring to their new house] because of the church up on the hill [laughs] which is the most lively church I've been to since 1979. We never stopped going to church but it wasn't …

Kevin: It didn't mean quite what it means now. We'd lost the joy.

Anne: We've proved, we've proved our faith is the, is, is, because we have proved, erm, the love of God and the strength of God to us in His, through His son Jesus so … I don't know how smart one can put it.

As this quotation makes evident, there is a constellation of factors that have enabled Anne and Kevin to move forward with their lives and cope with the loss of Anne's daughter. The move to their new house, which is close to a church they began attending relatively recently, has seen Anne and Kevin embedded within a new religious community, one which has facilitated, encouraged, and supported their faith. Other life course factors have played their part too. Retirement has enabled Anne to spend increasing amounts of time volunteering with the local church and their asylum seekers refuge programme. Kevin has been able to pursue similar activities, as well as helping to facilitate a number of interfaith forums. These circumstantial changes contrast with many of the other participants who had no other option but to return to work within weeks of suffering an attack or bereavement. While paid employment provided support to some participants, giving them direction and a rationale for following a daily routine, retirement has offered Anne and Kevin an opportunity to develop relationships within new communities.

Another group of participants, distinct from those considered above, described the importance of their faith almost entirely in terms of their religiously affiliated community and this was the case with all eight participants from Northern Ireland. Whether they had experienced persecution or harassment as a result of their faith (as several had) or they identified with, and supported, fellow members of their community, ways of talking about religion and community support were intimately connected.

116 Turning Points and Processes of Resilience

Survivor Solidarity

Many participants who spoke of the enormous support they continue to receive, and give, through connections made at the Peace Centre typically started by recalling how they attended a 'Sharing Experiences' residential weekend with the SAN and told their story to a group of people outside their family or friendship circles for the first time. In several interviews, when asked how, when and why they became involved in the organisation, participants would start with recollections from the first ever 'Sharing Experiences' event they attended. They would often reiterate this point in their lives as the one marking a major positive 'turning point', after which they felt better equipped to be able to deal with the adversities they were attempting to traverse, in part through a new-found recognition among fellow survivors. Conceiving of narratives as 'constellations of *relationships* (connected parts) embedded in *time and space*, constituted by *causal emplotment*' (Somers, 1994: 616, emphasis in original), this selective appropriation of 'Sharing Experiences' as the beginning of a new chapter in survivors' lives was repeated again and again. Not all friendships or networks among survivors were forged at the Peace Centre but most were, even if they primarily served to facilitate group storytelling, dialogue and activism elsewhere.

When asked if she felt ready to stop telling her story as part of peace and reconciliation events, Lynn drew on her many positive experiences with fellow survivors as a reason and motivation to continue meeting new groups in the hope that she might continue to learn from them:

> Not yet. Not yet. Haven't got there yet at the minute, I keep thinking of the things that people have inadvertently said that have touched me and changed a thinking in me or maybe got me an answer, you know. And people have come to me and said 'ohhhh you said such and such and such and such, you've no idea what that did to me' and that's what keeps me going, the fact that maybe inadvertently I will say something that will trigger something in somebody's mind or that at one of these weekends or something I will meet somebody that will say something and it'll help me.
> (Lynn)

This desire to leave open the possibility that future friendships with fellow survivors will continue to be formed, potentially influencing Lynn's well-being and sense of ontological security for the better, speaks strongly to the notion of 'causal employment' referred to above. Relationships with other survivors and the stories shared between them often represented seminal turning points within the data which again emphasised a sense of personal development and mutual understanding. Unsurprisingly, given the power of such relationships, several participants spoke of wanting to reciprocate the help and support they had received from others. This reciprocity represented something of a cathartic

Sources of Resilience for Survivors   117

exchange between individuals with a tacit knowledge of human suffering. As Chandani explains, the help and strength to be gained from such relationships and the support provided to others operates simultaneously:

> I think what I'm trying to do at the moment is to be available for other victims. So if I'm getting a phone call once a week from somebody who just listens to me, what have I experienced, what's happened to me, whatever, I wanna do that for other people. I've done it for two people in just the last week ... a 7/7 survivor who was really in a black place, a very dark place, they just couldn't see a way out, couldn't see a light at the end of the tunnel, er, and just talking things out, some things I was able to help him with, some things I could just advise him on and some things I just couldn't do anything about. Then I've met a Tunisia [attack] lady [Karen – also interviewed during this research] and I felt really rewarded for them to then turn around and say we're so glad you're part of our lives, we're so glad that you're there at the end of the phone Chandani and I thought well, do you know what, I've always been one to share, whatever I get I share, so this is my way of sharing my pain, my loneliness, my isolation and all my problems. So I would love to be able to ... at the moment I think all I'm thinking about is I need to make myself more available to other victims and again I think that would be part of my healing process. I've always been in a place where I've always been helping so I was feeling very useless that I wasn't able to help myself let alone anybody else but I'm finding that I can help, there are things that I can do to for other people, you know.
>
> (Chandani)

The Peace Centre clearly offers an ideal opportunity for survivors to meet, share experiences and exchange contact details and every event attended during fieldwork saw this kind of interaction take place. However, participants interviewed here from the earliest incident in 1971 up to the 2005 London bombings (eighteen in total) also spoke about building earlier networks before attending any events in Warrington. Often this took place completely informally, such as the close-knit community and familial ties spoken about earlier, but it sometimes took more organised and planned forms too. For example, a small group of survivors who had been travelling in the King's Cross tube train formed an informal support network with which Ganesh became involved. While it was informal, he was first made aware of it after his GP noticed an article about them featured in *The Sunday Times* and suggested it might be worth speaking to them. Here Ganesh describes the format and loose organisation of the group:

> They were, well, meeting is probably a bit of a stretch, erm, they were more like a, yeah, more like gatherings in a pub ... I was going to use the vernacular but basically they were piss ups [both laugh] so we were meeting

every couple of months or so whenever everybody felt like organising something. There'd usually be at least half a dozen or a dozen of us who'd meet up, sometimes more, there was no agenda or anything it was just a social thing. If people wanted, in the early days, yes people did want to talk about their experience, erm, so you know whoever wanted to talk about it would talk about it but, as I said, it wasn't a meeting it was just people, friends, getting together in the pub.

(Ganesh)

Interestingly, many members of the group took measures to move out of London and even out of the country altogether after 7/7, something Ganesh also tried to do, which led to some members drifting apart over the years. However, even withstanding this gradual fragmentation, the support derived from those ongoing encounters has formed the most stable and enduring base of support for Ganesh over the years in a way that sounded increasingly familiar across all interviews as the research progressed. Keeping this commonality in mind, this is how Ganesh described his personal experience of fellow survivor support:

For me, I think more than anybody else has been fellow survivors – that's been the main source of support. So there was that King's Cross United group I mentioned earlier, in the early days, people who were fellow survivors. There's probably not many of those people left from that group, maybe one or two, three of us altogether still from that original group and then there's some others who've joined our sort of regular get togethers, so I'd say there's probably two or three fellow survivors from 7/7 who've become more like, almost like a second family. We can talk to each other at any time of the day or night or whatever, even if it's nothing related to 7/7, because we've shared that really sort of awful experience together. After sharing something like that you feel like you can share anything else that happens, so they've been a tremendous support for me with other things that have happened as well, not just 7/7.

(Ganesh)

On largely ethical grounds, as advised by FfP staff, only three other participants were interviewed who suffered the effects of violence after the 2005 London attacks (i.e. from different events altogether in more recent years). It was nonetheless interesting to note that while the bulk of participants had the experience of the kind of informal survivor networks described by Ganesh, these more recent individuals did not. Their first and only experience of survivor-led support was through the Peace Centre. There could be several reasons for this. The Northern Irish peace process from the late 1990s and the 2005 London attacks both showed, in different ways, the value of engaging survivors of political violence in storytelling and dialogue. It is now relatively common for practitioners and NGOs to try and facilitate meetings among survivors as soon as possible but might not yet be recognised formally as a kind of 'best practice'. The other main contextual detail which clearly separates these three participants with the others is that they are either linked to isolated incidents (Amanda and George) or that they were the only survivor from a particular incident to attend Warrington at the time of interview (Karen). In Karen's case, she has kept in touch with several friends who also survived the beach shooting in Sousse, Tunisia, in 2015. She describes one of these relationships in a similar way to Jane who talked about meeting people for the first time on the day of the attack and then staying in touch with them ever since. So while she may be the only survivor from Tunisia to have attended the Peace Centre (at the time of the research), she was still in contact with individuals from there while benefiting from speaking to survivors of other attacks in Warrington.

While every participant's stories differ around who they know associated with political violence or how their friendships function, the overriding fact unifying their narratives is that meeting fellow survivors and keeping in touch with them has proved to be a major, if not the major, turning point in their journeys of recovery. There were some differences to the general means by which people stayed in touch presented above. Kelly, for example, was one of four participants who also mentioned that they found the Foundation's use of social media helpful, particularly some of their supportive Facebook posts following recent attacks and reminding participants of upcoming events. But these were also individuals who expressed their reliance on face-to-face survivor interaction rather than preferring online discussions.

The perceived impact of interactional dynamics in group discussions among survivors were understandably personal to individuals but, to reiterate, a clearly discernible motif that featured repeatedly throughout both fieldwork observations and interviews was the proclaimed power and value of a tacit empathy among survivors. The deeply moving and emotionally charged nature of storytelling workshops facilitated by the FfP simultaneously pose organisational challenges and potentially revelatory support for participants. John later described such tacit empathy as serving a dual function. On the one hand, the group dynamics he describes below brought more comfort and support to him than interactions with 'normal' people in his everyday life previously had for the same reasons articulated by other participants above. On the other, and of particular practical significance for group facilitation, was the fact that after initially sharing his story he needed to speak less of the raw and macabre details aloud, knowing others in the group understood his experiences implicitly.

> In my Sharing Experiences [storytelling talk] I kind of went through pretty much everything but if I'm talking to, say, Ganesh who was there anyway I don't need to say all the details because he was there, he knows, he's seen it, you know, you don't have to describe anything to them. But there are some people that still do describe everything and you're like, well, I know cos I

was there [laughs], you know, I don't need to be reminded of, you know, body parts or whatever, you know, erm, but people do, like I say, overshare sometimes.

(John)

John's reference to 'oversharing' here is pertinent and gives rise to a whole series of sub-questions and points of potential departure but, for the sake of brevity, two points particularly stand out. Firstly, it underscores the importance of not probing into case details participants are not comfortable offering voluntarily. Extended contact prior to interviews allowed for the gathering of sufficient context so that during interviews it was possible to spare participants the requirement of re-describing events in detail – precisely the point alluded to above by John. Secondly, his comments raise questions around storytelling as potentially causing either some sort of 'identity fix' or even secondary trauma. This question of habitual storytelling is returned to briefly in Chapter 6.

Focusing more closely on the supportive function of solidarity and sharing experiences among survivors, John went on to explain how participants at the FfP would form intimate bonds and close around each other in the event that one of them became upset – an emotive and 'hands on' form of support quite contrasting with the often cold and detached language of 'safeguarding' or professional counselling.

Cos, you know, everyone knows how it, how you feel or whatever and, and what you've seen or, especially with the 7/7 groups because, you know, they were all there and they shared your experience but … and yeah you just, you can, you just know that some things you talk about will set someone off. Or if someone has a moment it's fine – you know why. You know, it's not gonna be like 'oh my God so and so has burst into tears'. If that happens everyone kinda closes around you and you're all looked after for that moment until it's passed and everyone carries on again and it doesn't affect everyone.

(John)

Here John's comments echo the observation made by Overland (2013: 207) in her study of Cambodian survivors of the Khmer Rouge period referred to in Chapter 1: 'My impression is that, between equals in experience, perhaps fewer words and less depth suffice'. Whether participants relied heavily on familial ties, everyone clearly valued the safe space afforded to them by the Peace Centre and the opportunities it has given them (more on this below). It is clear from the data that it offers a convenient and well-organised space within which the kind of survivor solidarity that would probably happen elsewhere can flourish in a focused and semi-structured way.

Resilience as Doing: Practice-oriented Support

A variety of practice-oriented support systems or coping activities were cited by participants. In many cases, several of the following sources of practice-oriented support had been, or were being, accessed by individuals. This reflects both practical considerations, such as when particular forms of support may have been offered to survivors, and the heterogeneous nature of their remits which in some cases differ radically from each other. During the fieldwork phase of this research and through speaking to staff frequently, it became clear that participants utilising FfP resources also 'rotate' other support and activist organisations, therapeutic treatments, and more context-specific activities.

The Foundation for Peace

As highlighted above, the FfP itself represents something of an epicentre for many participants, through which they have met other survivors, community activists, and project leaders. The participants interviewed here all access and visit the FfP to differing degrees and with differing regularity, but all were unanimous in heaping praise on the work it does and expressing strong wishes that it remain open, active, and better-funded so that it can continue with the work it does. This support for the charity carried an emotional resonance which appeared in every interview, except for those few where participants had not actually attended but were close family and friends of those who did and who FfP staff had been in touch with. It was therefore the most common denominator among participants vis-à-vis the practice-oriented support sought. This is an obvious consequence of the sampling strategy and access revolving around the FfP. Several people spoke of having 'life changing experiences in this place' and one even stated that the Peace Centre had 'given him his life back'. In addition to those interviews which emphasised the importance of meeting fellow survivors, initially through the 'Sharing Experiences' residential event and then others such as 'Living with Trauma' awareness workshops or dialogue residential weekends, there were notable examples of individuals gaining some form of support through the FfP but whose experiences did not necessarily fit into the kind of catharsis discussed earlier.

Colin Parry spoke of the FfP, its inception, and creating it in the beginning following his son Tim's death in the Warrington bombing as a 'saving grace'. 'In the early days', he reflected, 'I think this [the FfP] has been the glue that's kept our family together, without a shadow of a doubt' (Colin). He described it as 'filling a void' and giving him 'a sense of purpose' at an otherwise confusing and distressing time. This 'void', for Colin, was most obviously the loss of his son. However, to a lesser degree, it was also the fact that while trying to come to terms with this loss he had relatively little family members to turn to. An only child, his mother had passed away and aside from his father there were only cousins and family he did not know. His father passed away shortly after Tim's

122 Turning Points and Processes of Resilience

death, heartbroken by the death of his grandson. Although he stressed how important and supportive Wendy's family were, he only really found himself able to talk about Tim during anniversaries, often with the media who ironically provided Colin with largely positive experiences in sharp contrast with most other participants (noted in Chapter 3). While most of our conversation about the charity revolved around its aims, ambitions, and the changing nature of third sector funding, including a move to more commission-based grants (see Simmonds, 2016) which has led to a diversification of the charity's work in recent years, it was clear that the Foundation has provided Colin and his wife Wendy with unique and personally driven support over the years. It seemed that the practical demands of raising funds and organising the centre's activities in the early days have provided the kind of outlet of emotion and anguish for Colin which he may, or may not, have experienced had he been involved in the Foundation's activities as a participant.

In a distinct but similar vein, Stephen explained that following the death of his son Nick in the London 2005 bombings he wanted to make a practical difference rather than seeking out ostensibly emotional support from the FfP. While he fully endorses and supports the SAN and the group sharing discussions that form part of that strand of the FfP's work, Stephen's interests lie more squarely in its violence prevention-based potential. As a trustee of the charity, he helps to provide strategic input into its activities but says he and his family 'never needed the crutch, the walking stick, of the SAN [Survivors Assistance Network]', later describing the SAN as 'palliative care' which fell short of 'cutting out the cancer' of terrorism (Stephen). He did not mean this negatively but was emphasising the fact that he and his wife 'never really felt the need for external help because in our particular circumstances we've got a network of friends and family that have filled that gap if you like' (Stephen). Here we can glimpse a way in which different sources of support are utilised and prioritised, or not, according to different interpersonal and familial factors as well as personality traits or innate characteristics.

One final point worth noting here is that the practical work performed by the Peace Centre staff served to both facilitate the kinds of solidarity, bonding, and tacit knowledge among survivors noted earlier, but that it also served to create and reinforce classifications of so-called resilient survivors (or, conversely, those not deemed to be sufficiently 'resilient'). During an observational visit to the FfP during 2015, I spoke at length with one of the senior staff members about how she perceived the relative 'pros and cons' of organising event-specific versus event-general workshops. Her view was that for 'Trauma Awareness' workshops, it was preferable to organise groups according to event (e.g. '7/7') or at least event type (e.g. 'isolated terror attack in England') while 'Dialogue' workshops or one-off talks, lectures, or visits could be safely organised using a mixture of participants with experience of diverse events. She also attributed importance to the length of 'healing time' survivors had accrued since first attending the FfP which, while seemingly arbitrary, clearly drew upon considerable professional experience of working with victims in a variety of settings. This staff member would often talk of FfP participants as 'resilient enough' (or not) to cope with particular workshops over others. Her selections seemed somewhat oblique and even arbitrary at the time but were later anchored to a concrete example by her after a 'Dialogue' workshop between Irish and English survivors and former perpetrators that she facilitated and I attended. Differences in storytelling style between participants noticeably hinged on humour and particularly the employment of 'dark' humour from some individuals, much to the visible discomfort of some of the others. There is, of course, an extensive literature on the use of 'dark' or 'gallows' humour in relation to group cohesion and coping mechanisms among emergency service personnel involved in what Scott (2007) terms 'sudden deathwork' (see, *inter alia*, Young, 1995; Rowe and Regehr, 2010) which was certainly apparent among some survivors here. The important point about the practical manifestation of resilience classifications noted here is that it consequently shaped participant recruitment to some extent (as noted earlier around more recent terror attacks). Not wishing (or able) to go against the professional knowledge and opinions of Peace Centre staff, who formed an important part of the ethical and safeguarding procedures of the project, I was unable to interview some survivors who may have seemed willing to participate but who the Peace Centre staff believed lacked sufficient 'robustness' so soon after experiencing an attack.

Often, this seemed sensibly cautious. At other times, the kinds of language used to describe somebody's apparent capacity to cope and represent themselves in certain contexts created some unease (see McGowan, 2020: 4). Well-meaning, and even objectively well-advised, decisions not to interview certain people over others cannot help but enact various forms of moral judgement and therefore moral practice. The significance of this for Hacking's (1995; 2002) idea of 'making up people', detailed in Chapter 2, is well illustrated here. Ostensibly 'less resilient' survivors may not get a chance to exhibit (or not) their resilient capacities, while those already deemed to 'be resilient' do, potentially only serving to substantiate the views held by those facilitating and organising the practical work of the Peace Centre and, consequently, the interviews made possible here. Insofar as survivors are rendered visibly 'resilient', including through the research process, this produces something of a 'looping effect' (Hacking, 1995). Actions among a particular group inform the classifications used to describe them. Subsequent actions among that group are potentially moulded by the interactions made available through such classifications; and 'classified people enhance and adjust what is true of them' (Hacking, 2007: 289). Consequently, the identification of so-called resilient survivors is never an objective, nor static, exercise. Far from gathering data and evidence 'out there' in the world, social research deals with 'moving targets because our investigations interact with the targets themselves, and change them' (Hacking, 2007: 293). Further examples of this phenomenon are considered below.

124 Turning Points and Processes of Resilience

Therapy and Counselling

Much of the data emphasising how important the Foundation has been for survivors also shows that many participants sought some form of therapy or counselling and reveals how instrumental the charity has been as a catalyst for participants going on to seek these forms of support. This is unsurprising in many ways, since the charity does not primarily employ trained counsellors or offer therapeutic services as part of its remit. They do, however, signpost individuals towards such services where appropriate. The nature of therapy participants had sought, or the regularity with which they had accessed it, was not always possible to ascertain from the interview data. However, it was clear that several participants had adopted a language that aligned closely with both therapeutic terminologies and the kind of lexicons used by FfP during their 'Living with Trauma' awareness workshops.

For many interviewees, this took the form of describing ways they *should* have been coping, or reference to former coping mechanisms as negative or maladaptive. John, for example, made repeated reference to how the Peace Centre had provided him with a conduit through which he was able to put more formal, practice-based coping mechanisms into effect. He spoke several times about how he *should* have been coping, in contrast to how he had been:

> As regards to this place and 7/7 I'm, you know, I'm glad it's here. I feel like I'm a different person but for the good whereas initially afterwards I was a different person for the worst because I wasn't, I had no coping mechanism for it [...] so I think that sort of attitude has come, for me, from this Centre, you know. [...] I would probably have gone through more of a process. Cos I know how unhealthy it's been. I think that, you know, that sort of coping with it was the way I was trying to cope with 7/7 anyway. In the last two years [through attending Foundation activities and receiving trauma therapy] I've felt that I've got so much better than I had in the previous nine. So it's been quite an eye-opener for me and doing these sessions and talking to people that have been there, and proper sort of trauma counsellors and stuff like that, you meet everyone that's been through a range of different things and you start realising how people should cope with it and how I should really cope with it. [...] Yeah so starting to come to terms with the way you deal with stuff, the way I deal with stuff, and maybe thinking twice about things and getting over those sort of moments, you know, the way you react maybe, a little bit of thinking beforehand, sort of thing.
>
> (John)

John was later diagnosed with PTSD, having been encouraged to attend for more medical-based expertise. This process began by learning more about trauma symptoms through one of the Foundation's weekend events. Similarly, George's expectations of how he was coping turned out not to cohere with how the Foundation recognised symptoms of trauma. Soon after his brother Peter was brutally murdered in Syria by IS fighters, he began talking about his experiences to police and schools across the UK. When he first attended the Foundation, he felt as though he could get more from the activities by contributing to the day's talks in a similar capacity, as someone with direct experience of terrorism rather than as someone in need of therapeutic support or interventions.

> So I'd gone down to Warrington, thinking that I was there to speak, and it's sort of an awareness weekend. And I thought, I was a bit like, oh, okay, maybe I've come to the wrong thing, because I'm doing fine. I'm not … I've got no problems. And then they put up these slides of symptoms of people who have gone through trauma. And I'm going, yup, yup, yup … oh fuck, I am not doing anywhere near as good as I thought I was. None of it was big; it was all small cracks, right.
>
> (George)

It is too simplistic to conclude from this that George had no issues coping beforehand, or that seeking therapeutic support was not helpful for him. As Chamberlin (2012: 364) notes particularly in relation to men, PTSD may provide an 'honourable explanation' for men breaking down under severe stress, offering a more coherent framework for their fears, vulnerabilities, and struggles. The fact that George continues with many of the coping activities he was doing before seeking medical assistance suggests that therapeutic interventions have not displaced or replaced his coping mechanisms from before.

Chandani is another participant who spoke of 'discovering' old emotions anew (*qua* Hacking, 1995), often referring to recently acquired knowledge courtesy of specialists or indeed staff at the FfP. Her story is considered in more depth in the next chapter rather than here but it was clear that recent interactions with therapists, counsellors, FfP staff, and committee officials working on an ongoing inquiry into IRA victims had all variously encouraged her to revisit old experiences which suddenly needed readdressing. In some cases, this journey of self-discovery leant even further towards therapeutic interpretation. This is evidenced most starkly by Jane. After surviving a bomb during the London 2005 attacks, she travelled to Cambodia to take part in controlled landmine detonations and helped to build houses for landmine victims. She still speaks of this as one of her coping mechanisms. She felt immediately compelled to try and make sure others did not suffer in a similar way to her. However, the way she describes her therapist's response to this activity shows that such immediate or direct action was met with some resistance by clinical expertise:

Jane: We all cope in different ways I think. Part of it is finding your coping way, erm … my psychologist, the first conversation I ever had with him he said 'do you have survivor's guilt?' I said no, no, no and I went oh yeah

I survived, anyway I have to go to Cambodia to do this and do that and yay and how can I have survivor's guilt and then he went ... 'oh my God ... this is the worst case of survivor's guilt I've ever come across' and he went 'in really severe cases that's how it manifests!' [laughs] And I went no, no, no don't be silly!

Will: In a way though, from what you've said to me, going to Cambodia and doing all that other stuff was part of your ...

Jane: It was therapeutic!

In the same way that George has continued with his activity, despite being made to recognise his emotions and reactions as being somehow disordered, Jane still recognises her trip to Cambodia as a major source of inspiration and support. It remains part of her narrative of recovery, and she still describes it in only positive terms. Noticing the word 'resilient' on an information leaflet at the Peace Centre, she later commented: 'Helping people, helping other people, makes you ... going through any kind of trauma motivates you to want to help others like I did in Cambodia – and that's resilience!' (Jane). While questions can be asked around whether therapeutic intervention can sometimes detract from a diverse range of natural coping responses, we must also recognise that people do not simply lose their sense of agency upon contact with therapeutic or medical expertise. Jane continued to engage with therapeutic treatment, having over 30 sessions of cognitive behavioural therapy, but she has always maintained that many of the things she did to cope prior to treatment also worked for her and continue to do so.

In all cases, it is possible to see how people are discovered and rendered visible by therapy, counselling, and organisations such as the FfP, as the following quote exemplifies: 'There is more help definitely, erm, *people are making them, agencies and people are more making them aware and going looking for these victims*' (Chandani, emphasis added). This was said in response to a question about whether there were more services available for victims in the contemporary era. Again this constitutes, in part, the 'making up' (Hacking, 1995, 2002) of resilient survivor communities – survivors must first be discovered, classified, encouraged, and shown to be making headway on a trajectory of coping.

Peace and Reconciliation Activities

Most sources of support identified in this chapter share many similarities with a range of more 'routine' life adversities, such as suffering natural bereavements, losing the stability and income from paid occupation, being injured in a serious accident or fighting other harms such as drug or alcohol addiction. That is not to say these harms are necessarily alike but that, from a sociological viewpoint, many of the necessary sources of support (such as strong family ties, having a stake in a local community, being able to talk to like-minded people, accessing counselling services, and so on) share similarities. As this chapter has shown, these sources of support are extremely wide-ranging and multi-layered. In her study of Cambodian resilience among survivors of the Khmer Rouge, Overland (2013: 204) states that 'it may be easier to say what the properties and resources found in this study were *not*, than what they were'. As this suggests, we are likely to find resilience in any and every corner of social life, in response to all manner of traumatic incidents, if there are sufficient sources of support from the kinds of areas discussed above. One area of activity, however, which is more unique to survivors of political violence, particularly in proximity to the Northern Ireland Troubles, is voluntary participation in peace and reconciliation activities associated with its ensuing peace process.

All participants from Northern Ireland have, at some point, taken part in peacebuilding activities or dialogue work as a result of experiencing violence first hand and most continue to do so. It differs slightly from participants in England insofar as their activities are geared towards a specific historical conflict. These activities fall into two broad categories. The first are commemorative practices, including annual peace marches, and dialogue-based events – some of which are facilitated by the FfP. The dialogue events attended during the fieldwork phase of the research differed in their format from the 'Sharing Experiences' weekends but were still residential, weekend-long events and are also conducted over three connected weekends. This means participants spend extended periods of time in each other's company and reap many of the benefits already discussed in this chapter. As well as marches and workshops, memorial events also represent important milestones for survivors. Examples of this include commemorations in Warrington, London, and Derry. Memorials and commemorative events, as practical expressions of resilience, are commonly found among participant groups associated with all conflicts referred to in this book, something reflective of a broader shift towards memorialisation as a performative ritual in, and with, the bombsite (Heath-Kelly, 2015; Paliewicz, 2017).

The second set of peace and reconciliation activities are those occurring outside the traditional remits of peace organisations. In Northern Ireland this included participation in real-life conflict-focused theatre productions, which a small group of the participants from this research have taken part in. This entailed providing their testimonies to a theatre production company who then weaved their narratives into a script (see McGowan, 2019). The survivors themselves then 'acted out' their scripts in an on-stage performance, often emphasising elements of the conflict typically conveyed through more conventional methods such as mediated dialogue. People who had participated in these performances, including participants interviewed here and others that were spoken to during fieldwork, said that the practice of performing public testimonies before their own communities was an incredibly powerful and even emancipating experience. It has also given many of them the encouragement and confidence to speak publicly elsewhere, thus boosting their self-esteem. In England and Scotland, a number of participants described their involvement in a range of voluntary activities including interfaith community workshops,

128 Turning Points and Processes of Resilience

asylum and refugee support forums, women's advocacy, anti-war initiatives, and awareness-raising talks. Space does not permit a detailed look at each of these and their respective remits. However, the nature of the Peace Centre, functioning as a hub where people from a diverse range of backgrounds and experiences come together, makes it an ideal site at which to observe this convergence of survivor activities. Each of these activities, in their own way, was described as a means of both promoting peace and 'keeping busy', in much the same way that Colin Parry described his original attempts to create a scholarship in Tim's name. That same desire to fill time meaningfully – to 'fill a void' and have 'a sense of purpose' (Colin) – underpinned the compulsion for people to pursue these voluntary activities, drawing on their intimate experiences of violence. Their self-awareness, confidence, courage, and motivation to do so were often first fostered at the Peace Centre. It continues to operate as an important springboard for survivors in this regard, particularly those who have attended their events multiple times and are perhaps ready to move on from 'Sharing Experiences', 'Living with Trauma', and other events pitched particularly at participants in earlier stages of bereavement, injury, and recovery.

Conclusion

This chapter has identified a range of what Overland (2013: 204) terms 'resilience resources'. The data has highlighted how important it is to consider the convergence of both individual and structural factors influencing a person's resilience; they cannot be separated. Whilst Herman (2001: 58–60) suggests that the impact of traumatic events partially depends on the resilience of the affected individual, she adds that people who are already marginalised, disconnected, or disempowered are also those most at risk from the psychological impacts of trauma and who are less likely to 'be resilient'. This has been suggested in empirical studies too. While not specifically focusing on the concept of resilience, Webel (2004) nonetheless concerns himself with a closely related question in his sociological study of terrorism victims, attempting to extrapolate from his participants what it is that constitutes the '*(largely unconscious) coping strategies* of the most and least traumatized victims of political terror' (2004: 91, emphasis in original). His findings suggest that the people who tend to cope best with trauma due to 'narcissistic-obsessional' tendencies, such as a devotion to self-protection, survival, and skills in utilising the tools and people around them to survive, are also the most likely to be adept at thriving and acquiring wealth, power, and social influence within market-driven capitalist environments (2004: 90). Thus, the way we perceive trauma (and related anxiety) and our levels of resilience towards it may be linked with how we think about, and approach, the more mundane and routine daily struggles and challenges in contemporary capitalist society. The obvious concern is that those who lack the requisite socio-economic resources, or who feel disconnected from the necessary economic and civic participation required of them under modern

Sources of Resilience for Survivors 129

consumer capitalism, will fall by the wayside compared with those whose existing access to such resources and participation equips them particularly well to respond to traumatic incidents. This chimes with political critiques of resilience and its presumptions within policy summarised in Chapter 1.

Despite the logic underpinning Herman and Webel's theses, it is not wholly supported by the data analysed here. Webel (2004: 138) concludes that whilst the nature of the traumatic event is an important variable in how people respond in the face of adversity it is not as important as individual personality characteristics. The 'narcissistic-obsessional' tendencies he describes, suggesting as they do a highly individualised and self-interested drive to survive and self-optimise at all costs, contrast sharply with the more prevalent tendency to seek out strength through collective support and solidarity among survivors, their communities, and their families as documented here. While individual personality traits are clearly important and necessary for building resilience at a collective level, these individual characteristics are exercised within and through social interaction with wider society. Identifying the sources of, and barriers to, resilience both within and beyond the individual is thus key in predicting who is most likely to feel the traumatic effects of PVT most strongly and for longer periods of time. In addition, links between community, class, and resilience are complex. Communities that are ostensibly less materially privileged may exhibit stronger communal ties, while social isolation can occur in spite of financial stability. The fact that several participants suggested feeling fortified or strengthened by their experiences, having overcome or surpassed their most difficult periods, is not an argument for adversity (as many critics of resilience-based economic policy would argue against) but does render Herman and Webel's analyses problematic, at least in this context.

Some of the findings highlighted here are by no means 'new'. The discussion of 'victims'/'survivors', for example, is one raised repeatedly within empirical literatures involving casualties of political violence, war, and terrorism (Scheper-Hughes, 2008; Siapno, 2009; Vezzadini, 2017). Within this set of familiar debates, however, the data analysed here both resonates and departs from them. For example, while Siapno (2009: 59) suggests that our decision to dichotomously classify injured or bereaved people as traumatised victims or resilient survivors carries serious implications, she mistakenly fails to challenge the fact that such decisions should not lie with researchers but rather the voices they choose to study. She rightly points out that such decisions matter in relation to the type of knowledge we produce, with the possibility that we 'miss' things out in the process. While the distinction between 'victim' and 'survivor' was spoken about in relation to individuals, their apparent capacities to traverse traumatic events, and their outlook on the future, this 'line' was not one drawn by the researcher but instead described by participants themselves. Consequently, this provides a natural point of departure for considering the extent to which problems with the way resilience is articulated and deployed by academics and policymakers are unique to resilience, and how far such methodological pitfalls apply to a

130 Turning Points and Processes of Resilience

panoply of concepts. It also challenges the policy and practice presumptions in contemporary culture which arguably orient automatically to assumptions of victimhood (Coles, 2007).

As is evident from the preceding discussion about both communal resilience and factors at an individual level, making some survivors ostensibly well placed to traverse adversity while others may struggle, the overriding impression from fieldwork and interviews is that most people will both struggle and cope in the longer term. It is difficult to isolate one set of supportive resources over others, such is their intertwined nature. Moreover, given the mutually inclusive nature of these resources, perhaps we are better speaking of 'intersecting resiliences' than one definitive, finite, or comprehensive formula for coping with trauma. Rather, they are complex, nebulous, shifting, and subject to the same fluxing interruptions of everyday life as we might expect from more ordinary circumstances. This chapter has deliberately separated various elements of support described by participants in order to render them more visible than they perhaps might appear in the everyday milieu in which they occur; to do so necessarily simplifies or obscures their multi-layered nature. Evidencing these intersections in more detail, Chapter 5 more explicitly introduces the temporal nature of support resources described by participants. Part of that chapter teases out some of the main factors driving temporal differences, while the latter half presents the ideal-typical cases of Chandani and Anne and Kevin's stories as a way of further explicating these differences. In doing so, it develops the notion of 'intersecting resiliences' introduced here.

References

Cavelty, M.D., Kaufmann, M. and Kristensen, K.S. (2015) Resilience and (in) security: Practices, subjects, temporalities. *Security Dialogue* 46(1): 3–14.

Chamberlin, S.M.E (2012) Emasculated by trauma: A social history of post-traumatic stress disorder, stigma, and masculinity. *The Journal of American Culture* 35(4): 358–65.

Coles, A.M. (2007) *The Cult of True Victimhood: From the War on Welfare to the War on Terror.* Stanford: Stanford University Press.

Furedi, F. (2008) Fear and security: A vulnerability-led policy response. *Social Policy and Administration* 42(6): 645–61.

Gilbert, E. (2017) Victim compensation for acts of terrorism and the limits of the state. *Critical Studies on Terrorism* DOI: https://doi.org/10.1080/17539153.2017.1411234.

Hacking, I. (1995) *Rewriting the Soul: Multiple Personality and the Sciences of Memory.* Princeton, NJ: Princeton University Press.

Hacking, I. (2002) *Historical Ontology.* Cambridge: Harvard University Press.

Hacking, I. (2007) Kinds of people: Moving targets. *Proceedings of the British Academy* 151: 285–318.

Heath-Kelly, C. (2015) Securing through the failure to secure? The ambiguity of resilience at the bombsite. *Security Dialogue* 46(1): 69–85.

Herman, J.L. (2001) *Trauma and Recovery.* London: Pandora.

McGowan, W. (2019) Performing atrocity: Staging experiences of violence and conflict. In R. Lippens and E. Murray (Eds.) *Representing the Experience of War and Atrocity.* Hampshire: Palgrave Macmillan. pp.203–25.

McGowan, W. (2020) 'If you didn't laugh, you'd cry': Emotional labour, reflexivity and ethics-as-practice in a qualitative fieldwork context. *Methodological Innovations* 13(2): 1–10.

Ministry of Justice (2012) *The Victims of Overseas Terrorism Compensation Scheme 2012.* London: Crown copyright.

Overland, G. (2013) *Post Traumatic Survival: The Lessons of Cambodian Resilience.* Newcastle upon Tyne: Cambridge Scholars Publishing.

Paliewicz, N.S. (2017) Bent but not broken: Remembering vulnerability and resiliency at the National September 11 Memorial Museum. *Southern Communication Journal* 82(1): 1–14.

Rock, P. (2002) On becoming a victim. In C. Hoyle and R. Young (Eds.), *New Visions of Crime Victims.* Oxford: Hart Publishing. pp.1–22.

Rowe, A. and Regehr, C. (2010) Whatever gets you through today: An examination of cynical humor among emergency service professionals. *Journal of Loss and Trauma* 15(5): 448–64.

Scheper-Hughes, N. (2008) A talent for life: Reflections on human vulnerability and resilience. *Ethnos* 73(1): 25–56.

Scott, T. (2007) Expression of humour by emergency personnel involved in sudden deathwork. *Mortality* 12(4): 350–64.

Siapno, J.A. (2009) Living through terror: Everyday resilience in East Timor and Aceh. *Social Identities* 15(1): 43–64.

Simmonds, L. (2016) The potential impact of local commissioning on victim services in England and Wales. *International Review of Victimology* 22(3): 223–37.

Somers, M.R. (1994) The narrative constitution of identity: A relational and network approach. *Theory and Society* 23(5): 605–49.

Ungar, M. (2004) A constructionist discourse on resilience: Multiple contexts, multiple realities among at-risk children and youth. *Youth & Society* 35(3): 341–65.

Vezzadini, S. (2017) Not ideal victims but real victims: Modes of response among survivors and families of victims of terrorism in Italy, 1969–1980. In O. Lynch and J. Argomaniz (Eds.) *Victims and Perpetrators of Terrorism.* London: Routledge. pp.70–89.

Walklate, S. (2011) Reframing criminal victimization: Finding a place for vulnerability and resilience. *Theoretical Criminology* 15(2): 179–94.

Walklate, S., McGarry, R. and Mythen, G. (2014) Searching for resilience: A conceptual excavation. *Armed Forces & Society* 40(3): 408–27.

Walsh-Dilley, M. and Wolford, W. (2015) (Un)Defining resilience: Subjective understandings of 'resilience' from the field. *Resilience: International Policies, Practices and Discourses* 3(3): 173–82.

Webel, C.P. (2004) *Terror, Terrorism, and the Human Condition.* Hampshire: Palgrave Macmillan.

Young, M. (1995) Black humour – making light of death. *Policing and Society* 5(2): 151–67.

Chapter 5

Exploring Temporalities of (In)Security and Resilience

> The starting-point of critical elaboration is the consciousness of what one really is, and is 'knowing thyself' as a product of the historical process to date which has deposited in you an infinity of traces, without leaving an inventory.
>
> (Gramsci, 2000: 326)

As Chapters 3 and 4 have shown, the impacts of political violence and terrorism (PVT) display many patterns, overlaps, and similarities with extant findings from studies of conflicts and critical incidents represented in the data, consolidating research on the Northern Ireland Troubles (Fay, Morrissey and Smyth, 1999; Tim Parry Johnathan Ball Trust, 2003; Dawson, Dover and Hopkins, 2017), the 2005 London bombings (Rubin et al., 2005), and other terror attacks globally (see García-Vera, Sanz and Gutiérrez, 2016 for a systematic review). Having presented such impacts and the sources of support utilised by survivors in negotiating them, this chapter delves more specifically into the temporal aspects of these accounts. What this means, specifically, requires some clarification.

One aspect of the data, inherently linked to issues of time and temporality, related to the actual 'at the time' experience of the violent event itself. Nearly all participants described 'their event' in some detail and many reflected on the passage of time on that day. The units of time used to describe their immediate feelings and reactions varied from seconds to days and were sometimes drawn upon to illustrate feelings of what Flaherty (1999) terms the perceived 'protraction' (slowing down) or 'compression' (speeding up) of time. Autobiographical examples from survivors of the kind of reflection alluded to by Flaherty (1999) can also be found in texts such as Parry and Parry (1994), Nicholson (2010), and Murakami (2003). While often interesting and always harrowing, the focus here is not on how the passage of time was perceived at the time of being injured, but rather on parts of participants' narratives that they then fitted into longer narratives about their life courses. Taking this longer view of time, it becomes possible to explore the extent to which 'resilience' appears pertinent, or even apparent, in survivors' narratives of managing harm and trauma. A key question to address is whether resilience, either in the form of coping or of

DOI: 10.4324/9781003154020-8

Exploring Temporalities of (In)Security 133

more positively transforming, is a process, whether this process appears to be linear, or whether there are critical moments or 'turning points' at which resilience is stimulated or generated. It also enables us to consider something Hacking (2003: 118) calls 'retroactive descriptions', that is, 'new descriptions given now, of events in the past'.

Attending to these questions, this chapter is broadly split into two halves. In the first half, factors are identified which shaped survivors' narratives in predominantly retroactive or, conversely, prospective ways. These factors include *who* perpetrated violence against survivors, how 'everyday' challenges throughout the life course have become enmeshed in, and related to, previous critical incidents, how survivors have mobilised and expressed themselves in the present, and what form their suffering primarily took (e.g. were survivors physically injured, bereaved, or eyewitnesses). These sections are not afforded equal weight but rather reflect their importance within the data. The second half of the chapter then focuses exclusively on the accounts of Chandani, Anne, and Kevin. These accounts are extrapolated from the broader sample as ideal-typical illustrations of primarily proactive and retroactive narration. The chief purpose of extrapolating ideal-type constructs when analysing the interview data was to make intelligible, and to collectively order, otherwise individual patterns of social action and perceptions. They were used in relation to both discrete themes within the data and individual survivors themselves, whose narratives encompassed multiple features of particular themes (in this case those relating to temporality). Rather than suggesting that the groupings of data presented here are universally valid, ideal-type constructs are formulated for their comparative insights, to draw linkages between individual cases, and are deployed as something of a yardstick, or compass instrument, capable of giving an impression of scales between discrete empirical cases (Psathas, 2005: 156).

Modes of temporality are inherently overlapping and mutually constituting. Returning to the relationship between phenomena and discourse (*qua* Hacking, 1995, 2002, 2004) sketched out in Chapters 1 and 2, this general point is confirmed in both fields.

Temporality features centrally in Sartre's (2003[1943]) phenomenological ontology, where time comes into being through human subjectivity, spontaneity, and consciousness. Time for human subjects is experienced (being 'for-itself'), in contrast with non-human objects (being 'in-itself'). Importantly for Sartre, the primacy given to subjectivity means that past, present, and future cannot help but implicate each other, whether projecting ourselves away from a past, through a present, or towards a future. Contra an epistemological idealism which might posit temporal modes of being as neat, separately knowable entities, Sartre speaks only of temporality ontologically as a reflective and existential experience with all the possibilities and contingency this entails. Hence, he states: 'The only possible method by which to study temporality is to approach it as a totality which dominates its secondary structures and which confers on them their meaning' (Sartre, 2003[1943]: 130).

134 Turning Points and Processes of Resilience

Similarly, in his extensive analysis of temporality within war on terror (WOT) discourse, Jarvis (2009) draws out three 'temporal shapes' manifest in the political rhetoric of the Bush administration following 9/11: radical discontinuity, linear temporality, and timelessness. While the first emphasises uniqueness in the present, the second emphasises continuity with the past performed into the future, and the third emphasises a sense of perpetuity drawing on historical struggle for legitimacy. Jarvis repeatedly points out that the scripting of temporality in particular ways shaped the parameters and conduct of the WOT, simultaneously enabling certain courses of action and foreclosing others. In saying this, he is not pitting discontinuity, linearity, and timelessness against one another as mutually exclusive, but rather suggesting that *within* each temporal shape the Bush administration was able to propose particular images of time. Each form of enabling or foreclosing of action occurred with repercussions for violence, identity, and politics, leaving us with a complex picture of discourse in which warnings of perpetual terror threats sit quite comfortably alongside declarations of guaranteed US victory, and the novelty of an emergent enemy is reiterated alongside simultaneous appeals to a nostalgic nationalism which remembers the inevitability of evil from time immemorial. In neither the phenomenological nor the discursive, account of time do we see a 'boxing off' of time frames as mutually exclusive.

It is clear that past, present, and future temporalities are implicated in the lives of all participants. The purpose of this chapter is to evidence the chief ways in which this manifests itself through their testimonies. The ideal-typical cases considered in the second half of this chapter are telling, however, either because surely conscious efforts are made to reinforce a particularly proactive and prospective narrative (Anne and Kevin), or because despite remaining upbeat, positive, and proactive, a narrative may be unavoidably and materially shaped by the past, even when describing present and future plans (Chandani). As the quotation from Gramsci at the beginning of this chapter suggests, history does not provide us with a fixed text from which to read; we have no inventory to refer to, from which we might reel off a catalogue of concrete and immutable seminal life moments. As he also suggests, it does, however, leave deposits and infinite 'traces'. This notion of 'trace(s)', variously interpreted and deployed, has been developed by Fassin (2011) and, subsequently, Walklate and McGarry (2015) to point to the body as a site of evidence, memory, and a vessel through which 'the hand of the (invisible) state' (Walklate and McGarry, 2015: 193) continues to act – sometimes seen, often unseen. Fassin (2011) points to the harrowing example of a young Haitian rape survivor whose subsequent French asylum application succeeded only on compassionate grounds owing to her contracting of AIDS from the attack. The trace of violence left in her body was recognised through practical and bureaucratic means as a consequence of structural rather than political violence. Hence, for Fassin, the body becomes a starting point from which we can work backwards and forwards; the traces of violence are, in essence, constituted by the practical work that those traces do.

Exploring Temporalities of (In)Security

We will see, particularly in the case of Chandani, that this practical work is often routine, mundane, and in contrast with the original act of violence around which these traces pivot, unspectacular in its nature if not its consequences.

Factors Influencing Retroactive and Prospective Narrative Formation

Violence 'From Above' and 'From Below': Official Inquests, Justice, and Peace Campaigning

While visiting the Peace Centre, observing its storytelling and dialogue-based events, and conducting the interviews analysed here, one of the obvious, though no less important, distinctions between interviewees was differences in who was responsible for perpetrating extreme violence against them or their family. While these incidents span a diverse time and place range, it is possible to group or categorise them as either institutional, authorised violence committed 'from above', typically by State actors (e.g. the shooting of innocent protestors by the British military in Northern Ireland in 1972), or as anti-institutional, unauthorised violence committed 'from below', typically by non-State actors (e.g. the 2005 London bombings) (Ruggiero, 2006: 1). It is tempting to simplify this categorisation further into 'State' and 'non-State' terrorism, although this distinction is often fraught in cases of State-sponsored terrorism or State collusion with paramilitary groups (see Green and Ward, 2004: 105–23; Chomsky, 2015). Such distinctions are nonetheless useful here in a heuristic sense because they have clear and palpable implications for the ways in which survivors articulated their sense of loss, injury, or (in)justice, and significantly influenced their outlook on coping, including what form coping has taken or what form they feel it should take.

Before exploring some of the nuances and intersections between survivors across both institutional and anti-institutional violence, one of the clearest themes to emerge from the data which differentiates them is the degree to which they felt satisfied that their knowledge of events was complete, or as complete as it could be. Searches for, and access to, accurate details about what happened, how it happened, and why it happened guided many survivors' processes of recovery. Such knowledge, or lack of it, could act either as a springboard from which coping was facilitated or as an obstacle to reconciling events and 'moving on' in a variety of purposeful ways. In both cases, completeness of knowledge, or satisfaction that factual details surrounding the event were as complete as they could be, was a key factor in shaping how participants positioned their present selves in relation to past experiences.

Official inquests serve an important function in this regard and while they do not always add new information to details circulated in the wider media they undoubtedly add authority and weight to a set of established facts, around which survivors are then able (or not) to relate, respond, add and build narrative,

136 Turning Points and Processes of Resilience

or simply know that inquest verdicts are there for them should they ever wish to revisit them. For several survivors, they served as an important point of reference during group storytelling at the Foundation for Peace (FfP) when explaining or emphasising certain points of their experiences, reiterating details from inquests again during their interviews. Any participants satisfied by the verdicts of official inquests were survivors of violence 'from below'.

Lynn was held hostage by the Irish Republican Army (IRA) in 1990 while her husband Jim, a civilian cook who worked in a British Army base, was taken from their family home and strapped into a van loaded with explosives. Chained to the pedals and steering wheel of the van, unable to escape, he was then forced to drive to an army checkpoint where the bomb was remotely detonated, killing Jim along with five soldiers. It was at the inquest that Lynn discovered that seconds before the bomb was detonated, Jim had shouted a warning to a larger group of soldiers who were heading over to the van as it pulled up to the checkpoint and that his actions had prevented an even greater loss of life. Lynn even met some of the badly injured soldiers at the inquest who had heard Jim's warning and run, ultimately saving their lives. Along with praise from the soldiers, Jim's murder also marked a milestone in ongoing hostilities in Northern Ireland. The sheer brutality of the IRA's proxy bomb campaign, which reached its peak in the autumn of 1990 when Jim was killed, alienated large sections of the public in Northern Ireland, including among the broader Republican community (Bloom and Horgan, 2008: 581). This public reaction not only generated solidarity and support for Lynn and her family, but also formed an integral part of how she has made sense of her husband's death in the years that have followed and how she frames the context surrounding the murder. The information Lynn acquired at the inquest, along with this public response, has strongly contributed to what she now describes as a series of seminal turning points for her. Knowing that her husband had saved lives was central to Lynn's account. Inquests were similarly described as major turning points by Stephen and Jane and also feature in Anne and Kevin's account later in this chapter.

Despite the challenges inquests may pose emotionally and temporally, they are a routine procedural feature of anti-institutional, non-State terror attacks which seek to make available a chain of information. In the cases considered here, they mark a point in time that can be returned to by survivors if they wish or avoided and, in theory, moved on from over time. This was not the only area within the data where issues of temporality are writ large. Another interesting theme to emerge in this regard was participants' often quite disparate pursuits of peace *or* justice, each carrying different rationales and consequences. In his essay on collective memory, Rieff (2016: 91) argues that 'peace and justice can sometimes be inimical to each other'. While questions of justice have been legally and politically linked to the precedent of remembering, the pursuit of peace, for Rieff, might be tentatively associated with the 'practice' of forgetting. The accounts analysed for this research ultimately repudiate such a simplistic dichotomy. Survivors focused on promoting peace rather than pursuing justice continue to engage in acts of remembrance for loved ones who were killed, for example. The passing of anniversaries was an important theme that was raised repeatedly in interviews, often discussed in the context of how much has happened since the incident or how well participants felt they were coping now. However, the distinction between justice and peace was nonetheless significant and often brought up in discussions about how survivors positioned their own wants, needs, and well-being, suggesting differing perspectives on past violence and future prospects. It is possible to draw attention to three main sub-themes arising from the data around justice and peace.

The first is an overriding focus on peace and looking to the future, often combined by an unwillingness to reflect on past wrongs for too long, particularly when asked to do so by the media, and an accepting resignation that justice is unachievable in any legal sense of the word. FfP founder Colin Parry explicitly differentiated the two in discussing the Foundation's work and the vision he and his wife Wendy had when establishing the charity:

> We don't act for justice, we're not campaigning for anything other than … peace, that's all we campaign for.
>
> (Colin Parry)

During our interview, we touched upon the work of other victim-focused groups who were still pursuing investigations or inquiries into the death of their loved ones or, in some other cases, miscarriages of justice which had seen falsely accused perpetrators charged with their murder. Respectfully distancing himself and the Foundation's work from such justice campaigns, Colin was clear in articulating the future-facing outlook of their work:

> what we do is not focused on the past. We know we're never gonna get justice for Tim, nobody's ever been arrested, nobody ever will be and therefore we're not pursuing the bomber, we're not pursuing some sense of justice, we pursue the cause of peace and now our son lives on and Johnathan lives on, their faces, names, through what we do.
>
> (Colin Parry)

As this quotation makes clear, the pursuit of peace is intimately bound up with a desire not to look back, but at the same time not forget or relegate the central importance of the loss of Tim and Johnathan in the Warrington bombing. Therefore, while peace and justice were manifestly separate in Colin's account, peace was certainly not a vehicle or a synonym for forgetting in any straightforward sense of the word. This was emphasised in Colin's discussion of the Northern Ireland conflict – a legacy intimately linked with the Foundation's genesis but one which he nonetheless expresses frustration at:

Colin: We're always looking forward I mean, and this is why Northern Ireland to this day still depresses me because inevitably all the focus is on past hurts and digging up atrocities which I know were awful, Bloody Sunday and Bloody Friday and this bombing and that bombing, erm, and it's almost as if all that's gotta be cleared before you can make any real lasting progress but you can't, you're never gonna heal the past, you've gotta accept that there's a line and now focus on the future where you can affect things, you can change things. You never forget but you can't be dragged down by what's happened to you. If you are then you're mired in something that's gonna bring you down.

(Colin Parry)

Colin's resignation that he and his wife were never going to get justice in any conventional legal sense for the murder of his son resonated with other accounts from survivors of anti-institutional, non-State terror attacks. As he states, while the perpetrators were not killed, they were never arrested; in addition, the conditional concessions afforded to paramilitary groups following the Good Friday Agreement (GFA) 1998 meant that while the attack was not forgotten the pursuit of peace necessarily altered the 'traditional' route of criminal justice. In the case of suicide attacks, or where the perpetrator was killed by security services, this sense of resignation was similarly expressed. George, whose brother Peter was killed in 2014 by the Islamic State of Iraq and the Levant (ISIL/ISIS) in Syria after being held hostage, suggested that while he would have wanted the man who murdered his brother to face justice in a court of law the fact that he was instead killed in a drone strike obviously takes that possibility away. Several participants who were either injured or had lost family members in the 2005 London bombings (Kevin, Anne, Ganesh, John) similarly drew attention to the fact that because no criminal justice could be pursued due to the bombers taking their own lives too, any lingering sense that they might pursue justice against perpetrators directly was soon forgotten and replaced by thoughts of how they might cope personally and move on in other meaningful ways.

In contrast with the active prioritisation of future peace and personal wellbeing, there were those with experience of harm through State violence (Paul, Barry, Bridget, Liz, Kathy, Louise, and Claire) who talked more explicitly about past events and justice – either its active pursuit through organised campaigning, or its clear absence in their journeys of coming to terms with the loss of a relative. Whether they felt like it was achievable in practice, justice took on a more palpable role, necessarily connecting them directly to recollections of the past. This is not to say that aspirations of peace were not expressed, but rather that the presence or absence of justice was highlighted as an obvious facet of their struggle. The need to continue directly engaging with the violence of the past was writ large in these interviews, articulated in both highly emotive and eminently practical terms. This is illustrated vividly in the following interview extract from Barry. His grandfather, a 73-year-old Catholic who worked as a school-crossing patrolman, was killed on 4 December 1971 by a bomb in McGurk's Bar in Belfast. Culpability for the attack, which was committed by loyalist paramilitaries, was initially attached to the victims of the bomb who were drinking inside the pub. The police and newspaper media reports had suggested that the bomb was an 'own goal' for republican paramilitaries and that the bomb had mistakenly detonated before being transported to its intended destination. In 1978, a member of the loyalist Ulster Volunteer Force was convicted for the murders and attempted murders of those in McGurk's Bar, although this received limited media coverage. In addition to trying to clear their family member's names, the McGurk's Bar justice campaign has pursued investigations into State collusion in the form of security force involvement in assisting and covering up the actions of the bombers, as well as shortcomings in the way the Royal Ulster Constabulary (RUC) investigated the case at the time (for more details see Police Ombudsman for Northern Ireland (2011); MacAirt (2012)).

Barry: Yes and understanding he's dead, he's just blown to bits, and then he becomes a bomber, and then he becomes a terrorist. So you have that stigma over our family and that almost like put you on a journey from 1971 to clear his name, that he wasn't a bomber, he wasn't making anything, he wasn't IRA. He was a pensioner, a pensioner who went out on a Saturday night to watch a football match and to have a pint of Guinness and he was killed because he was Catholic, because of his faith, you know what I mean? And that's, that almost like has motivated me and so – but along the way my grandmother has since died, my mother has since died, and my younger sister. So they've never seen justice, truth or acknowledgement and I … you almost like, it's like you almost feel compelled.

Will: To carry on?

Barry: Yes. I would love to go away and do something else for the rest of my life but you feel trapped. Not in a bad way but in a way you feel compelled because the dead can't speak for themselves, and we almost like have to be their voice. So you imagine then travelling that journey and along the way from '72, '73, you keep meeting all these other families and they're like 'oh you're the McGurk's Bar campaign, yous are doing a good job' and this is why we're joining different families together. So we've actually got a monument and you've got the portraits of about 360 families that have joined our campaign.

[…]

Some people want compensation, financial compensation, because they lost a bread winner. My granny ended up penniless and all the rest. So there's that type of truth and there are other people that want just acknowledgements. My grandmother would have says she never wanted anybody going to prison, she just wanted someone officially to come and rap on our door and say her husband, he was innocent, he wasn't a bomber. And she would have just accepted that as truth, as acknowledgement. So

140 Turning Points and Processes of Resilience

our people want to eyeball in court the people who were involved in the bombing, you know, because there was more than one person involved in McGurk's Bar. There was only one person ever found guilty. So there's that type of acknowledgement and justice that they're seeking and then there was … what we would look for is more the political culpability. Not so much the person who made or planted the bomb. We're more interested in the people who pulled the strings in different levels.

[…]

And there's still people who still believe today, even though you're trying your best, it's almost like it's a David versus Goliath type battle.

Will: So where's the campaign up to now as we speak?

Barry: Well we got a report, an official government report from what they call the police ombudsman, whose job is to investigate police misdemeanours in the past and he says in his report there was investigative bias in our case. In other words, the investigating officers had a bias towards blaming Republicans, as opposed to Loyalists. And the present day chief constable refused to accept it. He's refused to accept that the RUC was a different animal 40 years ago, 45 years ago. So we're now in court over 20 years this month to get the chief constable to accept that what the police ombudsman said was right, you understand. But it's a whole constitutional thing as well because they're supposed to be his line management, the police ombudsman's office is supposed to be telling him and he's refusing to accept their verdict.

Barry's explanations of how the victims of the McGurk's Bar bomb have been treated over the years and their struggle against various forms of media and police bias form part of the wider sectarian conflict associated with 'The Troubles' and cannot be assumed to have universal resonance for victims of PVT facing institutional barriers to justice. As the above extract suggests, multiple campaigns have united over the years driven by a variety of incidents and factors. However, it is insightful because it reveals something of the attachment victims may have to original events and unsatisfactory developments in their explanation and accountability. From describing the pain of imagining his grandfather, 'a 73-year-old pensioner – you imagine him with a wee cloth cap and his pipe' (Barry), killed in the bombing, unable to be placed in an open coffin for the funeral, to him being branded a terrorist, to then being prompted to remember other relatives who have now passed away without having all the answers they wanted about the murder; there's a clear adherence to a retrospective, chronological remembering and telling of 'the chain of events' underpinning a grief which pervades the present. This is accompanied by reiterating injustices from varying points in time – from the unfair media treatment, to the police ombudsman's report (see Police Ombudsman for Northern Ireland, 2011), to the unsatisfactory response to the families from the current chief constable at the time of our interview in 2016.

As Barry points out elsewhere, the McGurk's Bar bomb occurred after the summer of 1971 when the tactic of internment (imprisonment without trial) was used by the British military on over 300 people suspected of being members of the IRA. The following month, at the end of January 1972, another incident of seminal importance during 'The Troubles' occurred, in which 14 civilians were shot dead (and another 15 injured) by the British Army following a civil rights march in what became known as Bloody Sunday. Much like the institutional violence from the previous months, this event has become known as one of the most renowned and successful social justice campaigns to emerge from Northern Ireland in the second half of the 20th century. While death tolls may have been higher in other attacks at the hands of both loyalist and republican groups, it was the biggest single killing by State forces during 'The Troubles' and was perpetrated with relatively minimal Unionist input; that is, while Bloody Sunday can undoubtedly be seen as an attempt at the time to shore up Unionist rule, the British State actively carried out and managed the attack and its aftermath (McCann, 2006: 4–5). Liz and Kathy's brother Jack was shot dead during the attack, and their father was shot and wounded while rushing to his aid. As well as participating in the Bloody Sunday Justice Campaign for many years, they played a leading role in ensuring the annual Bloody Sunday March for Justice would continue following British Prime Minister David Cameron's public apology in 2010 for the atrocity. Some had suggested the march should end the following year, accepting this apology as victory for the campaign, but Liz and Kathy felt that it should continue if it was to achieve all of the campaign's original demands and continue to tap into broader social justice struggles elsewhere. The following dialogue between Liz, Kathy, and Paul reveals something of this almost unconditional continuity:

Liz: The Bloody Sunday Justice Campaign that started in the early 90s, you know, where, I, I became involved because the three demands of the campaign, which all of the family and all of the wounded signed up to, was the overturning of the first enquiry, Widgery [Lord in charge of the 1972 tribunal], the second was the declarations of innocence and the third was prosecutions. As of today, and as in the future, we are still on that path.

Kathy: We have never deviated, we have never deviated.

Liz: You know, and even after we get prosecutions … I am sure of that, I am sure – soldiers will come into court.

Kathy: Yes, absolutely.

Liz: I will never give up on that. Even after that then, how can, how can any of us lead a life where we can walk away from other injustices that's happening? […]

Kathy: And it's [the Bloody Sunday March for Justice] done in some terrible weather, and those people would still do that to remember because it's in their memory that there's people here that didn't get justice, still, all these years later.

142 Turning Points and Processes of Resilience

Beside those survivors explicitly campaigning for either peace or justice, within the interview sample there was also a third category of people whose views were more conflicted. For example, Chandani, who was severely injured by an IRA bomb in London in the early 1980s, supports collective notions of peacebuilding in theory but feels a profound sense of injustice at the GFA 1998. She talked at length about how, for her, the formal peace process in Northern Ireland has effectively blocked the possibility of justice for victims of IRA violence due to the release of political prisoners and the conditions placed upon reopening cases or taking them to court. Danielle, whose mother was also injured and later died following a separate IRA incident, reflecting on the differential focus on justice and peace among survivors and the emphases within the FfP, felt the relationship to be individually contingent. She described the relationship between justice and peace to be 'symbiotic', also acknowledging that while the retrospective pursuit of justice may be a major driving force for some survivors it may also take a huge toll on their health and their everyday lives. The data analysed here suggests that while all survivors of political violence face a great many hardships, victims of institutional, State violence may be forced into such lengthy pursuits if they want to secure the information they need and to make this publicly known.

The struggle for victims of State violence pursuing truth, justice, and accountability is well documented (Scraton, 2002, 2004; Rolston and Scraton, 2005). The data complements this picture by suggesting that victims of State violence are likely to remain bound to an unresolved past for longer, aggravating existing health issues and obstructing any real possibility of 'moving on' or achieving a sense of closure through conventional avenues.

Relating the Everyday to the Spectacular

In addition to the everyday campaigning activities of some survivors considered above, another kind of linkage to the past occurs through everyday adversities. This includes some of the impacts considered in Chapter 3 such as fear, anxiety, and relationship difficulties, as well as isolated experiences of adversity such as burglary. Jane would often relate any adversity that she has had to traverse in everyday life back to overcoming the trauma of 7/7, also pointing to the fact that experiencing trauma has enabled her to help other people now:

Jane: I always say to people God don't let it take a bomb up your arse to get out, to get your motivation out, cos it might just come to that but ... so yeah, I always think the people who do all of that kind of stuff without a bomb up their arse, they're the resilient amazing human beings. [...] Helping people, helping other people do, makes you ... going through any kind of trauma motivates you to want to help others like I did in Cambodia – and that's resilience!

Jane's explicit pairing of her response with 'resilience' was interesting, though perhaps to be expected, because of her participation in a number of eponymous workshops and seminars, both at the FfP and at local universities. While most other participants made no specific reference to it, Jane would relate many of her comments back to notions of resilience she had heard about at these events, which were either supported or challenged. It was clear that she subscribed to resilience as a desirable quality and one which could, in theory, be strengthened and 'worked on' externally. As her quotation above shows, however, she forged her own understanding of the term in which she sometimes offered quite a different perspective to therapeutic narratives.

Ganesh, whose comments featured in Chapter 3 when discussing the impact of 7/7 on a recent relationship breakdown, also experienced a recent burglary. As the following extract shows, his narrative about 7/7 was interspersed with reflections on less spectacular, though undoubtedly difficult, life experiences which were also linked by him to 7/7:

Ganesh: If you're exposed to one traumatic incident in your entire life, then you're very lucky if you've had no more than the one, but most people will have at least one or two, they might be minor, they might be major, who knows. Very few people go through life with everything being rosy and nothing bad ever happening. You might get over the first one where you think you've got over the first one and the next one comes along and you think, might be totally independent, unrelated, uncorrelated with the first one but the, er, when the second one comes along it does kind of, it might trigger some things, some emotions that you had associated with the first one. A third one comes along, similarly you might have some emotions triggered from earlier ones so even though they seem to be uncorrelated, erm, mentally and emotionally they become highly correlated. […] After 7/7 a few years later my house was burgled so that knocked me back again a little bit, probably more than it would other people because after 7/7 my home felt like the one safe place in the world and then when that last safe space is encroached on, invaded, then, yeah what have you got left?

One thing to be mindful of when interpreting an extract such as this is the possibility that 7/7 loomed large in participants' narratives partly because of the context in which it was provided. Whether Ganesh would be as likely to link 7/7 to this burglary, or to discuss it openly at least, with friends or relatives is unknown.

Despite this note of caution, the regularity with which adverse, though more mundane and 'everyday', events such as relationship difficulties (a common theme – see Chapter 3), job losses, or other common setbacks, were linked in some ways within participant's narratives to an ostensibly unrelated, random event suggests that resilience must be understood to operate in relation to more

144 Turning Points and Processes of Resilience

general well-being. The obvious conclusion to draw would be that there is a positive relationship between higher levels of well-being and ontological security and higher levels of resilience. Similarly, when negative life events produce similarly negative emotions, it may be sometimes easier to attach these feelings to a known, material source of sadness, anger, confusion, and so on.

Narrating Suffering and Journeys of Recovery

In addition to major differences due to perpetrators and the justice–peace divide this showed in the data, and the linkages between everyday experiences and the traumatic event in question, it is also important to highlight the fact that the way in which suffering and recovery is narrated also carries a temporal dimension. The fact that many survivors make sure to emphasise a 'journey', that is, to suggest emotional distance travelled in their lives, cannot be divorced from an appreciation of the role of time. 'Distance' in this sense was often explained in relation to temporal markers, for example, after so many days, months, or years after the attack.

During the data analysis phase of the project, there seemed some distinctions between 'cathartic' narratives of suffering, which typically had a retroactive focus, the kind of which will be expanded on in the second half of this chapter, and those focused on 'prevention'. An example of the latter approach was given in Chapter 4 by Stephen who felt that, despite the offer of support through the SAN, he found more comfort in supporting other FfP projects such as THINK and 'My Former Life' – strands of the charity espousing notions of resilience much more closely aligned with the logic of *Prevent* than *Prepare* (see Chapter 1; see also Hardy, 2015). The focus in these accounts was, correspondingly, one of preparation and futurity. Often there seemed there was an irony to the 'cathartic' approach by survivors who decided to repeatedly present their experiences at FfP events and even wider fora. George, for example, was 'touring' schools up and down the country speaking to pupils about his brother's death. Several other participants had given similar talks in schools in the past and would continue to respond to requests by organisation to partake in 'Sharing Experiences'-style events despite having done so before. One staff member privately expressed a degree of scepticism towards this approach which, they thought, was counter to a more linear, progressive, unidirectional change within survivors from 'traumatised' to 'recovered'. George's partner Amanda similarly expressed concerns during our interview that he was pushing himself too hard and not giving himself any time away from talking about a traumatic past, thus rendering it perpetually present in his life. Participants did not reproduce this viewpoint however, suggesting the ongoing lift such talks would give them.

Besides the division between cathartic accounts used to facilitate reconciliation workshops or survivor storytelling and the prevention-focused work, the distinction made by participants between 'victim' and 'survivor' identities

Exploring Temporalities of (In)Security 145

discussed in Chapter 4 also carried obvious temporal differences. The latter was typically used by participants who were constantly trying to emphasise 'moving on' or 'moving forward' in their narratives. This does not mean to say they were always successful; as the second half of this chapter shows, Chandani, who identified strongly with the language of being a survivor, would nevertheless have to face the past and retell stories about it without necessarily wanting to. However, where narrative form alone is considered, the language of 'victim' was associated explicitly by participants with 'wallowing' or with being somehow defined by the past. Practical ruptures to coherent retroactive/prospective narratives also include anniversaries of particular attacks or loved one's birthdays, which understandably refocus many survivors' outlook on the past, if only temporarily. While issues of temporality, including reflections on the past through to the future, occur along a continuum there are some interviewees who exemplify the extremes of this continuum, with differing degrees of agency. This will be shown explicitly in the second half of this chapter.

Embodied Proximity

The decision by survivors to embark on lengthy justice campaigns in order to reclaim something of the past or, equipped with satisfactory information, to focus on ways of reclaiming the future, implies (and indeed evidences) a large degree of agency. However, there are other important factors involved in how survivors articulated their experiences and the different ways this influenced their relationship with the events of the past – factors sometimes far beyond their control. Specifically, where present-day feelings of security, or indeed survivors' practical ability to live 'normal' lives, are concerned there is an embodied influence to survivors' memory which is often shaped by whether individuals were physically injured, eyewitnesses to a critical incident, or bereaved through the loss of a relative. These distinctions cannot be said to wholly influence survivors' present outlook but are often important for practical reasons, such as mobility and health concerns. While several participants suffer from long-term injuries, this impact on their ability to 'move on' from past incidents is most explicitly, though complexly, relevant for Chandani, whose story is considered in greater detail in the next half of this chapter.

In other cases, reference to this proximity to trauma and the nature this takes are more subtle and arguably stand out more for audiences (including researchers) trying to make sense of differing degrees of harm. Due to the space required to sufficiently contextualise and explore the following two 'ideal-typical' case studies, as well as the differential importance of the four factors influencing retroactive/prospective formation of participants' narratives considered here, the proximity of survivors to particular incidents is not explored further. It seems a key variable to flag up, yet was not a factor revisited or extrapolated with further interviews. Consequently, it remains unclear as to exactly how proximity of witnesses, injured survivors, and bereaved family members' narratives

Turning Points and Processes of Resilience

carry different temporal inflections, aside from the unsurprising, though no less key, finding that lasting injury or psychological trauma serve as daily reminders about events which fall further into the past with every passing day.

Retroactive and Prospective Ways of Shaping 'Resilience Narratives': Two Ideal-typical Cases

One of the problems with a thematic analysis and presentation of findings is that whether equivalence is given to all themes often remains unclear (probably sometimes for researchers as much as for their readers). Several interviews cover at length, for example, the impact on sense of safety while travelling or using public transport; in others, ontological (in)security is explicitly tied to economic security which has been disrupted following a critical incident – how is this articulated? What are the temporal dimensions of these narratives? Which feature most prominently in these accounts and how – reflections on the past, present, or future? Is anxiety or fear, as ongoing negotiated challenges to ontological security, 'linear' in these accounts? For example, did the discussions around being afraid to travel then proceed into actual action of avoiding travel? Or avoiding certain people or places? Or to an expression of support for stricter security measures? How are feelings towards perpetrators expressed and how far can they act to draw survivors into a perpetual search for answers hidden in the past? These questions have been alluded to in this chapter by highlighting factors that appear to influence the temporal reflections evident within each narrative, though have not dissected individual narratives in great depth here. To reiterate Chapter 2, the narrative does not denote a vacuous social construction(ism) divorced from action but rather concrete, objective events underpinned by circumstantial and perceptive changes in survivors' lives and outlooks (see Hacking, 1995: 250–1; 256–7). As Hacking also emphasises, 'the intentionality of an action is not a private mental event added on to what is done, but is the doing in context' (Hacking, 1995: 248). This is true of both interviews occupying the remaining focus of this chapter.

'Retroactive' has been used here to denote 'new descriptions given now, of events in the past' (Hacking, 2003: 118), rather than as the antonym of 'proactive'. Uncritically deploying the dictionary definition of proactive, for instance – '(of a person or action) creating or controlling a situation rather than just responding to it after it has happened' (Oxford Dictionaries, 2017) – risks the suggestion that participants narrating their stories in a predominantly retroactive manner *never* 'create' or 'control' the situations they now find themselves faced with, thus rendering them somehow passive. Just as problematic would be the assumption that participants narrating their stories in a predominantly prospective manner *always* create or control the situations they now find themselves facing. Neither assumption would be true, nor would they accurately capture the complex and multidirectional temporality evident in each survivor narrative. While Rothberg (2009) has advanced the notion of 'multidirectional

Exploring Temporalities of (In)Security   147

memory' in relation to the Holocaust and decolonisation, it resonates here at a personal level to refer to instances where critical incidents from the past swoop in and out of people's everyday lives, interacting and intermingling with seemingly mundane and routine life struggles at a 'lower', or at least less 'spectacular', level.

'They want to drag you back and we don't want to be dragged back' (Anne and Kevin)

Anne and Kevin exemplify an outlook focused almost entirely on moving forwards and looking to the future rather than the past. They lost their daughter (for Kevin, his stepdaughter) Lauren in the 2005 London bombings when Germaine Lindsay detonated a suicide bomb on the tube train that she had boarded. Chapter 3 briefly touched upon a difficult period of grief for Anne and Kevin, starting from the moment they heard the news, through the uncertainty of identifying Lauren's remains, attending Lauren's funeral, and later bringing themselves to read the inquest reports. Anne was able to describe this period of her grief, but she explained that it was almost like bringing to bear experiences from another lifetime. Anne and Kevin had already described this period to a group of survivors at a 'Living with Trauma' workshop that was observed during a fieldwork visit. In the months after Lauren's death, she became very withdrawn, staying at home for weeks without returning to her daily routine or seeing any friends or family. Despite being a common response to natural deaths, there were a range of factors which, in the early stages of grief, Anne felt really exacerbated her sense of helplessness and intense depression, which lasted for around one year. Among these, again echoing Chapter 3, was prolonged harassment and intrusion of privacy by the media.

After refusing interviews and television appearances, journalists mysteriously managed to acquire new mobile numbers for Anne when she tried to change numbers. It was later established that the *News of the World* newspaper had hacked phones belonging to 7/7 victim's families. They would ring up or appear at the doorstep of their previous home asking for interviews. The intrusion reached a climax at Lauren's funeral, where Anne was shepherded through the back of the church to avoid being seen by the press. She tried her best to disguise herself but a reporter recognised her and subsequently wrote untrue statements about her behaviour during the service. Initially, they had given a couple of interviews but they soon realised how damaging the constant focus on Lauren's death was. While they were beginning to make progress with how they were coping, the press would inevitably want to focus on the day it happened and how they felt in the hours and days subsequently. This happened in both tabloid media and also a planned interview with the BBC's 'Songs of Praise' television programme, who had asked Anne and Kevin if they would speak about the role of Christianity in coping with Lauren's death. It was this aspect of the media attention that Anne objected to the most.

Anne: Well they leave us alone now because it's, it's not newsworthy at the moment

Kevin: We're yesterday's chip wrappers which is a nice place to be actually

Anne: But you see the problem is, what makes it bad is they want to drag you back and we don't want to be dragged back

They both described becoming resolutely focused on moving forwards and not getting stuck in cycles of grief and anger. Consequently, dwelling on how they felt during the aftermath of 7/7, rather than how they were doing now or how they were occupying their time, was an aspect of media interaction that was irreconcilable with their outlook. They are neither in denial about Lauren's death nor are they against talking about her life. Anne recalls how she eventually 'snapped out' of isolationist grief and started contacting Lauren's friends in order to gather as many photographs of her daughter as possible. It was only now Lauren was gone that she realised how few she had taken herself over the years. This proved to be a catalyst of sorts, which gave her some drive and enabled her to set her sights on something other than staying at home with no outlet for her grief. She was given many photographs she had never seen before, including ones of Lauren and her boyfriend on holidays. The photographs became 'precious, very, very precious' (Anne) items for Anne and Kevin. They continue to enable a vivid visual memory of Lauren to flourish, taking positive precedent over imaginations of Lauren's death. Anne and Kevin spent hours showing me photographs and books of poetry they had written and compiled in the months after 7/7, including a memorial book for all survivors, but they nonetheless typify a kind of future-facing resilience at their individual and familial level.

Kevin's individual response to the 7/7 attacks was to find out more about Islam (he holds a doctorate in theology) and to try and understand the alleged motives of the bombers. In time, he and Anne both became very active in their local community, promoting interfaith events at their church, and speaking out publicly about Islamophobia towards Muslims which was heightened following the 7/7 attacks. They also work for a refugee and asylum support charity that gives food, clothing, and advice to newly arrived refugees and those processing asylum claims. At the time of our interview, which was held at their home, a young man from Gaza was staying with them for a few weeks while he finished his application. There is a temporal paradox here. These varied activities are often related back to the death of Lauren if people ask what motivates Anne and Kevin. Their aim, however, is to focus on helping others and looking to the future, so there is an explicit focus ahead that implicitly draws its energy from the past. Their desire to combat Islamophobia was also linked by Anne to her experience of forgiving the 7/7 perpetrators, a process which she described as the last hurdle in moving on from the attack and its debilitating effect on her well-being. This occurred during a trial several years later in which three men accused of assisting the bombers were acquitted, as the following dialogue with

Exploring Temporalities of (In)Security   149

Kevin suggests. Importantly, the trial facilitated a sense of closure regardless of the legal outcome, while the later inquest reports, which were released in 2012, had the opposite effect:

Anne: One of the hardest things I've ever done ... do you remember that sometime later, erm, I've no idea how long later, they put four or five men up for trial accused of assisting the four bombers?

Kevin: Kingston Crown Court, yeah, remember it well

Anne: Yeah. And I actually was [long pause] led to pray for them ... and I have never done anything quite so hard in my life, it left me feeling absolutely exhausted. At this point they were still on trial but it was the right thing to do and I was very glad I could do it. In fact, they were acquitted weren't they all of them, erm ...

Kevin: Well the case was actually dropped

Anne: Whether they were guilty or not was beside the point. I could pray for them. The fact that they had been influenced – because they were fairly radical weren't they, they had given evidences of being ... and I could pray for them because, as it came out so clearly with Northern Ireland, there but for the grace of God go I. When you listen to Sara and Scott [former Northern Irish combatants they had met during dialogue workshops at the FfP] talking about how they got involved – If we had been in those same circumstances, those same people, we would have probably, almost certainly done exactly the same thing and so to be able to see these people, who may or may not have helped people kill my daughter, in a way as victims themselves, victims of what has been done over the years to them by various sources, was very releasing to me. I think that probably was the end of the line of anything holding me back to the event. After that I could move forward and I really resent those who would wish me to go back there and it's not heartlessness. I still have pain, I still miss, but I don't want to be defined by that event. I mean that was one of the reasons we were here [the new home they moved into following sustained harassment from the media] for nearly a year if not more than a year before we told anybody wasn't it? Because we do not want ... we don't ... We are not '7/7 bereaved people', we're Anne and Kevin.

Will: Yeah. From that moment then when you left behind anything that was gonna hold you back or had been holding you back, erm, from that point to now has anything taken you back or brought you back, have there been sort of, not stumbling blocks but have there been things along the way that have ...

Anne: No. [pause] The inquests I think. Reading that people walked over the bodies. That was very, very painful. Erm ... reading the inquests and you see we have no idea whether Lauren was killed immediately or whether she was the one that was calling for help and didn't get help, we will never know. All I know is it happened at ten to nine and by half past ten, quarter

150　Turning Points and Processes of Resilience

> to eleven everybody had been certified dead that was dead. So it could have been that long we don't know, her left leg was blown off, erm, so she might have bled to death very quickly, she was asthmatic, the shock to her lungs may have killed her. We hope so. But we don't know. But the inquests … that's why we had to stop reading, or I had to stop reading them, because that was dragging me back.

In finding space to pray for the perpetrators and see them as victims of structural forces, we might say that for Anne the suicide attackers responsible for 7/7 became 'transformed from being a dangerous other (not to be pitied) to being the subjects of pity' (Walklate, 2011: 189). The way Anne talks of her desire not to be labelled a '7/7 bereaved person' and her description of the inquest readings as 'dragging her back' suggest mechanisms by which she is able to formulate adaptive breaks with the past and points at which that adaption was challenged. This suggests that processes of resilience may not solely be about bouncing back and 'building up' but also turning away.

The intersection between the trial, familial support from Kevin, their determination not to become defined by a '7/7 identity', and Anne and Kevin's Christian faith also evidences some interesting strategies of 'consciousness blocking' or other forms of mental adaptation. Agamben's (1999: 17) analysis of testimony chimes with several of Anne and Kevin's above comments. Anne refers to the 'end of the line of anything holding me back to the event' and 'moving forward' which are key phrases here. While 'the event' signifies '7/7' and the cause of death of Lauren, it is difficult to know whether this is the focal point of what she refers to as 'the event'. In the above context, it would also allude to the grief and bereavement that Anne herself felt when she suffered from depression. Exactly which point in time is the focal point or 'event' to which they do not wish to be dragged back, or whether these two are inseparable for them, remain moot. Importantly, Anne and Kevin fall much closer to 'witnesses' as those who have lived through something (in this case bereavement) directly, as opposed to onlookers to a legal dispute or trial, yet they did not bear direct witness to 'an event from beginning to end' (Agamben, 1999: 17). They themselves were not physically on the train carriage as the bomb exploded and who survived to tell others what it was like. While Agamben's analysis concerns the testimony of Primo Levi and his experiences of Auschwitz, his identification of the lacuna between deceased victim and witness, in which truth is not contingent upon 'judgement' in the legal sense but rather emanates from a recognition of how messy the distinctions between victim and perpetrator are (Agamben, 1999: 17–18), resonates here in Anne's reflections. Agamben (1999: 22) himself is not averse to using examples 'which are very far from each other as to the gravity of the facts they concern but which coincide with respect to the *distinguo* they imply'.

Anne's own words about forgiveness (not cited directly here) virtually mirror those of Agamben's on the 'lacuna' or absences within testimony. He talks about the proxy role played by survivors on behalf of those who die. They cannot speak for the dead since they themselves did not experience death, and the dead themselves cannot speak about exactly what death is like. Anne's remarks about forgiveness suggest this lack of ability to speak for those who no longer can:

Anne: I don't have to forgive Germaine Lindsay for killing Lauren. Lauren has to do that. That's the dreadful thing about murder, because the person you've killed can't forgive you, in this life anyway, but what I have to forgive is my pain and my loss. Now if you keep it to what has been, the trespass against us, against me, the harm that's been done to me, then it's much easier to forgive and I think that is the problem with people who cannot forgive, they're not actually analysing what has the harm been to them.

The fact that both perpetrator and victim are dead in this case does not detract from the paralleled ways in which Anne rationalises her decision, as a Christian, not to forgive unconditionally. This way of rationalising bereavement via faith and forgiveness necessarily means that resilience is understood, for Anne, as something entirely contingent upon 'looking' and 'moving' forwards in time and not revisiting past factual events (as distinct from real-time emotional events such as periodic grief – 'I still miss'). Anne's inability or unwillingness to 'speak for Lauren', therefore discharging her responsibility to forgive in a direct sense, again relates to the way Agamben frames testimony:

The witness usually testifies in the name of justice and truth and as such his or her speech draws consistency and fullness. Yet here the value of testimony lies essentially in what it lacks; at its center it contains something that cannot be borne witness to and that discharges the survivor of authority. The 'true' witnesses, the 'complete witnesses', are those who did not bear witness and could not bear witness.

(Agamben, 1999: 34)

Simultaneously forgiving the grief felt directly as Lauren's mother, Anne's refusal to speak for Lauren discharges her of some responsibility to forgive her perpetrators unconditionally. Forgiveness, at least in a narratological sense, constitutes one way in which negative attachments to the past are transcended. Other participants, including Colin and family members of the Bloody Sunday victims, struggled with forgiveness but the fact that it featured heavily within discussions suggests further research is warranted into forgiveness as 'an emotion-focused coping strategy' (Worthington and Scherer, 2004). Again, for Anne, it remains a key way in which negative attachments to the past are transcended and it was an outlook that proved pertinent for Lynn, also a Christian, who felt inspired after hearing Anne's rationale for forgiving in this way.

152 Turning Points and Processes of Resilience

'If I'd still have been working, I'd be flying high by now' (Chandani)

'Somehow I had to send myself back, with words as catalysts, to open the memories out and see what they had to offer' (Bradbury, 1957: viii).

Chandani began attending FfP events in 2015 after seeking practical help from staff at the Foundation. She was taking her nephews to the Harrods store in London just before Christmas, 1983, because there was a Father Christmas giving out presents and her sister's children wanted to see him. Chandani was about to start a new job in Geneva, having previously worked for an American company, and this would be one of the last times she would get to see her sister and nephews before leaving. They were leaving the store when suddenly a loud explosion sent them to the ground covered in broken glass and shrapnel. A large car bomb had been detonated by the IRA which killed six people and injured around 90. Chandani was taken to hospital and treated for serious injuries to her shoulders and back, as well as comparatively superficial injuries to most of her body, including shrapnel cuts and burns. She described meeting Margaret Thatcher who visited survivors in hospital, where she remained for several weeks. Eventually, Chandani returned to work. She found this very difficult due to the long hours she had to work and the pressure she was under to organise important meetings, conferences, and functions for her company. Not long after returning to work she travelled to Paris with work where she was required to organise an event for hundreds of delegates. She described taking pain killers 'like sweeties' and constantly returning to her room to apply heat to her back to try and get some relief from the constant agony the bomb blast had left her with. Much of her job was like this – travelling, long hours, days of standing and walking around events and exhibitions, and often very little sleep. Eventually, this punishing schedule took its toll. She was forced to leave her job just months after returning to work.

One thing Chandani emphasised a number of times was that she did not struggle to find other jobs. She was successfully promoted in her old job and was highly valued by the company who were sorry to lose her. She soon found work doing less hours and retrained a number of times, including as a beautician, then as a teacher, in a bid to find a job that would allow sufficient flexibility for her to work around her physical pain. She did this for 15 years, often struggling to keep jobs for more than a few weeks or months. Eventually, around the turn of the millennium, after working continually against her doctor's orders, she stopped working altogether and began receiving disability benefits. For Chandani, this was not a positive outcome but a necessary one and it enabled her to rest and to undergo further treatment for her spinal injuries. Despite wanting to return to work, this did not happen and by 2012 Chandani was still in receipt of benefits. The introduction of the Welfare Reform Act in 2012 led to her disability benefits being suspended while she attended a number of lengthy, 'very painful' tribunals to prove her eligibility and reapply for her

Exploring Temporalities of (In)Security   153

incapacity benefit, which proved unsuccessful. Since then she has been periodically reassessed in order to qualify for piecemeal welfare support, despite her doctor repeatedly validating the seriousness of her injuries. There have been various knock-on effects of these economic disruptions, including problems securing housing and experiencing racist abuse in the new neighbourhood she was forced to move into. Again, while very fortunate to have survived the bomb attack, Chandani is still struggling with the physical consequences of it over 30 years later.

Chandani sought the help of her local MP who later told her about an upcoming Northern Ireland Affairs Committee in Parliament. The purpose of the Committee was to establish what support had been offered to victims of IRA-perpetrated violence, specifically attacks that had used the explosive Semtex which the UK government maintains was supplied by Libya under the leadership of Colonel Gaddafi. The aim of the Committee was also to potentially secure compensation from Libya for these victims, the outcome of which was ultimately unsuccessful but had not been made fully public at the time of writing (see McClafferty, 2021). When Chandani heard about this Committee and was encouraged to submit evidence, she had to work to a relatively tight deadline. Evidence was to be submitted electronically and she had no computer. She contacted the Foundation in Warrington who quickly helped her to prepare and send her statement to Parliament. In a bid to secure her financial security, Chandani found herself embroiled in a number of battles to prove her victimhood. After submitting written evidence, she was also required to attend in person and give oral testimony. Again, the FfP helped with this. Soon she was encouraged to tell her story in Warrington at a Sharing Experiences weekend.

At several points Chandani described the experience of travelling to give evidence to the Select Committee and meeting MPs and lawyers as 'daunting', partly because she was anxious to fulfil performative and emotional etiquette correctly. This prompted me to ask her whether suddenly having to tell and retell her story in varying degrees of detail to the committee (and subsequently at FfP), having spent so many years going about her daily life, was an enjoyable experience:

Chandani: No. Initially it was hard. I didn't want to because it was taking me back where I didn't wanna go, erm, and having blanked it successfully for so many years then to go back and recall all those little details and incidences and what comes in your head and the triggers and the smoke and the smell, erm, you know it was, it was something I didn't wanna do, erm, and I have got very upset with certain people when I've been trying to do this and [FfP staff member] is a witness where I've just completely broke down, erm … but again, like I said, I know I have to do it, it's healing and I don't wanna pretend it didn't happen. I don't wanna ignore it anymore, it's shaped me, it's shaped my life, so I have to acknowledge it but I wanna move on from it as well. I, I hope to get to a point where whatever help I can get and I feel a little bit safer, that ok I'm not, you know, there, there are people there for me. When I'm not so cut off and everything then I wanna stop talking about it at one stage, like down the line. I'll only do it for a reason and for people who need to know, er, and people who need to understand me then, you know. I don't need to do it with everybody. So I'm really careful with that as well.

The making and moulding of PVT survivors and their experiences can occur in subtle and unexpected ways with unintended consequences. As Chandani's public testimony shows, while she was given a platform from which to speak, her autonomy was heavily shaped by the need to garner particular forms of social and economic capital. Reflecting on the South African Truth and Reconciliation Commissions, Ross (2003) highlights the complex nature of testimony and storytelling which may be highly useful to some survivors, even those who do not directly participate, but not to others. She problematises the way in which storytelling was facilitated in a very specific context which was expected to produce certain explanations of events as they happened. Paradoxically, by privileging storytelling as a form of testimony and thus handing power to survivors, it may be assumed to represent an authentic account of the self 'constituted by a single "story" that can be appropriated by others' (Ross, 2003: 333). Hence, for victims of PVT it is not merely instances of direct coercion or manipulation, which may take their toll but also cases where victims are requested, usually by an official or state agency, to make public their experiences of terror.

Unlike policy-focused 'resilience', which tends to stress futurity, Chandani's case points to the ways in which resilience also entails coping with the retrospection of retelling past events – not because she chose to, but because she had to. Her own agency in negotiating this has intersected with changes to welfare, victim compensation, and geopolitical contexts at a structural level. Having spent years not discussing her incident, instead wanting to hold down jobs, she has now given testimony in a variety of new settings which she is finding incredibly difficult but necessary in order to secure some sort of financial stability. Factors beyond her immediate grasp, including practical necessities of housing and mobility, are contributing to a scenario, which is partially fixing her to an event in the past. Interestingly, she talked about 'discovering' for the first time that she had not been dealing properly with her emotions in the past. As an interviewer, it was sometimes difficult to reconcile this response with earlier discussions where she talked about how she had continued working and had continued to be an active member of her former community. To an outsider it would be easy to conclude that she was one of the strongest, most determined and, in many ways it seemed, resilient participants working with the FfP. The following extract does not detract from this conclusion. However, it does evidence something of a shift in the way Chandani began to feel about her own coping strategies once in contact with the Peace Centre, the recently commissioned Northern Ireland Affairs Committee, and a number of clinical professionals.

Chandani: I think since the NI committee, since recalling all these things, since doing Sharing Experiences at the Peace Centre, things are really now affecting me as they should have then. I've been told almost things go into hibernation as far as my emotional, you know condition was, because I didn't address any of it at that time so I've been told, yes, emotions, feelings, can go into hibernation till you try and confront it again.

Again, there are additional factors to consider aside from participation in organisational and medical settings. The changing nature of memory and emotion over the life course could also play a factor. Emotions and feelings may well have gone into some form of 'hibernation', as Chandani puts it, but they may also have fundamentally changed from when she first experienced them. Her injuries, which led to her unemployment and welfare difficulties, also meant that her community ties were severed. It is likely that material adversities such as this, linked as they are to past trauma, have meant that clear-cut anchors with which to make sense of emotional hardships are returned to again and again. Chandani's experiences appeared on a continuum within the data as far as interpretation and reinterpretation of coping mechanisms are concerned. Her story is one of self-discovery, ageing and, in many ways, a curiosity to find out more about her own feelings. She would ask professionals along the way for their knowledge about particular issues and apply that knowledge to her own suffering.

Chandani's story is insightful on a number of levels. Like Anne and Kevin, she was described as being particularly 'resilient' by the second gatekeeper-staff member at FfP and, similarly, made no explicit reference to 'resilience' herself – not to being 'resilient', to feeling 'resilient', to acting, behaving or responding 'resiliently'. Beneath this obvious point, however, it *did* become apparent from spending time and speaking with Chandani why the gatekeeper may have come to this conclusion. Not only did the gatekeeper have a personal interest and occupational background in mental health and well-being-related training and knowledge of therapeutic practice where the language of 'resilience' is commonplace (see Chapter 1), Chandani simply gave off a very warm, friendly, and positive air. During each event that we attended together, she would typically be found in the midst of conversation with others, smiling, laughing, and often expressing herself in a way that, quite simply put, made others smile too. Towards the end of our interview, I asked whether she felt that things were better for survivors of more recent events, such as Karen and John who she knew well through FfP and had mentioned already, than they had been for her. Acknowledging her own struggle briefly, she quickly talked about wanting to support Karen through her fears around travelling:

156 Turning Points and Processes of Resilience

Chandani: It is nice to meet these people because you know, you can maybe give to them. I've said to Karen, Karen don't, she finds it difficult the travel and things and I always say well don't do what I did, don't get in the wars, please don't, if you want I'll make the journeys with you.

In many ways, Chandani's outlook exemplifies a number of clichés, such as 'making light of her situation or circumstances', 'seeing the glass as half-full rather than half-empty', or 'always looking on the bright side'. This seems to be part of her inimitable character that comes naturally to her; she thinks of others before herself, she is kind (as fellow participants Karen and John frequently attest), and she is perpetually grateful for everything she has. However, recent interventions alluded to above have moulded her experiences in ways that often seemed at odds with this naturally, inherently 'resilient', or at least, resourceful individual. New ideas to her, which she has applied to old actions (Hacking, 1995: 247), have been difficult to reconcile with her previous trajectory. As she says above, 'having blanked it successfully for so many years' (Chandani), being forced into a process of public testimony is not without its difficulties and cannot possibly be beneficial for every survivor. To repeat part of her quotation from above, 'to go back and recall those little details and incidences and what comes in your head and the triggers and the smoke and the smell, erm, you know it was, it was something I didn't wanna do' (Chandani).

There are many survivors with an overt focus on the past. As this chapter has shown, one of the main factors underpinning this is the pursuit of justice, often for instances of State violence. Others, including Chandani, would clearly prefer to 'move on' from these events and rebuild their lives anew. Chandani's story has been reflected on here as an example of retroactivity. Her case is more complex than simply 'looking back'. The fact that there have been so many practical hurdles, which have forced her to reconcile publicly with a past that she would not have otherwise, more powerfully illustrates that while survivors do have autonomy and agency when crafting their long-term response to terror, this agency is nonetheless structurally contingent. In this way, her case absolutely exemplifies the differential 'push' and 'pull' factors noted in Chapter 4 which are simultaneously at play, including at individual, economic, and practice-based levels, and their multi-layered nature in fortifying resilience at certain times while challenging it at others (Walklate, McGarry and Mythen, 2014).

Conclusion

This chapter has identified a number of different ways in which survivors' experiences of political violence play out in temporally diverse directions. In doing so, it has drawn attention to turning points in survivors' narratives of coping with trauma and loss, further highlighting sources of support, frustration, and struggle for participants. In many accounts, fundamental narratives around how survivors were coping with injury or loss, sometimes many years, even decades, later and how they reflected on their future prospects hinged positively and negatively on factual details of the incident in question. As Rock (1998: 99) notes in his classic study of homicide victims and organisations formed by them: 'Survivors thereby sought information, a restoration of control, and an end to the marginality which magnified their feelings of powerlessness and kept them apart from important sources of understanding'. The differential production and management of knowledge surrounding the death of a loved one, as the above analysis reveals, has acted to trap victims of institutional violence in a perpetual and incomplete search for truth about past injustices, which can generate markedly different reflections on both history and prospects for the future.

Transcending the institutional/anti-institutional violence (Ruggiero, 2006: 1) divide is a recognition among several participants that the past in which they suffered is nonetheless a major part of who they are and, indeed, that they cannot imagine being better equipped to overcome any hurdles the future may hold because of overcoming such hardships. In other instances, particularly the cases of the Bloody Sunday and McGurk's Bar justice campaigners, the very same thing causing anguish and frustration for bereaved families is feeding the desire to continue fighting for justice. Both approaches among different survivors – focusing on the future and the past – display immense strength and capacities for coping with stressful bereavements. Thought of in this way, coping, or 'resilience', is situated within a dialectic relationship with adversity. Aguirre (2007) has suggested a dialectic process exists between resilience and vulnerability in relation to social organisations faced with natural disasters and hazards; the duality of the two means that while they are mutually reinforcing, feeding off each other, they cannot be reduced to one another. Rather than using the word 'vulnerability', which implies either risk based on past harm or risk of future harm, we might more usefully think of a dialectic relationship between 'harm' and 'recovery'.

As this chapter has shown, some survivors express an attachment to past violence driven by a pursuit for justice. Others stress the need to cope personally and a desire to actively move on from past events. Neither is inherently 'better' or more desirable; each is qualitatively different. Clearly, survivors with the latter outlook, often accompanied by active practice through the promotion of personal growth and peacebuilding with various groups, represent a general disposition that would seem to cohere relatively strongly with notions of adaptation envisioned within resilience discourse and policy frameworks. However, the heterogeneity of the data in terms of radically differential time lapses between critical incidents and the present, the survivors' varied contact with, and knowledge of, organisations and practitioners espousing the language and tenets of 'resilience', and a varying subtlety with which coming to terms with past events was described in group storytelling and interviews, all suggest an innateness to survivors' varied coping mechanisms. Indeed, rather than representing 'resilient subjects' created and objectified by 'governmental philosophy and practice' (Cavelty, Kaufmann and Kristensen, 2015: 7), the accounts analysed here and in Chapters 3 and 4 are rich in multidirectional, empowering, perhaps even emancipatory engagements with deeply harmful violence from the past. Over time, this violence presents surmountable challenges to present and future ontological security, representing partial and temporary 'contradictions of resilience practices' (Cavelty, Kaufmann and Kristensen, 2015: 12).

Adding to debates identified in Chapter 1, particularly criticisms of resilience discourse raised by Schott (2015) which are revisited in Chapter 6, this chapter has identified four key factors which proved pivotal for the way time was described and mediated by participants in relation to their experiences. This includes: who perpetrated the violence against them; how more 'everyday' challenges throughout the life course have become enmeshed in, and related to, previous critical incidents; how survivors mobilise and express themselves in the present, and the form that such mobilisations have taken; and finally the specific form their injuries and suffering took. In each case, temporality is shown to exhibit an eminently subjective dimension, as Flaherty (1999: 1–2) argues: 'Our clocks and calendars mark time, but they do not make time. Only human beings make time by sifting the fragmentary dynamics of experience through the reflexive "unity of consciousness"' (Flaherty, 1999: 1–2). Due to the difficulty of evidencing the importance attached to each of these four factors, they were summarised in corresponding order and length relative to their strength within the interview data. In a further effort to show the range and variance within the data, Anne and Kevin's story was considered in more detail alongside Chandani's to compare and contrast the ways in which each carried different temporal emphases. A number of interviews could have been used to show a more explicit focus on the past, such as those concerned with ongoing justice campaigns, particularly in Northern Ireland. Instead, Chandani's story was selected because of how clearly it shows the routine and practical, yet complex, drivers of temporality within survivor narratives. These observations, combined with insights about how survivors have differently mobilised and taken up activist causes with different temporal gazes, provide an extensive empirical backcloth from which to revisit many of the theoretical claims made of resilience in Chapter 1. It is to this task of synthesising empirical analysis and theoretical discussion that the third and final part of the book now turns.

References

Agamben, G. (1999) *Remnants of Auschwitz: The Witness and the Archive.* New York: Zone Books.

Aguirre, B.E. (2007) Dialectics of vulnerability and resilience. *Georgetown Journal on Poverty Law & Policy* 14(1): 39–59.

Bloom, M. and Horgan, J. (2008) Missing their mark: The IRA's proxy bomb campaign. *Social Research* 75(2): 579–614.

Bradbury, R. (1957) *Dandelion Wine.* London: Harper Voyager.

Cavelty, M.D., Kaufmann, M. and Kristensen, K.S. (2015) Resilience and (in) security: Practices, subjects, temporalities. *Security Dialogue* 46(1): 3–14.

Chomsky, N. (2015) *Culture of Terrorism*. 2nd edition. London: Pluto Press.

Dawson, G., Dover, J. and Hopkins, S. (2017) *The Northern Ireland Troubles in Britain: Impacts, Engagements, Legacies and Memories*. Manchester: Manchester University Press.

Fassin, D. (2011) The trace: Violence, truth and the politics of the body. *Social Research* 78(2): 281–98.

Fay, M-T., Morrissey, M. and Smyth, M. (1999) *Northern Ireland's Troubles: The Human Costs*. London: Pluto Press.

Flaherty, M.G. (1999) *A Watched Pot: How We Experience Time*. New York: New York University Press.

García-Vera, M.P., Sanz, J. and Gutiérrez, S. (2016) A systematic review of the literature on posttraumatic stress disorder in victims of terrorist attacks. *Psychological Reports* 119(1): 328–59.

Gramsci, A. (2000) Philosophy, common sense, language and folklore. In D. Forgacs (Ed.) *The Antonio Gramsci Reader/A Gramsci Reader: Selected Writings 1916–1935*. London: Lawrence and Wishart. pp.323–62.

Green, P. and Ward, T. (2004) *State Crime: Governments, Violence and Corruption*. London: Pluto Press.

Hacking, I. (1995) *Rewriting the Soul: Multiple Personality and the Sciences of Memory*. Princeton, NJ: Princeton University Press.

Hacking, I. (2003) Indeterminacy in the past: On the recent discussion of chapter 17 of rewriting the soul. *History of the Human Sciences* 16(2): 117–24.

Hardy, K. (2015) Resilience in UK counter-terrorism. *Theoretical Criminology* 19(1): 77–94.

Jarvis, L. (2009) *Times of Terror: Discourse, Temporality and the War on Terror*. Hampshire: Palgrave.

MacAirt, C. (2012) *The McGurk's Bar Bombing: Collusion, Cover-Up and a Campaign for Truth*. Aberdeenshire: Frontline Noir.

McCann, E. (2006) *The Bloody Sunday Inquiry: The Families Speak Out*. London: Pluto Press.

McClafferty, E. (2021) Frozen Libyan assets will not be used to compensate IRA victims. [online] Available at: www.bbc.co.uk/news/uk–northern–ireland–56503781 [Accessed 06/04/2021].

Murakami, H. (2003) *Underground: The Tokyo Gas Attack and the Japanese Psyche*. Translated from Japanese by Birnbaum, A. and Gabriel, P. London: Vintage.

Nicholson, J. (2010) *A Song for Jenny: A Mother's Story of Love and Loss*. London: HarperCollins.

Oxford Dictionaries (2017) Definition of *proactive* in English. [online] Available at: https://en.oxforddictionaries.com/definition/proactive [Accessed 29/12/2017].

Parry, C. and Parry, W. (1994) *Tim: An Ordinary Boy*. London: Hodder and Stoughton.

Police Ombudsman for Northern Ireland (2011) *Public Statement by the Police Ombudsman under Section 62 of the Police (Northern Ireland) Act 1998: Relating to the complaint by the relatives of the victims of the bombing of McGurk's Bar, Belfast on 4 December 1971*. Available online: https://policeombudsman.org/getmedia/893d20b0-5ed6-4b37-8568-264dd d857428/McGurk-s-Final-Report.pdf?ext=.pdf [Accessed 26/03/2017].

Psathas, G. (2005) The ideal type in Weber and Schutz. In M. Endress, G. Psathas and H. Nasu (Eds.) *Explorations of the Life-World: Continuing Dialogues with Alfred Schutz*. Dordrecht: Springer. pp.143–69.

Rieff, D. (2016) *In Praise of Forgetting: Historical Memory and Its Ironies*. New Haven: Yale University Press.

Rock, P. (1998) *After Homicide: Practical and Political Responses to Bereavement*. Oxford: Oxford University Press.

Rolston, B. and Scraton, P. (2005) In the full glare of English politics: Ireland, inquiries and the British state. *British Journal of Criminology* 45(4): 547–64.

Ross, F.C. (2003) On having voice and being heard: Some after-effects of testifying before the South African Truth and Reconciliation Commission. *Anthropological Theory* 3(3): 325–41.

Rothberg, M. (2009) *Multidirectional Memory: Remembering the Holocaust in the Age of Decolonization*. Stanford: Stanford University Press.

Rubin, G.J., Brewin, C.R., Greenberg, N., Simpson, J. and Wessely, S. (2005) Psychological and behavioural reactions to the bombings in London on 7 July 2005: Cross sectional survey of a representative sample of Londoners. *British Medical Journal* 331(7517): 606–11.

Ruggiero, V. (2006) *Understanding Political Violence: A Criminological Analysis*. Maidenhead: Open University Press.

Sartre, J.P. (2003[1943]) *Being and Nothingness: An Essay on Phenomenological Ontology*. London: Routledge.

Schott, R.M. (2015) 'Not just victims … but': Toward a critical theory of the victim. In H. Marway and H. Widdows (Eds.) *Women and Violence: The Agency of Victims and Perpetrators*. Basingstoke: Palgrave Macmillan. pp.178–94.

Scraton, P. (2002) Lost lives, hidden voices: 'truth' and controversial deaths. *Race & Class* 44(1): 107–18.

Scraton, P. (2004) From deceit to disclosure: The politics of official inquiries in the United Kingdom. In G. Gilligan and J. Pratt (Eds.) *Crime, Truth and Justice: Official Inquiry, Discourse, Knowledge*. London: Routledge. pp.46–70.

Tim Parry Johnathan Ball Trust (2003) *The Legacy: A Study of the Needs of GB Victims and Survivors of the Northern Ireland 'Troubles'*. Warrington: Tim Parry Johnathan Ball Trust.

Walklate, S. (2011) Reframing criminal victimization: Finding a place for vulnerability and resilience. *Theoretical Criminology* 15(2): 179–94.

Walklate, S. and McGarry, R. (2015) Competing for the trace: The legacies of war's violence. In S. Walklate and R. McGarry (Eds.), *Criminology and War: Transgressing the Borders*. London: Routledge. pp.180–97.

Walklate, S., McGarry, R. and Mythen, G. (2014) Searching for resilience: A conceptual excavation. *Armed Forces & Society* 40(3): 408–27.

Worthington, E.L. and Scherer, M. (2004) Forgiveness is an emotion-focused coping strategy that can reduce health risks and promote health resilience: Theory, review, and hypotheses. *Psychology & Health* 19(3): 385–405.

Part III

Repurposing Resilience

Chapter 6

Temporality, Resistance, and Solidarity

The Making and Moulding of Resilient Survivor Communities

> Perhaps it's true that things can change in a day. That a few dozen hours can affect the outcome of whole lifetimes. And that when they do, those few dozen hours, like the salvaged remains of a burned house – the charred clock, the singed photograph, the scorched furniture – must be resurrected from the ruins and examined. Preserved. Accounted for.
>
> Little events, ordinary things, smashed and reconstituted. Imbued with new meaning. Suddenly they become the bleached bones of a story.
>
> (Roy, 2017[1997]: 32–3)

Against the widely contested discursive backdrop discussed in Chapter 1, one of the primary aims of this book was to document what survivors themselves understood by resilience in the context of their experiences of harm and trauma. Fleshing out the findings presented across Chapters 3, 4, and 5 and resituating them within the literature and debates concerning resilience considered earlier, this chapter focuses on three distinct conceptual issues firmly grounded in the data which, it is argued, have received scant or unsatisfactory attention elsewhere.

The first of these issues concerns the changing negotiation and mediation of harm and trauma over time. This includes the ways in which resilience appears to be accelerated or fortified at certain moments and yet challenged at others – a complex picture often rendered over in both policy narratives and their critiques. The second is how anger, contestation, and resistance feature within survivors' narratives. It is argued that while resistance is often claimed to be antithetical to resilience, we should not insist on their mutual exclusivity. Finally, the collective dynamics identified in this research around survivor communities and principles of solidarity are critically examined. While resilience has frequently been positioned as incumbent upon communities from a policy perspective, this chapter also considers the practical ways in which 'resilient communities' (in this case constituted by 'terrorism survivors') are brought into being. In short, they are 'made up' practically, as well as discursively.

Each one of these issues has its own links to the broader resilience literature and policy agenda but none, it is argued, has received satisfactory or sustained

DOI: 10.4324/9781003154020-10

164 Repurposing Resilience

attention in either. In relation to terrorism and security studies, these lacunae are particularly noticeable due to the dearth of empirical research available to substantiate or challenge assumptions put forward by theorists, civil society groups, and policymakers. While Chapters 3–5 have largely focused on the data without drawing too heavily on theoretical debates, the aim of this chapter is to revisit some of the discussions alluded to in Chapter 1 in light of this analysis. It does so in order to show that both policy narratives of resilience and the critics who eschew them often fall foul of the same tendency to oversimplify our understandings of resilience. As attractive as these critiques often are, they have proven unsuitable for making adequate sense of the stories and accounts shared by the survivors interviewed during this research.

Accounting for Time within Practices of Resilience

For the survivors interviewed in this project, the desire and need to overcome personal, familial, communal, physical, and psychological suffering, that is, to achieve a higher degree of ontological security, to go on 'going on' (Giddens, 1991: 35) in their present, everyday lives and maintain this into the future, is mediated along temporally complex and intersecting lines. Attempting to account for the complexity of time within participants' narratives is an important step towards making sense of the apparent tension between conflicting conceptualisations of resilience, particularly between security policy advocates and critical theorists. Temporality is an essential, if not the essential, point of departure for thinking through the 'contradictions and multiplicities' (Cavelty, Kaufmann and Kristensen, 2015: 12) found among resilience practices. As Dawson (2007: 5), commenting specifically on conflict in Northern Ireland and the multifaceted struggles of those affected by it, avers:

> [...] a medley of attachments to the past are also in play, manifesting, for example, in grieving for loved ones and comrades who have lost their lives to a war; in a sense of continuing commitment to a superseded regime or to the social movements and military organizations party to a conflict; in the psychological effects of trauma, evidence of the powerful hold exercised by the past within the unconscious levels of the psyche; in nostalgia for the security of a known and lost world, or for the solidarities and intensities of armed combat; in the need to uncover and know the truth about events of deep personal or social import that remain obscure and continue to haunt the imagination; and in impulses to shape present or future actions to make good what has been lost or repair what has been destroyed in the course of conflict.

Several of these observations apply to far more mundane phenomena than war and terrorism but the above quotation is nonetheless an insightful starting point for thinking through the multidirectional nature of memory, examples of which were pointed to from the data in Chapter 5. Rothberg (2009) employs the notion of 'multidirectional memory' in relation to the Holocaust and decolonisation; it is instead deployed here at a personal level to refer to instances where critical incidents from the past swoop in and out of people's everyday lives, interacting and intermingling with seemingly mundane and routine life struggles at a lower level. The temporal intersections suggested above by Dawson in relation to trauma and security pose an important, if relatively underexplored, set of questions for the contemporary resilience-based policy imagination which is arguably skewed towards linear (i.e. straight, uninterrupted, chronological) projections of futurity (Schott, 2015: 187).

As Chapter 1 contextualised, counterterrorism and security discourses espousing notions of citizen resilience and empowerment, often framed as the normative antidote to potential vulnerability and trauma, have been widely maligned across a range of critical security studies. Critics have highlighted the temporal disconnect between abstract, anticipatory frameworks of governance premised on futurity, on the one hand, and specific, material, tangible harms located in the past and permeating the present, on the other (Schott, 2015: 187). In exploring more diverse understandings of resilience, these critiques should encourage us to ask how does serious injury or bereavement, which has occurred in varying distances of the past, pervade present-day life for survivors and the families of those bereaved? What are the temporal factors or forces at play in their narratives? What effect might time be having within these stories? How does time shape narratives and how do they, simultaneously, shape time? How is coping with physical and emotional suffering strengthened, challenged, or otherwise expressed and in what ways are they contingent on time, or subject to change over time?

In considering these questions, this thesis has identified four primary factors which proved influential for the way time was described and mediated by participants in relation to their experiences. As Chapter 5 showed, these factors are: who perpetrated violence against them; what form did their suffering take; how have 'everyday' challenges throughout the life course become enmeshed in, and related to, previous critical incidents; and how have survivors mobilised and expressed themselves in the present? In that chapter, it was demonstrated that survivors of critical incidents and their families may reflect upon events differently if violence was perpetrated by non-State, rather than State, actors. They may also have varying degrees of direct, embodied trauma or memory of events depending on whether they were bereaved, eyewitnesses, or physically injured survivors. Irrespective of this, one of the most common themes to emerge and one which unified participant narratives across the State/non-State distinction was the way in which everyday challenges are often rationalised, made more or less difficult, and psychologically positioned in relation to previous, violent, traumatic incidents. This was often dovetailed by ways in which survivors mobilise and express themselves through various activist and social enterprises, much like the Parry's have (this is revisited in more detail towards the end of this chapter).

166 Repurposing Resilience

It is often asserted that people's everyday lifestyles, biography, and personality traits pre-existing critical incidents can strongly affect their ability to cope with adversity and trauma (see, for example, Herman, 2001: 58–60; Webel, 2004: 90; Overland, 2013: 204), but equally, the critical incident can affect people's resilience to those mundane events such as normal family bereavements, divorces or other relationship separations, personal injury, or job and money worries, in otherwise 'normal' contexts. Often, anytime other struggles are facing them the critical incident becomes a narrative anchor point with which to reconcile hardships, and once talking about the incident again reference is all too soon made to the everyday foundations upon which general well-being and ontological security either rest or are shaken by. This was evident, for example, from talking to John and Ganesh who both attributed difficulties in their relationships and subsequent divorces to the 7/7 bombings. Furthermore, John, who has since formed a relationship with a new partner, also attributes his newly honed ability to talk through his problems more openly with family to his experience of trauma. The critical incident carries no inherent or static meaning free from wider context but is positioned relationally and made sense of depending on how relationships are shaped by it. It can add positive and negative dynamics to new and old relationships. Inherent personality, lifestyle traits and personal, everyday life struggles are the stuff of resilience; sometimes they fortify it, at other times they test it to the limits. The actual critical incident in question swoops in and out of people's lives, probably for the rest of their lives, interacting and intermingling with more seemingly mundane and routine life struggles at a lower level. Several participants talked about needing to be 'blown up' to realise the strength they possessed to tackle these lower level struggles and how going through this trauma was ultimately what has made them stronger. Some even expressed incredulity at how people cope with more everyday struggles who have not first been through an ordeal of greater magnitude. These observations problematise the notion that we can 'map out' resilience training when, in reality, what people need to be/are being resilient to changes and morphs over time.

Much of the theoretical work around resilience and time is focused on society at an explicitly collective level. However, Bourbeau (2013) leaves sufficient space within his typology to think through its implications at an individual level too (see also Walklate, McGarry and Mythen, 2014). Commenting on resilience within different temporalities, Bourbeau (2013: 10) states:

> Resilience can refer to how well a society [or individual] is navigating through some past adversity such as 9/11 (retrospective), how successfully a society is navigating through some current adversity (concurrent) or the likelihood that a society will successfully navigate through disturbance in the future (prospective).

This is certainly true but arguably does not go far enough. In addition to the description of resilience in discrete relation to a range of temporal frames,

Temporality, Resistance, and Solidarity 167

resilience itself operates *across* and *between* these time frames, shapes them, is shaped by them, and is likely to be in constant flux through time. Coping in the present with an adverse event from the past is consigned to history as soon as it is experienced, as time moves on. Ontological security may be an ongoing aspiration but it is not an achievement finally arrived at or suspended in time. This research suggests that the negotiation of major adversities can and does operate retrospectively, concurrently, and prospectively, to use Bourbeau's (2013: 10) useful terms, in overlapping and simultaneous ways. While it may be useful to isolate them as discrete states of consciousness (e.g. traumatised individuals experiencing flashbacks to the past), linguistic forms (e.g. ways survivors talk about events and how they situate them within their narratives), or symbolic actions (e.g. through commemorative practices or trying to achieve personal goals), in reality they entwine and coexist.

Knowledge of the past is made present in the psyche of the survivor through their determination to render it absent. Anne, for example, in maintaining a strong commitment to moving on from past grief is indirectly, perhaps even subconsciously, invoking that very past. In stating that '… they want to drag you back and we don't want to be dragged back', Anne is forced to acknowledge what it is she risks being dragged back to. Paradoxically, the more survivors focus on moving away from the past, the more they are forced to acknowledge it again and again. This was particularly noticeable among participants who routinely embark on storytelling exercises such as the Sharing Experiences and Living with Trauma weekends, or various peace and reconciliation activities in Northern Ireland, where 'their story' is told and retold. Such practices arguably challenge the notion that survivors who feel confident and comfortable enough to talk to fellow survivors about their experiences have 'moved on' in any typical sense of the term; they at least suggest that a closer examination of the form and function of storytelling practices is warranted in future research.

In addition to the temporal binary of past/present, new ways of describing past experiences, including changing lexicons associated with trauma and victimisation, afford a retroactive reappraisal of past events in ways which would have been, in some cases, previously impossible (Hacking, 1995). An example of this was provided by Paul when reflecting on his injury from Bloody Sunday and the suggestion from a fellow participant that lots of survivors from the shootings had PTSD: 'Well like I said earlier, people didn't talk about that [PTSD] in 1972' (Paul). This hint at a previously unknown classificatory language chimes strongly with Ian Hacking's comments on time, memory, and the new ways of world-making made available through emergent and shifting knowledge practices:

> I came to this topic when thinking about how kinds of people come into being. How do systems of knowledge about kinds of people interact with the people who are known about? […] New meanings change the past. It is reinterpreted, yes, but more than that, it is reorganized, repopulated. It

becomes filled with new actions, new intentions, new events that caused us to be as we are. I have to discuss not only making up people but making up ourselves by reworking our memories.

(Hacking, 1995: 6)

This challenges Cavelty, Kaufmann and Kristensen's (2015: 9) suggestion that 'resilience emerges as a chimera that relates to the past and the future, but never exists in the present'. On the contrary, resilience practices emerge and disappear, are shaped and made possible by normative (and therefore present) assumptions, expressions and cultural references. Furthermore, while in non-specific terms 'the discourse of resilience is a discourse of futurity' (Schott, 2015: 186 – see Chapter 1), the reality for survivors coping with their own inescapably specific traumatic events and bereavements is that whatever form resilience might take for them remains just as contingent upon a complex admixture of temporalities as ever. This challenges the viewpoint that resilience has come to *successfully* replace post-Holocaust discourses, said to be 'oriented towards the past – the nature of past crimes, recovery after trauma, and the responsibility of the present for acknowledging past wrongs in order to prevent future atrocities' (Schott, 2015: 186). The data analysed here suggests infinite possibilities where resilience and time are concerned, supporting Heath-Kelly's (2015: 73) assertion that resilience is temporally ambiguous. It also takes seriously her warning that most research to date has failed to take different resilience temporalities seriously, thus perpetuating a range of issues well known to critical security studies: 'If critical research continues to focus only on anticipatory technologies, accepting the resilience temporality as it is performed in policy, then we risk buying into the rhetoric of prevention even as we critique it' (Heath-Kelly, 2015: 83). This research is an attempt to fill this lacuna and resist the rhetoric and risk alluded to by Heath-Kelly.

Making Space for Anger, Contestation, and Resistance within Studies of Resilience

In addition to debates around time, the data presented in this book contributes to a range of discussions pertaining to resilience and its relationship with resistance. As Chapter 3 highlighted, emotions such as anger which can facilitate and fuel political resistance are often seen as antithetical to resilience despite being fairly typical responses to bereavement (particularly, though not exclusively, in the short term). Some theorists have gone as far as insisting that resilience and resistance simply cannot coexist. Although such work typically refers to the use of resilience as a neoliberal organising metaphor, it is worth revisiting this claim in light of the data analysed here. While Neocleous (2013) makes no allowance whatsoever for a favourable consideration of resilience, Diprose (2015: 45) is more measured (though no less resolute) in her rebuke, maintaining that 'resilience is no basis for contentious politics'. Reflecting on personal ethnographic research experiences and work with grassroots campaigners and voluntary sector organisations, Diprose writes of how her initial association of resilience with 'small spectacles of self-determination' (2015: 44) became politically, indeed morally, untenable. Posited as the solution to marginalised communities' – rather than the coalition government's – economic woes since the recession, Diprose emotively discusses some of the ways in which resilience rhetoric has urged people in dire need of greater social welfare, or simply more favourable job prospects, to cope with precarity, internalise inequality, accept responsibility, all while allowing society's professional 'risk managers' indeterminate breathing space from accountability. Rather than asking 'why research resilience at all?', as Neocleous does, Diprose convincingly presents a case for questioning whether we, as a society, should be striving for resilience as an end goal; that is, should we not be aiming a little higher than merely surviving? Does resilience not set rather a low bar?

Neocleous goes further than this, stating that 'resilience is by definition *against resistance*' (2013: 7, emphasis in original). This is, of course, true insofar as adaptation is not making an absolute break with the past. But is resistance itself such a clear cut phenomenon? Around the time this research was originally conducted, the fatal shooting of black teenager Mike Brown in Ferguson, Missouri, and the subsequent demonstrations from the black community against police violence provided just one example to problematise this relationship. At an individual and community level, there was no doubting the emotional strength and political energy exhibited in Ferguson as protestors fought back against injustice using both non-direct and direct action. By seeing these events as communal solidarity and mutual aid it is no leap of faith to argue that through struggle and resistance the community in Ferguson has exhibited tremendous resilience in the face of adversity. Similar observations could be made about protests against the North Dakota Access Pipeline or justice campaigns such as those linked to Hillsborough or Bloody Sunday. However, as Diprose (2015) maintains, resilience borne of solidarity and political protest is not necessarily a positive outcome if it substitutes the resolution of tangible, material struggles; that is, it often enables grassroots organisations a resource through which they can regroup, in spite of any real political change. It is a powerful critique.

As Bourbeau (2013: 8) similarly suggests, coping, adapting, or bouncing back from adverse events is not always virtuous or beneficial:

> Resilience is not always a desirable feature of social, political or economic life. Being resilient might in fact mean being an obstacle to positive change in some cases. [...] [T]here might be good reasons for wanting to transform a social structure, a given situation, a regime, a norm, an economic system of exploitation, etc., and that being resilient to these changes could be considered as negative.
>
> (Bourbeau, 2013: 8)

170 Repurposing Resilience

The problem with rejecting resilience in the way Neocleous (2013) does is that it casts resilience as a monolithic experience, narrowly constituted by a single and very particular form of subjectivity. He begins his article with a contribution sent into a newspaper advice column by a 24-year-old woman who tells of her anxiety at living with a bullying, abusive boyfriend. Trapped in a relationship she regrets getting into, unable to afford her landlord's fees should she cancel their flat lease, and fearful of losing her job should she move home to stay with her mother, she laments: 'If I could only learn resilience, I feel like maybe the practicalities wouldn't be so daunting'. The article then highlights the rise in military resilience training, drawing on examples from the 'Comprehensive Soldier and Family Fitness' programme (on soldier fitness programmes and resilience see also Howell, 2015a and McGarry, Walklate and Mythen, 2015), leading to the following observation:

> When the only thing a sad, lonely and oppressed young woman thinks might help her *turns out to be the very same thing* being taught by the world's largest military power, something interesting is going on, something that takes us from mundane tips about how to live well to the world of national security, emergency planning and capital accumulation.
>
> (Neocleous, 2013: 3, emphasis added)

The suggestion that the State's pursuit of capital and security is aided by resilient (i.e. for Neocleous, pacified) subjects is undoubtedly true (Walklate, Mythen and McGarry, 2012; Jackson, 2013), but Neocleous equates one girl's desire to feel happy again, which in her own terms she describes as a yearning for 'resilience' or the ability to tackle her depression as a result of abuse and socio-economic adversity, with the use of the term by an army magazine to make soldiers and civilians stronger, tougher, or hungrier for a yet unseen conquest. This linkage is an interesting and provocative connection to ponder, but to say that this 'thing' that the girl yearns for 'turns out to be the very same thing being taught by the world's largest military power' is deeply problematic, not least of all due to the equation of common or everyday uses of language with military policy. Yet again, we are confronted with that now-familiar, though no less complex, tension between discourse in the abstract, language, and action (Hacking, 2004; see also Sartre, 1968). The way Neocleous presents resilience to us is that as a concept, it inherently describes the preparation of individuals by the State for any number of social, economic, militaristic, and coercive measures imaginable which it has at its (pre)disposal. That the State (and privately owned capital) may benefit from the pacification of citizens is not in question, but the dismissal of the term as also being capable of signifying an important process in overcoming victimisation, in some ways removes part of the necessary autonomy of victims needed to overcome trauma. As feminist philosopher and rape survivor Susan Brison (2002: 38) puts it, 'the self is both autonomous and socially dependent, vulnerable enough to be undone by violence and yet resilient enough to be reconstructed with the help of empathetic others'. Can we realistically assert that individual actors necessarily share the same understandings of resilience as those who both promote and critique it? Or that resilience cannot be both empowering and disabling, perhaps even simultaneously in some cases?

Without question, political critiques of resilience discourse are valuable and warrant careful consideration, but too often they fall into the trap of reading discursive signs one dimensionally. As Jessop (2010: 340) argues, analysis of discourse does not necessarily equate to a thoroughgoing discourse analysis, and accounts sometimes represent little more than reductionist caricatures of the social world in which 'agents can will almost anything into existence in and through an appropriately articulated discourse'. This critique is levelled powerfully by Howell (2015b) at much of the governmentality literature on resilience for falling into exactly this methodological trap; 'resilience discourse' is taken to mean simply any language which uses the words and phrases associated with articulations of 'big policy' – 'rather than a constellation or assemblage of discursive practices' (2015: 68). Her criticisms of such 'thin' notions of discourse focus, particularly, on the determinism frequently driving 'responsibilisation' debates. While this research is valuable, it frequently

> ends up in an analytical bind one end of which is to treat resilience-oriented governance as successful and a *fait accompli*. This is far from the case. Rather, failure is always to a greater or lesser degree intrinsic to governance [...] precisely because governance, and in this case specifically resilience, is always to some extent fantastical and utopian.
>
> (Howell, 2015b: 70)

This research has found no evidence that individuals who have suffered serious injury or bereavement through political violence miraculously achieve a state of 'resilience' which is then constantly maintained. The reality is certainly far more mundane, nuanced and human than Cavelty, Kaufmann and Kristensen's (2015: 3) deliberately provocative and satirical caricature of resilience as a kind of 'new superhero in town'.

The opposite is also true in that no participant could be said to totally lack resilience. Everybody interviewed exhibited tremendous courage, strength, and resolve in different ways. Some participants expressed this resolve through a commitment to their family, others to achieving life ambitions, many worked hard to overcome personal fears, anxieties, and inhibitions, while some channelled their energies into pursuing activism, resistance, and promoting social justice. That is not to say that everyone falls on their feet after suffering from political violence and therefore support is simply redundant. Rather, a distinction should be drawn between pain, anger, and grief that is directed outwardly and that which is directed or experienced inwardly. Neither response guarantees that victims will become managed subjects 'to be worked with

172 Repurposing Resilience

and upon in order to correct ignorance, vulnerability and misunderstanding' (O'Malley, 2006: 52) (and trauma) through top-down resilience strategy. It is not as predictable or causal as some of the 'resilience-as-responsibilisation' (*qua* Joseph, 2013) literature may suggest. It is, however, possible to see how each response coheres with different visions, projections, and imaginations of 'the resilient subject'. Inwardly directed grief and anger, for example, where survivors' predominant struggles are personal, self-directed, and private, chimes with accounts which have twinned resilience and trauma (Howell, 2012). Here, resilience is positioned as the answer to psychological suffering, thus inflecting the logics of resilience thinking with the pathological – a lineage inherited and extended from PTSD treatments and discourse. On the other hand, there is outwardly directed grief and anger, where survivors' struggles also include a large element of public protest and resistance, thus making visible, tangible connections and demands between their harm and injustice. Here too resilience has been closely twinned with trauma, but might instead resonate with accounts of pacification (Neocleous, 2012). These two general positions, indicative rather than exhaustive, are not mutually exclusive.

That neither extreme can be evidenced through this research – neither the resilient superhero, nor the permanently immobilised victim, coheres with Bourbeau's following observations:

> Resilience is always a matter of degree; complete immunity towards disturbances and shocks does not exist. As such, societies can be more or less resilient both diachronically and synchronically. Resilience is also constantly in flux. It is not a fixed attribute or an unchangeable characteristic of a society or an individual. No society is always resilient, and resilience does not express itself in a flat, stable or variation-free way. Resilience does not imply finality as the process can never be fully completed; the process is inherently dynamic and always in movement.
>
> (Bourbeau, 2013: 11)

The problem of abstraction associated with some so-called governmentality perspectives, some of which were outlined in Chapter 1, has been increasingly flagged up in more nuanced critiques of both the 'critical' literature examining resilience and 'big policy' doctrines which both have a tendency to imagine resilience as a homogenous phenomenon (as aptly pointed out by, *inter alia*, Schott, 2013; Brassett and Vaughn-Williams, 2015; Cavelty, Kaufmann and Kristensen, 2015). These approaches allow us to think beyond the narrow confines of an imaginary '*coherent* underlying logic' (Brassett and Vaughn-Williams, 2015: 39, emphasis added) at the heart of many resilience critiques, making possible a truly critical exploration of victimhood (Schott, 2013). Analyses critical of capital accumulation and State practices often assume the interpretation of these practices on behalf of the individual in a disappointing departure from early critical political economy, which was as attuned and

Temporality, Resistance, and Solidarity   173

committed to understanding being, existence and praxis as it was discourse, knowledge (both histories of ideas and contemporary applications of bourgeois science and technology), and ideology (Sartre, 1968). Foucault, to whom many turn when analysing discourse, commented specifically on this issue when reflecting on ideology and power:

> As regards Marxism, I'm not one of those who try to elicit the effects of power at the level of ideology. Indeed I wonder whether, before one poses the question of ideology, it wouldn't be more materialist to study first *the question of the body and the effects of power on it*. Because what troubles me with these analyses which prioritise ideology is that there is always presupposed a human subject on the lines of the model provided by classical philosophy, *endowed with a consciousness which power is then thought to seize on*.
>
> (Foucault, 1980: 58, emphases added)

This serves as a useful reminder to both critics and proponents of Foucault, who the latter have regularly used to underpin the 'resilience-as-responsibilisation' thesis. Making assumptions about the kinds of discursive practices resilience is said to give rise to thus risks misinterpreting Foucault and the way he believed power might relate to individual bodies. As the preceding discussion has illustrated, the kind of power dynamics concerning Foucault is often evident in accounts both rejecting and revering the resilience 'turn' – a tension this book has aimed to transcend through close empirical observation. Often, however, both camps have been guilty of recognising only one side of Foucault's 'truth' around power-knowledge, thus producing caricatured representations of his philosophy to support their position. To reiterate:

> Unlike Marx, and indeed Kant, Foucault made no effort to establish what is true and false, founded or unfounded, real or illusory, desirable or undesirable, legitimate or abusive. Foucault recognised no criteria by which a thought-system could be judged true or false, or better or worse. Any thought-system is logical according to its own logic. Different historical thrown-nesses just made them different.
>
> (Brocklesby and Cummings, 1996: 748–9)

To be sure, this critical appreciation of difference inextricably links to Foucault's appraisal of *knowledge practices*, particularly the roles played by both expert therapists and intellectuals – two key sets of actors producing and debating knowledge concerning 'resilience'. For Foucault, the increasing danger is that these actors have become inimical to 'local knowledge, and local knowledge is generally held by locals with general knowledge, not by consultant experts with specific theoretical knowledge' (Brocklesby and Cummings, 1996: 749). As a theoretical aside, Foucault's work clearly remains an important literature

174 Repurposing Resilience

to understand, not least of all given its huge influence on scholars of resilience. However, it is not the only framework for wrestling with this tension between discourse and practice, or knowledge and existence. The mature Sartre (1968, 2008[1972]), for instance, utilises Marx and Engels' work in his development of an explicitly Marxist existentialism. Contemporary scholars utilising Foucault often, regrettably, misinterpret his reticence towards Marxist analysis as a cue to abandon critical political economy altogether.

As Brassett and Vaughn-Williams (2015: 46) rightly argue, the 'worrying consensus across government, business, and some quarters of academia that resilience is an unquestionably "good" value to be striven for, invested in, and cultivated throughout society at whatever cost', is unhelpfully mirrored by equally abstract analyses of resilience values as *inherently* bad. Just as institutional manifestos on resilience attempt to account for an impossibly disparate array of socio-economic issues, polemic arguments that frame resilience as governmentality 'pure and simple' also miss the mark. Judging the utility or desirability of one's resilience to zero-hour employment contracts or dealing with the aftermath of a terrorist attack are not the same thing, or even comparable. As this research has shown, dealing with the aftermath of different *kinds* of terrorist attack is likely to differ radically. If they are described in parallel terms with no empirical evidence, we have to question the robustness and credibility of such claims. If we accept that resilience is a desirable attribute for participants here, insofar as its absence would almost certainly be a negative thing, how do we then account for individuals or groups who have traversed a range of harms through recourse to political resistance? The pursuit of justice is an interesting psychosocial variable to consider against the group of interviewees discussed earlier who have made every effort to transcend the past. Their focus on peace and trying to remain focused on the future sits relatively comfortably alongside policy projections of who might be imagined as 'the resilient subject'. However, family campaigners fighting for justice for their loved ones over four decades after a critical incident such as this are clearly displaying immense resilience (a fact which, at least in this specific context, directly challenges claims that resistance and resilience are necessarily antithetical (Neocleous, 2013: 7; Diprose, 2015: 48)). In addition to the solidarity and strength required at a familial and communal level though, what can such narratives reveal about the potential impacts of political violence at a personal level for individuals engaged in perpetually remembering past violence for the purpose of securing justice? Again, how does this change the temporal emphases we might associate with 'resilient subjectivities'? Shortcomings of some of the critical literature highlighted here are not raised as an endorsement of resilience; rather, they are posed to ensure that readings of the data presented in this book remain open and contestable. As Cavelty, Kaufmann and Kristensen (2015: 7) argue: 'Resilience may indeed be depoliticising, but positing it as the opposite of resistance simplifies the complex workings of power, empowerment, disempowerment, and the linkages between them'.

The Terrorism Survivor and Group Solidarity: 'Making Up' Resilient Survivor Communities

An interesting feature of the data to note with regard to community resilience is that in much of the literature commenting on the capacities of individuals and communities to recover from disaster, community is often described as an *already-existing entity* to which disaster befalls. Community is therefore typically imagined as being constituted by ecological, geographical, or demographic groupings, this commonality forming the basis of a community's capacity to organise, prepare, and adapt to adversity. Adversity is imagined as inherently prospective and is prefaced by notions of community which, no matter how concrete or abstract they may be, are formed prior to harm occurring. Resilience is therefore seen as an intrinsic capacity of that community (Manyena, 2006: 446). Herman's (2001: 70) summation of how individual resilience and recovery relates to community typifies this viewpoint: 'The response of the community has a powerful influence on the ultimate resolution of the trauma'. In short, community prefaces trauma support. Pre-existing communities are seen to support individuals, rather than individuals being seen to constitute, create, and sustain communities.

In contrast, notions of community and group solidarity described in this research suggest that adversity and harm can preface, fortify, and perhaps even create and constitute, the conditions for communities to form and to flourish. This is alluded to by Anderson (2015: 61, emphasis added) when he notes that 'the "resilient subject" is, among other things: […] a subject who is a member, or may *become* a member, of different kinds of community'. 'Community' has long been theorised as a heterogeneous, multifaceted categorisation with contested definitions, including conceptions of community which are constituted by social interaction, as well as mediated communication, among individuals with both shared and divergent values (Delanty, 2003). However, while this makes ample space for theoretical understandings of community beyond simply ecological or geographical areas, the security literature concerning resilience to trauma has been surprisingly slow to recognise the organic creation of survivor communities.

Although adversity and harm can help to create the conditions for new communities to emerge organically, this is not all that is required. Closer analysis of, in this case, survivor communities reveals a more nuanced, complex picture. While it may seem an obvious point, the organic creation of a community nonetheless requires that someone create it. Almost by definition, this is rarely the work of one individual. While the word 'organic' is perhaps a useful way of distinguishing between collective forms of resilience which have emerged from below, as opposed to strategies of contingency planning being directed at pre-existing communities from above, it does not mean that such survivor communities emerge accidentally with no concerted effort, planning, or strategy. Survivors interviewed here have been proactive in supporting others and bringing individuals from diverse backgrounds together who may not have otherwise met. As Chapter 2 contextualised, the building of the FfP and later the physical Peace Centre were the result of a long, committed and concerted effort by Colin and Wendy Parry with support from various local groups, dignitaries, political actors, donators, and funders.

Much of this work was serendipitous in nature and they learned as they went along. Initially their aims and expectations were relatively modest in comparison with their current reach; as Colin explained:

> Although we didn't think it at the time, I think that day [when they made a visit to a small organisation in Coleraine, Northern Ireland called The Peace People] took a root, and then if you fast forward five years on in '98 we founded the charity in its barest, smallest form imaginable, just operating from our spare [Tim's] bedroom.

The way in which they financed and launched the current range of programs is covered in Chapter 2, but an important point to consider is that it was the events of March 1993 and their desire to make an intervention and a change that led to survivors identifying with and meeting each other ever since. They provided an initial linguistic and logistical framework of activities around which others could organise and consolidate with like-minded individuals. Narratives around the Warrington bomb, Tim and Johnathan's tragic, untimely death and the desire to work towards peace were, and continue to be, told to new participants and retold to returning survivors as an important facet of 'bringing into being' the SAN. As Gabriel (2000) illustrates, the telling of stories in such contexts is a key component in establishing an organisation's rationale and, in this case, brings highly personal, emotive experiences to bear on the creation of a supportive community. Injured victims and grieving loved ones become recast, in certain settings at least, as 'terrorism survivors', a term capable of transmitting signification and meaning far beyond the lived experiences of individuals harmed by terrorism. It resonates in ways that may be more amenable to creating and sustaining communal activity.

To underscore the practical contingencies of this process, during fieldwork several members of staff reiterated that the Foundation is the only dedicated national charity working specifically to support 'survivors of terrorism' and politically motivated violence. Particular emphasis would be put on this when discussing and applying for funding, such as their recently commissioned work around prevention and radicalisation which is run separately to SAN. There are other charities said to offer 'generic' support to a broader range of injured parties, such as the British Red Cross and Victim Support, whose work is sometimes seen to be almost encroaching on the Foundation's unique remit, but these three organisations are the only charities listed in the UN's Directory of Organisations Supporting Victims of Terrorism (see United Nations, 2021). In reality, the Foundation also works with a range of other actors including former perpetrators, veterans, emergency responders, and relatives of witnesses. This became particularly apparent when trying to recruit participants not solely linked to military or paramilitary experiences. Indeed, some of these actors form the cornerstone of activities such as the Dialogue for Peace programme. This sometimes creates a somewhat contradictory and paradoxical dynamic whereby this very diversity among participants leads to fascinating and critical discussions among them within workshops around the problematic and reifying labelling of 'terrorism', 'terrorists', 'perpetrators', and 'victims' – the very labels required to publicise and 'sell' the work the organisation does. This was observed during fieldwork where certain labels and names would be used around one group of participants but then quickly changed or adjusted for another. 'The terrorism survivor', that is, the survivor of a terrorist act, is one such term – reified and rendered visible for the purposes of organisational branding, storytelling, and funding but frequently contradicted or re-rendered problematic in practice.

The notion of creating or entering a new community that was previously closed off or inaccessible is evident in Colin and Wendy Parry's moving account of Tim's death. In their words, they 'became members of an exclusive club; a club that no one ever asks to join; a club that never has a waiting list. We belong to the bereaved parents' club' (Parry and Parry, 1994: 343). The word 'became' and the notion of 'becoming' is again indicative of a starting point rather than an end, reinforcing the above observations about the creation or emergence of community (described here as a 'club') rather than its pre-existence. Again, this alone could not have guaranteed the emergence of the Survivors Assistance Network but Colin and Wendy's account shows examples of both incredible individual–familial resilience and also a mix of moral and entrepreneurial motivation which was evident in many participant's interviews too. To borrow from Hacking (1986), the 'making up' of a resilient community and, in this case, 'the terrorism survivor' as an actor within that community, is partly dependent on the identification and demarcation of a particular kind of suffering, one borne out of direct and painful experience. Colin and Wendy's reflections on this reveal how, as parents and as human beings, they had always felt compassion when witnessing or hearing of the tragic loss of life but after losing Tim, turning a blind eye was no longer an option anyway and they felt compelled to try and make a change through the work we see today:

> Whether through war, starvation or just terrible misfortune, it is always the death of children which affects us most. When their innocent lives are cut short, we feel it deeply. We also feel the parent's pain and shudder at the thought of it ever being our own child. Sometimes the tragic scenes on our television screens are so harrowing and so shocking that it is too much to bear and we look away. But when we do watch, our feelings of sympathy are occasionally tinged with the feeling of 'there, but for the grace of God, go I'. Until 20 March 1993, Wendy and I had only ever felt the pain and

suffering of other parents who had lost their children, whether they were black or white, Catholic or Protestant, boy or girl. When the scenes on television became too much for us to bear, we too could turn away. But not any more.

(Parry and Parry, 1994: 343)

There are some interesting parallels here with the work of Becker (1963) and particularly his discussion of the moral entrepreneur. Substantively, his work differs in several major ways. He was referring to the moral crusades of rule creators and rule enforcers, focusing on examples of perceived immoral behaviour being singled out by determined actors driven by personal, moral needs, and desires. His examples mainly relate to the creation of new laws and the role of law enforcement agents in persuading others, or themselves, that their causes are noble, just and necessary. Leaving aside these examples and Becker's focus on 'deviance', the notion of entrepreneurial activity driven by moral needs and desires remains a useful point of departure for thinking about why and how individuals, families, and groups affected by actual or perceived injustice, violence and trauma commit to a lifetime endeavour such as the FfP. It also raises a number of interesting questions in the current conjuncture. What is the relationship between this entrepreneurial spirit and resilience? What are the structural, as well as personal, drivers behind moral entrepreneurialism? What, if any, are the broader links between this kind of endeavour and questions relating to the broader cultural and political economy of victim rights (*qua* Ginsberg, 2014)? These questions carry particular resonance for the voluntary (victim support) sector at a time when austerity measures have coincided with shifts to almost entirely commission-based funding arrangements (see Simmonds, 2016). Arguably compounding this is the fact that while resources and funding are becoming harder to come by, the Foundation's supportive function is in demand more than ever due to both recent attacks around the UK and, more generally, the systematic outsourcing of mental health services by the central government. Whether this tension will morph and mould their activities directly, it is clear that throughout the organisation's history it has moved with the times, tweaked its remit along the way and itself proven to be highly resilient.

Refocusing for the moment on the question of resilience, despite addressing the question of morality Becker's work arguably lacks a sufficiently sustained analysis of the ways in which emotions function within personally and morally driven entrepreneurial dynamics. Morality, in Becker's analysis, figures predominantly as a form of indignation which is then channelled towards various forms of prohibition designed to change the behaviour of others. In contrast, the evidence presented here, including interviews with Colin Parry and other survivors who have turned their attentions towards various forms of social enterprise, strongly suggest a self-supportive function first and foremost. It also points to an overriding sense of compassion. While Becker's lawmakers could argue that they too are acting out of compassion, most survivors interviewed

Temporality, Resistance, and Solidarity 179

here explicitly advocated for peace, love, empathy, and compassion as a way of avoiding more draconian or forceful military responses further down the line. Of course, appeals to recruit further participants and promote the organisation's activities are mediated along moral lines. The promotion of peace, while roundly and normatively accepted as a highly desirable, perhaps even honourable, endeavour is nevertheless a moral and therefore ethical one. Furthermore, in 'enacting resilience' through such social enterprises there is a more or less explicit motivation to also change the language and behaviour of others.

The potential influence of language upon classificatory practice and therefore on subsequent action is made clear by Hacking (1995: 239, emphasis added):

> A new or modified mode of classification may systematically affect the people who are so classified, or the people themselves may rebel against the knowers, the classifiers, the science that classifies them. [...] Inventing or molding a new kind, a new classification, of people or of behaviour may create new ways to be a person, new choices to make, for good or evil. *There are new descriptions, and hence new actions under a description. It is not that people change, substantively, but that as a point of logic new opportunities for action are open to them.*

Hacking's claim that people do not change substantively, despite now being able to engage in new forms of practical activity as a result of new descriptions of self, is a contentious one, especially for survivors with traumatic experiences of past violence. This is partly because while Hacking, drawing on Elizabeth Anscombe's *Intention*, speaks of 'descriptions' and 'redescriptions' of events, he appears more anxious than Anscombe was to arrive at a conclusion in which one of two or more 'rival' descriptions 'wins out' (see Sharrock and Leudar, 2002: 109–10). It is one thing to claim that past events do not change, but our descriptions of them do. It is quite another to suggest that people do not substantively change as a result. Hacking is often purposefully hesitant and ambivalent in several of his claims – a refreshingly transparent rhetorical device which would certainly enhance many more dogmatic arguments concerning interpretive phenomena – so it is for readers to follow up his work and form their own critically informed understanding of this possible contradiction, or at least tension, in his argument. In any case, Hacking's observations around 'new opportunities for action' resonated particularly strongly during fieldwork when it became clear just how reliant several survivors have become on the FfP and other support groups which allow them to tell and retell their stories. Some would tell almost polished narratives which replicated previous ones (Anne and Kevin, for example), while others would consciously tell different versions of the same story. Lynn pointed out, for example, that:

> we [survivors] tell these stories but the story changes every time. I could sit here and start this interview all over again and not repeat anything – there's

just so many different stories and there's so many ways to look at things, you know I mean?

The benefits of finding a space where being a 'survivor of terrorism' is not seen as alien or awkward in conversation have been discussed extensively already (see Chapter 4). For some participants, this is perhaps more accurately described not as being a 'survivor of terrorism' but becoming one (Rock, 2002). There may be, however, another side to this which two different members of staff hinted at over the course of the fieldwork. What about participants who not only become 'survivors of terrorism' but do not move beyond this point? Is it possible that they could become 'trapped' in some way? If they are forever seen as 'the terrorism survivor', what happens if they stop associating with that label? For many participants, telling their story to others becomes a conduit through which a range of emotions and states of being are articulated. For others, their very material and financial stability remains contingent upon it. It provides a familiar frame in which to discuss ongoing, changing and temporally dynamic emotions and coping mechanisms. It may not even be about the story in and of itself but it is the story that provides a framework around which other issues can cohere. The balance between storytelling as cathartic and storytelling as 'trapping' participants in a perpetual cycle of dependency on the FfP as a facilitating space might well shift over time as the charity becomes busier and referrals increase (which, at the time of writing, they are). This was suggested by a staff member who voiced concerns that indeterminate reliance on the SAN could, in time, lead to a form of displacement or surrogacy for support rather than appropriate support in every case.

There is a two-way constitution of community at play at the FfP, with both survivors and organisation contributing, as the following quotation from Colin Parry suggests:

> For me the saving grace was this [the Foundation] which has grown into this wonderful thing now. We never had any idea it would in the early days ... but this has been the glue that's kept our family together, without a shadow of a doubt. [...] Yeah it fills a void you see, you've got a sense of purpose that's not just good for you, it's good for others too. Now it's not about building your ego or taking on airs and graces, but you know you can look anybody in the eye and say that what we're doing is genuinely good. There's no negatives to this, it's all good, whether it's that much good or that much good [gestures with hands] depends on the beneficiary and what they get from it and what they put into it but it's good [emphasis] – it is good.

While survivors themselves create and sustain communities as they grow, as the FfP surely has, they begin to represent community in a more traditional sense of the word and are there to facilitate aftercare support to more recently

Temporality, Resistance, and Solidarity 181

traumatised individuals. In this way, community functions in both 'bottom-up/ top-down' capacities and 'pre/post-traumatic incident' ways and spaces. It is both organic, in some respects, and garnered or promoted, in others. This is not a fixed or static process but rather loops over time (Hacking, 2004) as the organisation develops and as survivors themselves react and behave in relation to changing organisational labels and language. As part of Chapter 4 explained, organisations and services proactively seek out survivors and render them as such, reifying to varying extents the process of 'becoming victims' (Rock, 2002), and so we must bear in mind this proactivity as well as the purely organic coalescence of 'survivor communities'. These are important processes to identify if we are to start unpacking the ways in which resilience functions, and is fostered, at a collective level. It is clear that theoretical resilience models which work in a linear, step-by-step fashion and which culminate in a definitive 'end product' (the 'adaptive, shock resistant, resilient survivor') are likely to remain just that – theoretical. In practice, there is a multiplicity of interaction, naming and classifying of, by, and between actors involved who influence and shape the support of others in different ways and at different times. Survivors interviewed here have varying experiences of visiting the FfP and, consequently, have varying affinities, knowledges, and impacts upon the language it uses and different interpretations of it based on their experience.

Over a decade on since the financial crisis of 2008–9 and the subsequent implementation of austerity measures in the UK, it seems an apposite time to reflect on the real, imagined, and unintended ways in which resilience has been bestowed upon, expected of, or directed by notions of 'community'. As this chapter has argued, this warrants a close examination of situated, empirical, and case study examples which may offer fresh insights for theoretical scholars to work with. Prioritising neither psychological factors over social ones and vice versa, recognising that both are important and neither 'stay still' for very long, and questioning the conception of community as a pre-existing (both material and imagined) entity to which resilience is bestowed, directed, or expected, this research tentatively suggests that the creation of new communities could in and of itself constitute *resilience in action*. This idea is posited in light of data collected from what we might understand as a 'survivor community'; exploring how notions of *resilience as doing* resonate and play out in other settings is one avenue to explore against a more than sufficient backcloth of theoretical 'scene setting'. This dovetails and contributes to an emergent empirical literature on resilience, solidarity, and community (see Wright, 2016; Vrasti and Michelsen, 2017; Zebrowski and Sage, 2017).

Conclusion

This chapter has highlighted three interrelated areas of surprisingly neglected significance for critically understanding resilience as a complex and multifaceted phenomenon (Walklate, McGarry and Mythen, 2014): temporality, resistance,

182 Repurposing Resilience

and solidarity. In practical terms, these respective issues were manifest in the data considered in previous chapters through discussions of time, anger, and community. Time, for survivors, is something that both elapses and is disrupted. It is also a variable feature in survivors' narratives, including how they narrate their past, present, and future selves (McAdams, 1993; 2006). Time is both a specific factor that opens up and forecloses all kinds of practical activity, such as a reengagement with political or religious commitments that become easier as survivors retire from paid employment, or a disengagement from employment, hobbies and other forms of social engagement as survivors' long-term injuries worsen their quality of life.

Anger, on the other hand, is not simply something that happens in spite of survivors' involvement in its production, negotiation and, sometimes, transcendence. Rather, it often takes centre stage in survivors' sense of agency, violation, empowerment, and mission. As an emotion, anger can function adaptively or maladaptively, opening up new and energised forms of activism and social justice, or paralysing (temporarily or permanently) individuals' ability to cope, adapt, or reconcile with their loss or injury. Surprisingly scant attention is currently paid to anger as a positive and productive force, both within studies of resilience, which afford little space to ostensibly 'negative' or 'regressive' behaviours appearing to contradict therapeutic and linear models of recovery, and in everyday life more generally. Martha Nussbaum's (2016) widely read *Anger and Forgiveness*, for example, has anger as a stupid, magical, and narcissistic emotion with very few positive manifestations. Important exceptions to this include Lindebaum and Geddes' (2016) and Lindebaum and Gabriel's (2016) contributions to organisational behaviour studies, as well as some research into social justice campaigns and the kinds of experiences motivating survivors to seek justice. Even within the latter though, anger is rarely singled out as a productive emotion but rather assumed to be a motivating (i.e. purely instrumental) dynamic. For this reason alone, it is hardly surprising that resilience and resistance have only recently become acceptable and complementary bedfellows in the eponymous literature (see Ryan, 2015; Bourbeau and Ryan, 2018; see also Michelsen, 2017) and, more frequently, continue to be positioned as diametrically opposed and fundamentally incompatible (Neocleous, 2013; Diprose, 2015).

On the face of it, abstract tenets of resilience (as adaption) and resistance (as conflict and change) do indeed appear principally incompatible. But herein lies the problem. When we examine the emotional impacts of violence and the practical manifestations of these emotional impacts over time, we see that it is anger – 'what drives us is a good bit of rage!' (Liz; see Chapter 3) – that often bridges the gap between event and response, between 'injurability and agency' (Schott, 2013), and between victimisation and survival. While Nussbaum's (2016) analysis might not help us here, Audre Lorde's (1997[1981]: 284) is characteristically sharp at finding this intimate and productive link between injustice and emotion:

> My anger has meant pain to me but it has also meant survival, and before I give it up I'm going to be sure that there is something at least as powerful to replace it on the road to clarity.

Note this link is conditional, since the destination is not a place of narcissistic stupidity (Nussbaum) but 'clarity' of thought and knowledge (Lorde). To deny the link between resilience and resistance is to bifurcate what are, in reality, intimately connected ways of being a person. Drawing attention to the harms and injustices that have driven survivors to become active political agents is neither to concede to the precedents of overly medicalised models of trauma diagnosis and therapeutic intervention, even where these are wholly necessary support mechanisms, nor does it necessarily dilute or detract from the demands and changes being fought for.

Further reasons for this straw bifurcation emanate from toxic forms of masculinity, including within 'progressive' political movements, whose eagerness to display a combative and impervious front often reproduces the kinds of hegemonic masculinity more frequently (if naively) associated with the centre-right. 'Similarly', writes Butler (2020: 201),

> the prejudice against nonviolence as passive and useless implicitly depends upon a gendered division of attributes by which masculinity stands for activity, and femininity for passivity. No translation of those values will defeat the falsehood of that binary. [...] Sometimes continuing to exist in the vexation of social relations is the ultimate defeat of violent power.

Non-violence, for Butler (2020: 27), should not be thought of 'simply as the absence of violence, or as the act of refraining from committing violence, but as a sustained commitment, even a way of rerouting aggression for the purposes of affirming ideals of equality and freedom'. This 'rerouting' echoes Lorde's comment above. Both speak to a process of harnessing, channelling, and redirecting power intelligently, emanating from and energised (but not characterised) by raw emotion. Acutely gendered idealisations of 'resistance' among critical scholars and activists are matched by equally reductive accounts of injury, harm, and recovery by the mainstream media, who often give predominant airtime and column inches to those who look and sound most like the kind of 'ideal victim' (Christie, 1986) envisaged within adversarial criminal justice – innocent and passive, articulate but not overly outspoken. Certainly any attempt to mobilise and assert a sense of anger, especially one directed at resisting liberal security state apparatuses, is likely to be pathologised as unprocessed trauma or simply ignored.

Lastly, the chapter has contributed to an emergent empirical and conceptual literature exploring the relationship between resilience, solidarity, and community (Wright, 2016; Vrasti and Michelsen, 2017; Zebrowski and Sage, 2017). More specifically, it has highlighted solidarity as one practical manifestation, or

184 Repurposing Resilience

'making up', of community. It was argued that while the relationship between resilience and temporality is often ignored, and the relationship between resilience and resistance denied, the automatic pairing of resilience and 'community' has been a recurring and even ubiquitous feature of social policy and political discourse, as well as many academic studies of resilience from a panoply of disciplinary fields. This has often produced and reproduced a static and reductive account of community as a pre-existing entity to which top-down exhortations of 'pulling together' or 'keeping calm and carrying on' are directed. Not only is this account inadequate when it comes to describing the practical manifestations of resilience, including the coming into being of new forms of community (such as survivor communities) after periods or moments of adversity have taken place, but it also strips much of the organic, creative, and even radical potential out of the resilience-community debate. Of course, this is unsurprising given the metaphorical uses of 'resilience' and 'community' which came to be routinely espoused after the 2007–8 financial crisis as a rhetorical sweetener to the bitter pill of austerity. Contrary to the insidiously saccharine declaration that 'we are all in this together', as former UK Prime Minister David Cameron did as he simultaneously administered deeper and deeper cuts to public services, the more nuanced picture of community detailed in this chapter suggests instead that some people are indeed in it together, but that these pockets of peer-support, solidarity, and tacit empathy take comparatively local, emergent, and exclusive forms. That is not to say that survivor communities do not grow, expand, welcome in, or join up with other communities, we know they do, but rather that they begin with a much more specific and situated set of conditions.

In sum, 'temporality', 'resistance', and 'community' are important, but abstract, ideas to consider if we are to form a fuller and richer understanding of resilience. This chapter has brought these ideas to life by paying close attention to the specific *form* each appears to be taking for survivors of political violence and terrorism. This includes time, anger, and solidarity, respectively.

References

Anderson, B. (2015) What kind of thing is resilience? *Politics* 35(1): 60–6.

Becker, H.S. (1963) *Outsiders: Studies in the Sociology of Deviance*. New York: The Free Press.

Bourbeau, P. (2013) Resiliencism: Premises and promises in securitisation research. *Resilience: International Policies, Practices and Discourses* 1(1): 3–17.

Bourbeau, P. and Ryan, C. (2018) Resilience, resistance, infrapolitics and enmeshment. *European Journal of International Relations*. 24(1): 221–39.

Brassett, J. and Vaughn-Williams, N. (2015) Security and the performative politics of resilience: Critical infrastructure protection and humanitarian emergency preparedness. *Security Dialogue* 46(1): 32–50.

Brison, S. (2002) *Aftermath: Violence and the Remaking of a Self*. Princeton: Princeton University Press.

Brocklesby, J. and Cummings, S. (1996) Foucault plays Habermas: An alternative philosophical underpinning for critical systems thinking. *Journal of the Operational Research Society* 47(6): 741–54.

Butler, J. (2020) *The Force of Nonviolence: An Ethico-Political Bind*. London: Verso.

Cavelty, M.D., Kaufmann, M. and Kristensen, K.S. (2015) Resilience and (in) security: Practices, subjects, temporalities. *Security Dialogue* 46(1): 3–14.

Christie, N. (1986) The ideal victim. In E. Fattah (Ed.) *From Crime Policy to Victim Policy: Reorienting the Justice System*. London: Macmillan. pp.17–30.

Dawson, G. (2007) *Making Peace with the Past? Memory, Trauma and the Irish Troubles*. Manchester: Manchester University Press.

Delanty, G. (2003) *Community*. London: Routledge.

Diprose, K. (2015) Resilience is futile. *Soundings: A Journal of Politics and Culture* 58: 44–56.

Foucault, M. (1980) Body/power. In C. Gordon (Ed.), *Power/Knowledge: Selected Interviews and Other Writings 1972–1977*. Translated from French by Gordon, C., Marshall, L., Mepham, J. and Soper, K. New York: Vintage Books. pp.55–62.

Gabriel, Y. (2000) *Storytelling in Organizations: Facts, Fictions, and Fantasies*. Oxford: Oxford University Press.

Giddens, A. (1991) *Modernity and Self-Identity: Self and Society in the Late Modern Age*. Cambridge: Polity Press.

Ginsberg, R. (2014) Mighty crime victims: Victims' rights and neoliberalism in the American conjuncture. *Cultural Studies* 28(5/6): 911–46.

Hacking, I. (1986) Making up people. In T.C. Heller et al. (Eds.) *Reconstructing Individualism: Autonomy, Individuality, and the Self in Western Thought*. California: Stanford University Press. pp.222–36.

Hacking, I. (1995) *Rewriting the Soul: Multiple Personality and the Sciences of Memory*. Princeton, NJ: Princeton University Press.

Hacking, I. (2004) Between Michel Foucault and Erving Goffman: Between discourse in the abstract and face-to-face interaction. *Economy and Society* 33(3): 277–302.

Heath-Kelly, C. (2015) Securing through the failure to secure? The ambiguity of resilience at the bombsite. *Security Dialogue* 46(1): 69–85.

Herman, J.L. (2001) *Trauma and Recovery*. London: Pandora.

Howell, A. (2012) The demise of PTSD: From governing through trauma to governing resilience. *Alternatives: Global, Local, Political* 37(3): 214–26.

Howell, A. (2015a) Resilience, war, and austerity: The ethics of military human enhancement and the politics of data. *Security Dialogue* 46(1): 15–31.

Howell, A. (2015b) Resilience as enhancement: Governmentality and political economy beyond 'responsibilisation'. *Politics* 35(1): 67–71.

Jackson, W. (2013) Securitisation as depoliticisation: depoliticisation as pacification. *Socialist Studies/Études socialistes* 9(2): 146–66.

Jessop, B. (2010) Cultural political economy and critical policy studies. *Critical Policy Studies* 3(3–4): 336–56.

Joseph, J. (2013) Resilience as embedded neoliberalism: A governmentality approach. *Resilience: International Policies, Practices and Discourses* 1(1): 38–52.

Lindebaum, D. and Gabriel, Y. (2016) Anger and organization studies: From social disorder to moral order. *Organization Studies* 37(7): 903–18.

Lindebaum, D. and Geddes, D. (2016) The place and role of (moral) anger in organizational behaviour studies. *Journal of Organizational Behaviour* 37(5): 738–57.

Lorde, A. (1997[1981]) The uses of anger. *Womne's Studies Quarterly* 25(1/2): 278–85.

Manyena, S.B. (2006) The concept of resilience revisited. *Disasters* 30(4): 433–50.

McAdams, D.P. (1993) *The Stories We Live By: Personal Myths and the Making of the Self.* New York: The Guildford Press.

McAdams, D.P. (2006) *The Redemptive Self: Stories Americans Live By.* Oxford: Oxford University Press.

McGarry, R., Walklate, S. and Mythen, G. (2015) A sociological analysis of military resilience: Opening up the debate. *Armed Forces & Society* 41: 352–78.

Michelsen, N. (2017) On the genealogy of strategies: Resilience in the revolution. *Resilience: International Policies, Practices and Discourses* 5(1): 61–77.

Neocleous, M. (2012) 'Don't be scared, be prepared': Trauma-anxiety-resilience. *Alternatives: Global, Local, Political* 37(3): 188–98.

Neocleous, M. (2013) Resisting resilience. *Radical Philosophy* 178(6): 2–7.

Nussbaum, M.C. (2016) *Anger and Forgiveness: Resentment, Generosity, Justice.* New York: Oxford University Press.

O'Malley, P. (2006) Criminology and risk. In G. Mythen and S. Walklate (Eds.) *Beyond the Risk Society: Critical Reflections on Risk and Human Security.* Berkshire: Open University Press. pp.43–60.

Overland, G. (2013) *Post Traumatic Survival: The Lessons of Cambodian Resilience.* Newcastle upon Tyne: Cambridge Scholars Publishing.

Parry, C. and Parry, W. (1994) *Tim: An Ordinary Boy.* London: Hodder and Stoughton.

Rock, P. (2002) On becoming a victim. In C. Hoyle and R. Young (Eds.) *New Visions of Crime Victims.* Oxford: Hart Publishing. pp.1–22.

Rothberg, M. (2009) *Multidirectional Memory: Remembering the Holocaust in the Age of Decolonization.* Stanford: Stanford University Press.

Roy, A. (2017[1997]) *The God of Small Things.* London: 4th Estate.

Ryan, C. (2015) Everyday resilience as resistance: Palestinian women practicing *Sumud.* *International Political Sociology* 9(4): 299–315.

Sartre, J.P. (1968) *Search for a Method.* New York: Vintage.

Sartre, J.P. (2008[1972]) *Between Existentialism and Marxism.* London: Verso.

Schott, R.M. (2013) Resilience, normativity and vulnerability. *Resilience: International Policies, Practices and Discourses* 1(3): 210–18.

Schott, R.M. (2015) 'Not just victims … but': Toward a critical theory of the victim. In H. Marway and H. Widdows (Eds.) *Women and Violence: The Agency of Victims and Perpetrators.* Basingstoke: Palgrave Macmillan. pp.178–94.

Sharrock, W. and Leudar, I. (2002) Indeterminacy in the past? *History of the Human Sciences* 15(3): 95–115.

Simmonds, L. (2016) The potential impact of local commissioning on victim services in England and Wales. *International Review of Victimology* 22(3): 223–37.

United Nations (2021) Directory of Organisations Supporting Victims of Terrorism [online] Available at: www.un.org/victimsofterrorism/en/directory [Accessed 26/01/2021].

Vrasti, W. and Michelsen, N. (2017) Introduction: On resilience and solidarity. *Resilience: International Policies, Practices and Discourses* 5(1): 1–9.

Walklate, S., McGarry, R. and Mythen, G. (2014) Searching for resilience: A conceptual excavation. *Armed Forces & Society* 40(3): 408–27.

Walklate, S., Mythen, G. and McGarry, R. (2012) States of resilience and the resilient state. *Current Issues in Criminal Justice* 24(2): 185–204.

Webel, C.P. (2004) *Terror, Terrorism, and the Human Condition*. Hampshire: Palgrave Macmillan.

Wright, K. (2016) Resilient communities? Experiences of risk and resilience in a time of austerity. *International Journal of Disaster Risk Reduction* 18: 154–61.

Zebrowski, C. and Sage, D. (2017) Organising community resilience: an examination of the forms of sociality promoted in community resilience programmes. *Resilience: International Policies, Practices and Discourses* 5(1): 44–60.

Chapter 7

Am I Invictus?

The phrase 'I Am Invictus' was used repeatedly throughout the media campaign and event branding of the 2014 'Invictus Games' – a televised multi-sport event launched by Prince Harry in which over 400 'wounded, injured, and sick servicemen and women' from 13 nations competed. The event, which has taken place on four successive occasions with more scheduled, was dubbed a 'celebration of resilience and passion', drawing on 'the power of sport to inspire recovery, support rehabilitation, and generate a wider understanding and respect of those who serve their country' (see Invictus Games, 2014). Inspiration for the event's name came from an eponymous poem by William Ernest Henley (1849–1903), which tells a tale of defiant endurance in the face of a cruel and challenging destiny:

> *Invictus*
> Out of the night that covers me,
> Black as the Pit from pole to pole,
> I thank whatever gods may be
> For my unconquerable soul.
>
> In the fell clutch of circumstance
> I have not winced nor cried aloud.
> Under the bludgeonings of chance
> My head is bloody, but unbowed.
>
> Beyond this place of wrath and tears
> Looms but the Horror of the shade,
> And yet the menace of the years
> Finds, and shall find, me unafraid.
>
> It matters not how strait the gate,
> How charged with punishments the scroll.
> I am the master of my fate:
> I am the captain of my soul.

While 'fell clutch of circumstance' and 'bludgeonings of chance' undoubtedly strike a sombre chord in the context of some of the harms documented throughout this book, no direct comparison is drawn here between injured service personnel and the participants in this project. Ironically though, the poem was cited by both Oklahoma City bomber Timothy McVeigh just prior to his execution in 2001, and Brenton Tarrant, the fascist perpetrator of the 2019 Christchurch mosque shootings in New Zealand, who included the poem in his sickening manifesto. These are not the only occasions when 'poems of resilience' have been 'twisted for terrorism', as a headline in *The Atlantic* put it, although the message underpinning these works is hardly an obscure one (Kornhaber, 2019).

Rather, the statement – 'I am Invictus' – reflecting an assertive, even combative stoicism, is a telling insight into the kind of person routinely idealised and envisioned in much of the resilience discourse outlined in Chapter 1. Declaring ourselves the 'masters of our fate', or 'the captains of our soul', as the poem does, exemplifies this idealised self. But 'the self' is, of course, not a one-dimensional entity. Competing notions of 'the self' include who we *think* we are, as well as comparatively unfelt or unconscious factors unknowingly shaping us, along with real-time, existential and in-the-moment qualities of experience (see Laws, 2020). Chapter 1 encouraged readers to remain cautious and sceptical towards declarations of resilience, without dismissing their importance for making sense of it. While 'the soul' can usefully be thought of as that inner space harbouring a range of complex and often contradictory emotions, sentiments, responsibilities, and freedoms within a person (Hacking, 1995: 6), the version of the soul espoused in *Invictus* is one of strength, endurance, and unwavering stoicism. In fact, it says less about the soul in question than it does make a declaration of moral character – something not exclusively, but predominantly, the preserve of the political right (Sayer, 2020). This portrayal of idealised emotion should be seen not simply as an expression of psychological strength but rather as part of a broader cultural, political, and moral economy (*qua* Ahmed, 2004).

Stoicism, as Russell (2004[1946]: 241) writes, 'is emotionally narrow, and in a certain sense fanatical'. Unsurprisingly, it 'appealed to rulers' (Russell, 2004[1946]: 241) in the Greek and Roman empires it is typically traced back to *I AM Invictus*. No room here for ambivalence, no space to falter, and no accident that the kind of person being promoted through a celebration of military service should embody such a warrior-like caricature. It would be easy to leave the analysis of the poem there, as further evidence of the promotion of 'soldier fitness' propaganda and its transference into civilian self-help agendas (see Neocleous, 2013; Howell, 2015a; McGarry, Walklate and Mythen, 2015). The final two lines of the poem, however, also point to a more fundamental sociological problem and a tension in the political imaginary of resilience between agency and structure, and between the contingent and determined nature of the social milieu in which we act out our lives. Not only is talk of captaining our

190 Repurposing Resilience

own souls an oversimplification of the soul itself, but as a hyper-individualistic ethic of resilience it also fails to truly acknowledge our social and political inter-dependency (Butler, 2020). If the data presented throughout this book conveys one resounding message, it is sure that if any one of the most 'resilient' individual survivors, whose voices we have heard, were stripped of their familial, com-munal, and social selves, then they would scarcely be able to cope with adversity in the ways that they have. Resilience then, despite often being seen as the pre-serve of neoliberal ideology, could not exist, could not function in practice, if hyper-individualisation were realised in its purest, most extreme form. Thinking about our contemporary mental health crises, particularly after the great social experiment of 2020–21, COVID-19, this link becomes even clearer. If one good thing can come from this period, hopefully it is a wider recognition of the fact that so much of what constitutes mental distress stems not from within our own heads, but from the societies in which we live (Ferguson, 2017).

As the title of this final part of the book suggests, there is merit in engaging with a 'repurposing' of resilience. Chapter 6 lays the groundwork for such a task, exploring the interrelated issues of temporality, resistance, and solidarity, all of which represent either thorny or neglected terrain in many accounts of resilience. There are clearly limits to repurposing or reimagining any idea or concept though. If resilience can mean anything, then surely it loses, rather than gains, utility? By the same token, we cannot control phenomeno-logical activity simply by developing more and more elaborate, inclusive, or sophisticated definitions (Williams, 1988: 24; Sacks, 1989: 256). Developments in the study of trauma show, however, that the opposite can also be true within highly specific work silos. In the afterword to the second edition of *Trauma and Recovery*, Judith Herman expressed concern that the scientific study of PTSD was becoming too narrowly focused on biological findings produced in clin-ical settings lacking any 'closeness and mutuality' (Herman, 2001: 240) between researchers and survivors. As the scientific (precise, measurable, defined) study of trauma achieved 'legitimacy' among scientific communities, so too did its study in some quarters become narrowed to obscurity (Herman, 2001: 240). Clearly, then, we must be mindful of how inclusive or exclusive a term resili-ence should be. Herman's (2001: 241) hope for an interdisciplinary approach to studying stages of recovery strikes this balance by describing naturally occurring methods, leaving equal space for individual, collective, and communal processes in all their psychological, social, and political diversity:

> Insight into the recovery process may also be gained by drawing upon the wisdom of the majority of trauma survivors worldwide, who never get formal treatment of any kind. To the extent that they recover, most survivors must invent their own methods, drawing on their individual strengths and the supportive relationships naturally available to them in their own com-munities. Systematic studies of resilience in untreated survivors hold great promise for developing more effective and widely adaptable methods of therapeutic intervention.

The first section of this chapter presents five distinct framings of resilience which have been distilled from the preceding analysis and which each, in their own way, speak to one or more of the overarching themes discussed in Chapter 6. In doing so, it also considers some of the epistemological challenges associated with an empirical project of this nature. The aim is not to shoe-horn the findings into pre-existing theoretical frameworks, but rather to capture the more complex and varied characteristics of resilience alluded to above. This stands in stark contrast to the simplistic accounts of resilience explored in Chapter 1, resonating more strongly with the work of Scheper-Hughes (2008) and Overland (2013) whose findings are revisited in the second section. The third section briefly highlights some of the problems of supporting or engaging with victim and victim-related policy. Attention is drawn to these issues here before a series of key recommendations for policy and practice are made in the fourth and final section of the chapter.

From the General to the Specific and Back Again: Five Framings of Resilience

This book has drawn together a range of emergent themes from the data which point specifically to ways in which survivors have coped with their adversities. Exploring the disparate array of coping mechanisms and sources of support discussed by individual participants thematically, the aim has been to negotiate a pathway through both 'general' and 'specific' features of our subject matter. Some general features might include things like anti-resilience discourses which have highlighted its propensity to reproduce neoliberal logic, or the kinds of remarkable benefits resilience is said to bring by post-traumatic growth therapists. Specific features include events, observations, or viewpoints involving individual participants, whose 'truths' may back up or challenge these more overarching accounts. Plotting a course through this 'general' to 'specific' slalom is, of course, a task not unique to empirical analyses of resilience but one which nonetheless carries significant methodological implications within this context, as Anderson (2015: 64) makes clear:

> How do we take seriously the multiplicity of a phenomenon, while avoiding the problem of numerous, individual, case studies of resiliences in practice? How do we make resilience into an object of inquiry rather than reproduce consoling [...] accounts that repeat what is already well known in other critiques of (neo)liberalism? The question is far from unique to resilience; indeed, it turns on how we deal with generality and specificity.

Following Anderson (2015) and Howell (2015b), presumptions about what resilience is, or might be, including the prevalent coupling of resilience and neoliberal ways of governing (*qua* Joseph, 2013), were purposefully 'bracketed off' from the writing up of the data. In line with the kind of abductive analysis (Tavory and Timmermans, 2014) used to operationalise some of Hacking's ideas (see Chapter 2), it would be unrealistic to claim that these popular critiques of resilience can be bracketed off from the collection and reading of data, but certainly an effort has been made in previous chapters to draw attention to data which is compelling, whether that affirms or challenges these critiques. The task has been to identify resilience in practice, as it is described and purportedly performed, rather than deciding, *a priori*, the function it may be serving for anyone other than participants themselves (see Chapter 2).

This task has thrown up a number of difficulties and questions, particularly around identifying something without concrete prior definition. This project's research questions focused on what survivors themselves understood by resilience and what fundamental 'resilience resources' (Overland, 2013: 204) are harnessed by them in the aftermath of political violence. This begs the question; how do we know 'resilience' when we see or hear it? Except for a few individuals, participants did not typically talk of 'resilience', of 'being resilient', or of 'building resilience'. In contrast to 'trauma' and 'PTSD', direct references to 'resilience' appear relatively sparsely within the interview transcripts (at least in this specific context, Howell's (2012) suggestion that PTSD's diagnostic authority may have been encroached on by resilience would appear to be premature). Unlike the young woman cited by Neocleous (2013: 2) in his dismantling critique of resilience policies and discourse, participants interviewed here did not express an explicit desire to 'learn resilience'. Many did, however, talk of 'turning points' in their lives, of developing more or less positive outlooks, or of being able to confront problems they once felt unable to. Moreover, others talked about achieving things they never imagined they could or living a life happily despite thinking they could never be happy again. While it is possible to highlight these narratives and point to the sources of support cited therein as examples of resilience in practice, the difficulties outlined above remain. Every participant spoken to during this project could, in some way, be said to be resilient. They sat down and talked at length to a relative stranger, some several times during the course of the fieldwork, about harrowing and personally distressing events out of choice. They exercised agency in choosing to volunteer information about their lives because they wanted to and felt able to. But if this alone is resilience then how do we tease apart its disparate forms? Is resilience 'merely' surviving? Or to put it more provocatively, what exactly is the opposite of resilience? Despite people's ability to participate willingly in telling their stories how they choose to, at what point can *we* decide when they are not exhibiting resilient characteristics?

The fact that participants did not typically speak of resilience in explicit terms was a positive and encouraging sign from a methodological perspective. In a research project of this nature, it is very difficult to know when participants are simply reproducing the official discourse and rhetoric of the organisation (FfP) and its staff. The few participants who spoke explicitly and repeatedly of resilience, for example, had been recruited by a 'secondary' gatekeeper who had inadvertently (and explicitly) told them that I was specifically interested in 'resilience', whereas others were simply told that I was researching the experiences of victims of political violence. Regardless of this methodological issue, trying to decipher whether survivors' language 'truly' reflected their own views or has been moulded by contact with the Foundation is virtually impossible and almost certainly futile. Interaction between an organisation such as the Foundation and its participants is not unidirectional, nor is its meaning constant. Notions around what 'trauma' or 'resilience' might look and feel like are co-produced by both parties and as Hacking (2004: 280) avers, 'Naming has real effects on people, and changes in people have real effects on subsequent classifications'. Each event brings with it a different set of participant dynamics from a diverse set of critical incidents; each commissioned project or funded programme brings with it a newly tweaked list of criteria to work around and towards.

In wrestling with these difficulties, the starting point for identifying resilience within participant narratives must be those instances or processes described by individuals where they have flourished, where they have attained or reclaimed a sense of ontological security (Giddens, 1991: 35), or simply where difficulties in life thrown up by their experiences of political violence have been negotiated or overcome. Equally important is the possibility, identified in a significant minority of interviews, that survivors do not express such desires or needs. Recognising that the resolve of survivors of political violence, even those who appear to embody the kind of strength and resilience being advocated by the FfP, waxes and wanes over time is an important way of making sense of this. These positions are rarely so clearly defined in practice and most participants, at some points during the fieldwork observations and interviews, expressed overriding emotional impacts (primarily anger) which, at times, did not neatly cohere with how policy narratives, therapeutic interventions, or academic theories might imagine the 'resilient subject' to look and sound like. These disconnects were highlighted in Chapter 6.

Fundamentally, participant's understandings of overcoming or negotiating adversity fall into five main categories. These categories are not the specific sources of support described in Chapter 4 but rather predominant or overriding ways in which overcoming adversity was framed. These include resilience as: *A Reformulation of Self or Experience*; as *Group Solidarity*; as *Tacit Peer Support*; as *Transcending the Past*; and, finally, as *Resisting Injustice*. Each coheres in different ways with a range of impacts of PVT described in Chapter 3 and the sources of support covered in Chapter 4 but each are amalgamations of participant narratives, observations made during fieldwork, and iterative readings of the data vis-à-vis the resilience literature. While Chapters 3–5 presented the data analysis of participants' direct personal experiences ('the specific'), the understandings of resilience presented here result from comparative and conceptual grouping ('the general') and dovetail the conceptual critiques made in Chapter 6. The 'specific' and 'general' referred to here (responding to Anderson, 2015) represent direct 'objects' of study versus the 'idea' of resilience as contested

194 Repurposing Resilience

by a range of policymakers and academics (respectively) (*qua* Hacking, 1997). Rather than re-presenting the same themes discussed in previous data-led chapters, this section extrapolates the implications those themes and data have for how resilience is understood in the context of PVT trauma, harm, and victimisation. There exists a range of links between them and it is important to recognise the potentially limitless diversity and fluidity between them for both this project's participant sample and those of future empirical work.

As ever, every epistemological and methodological position invites some form of critique and it is important to be aware of how similar approaches have been deployed in the past and why they have drawn criticism. In an astute article entitled *What Kind of Thing is Resilience?*, Ben Anderson (2015: 60–1) draws attention to the sheer volume, variety, and interdisciplinarity of contemporary studies of resilience, reasoning that:

> This means that there is both an empirical diversity of resiliences and a diversity of types or forms that are extracted, in analysis, from that empirical diversity. The typical way of dealing with this diversity is to, first, briefly acknowledge it before, second, erasing it by identifying what is common across articulations of resilience. Resiliencies are read for their common characteristics and differences become a secondary matter of the specific articulation of resilience in this or that practical context. What is produced by this style of analysis is a 'resilience' that never actually exists in practice. It is a purified, ideal type, resilience suitable for the evaluative moment of critique. Resilience can then be denounced. This is made possible by a methodological procedure that takes a specific articulation of resilience – say in a policy as represented by a policy document – and treats it as somehow exemplifying characteristics of resilience in general.

Whether this kind of procedure is an inherent feature, or abuse of, the Weberian–Schutzian ideal type construct as an analytical device (see Psathas, 2005) represents a debate beyond the remit of this chapter. The kind of erasure alluded to by Anderson in the creation of these 'evaluative moments of critique' will certainly be familiar to anyone who has studied resilience for any length of time. Endless ground clearing, straw arguments, polemics, or abstract technical debates are often the stuff of resilience scholarship. So much so, that the concluding chapter of this book revisits the very issue of researching such a 'noisy' concept from a personal and reflective viewpoint.

Nonetheless, given the utility of the ideal type construct within this work, it is important that we take Anderson's 'methodographic' (see Greiffenhagen, Mair and Sharrock, 2011) comments seriously. In grouping resilience into five framings here, my intention is not to argue that they 'somehow exemplify characteristics of resilience in general' as Anderson warns of above, and it is imperative that readers do not apply them in this way. They are, however, invited to read them comparatively for similarities, differences, and possible insights that might be drawn when analysing their own data, or for people making sense of their own stories of resilience. For anyone attempting or advocating for a repurposing of resilience, Anderson's closing remarks serve as something of a methodological manifesto and deserve to be reproduced at length here before we delve into the five framings of resilience finally arrived at:

> To conclude, my argument has a series of consequences for how we encounter resilience: how resilience shows up as an object of inquiry that might object to how we enrol it into our consoling stories that purport to reveal the contemporary condition.
>
> 1   No one policy or programme or articulation can exemplify 'resilience' and claims about resilience in the singular and in general miss the particular consequences and implications of this or that variety of resilience.
> 2   Resilience never happens on its own in pure form. It co-exists in complex fields alongside other ways of governing life and, as such, is part of a series of intensifications, redeployments and (dis)continuities.
> 3   The newness, or not, of resilience is always a question to be asked and one that will vary across different varieties of resilience. Perhaps in some cases resilience is a minor change in longstanding logics of preparedness. Perhaps in other cases resilience is merely the latest variant of risk-based logics?
> 4   Connections between resilience and something else – say neoliberal ways of governing – should not be the premise of inquiry, but must be demonstrated.
>
> These methodological axioms constitute a declaration of ignorance before empirical work: we do not know what resilience is and we do not know what resilience does. The aim is to make resilience into an object of inquiry that could, perhaps, object to contemporary 'critical conventional wisdom' (Collier, 2011: 9).
>
> (Anderson, 2015: 64–5)

These principles form an important basis upon which to work, including on the potential transformation or repurposing of resilience as a viable and valuable object of empirical inquiry and not simply a proxy concept for pre-existing conflicts in formal analytic theory.

Resilience as a Reformulation of Self or Experience

At an individual, psychosocial level, overcoming harm and trauma for survivors most commonly revolved around reformulating the way they described their lives or experiences in order to reclaim a sense of control and autonomy. This revealed a concerted, reflexive effort to make sense of immense life changes and

196 Repurposing Resilience

recast them in more positive or self-directed ways. One of the most striking aspects of almost all of the interviews was the extent to which survivors seemed so sanguine about such tragic events. In reality, it has taken most of them years to resituate tragic events within their biographical narratives. An apparent focus of their sense-making was accepting and dealing with these changes to their personal lives rather than trying to return to a previous state as though unchanged. Resilience, in this sense, manifested itself as an ongoing, transformative, and cumulative experience. In addition to identifying with more positive and empowering language, such as 'survivor' rather than 'victim', participants spoke of how an amalgamation of negative experiences had, paradoxically, produced much stronger individuals capable of traversing past and future adversity. Gramsci's (2000: 326) observation about how historical processes deposit within people 'an infinity of traces, without leaving an inventory' rings true insofar as people's life experience, including their capacity to cope with trauma, is an intangible product of their past – if not intangible, then certainly greater than the sum of their parts. Invoking past experience and applying it to present struggles typically involves a reinterpretation and redescription of that experience in light of more recent memories, knowledge, and acquired language. The amount of time to elapse following critical incidents is interesting to note here, with survivors of more recent terror attacks often exhibiting less of a tendency to paint events in such a positive light. There were enough exceptions to this, however, that the passage of time was not entirely decisive for whether or not individuals began to reformulate their experiences in more optimistic ways. Creating a sense of optimism and acceptance at the individual level underpinned so many narratives and is clearly a catalyst for coping with post-conflict harm.

Resilience as Group Solidarity

Beyond individual interpretations and reformulations of past experiences, the notion of resilience also resonates collectively through group solidarity. This can occur within families, geographical or religious communities, or indeed within groups of survivors. The final section of this chapter looks more closely at the constitution of survivor communities but group solidarity operates in many more collective contexts than victim advocacy, activism, or media campaigns. These include all-important forms of identification and communication, facilitating 'collective effervescence' in a Durkheimian sense, but supportive associations can and do operate at far more mundane, everyday levels through, for example, workplace or leisure activities. As Chapter 6 highlighted, some participants from different parts of the UK commented on the difference they perceived between the working-class, often rural or semi-rural communities of Northern Ireland and the more sprawling, anonymous and potentially atomised urban neighbourhoods of the larger English cities.

Probably more significant than this for group solidarity is the fact that in Northern Ireland the very conflict which survivors have negotiated has partly ensured the continued relevance and resonance of group identities along both religious and political lines. Knowledge of violent harm and trauma among whole communities suggests quite different cultural processes of resilience taking place in everyday practice. It was clear that for participants who had fallen victim to somewhat more isolated or random acts of terror, the most important and significant source of group support would come from within the family; where no family support was present it would come from the FfP. This was also of the utmost importance for participants from more 'tight knit' and well-connected communities but it was not their only, or even their primary, support group that they could access. This is one side-effect of being cast as a 'suspect community' (Hillyard, 1993; Pantazis and Pemberton, 2009; Mythen, 2012; Breen-Smyth, 2014). An obverse of casting such communities as 'outsiders' (Becker, 1963) is that community relations *amongst* 'outsiders' are consolidated and strengthened. There is a dialectic at play between being victimised as suspect communities and needing to pull together. Describing 'community' in these terms, that is, one characterised by conflict and its response to it, is to refer to it in 'ideal typical' terms. Furthermore, as Breen-Smyth (2014) suggests, suspect communities can themselves be characterised by imagined (*qua* Anderson, 2006), as well as embodied, boundaries.

Resilience as Tacit Peer Support

Within these understandings of group solidarity as 'resilience resources' (Overland, 2013: 204) is the more specific practice of providing and/or receiving peer support from fellow survivors of political violence. The cathartic experiences reported by many participants in Chapter 6 which simultaneously represent self-help and help to others highlight the potential benefits of coordinated peer support. Examples of this include the Survivors Assistance Network itself at the Foundation which has facilitated networking between survivors in the UK. Other activities which have fostered resilience through specific supportive endeavours to other injured, traumatised, or violently oppressed individuals include Jane's aid work in Cambodia which included safely detonating landmines and helping to build homes for landmine survivors. In a different, but related, vein Anne and Kevin helped to establish and run a project through their local church offering help and food to refugees and asylum seekers. Along with George and Amanda they also helped to set up and actively contribute to a variety of interfaith forums in a bid to overcome a rise in post-'7/7' Islamophobia in their local communities. While these activities share some links with more general group solidarity, they are distinguished by a belief among survivors that having lived through periods of violent conflict or isolated attacks they are particularly well equipped to support others due to enhanced levels of empathy. While family members, colleagues, and friends can provide tremendous support, they are unlikely to share the same tacit knowledge about the impacts of political violence, particularly the psychological challenges. This

198   Repurposing Resilience

carries significant, yet relatively straightforward, policy implications for authorities and support provision in the aftermath of recent terror attacks in the UK and beyond. If local victim support services were able to put survivors in touch sooner and facilitate ongoing networking, in much the same way as survivors of the London 2005 bombings organised themselves through the King's Cross United group, there is evidence here to suggest that the psychological isolation which often accompanies such victimisation could be mitigated to some extent. The reality of this happening, of course, rests partly in the hands of increasingly frugal funding bodies and state departments committed to the implementation of austerity measures. Consequently, the potential for promoting resilience in the form of peer support activities is intimately connected to the broader political economy within which such activities might potentially sit.

Resilience as Transcending the Past

This book has argued that survivors of political violence have different relationships with the past. There are a number of reasons for this which have been covered in Chapters 5 and 6. In terms of the implications this data has for conceptualising resilience, it is interesting to again flag up David Rieff's (2016) essay on collective memory and to consider some related concerns for individual survivors of political violence. Notwithstanding barriers in the way Rieff advocates for the selective 'forgetting' of certain conflicts in the interest of the greater good (see McGowan, 2017), his distinction between 'justice' and 'peace' and the way each sets a different temporal precedent resonates with survivors' accounts analysed throughout this book. As Chapter 5 showed, within this interview sample the pursuit of justice is more strongly associated with state-perpetrated violence. The act of pursuing justice requires a range of legal, cultural, and symbolic acts and gestures ensuring links with the past are not severed. For participants with experience of non-state terrorism who are never going to achieve justice in the traditional legal sense, primarily because the perpetrator is either dead or because authorities are not pursuing them (e.g. due to the Good Friday Agreement), talk of achieving personal, inner peace, and not being mired in the past was far more significant than any consideration of perpetrators and their potential fate. The strength required to transcend the past leaves no room to harbour such thoughts. Fighting for justice, no matter how realistic its realisation may be, entails expending a lot of emotional labour which can sometimes be antithetical to resilience. The stress and anxiety which can be induced by reading inquest reports, visiting hearings in court, or simply talking about the events again and again can rupture any semblance of inner peace and elongate suffering in a variety of ways.

Much has been written about the notion of secondary victimisation, particularly within criminology and victimology. A different, but related, area of future inquiry is surely how dis/non-engagement with criminal justice campaigns and systems on the part of victims may facilitate resilience, allowing individuals to negotiate the after-effects of violence while retaining a much stronger sense of autonomy. This is one way for victims to retain a degree of control over their lives and makes good some of the issues identified over four decades ago by Christie (1977). Often, the more victims try to disengage, the more various campaign groups or even the criminal justice system itself tries to 'help' them to re-engage, so central is the position of the victim in contemporary Western society. In other examples, such as historic sexual abuse cases, we sometimes see victims eventually coming forward having maintained a personal policy of non-disclosure. Why is this? What are the implications of disclosure for their well-being? Was non-disclosure previously offering a way of coping in the face of otherwise unimaginable emotional turmoil? Was their resilience strategically fortified by maintaining public silence? These questions are not posed in order to compare terrorism and everyday gendered violence (although see Sjoberg and Gentry, 2015 for a discussion around why and how we might) but rather used to highlight the fact that, contra the various political, legal, and cultural expectations often placed upon victims of violence to behave in certain ways, strategies are sometimes deployed which attempt to transcend, or at least negotiate, past experiences in ways which minimise the otherwise constant exposure to them. While the language of 'remembering' and 'forgetting' used by Rieff (2016) to describe 'justice' and 'peace' respectively is a little too simplistic, not least of all because it sets up an unrealistic either/or dichotomy, it prompts us to think through the potential implications of moving beyond retrospective introspection. While participants who had apparently managed to do this seemed to exhibit a calmer acceptance of their historical circumstances and were working to transcend them, the ability to 'move on' psychologically is not something people can simply control at will. This is the shortcoming of Rieff's (2016) suggestion that 'active forgetting' may in fact help to mitigate against future conflicts more than collective remembrance does. If forgetting is consciously practiced as a wilful act it can hardly be said to be forgetting at all. Achieving inner peace through transcending past memories is not something all survivors experience or have control over. Those who did from within the sample used here, however, exhibited significant individual resilience and were often talked about as particularly strong and successfully coping by the organisation.

Resilience as Resisting Injustice

In contrast, other survivors may gain strength from focusing on the past. This represents another example from within 'a vast variety of resilient subjects' (Cavelty, Kaufmann and Kristensen, 2015: 8), underscoring the pluralistic nature of survivors' coping mechanisms. Responding to past violence by resisting injustice and working to make societal change often can either target specific events or come to include others. For example, some survivors are involved in very narrow justice pursuits geared towards achieving greater transparency alongside memorialisation and commemoration of the dead. Others become involved in activism through one such issue but then find themselves working across a much broader range of social justice campaigns, often linking campaign groups as a gesture of solidarity. As a driving force for several survivors, social justice campaigning and challenging perceived injustices head on through activism allows them to draw upon past experiences to help others, but also to give positive, motivational meaning to tragic events as they share practical experiences of dealing with the courts, police, coroners, and so on. While campaigning is the apparent motivator, it is concomitantly achieving several forms of resilience listed above in an overlapping, multi-layered way.

Fundamentally, however, survivors drawing upon their experiences in this vein want some form of change and usually greater recognition too. This coheres closely with what Bourbeau (2013) has termed 'resilience as renewal'. As he explains, 'resilience as renewal means that disturbances would play a triggering role in a sustained and systematic effort to change profoundly a given policy or how a society understands and interprets a particular set of issues' (Bourbeau, 2013: 16). This conception of resilience makes space not only for activism or counter-hegemonic peace activities but also for survivors committed to 'prevention-based' work as some are.

Survivor Resilience(s)

Manyena (2006: 433) reminds us that the etymological origins of 'resilience' centre on an ability 'to jump back'. To reiterate, a search of different etymological dictionaries reveals competing origins; while some suggest a 'springing forward' they nonetheless emphasise the act of rebounding, typically with reference to a physical state rather than a temporal direction. Indeed, the notion of 'bouncing back' has underpinned scores of resilience definitions. As Walklate, McGarry and Mythen (2014: 411) point out, metaphorical uses of resilience such as this enabled the transference of its use from ecology and complex systems theory to a whole range of other disciplines and applications. Where people, as opposed to engineering materials, are concerned resilience has also been said to refer to a process of 'bounce-back-ability' in which those individuals return to a former state unchanged (see Manyena, 2006: 438). This view of resilience has, however, been significantly critiqued, even in the social ecology literature in which it has its origins. Similarly, from a position of critique, the data analysed here reveals the inadequacy of such conceptions. Contra the dubious logic underpinning a belief that an individual could live through major adversities and come out totally unchanged (positively or negatively), the data analysed in previous chapters contained narratives suggesting that people actively draw on such experiences to positively reinforce change in their lives. Consequently, this data can help expand our knowledge of what survivors of political violence understand by resilience in the context of their experiences of trauma, as well as revealing the fundamental resources required by survivors to enable and build resilience in the aftermath of such violence. These exhibit both 'inherent' and 'structural' dimensions (Walklate, 2011), both of which play differential roles depending on individual character, circumstances within which harm occurs, and existing social relations between survivors, their families, and their communities. Resilience is more likely to bring transformation than continuity and is exercised with varying degrees of conscious agency.

The findings of this research are time-place specific and products of both the researcher and participant's respective (and shared) geopolitical and cultural influences, thereby making no universal claims about resilience in other contexts or places. Interestingly, however, the five forms of resilience summarised above strongly overlap with both Scheper-Hughes' (2008) and Overland's (2013) interpretations of resilience based on their own empirical observations. Drawing on decades of ethnographic research in South America and South Africa, among other countries, the characteristics of resilience identified by Scheper-Hughes (2008) include: 'Normalisation'; 'Narrativity'; 'Reframing'; 'Instrumentality/ Improvisation'; and 'Black Humour'. Each carries resonances associated with the unique ethnographic examples used by Scheper-Hughes to shore up her findings, but overall themes of exercising agency in narrative representation and the desire and ability to drive forward feature prominently and resonate with the analyses presented in this, and preceding, chapters. A more complex and moot comparison between this study and Scheper-Hughes' (2008: 50) findings lies in her

> topsy-turvy view of the phenomenology of trauma suggesting that the subjective experience of the immediate symptoms of an explosion, a violent assault, a rape, even torture may produce paradoxical 'symptoms' that can be viewed as signs of resilience and strength rather than breakdown.

As she goes on to elaborate:

> The immediate experience of trauma produces altered states that are not totally dissimilar from states of ecstasy or what William James called 'Varieties of Religious Experience'. We can call them transcendental. When Albie Sachs refers to his 'addiction' to the excitement of waging a revolution – one that resulted in his near death and loss of limb – or when anthropologist Meira Weiss says that in Jerusalem, following a spate of bomb-ings in the city, people grow bored and 'antsy' in-between the blasts, they speak of violent events with a blend of horror and exultation. If there is survivor guilt, and there is, there is also 'survivor high' and it bears some serious examination.

A dilute version of this 'survivor high' was perhaps evident among survivors interviewed here who continue to actively thrive on telling and retelling their stories of trauma and suffering, for whom life in-between 'public appearances' may represent comparative mundanity, but these were the passing thoughts of an intrigued researcher rather than concrete findings rooted in the interview data. In any case, Scheper-Hughes' inversion of trauma and resilience signifiers reminds us of the fine line (or is it an overlap?) between innate strength and forced stoicism and that our interpretations of such signifiers can only, ultimately, amount to a secondary approximation of someone else's inner life world.

Similarly, in summing up her findings on the resilience of Cambodian survivors of the Khmer Rouge, Overland (2013: 192) conceives of resilience under the following categories: 'Nomos and worldview' (including religious worldviews, karma theodicies, and acting in accordance with codes of moral virtue); 'Social Integration' (including a belief in the importance of family and community); and 'Self-reliance/Agency' (including individual responsibility, self-reliance, hard work, perseverance, struggle, and fight). Again, her categories carry particular meaning when read in tandem with her participants' accounts, but the importance of faith and religion, familial and communal bonds and the starting point of individual strength of self-belief among survivors also speaks strongly to the categories generated by this study's data. The interview data analysed here echoes Overland's (2013: 206, emphases in original) study in that she finds 'no confirmation of expectations that work, or family, or religion as *individual factors* would support resilient recovery', but rather that collectively these formed 'parts of a constellation of resilience resources and a coherent system of meaning. Most significant of all, this was the interviewees' *own* coherent system of meaning'.

Given what we know about how encompassing 'resilience' can be when deployed as a metaphor for tolerance to austerity (Harrison, 2013), the management of economically destitute communities through responsibilised control-at-a-distance, and security strategies interceded through a 'politics of catastrophe' (Aradau and van Munster, 2011), it is unlikely that the term is about to disappear from political usage. However, that '[w]e get nowhere politically by simply attempting to condemn concepts', thus further 'ossifying' already essentialised positions (Chandler and Reid, 2016: 117), invites thinking anew. Approaching these problems differently, might a way of further prizing open some of the discursive contradictions found within resilience rhetoric be to push at the taken-for-granted boundaries of what is allowed to constitute resilience? How do the discursive claims of 'resilience' stack up against the material realities of those individuals and communities in question? Why not let us engage in our own discursive refashioning? Given how arbitrary and speculative both institutional and academic discussions around resilience often are, from policy agendas to polemic debates, such a project must strive not to simply reproduce this state of affairs but at least try to negate it methodologically. As Anderson's (2015) principles discussed earlier in this chapter emphasise, connections between resilience and 'something else', be that neoliberalism, resistance, solidarity, or temporality, must be a demonstrable outcome of empirical work and not simply prior theorisation or presumption.

Having spent the first two-thirds of this chapter drawing together the conceptual findings of this project, in particular teasing apart the different ideal types of resilience being exhibited by survivors, attention now turns to what we might do to best support survivors in similar situations. Engaging with policy is a controversial endeavour whatever the topic area and this is certainly the case when it comes to victims and terrorism, respectively. As Chapter 2 argued, when these two things come together 'victims of terrorism', both as a concrete set of people and as a more abstract motif in discussions about national security, become incredibly powerful political capital indeed. Cognisant of this, it is necessary to consider some of the principles that should underpin our research and the translation of that research into recommendations for policy and practice in an environment littered with potential pitfalls. It is to this discussion that the chapter now turns.

Responding to Harm and Bereavement: The Politics of Engaging with Victim Policy

In the final section of this chapter, I make a series of recommendations for policy and practice. In doing so, I am not calling for the prioritisation of victims' voices in a way that pits their needs against the needs of others, or suggesting that they require special sympathy or rights because of, and certainly not conditional upon, their status 'as victims'. Readers should be alert to the discursive and symbolic power of 'victims' and certainly think through some of the potential implications that engaging with 'victims' as an eponymous area of study might have for their work before seeking policy relevance.

How might we engage in questions pertinent to this Victims, Culture, and Society book series in relation to the fascinating but fairly bleak picture painted by Ginsberg (2014) of victim rights and policymaking aimed at ameliorating their experiences of harm, trauma, and bereavement? Ginsberg (2014) convincingly highlights a worrying 'neatness of fit' (Walklate, 2019: 88) between calls to prioritise the voices and sovereignty of victims and neoliberalism. He demonstrates how in recent years a panoply of policy shifts have placed victims at the centre of criminal justice processes, from allowing victims and their families to influence sentencing outcomes to naming specific laws after deceased victims. This gives rise to a form of policymaking that 'requires the constant representation of pain to ensure the ongoing sovereignty of the victim whilst simultaneously ensuring "victims" voices become "reshaped, packaged, commodified"' (Walklate, 2019: 88). How do we engage in victim-focused policymaking, or indeed the moral terrain of any major criminal justice or penal field, without succumbing to the 'corrosive, life-sapping, law and order discourses articulated by the majority of contemporary politicians and media commentators and the pragmatic expediency of many in the liberal reform lobby' (Sim, 2018: 184)?

Engaging with policymakers, full stop remains an important yet controversial and contested endeavour for critical terrorism studies (CTS) scholars (see McGowan, 2016), for whom, among others, it is hoped this book will prove interesting, provocative, and useful:

204 Repurposing Resilience

The question of whether CTS scholarship should be more or less 'policy-relevant' (if at all) is integral to its disciplinarity [...]; indeed, it is neither prudent nor possible for CTS to adopt any universalising posture in this regard. Yet, in the midst of these debates, we should not forget that whatever one's position on its potential merits, the enactment of policy yields incredible effects on the lives of those variously associated with terrorism: including victims, ordinary citizens, and 'terrorists' themselves. As a meaningful topic of inquiry, policy-relevance, then, is perhaps more essential than most.

(Fitzgerald, Ali and Armstrong, 2016: 9)

To contribute practical ideas for a potential policy audience then, based upon the observations underpinning this research, is also to make two interrelated observations, claims, and assumptions about resilience in actual practice. One concerns the co-option of critical research agendas, and the second centres more conceptually on the contested and complex nature of violence itself to which these discussions of policy are directed.

Firstly, scholars do not automatically concede or hand over their intellectual autonomy because of how policymakers may interpret or apply their suggestions, providing they do not subsequently chase mainstream policy approval by making their findings, outputs, or recommendations more palatable (the 'making up' of liberal social scientists and its 'looping effects' represents a whole new project for someone to document). Despite the fact that this co-option of social science regularly characterises mainstream political engagement with it:

[...] praxis should not be equated with a reductive understanding of policy-relevance where academics abandon their criticality in favour of professional advancement. Instead, [...] CTS should work with the state in the pursuit of emancipation because they are not unitary actors but contain both 'emancipatory and counter-emancipatory agendas'. Moreover, the heterogeneity of state actors, some of whom may have emancipatory agendas can be exploited to bring about wider political change.

(Fitzgerald, Ali and Armstrong, 2016: 5)

Despite claims concerning the incompatibility between resilience and resistance discussed in Chapter 6 (see Neocleous, 2013; Diprose, 2015), critical scholars may actually be taking the path of least resistance when they dismiss resilience discourse and the practical work it can engender (both good and bad) by disengaging from its debate altogether. Fitzgerald, Ali and Armstrong (2016: 9) aptly describe this as 'an ethos of "discomfort" where working alongside state actors, though complicated and potentially problematic, is nonetheless essential in working towards emancipation'.

Second is a recognition of the necessarily contested political nature of violence and our potential response to it that requires that we find the imagination,

Am I Invictus? 205

courage, and nuance to be able to transcend binary thinking (*qua* Butler, 2004); to condemn both acts of violence that routinely harm, injure, and kill people in the name of counterterror and State repression, while simultaneously accepting the reality of harm, injury, and lethal force that is occasionally inflicted on victims of political violence and terrorism by comparatively weaker, non-State aggressors too. Transcending binary thinking in this way also reflects a belief that even controversial, divisive, and potentially depoliticising concepts (reminiscent of some of the resilience discourses outlined in Chapter 1) have an afterlife – that is, a life after their original creation, articulation, and discursive manipulation.

Taking these two interrelated observations, claims, and assumptions about resilience in actual practice seriously, then, is to recognise it as contingent, not static, phenomena. This is not to argue that resilience is a desirable framework for policymakers to persist with, or that it does not at times serve the very depoliticising functions its critics rightly highlight. It is, however, to recognise both the diversity of voices engaged in this debate and to pay due attention to the unexpected, innocuous, and even positive effects that resilience discourse may incidentally have in practice. Again, this is to acknowledge that responding resiliently to a terror attack is not the same as being told to be resilient to poverty or austerity.

Key Recommendations for Policy and Practice

In no order of importance or priority, the following points briefly outline recommendations for policy and practice, including areas to direct a renewed focus on, based on the research findings presented in this, and preceding chapters, and should be read with the above provisos firmly in mind:

1   *A Duty of Care for the Media*

More should be done to ensure that survivors and their families are granted their right to privacy, including in the immediate aftermath of an attack, during annual or commemorative coverage of prior attacks, and at any time the media wishes to contact families for interviews or comment. The findings about media intrusion presented here were recently echoed in Lord Kerslake's report into the Manchester Arena bombing and by comments from victim's families (see The Kerslake Report, 2018; BBC, 2018). The need for more measured and proportionate reporting has also been raised recently by English (2017).

2   *Information Sharing Among Emergency Services*

Information sharing across and between agencies and emergency services is, similarly, an area for potential improvement. While emergency responders carry out a courageous and vital job in some of the most difficult circumstances, experiences from some survivors point to instances of poor communication. This was an issue reported by Ganesh in relation to 7/7, who despite giving his details to multiple officials was not contacted at all for two weeks. Living outside London, he can only assume that his details were not shared between different police forces. This led to a lack of information about the investigation and a costly delay in appropriate medical treatment. This issue was again raised in The Kerslake Report (2018) into the Manchester Arena attack which found evidence of poor communication between emergency service agencies and also in relation to the Grenfell fire and subsequent inquiry.

3 *Languages of Recovery within Victim Support Policy*

The language used to describe 'resilience' in policy, third sector practice, and therapeutic settings should emphasise the potentially non-linear nature of coming to terms with political violence and terrorism. Current emphasis overwhelmingly suggests a finite, future-oriented, and linear process where recovery is positively incremental. This describes an ideal response but may not capture the reality for many.

4 *Victim Compensation*

Despite the recent adoption of dedicated victim compensation schemes for terrorist attack victims, the function of victim compensation remains poorly understood and controversial among survivors in this context as this research has shown. This is evident in recent examples of victims attempting to claim compensation from holiday providers, as with victims of the attack in Sousse, Tunisia, and legislation around compensation being used instrumentally in international diplomacy between nation states, as in the US with the Justice Against Sponsors of Terrorism Act. One area for practical and immediate reform is the material support and resources afforded to survivors and their families which could better enable them to attend inquests without the financial pressures associated with travel, accommodation, time taken off work, loss of earnings, and childcare costs. This should not be issued instead of, but as well as, compensation and certainly should not be limited to 'victims of terrorism' but made available to anyone harmed by State, corporate, or institutional harm. The practical and applied nature of such gestures may also help to assuage feelings of guilt and even revulsion felt by many survivors for 'having a price put on a loved one's life', or for accepting expendable money from often unknown or dubious sources from survivors' perspectives, while also potentially improving information flows between arbiters (almost exclusively the state) and survivors. There is thus clear potential and priority for future research to consider both the impact and function of victim compensation schemes for victims and their geopolitical significance more broadly (see Gilbert, 2017).

5 *Fostering Survivor Solidarity and Peer Support Programmes*

Reiterating the importance of survivor solidarity and the chance for survivors to share their experiences within understanding and empathetic groups, every effort should be made to put survivors in contact with fellow survivors via support organisations at the earliest practicable opportunity. While some networks may spontaneously put survivors in contact with each other on an *ad hoc* basis, and some existing organisations may offer *advice*-led support to survivors over the phone, email, or through often isolated caseworker visits, the combination of peer-to-peer AND organisationally facilitated support for such a heterogeneous range of survivors of PVT offered at the FfP remains unique.

6 *Coroners and Inquests*

Coroners and the function played by inquests was discussed by numerous participants here as both important and challenging milestones in ascertaining exactly what happened to loved ones. Some of these participants seemed satisfied with the way that inquests were carried out, while others felt them to be long, drawn out, and exclusionary processes for bereaved family members. As with other high profile or mass fatality incidents, the psychosocial needs of the bereaved are often subordinated to the professional priorities of regulatory State agencies (Davis and Scraton, 1999). In the event that the perpetrator is the State, this subordination may not simply be a case of lengthy administration and unavoidable bureaucracy but could involve corruption, collusion, and deliberate stalling, as has been the case with regard to public inquiries (Rolston and Scraton, 2005). As with several of the other policy recommendations made here, this issue should not be thought of in isolation but in relation to death and bereavement more broadly. Given their archaic form, and taking into account persistent concerns raised over the judicial discretion, devolved funding, and lack of accountability of the coroners' service in England and Wales (see Pitman, 2012), there is an urgent need for a radical reimagining of the coronial service, including in relation to both inquests and public inquiries. Problems here concern not just the potentially lengthy processes the bereaved must navigate when it comes to coroners' inquests (Pitman, 2012: 1), but extend to the lack of independent oversight and enforcement of post-death investigations and related recommendations stemming from inquiries too. An independent and public body with statutory power to oversee this process could help to ameliorate the disproportionately long-term harm, secrecy, and emotional torture inflicted on victims of institutional and State violence (see Inquest, 2021), and the whole system could be much improved for bereaved families in general. The charity Inquest also call for non-means tested funding for bereaved families to attend inquests of institutional and State-related deaths, something already suggested above in relation to compensation.

Conclusion

This chapter, along with the last, has drawn together the themes identified in Chapters 3–5, grouping unified understandings of resilience and highlighting the implications that this work has for the way we might think about resilience in relation to time, resistance, and community. In discussing these issues at a somewhat more abstract level than those previous chapters, the aim here has not been to make absolute claims or to reify what are, in reality, highly fluid and sometimes transient practices in self-understanding when analysed on a case-by-case basis. In thinking through the range of emotions associated with injury, bereavement, and trauma, or trying to locate these injuries and survivors' responses to them in time, we necessarily find ourselves trying to make sense of individuals' 'inner lives', embedded within a collective and structural milieu (Mills, 2000). This is obviously a complex and, according to Hacking, perhaps even indeterminate task. Scholars of violence, particularly those relying on the epistemic weight and authenticity of survivors' testimonies, are well placed to 'talk up' rather than 'talk down' the complex and contradictory sentiments such narratives often furnish. Describing something of the messiness expressed from deep within survivors' selves seems a far more important and worthwhile job than layering yet more redescriptions onto our data in order to theoretically repackage it into more totalising eponymous subfields of inquiry, such as studies of 'emotion', 'identity', or 'victims'. While talk of 'the soul' may sound abstract compared to 'emotion' or 'identity', Hacking's understanding of the soul perfectly captures the mix of inner, tacit experiences pointed to by participants here, providing a more nuanced and compelling depiction than *I Am Invictus*, discussed at the beginning of this chapter:

> The soul that was scientized was something transcendental, perhaps immortal. Philosophers of my stripe speak of the soul not to suggest something eternal, but to invoke character, reflective choice, self-understanding, values that include honesty to others and oneself, and several types of freedom and responsibility. Love, passion, envy, tedium, regret, and quiet contentment are the stuff of the soul. [...] I do not think of the soul as unitary, as an essence, as one single thing, or even as a thing at all. It does not denote an unchanging core of personal identity. One person, one soul, may have many facets and speak with many tongues. To think of the soul is not to imply that there is one essence, one spiritual point, from which all voices issue. [...] It stands for the strange mix of aspects of a person that may be, at some time, imaged as inner – a thought not contradicted by Wittgenstein's dictum, that the body is the best picture of the soul.
>
> (Hacking, 1995: 6)

Human resilience, or the ability and practice of negotiating adversity, is constituted by this 'strange mix' referred to by Hacking. Consequently, we are unlikely to find two identical processes, or 'two identical stories', of making up people (Hacking, 2002:114), including of resilience among individual survivors. Documenting the making and moulding of resilient selves is, chiefly, a job of description. While much theoretical and even empirical work around resilience has sought to find definitive either/or categories to work with, or to propose typologies which can fit any range of human experience into, the patterns in the data pointed to here are only intended to group the experiences of participants in this study. This is not to say they might not resonate in other social settings or future studies (some of the more mundane features of coping surely will), but it is important that observations of 'resilient practice' are situated, contextualised, and appraised in a modest and considered way.

Imagining what 'the resilient subject' looks and sounds like is to presume a coherence rarely found in the messy realities of everyday life. It is an inescapably normative judgement that is difficult to avoid. Arguably, the power of 'terrorism' as an 'organizing concept' (Crenshaw, 1995: 9) makes it even more difficult to 'bracket off' dominant understandings of trauma and our responses to it. Even when 'terrorism' fails to adequately capture the complex and antagonistic nature of real-world events, researchers, organisations, and policymakers cannot help but be influenced by the gravitas it commands for a range of different reasons (see Chapter 2). As Crenshaw (1995: 7) argues, 'concepts follow politics' on this terrain. However, following Hacking's epistemological lead discussed in Chapter 2 and deployed throughout this work, they also follow, influence, and are in turn influenced by, social action independent of top-down politics, and top-down politics frequently follow people's reactions to labels such as 'terrorism'. This chapter has argued that processes that are more temporally complex than theoretically neat recovery steps, or which channel anger in order to pursue active and contentious personal or political goals, are still functioning as processes of resilience.

It seemed that participants were often trying to verbalise that which was almost impossible to put into words. The kind of quiet self-understanding alluded to by Hacking's discussion of the soul above is something familiar to us all. However, verbal articulations of the human condition necessarily fall into familiar forms of description. Only those with similar experiences have a tacit understanding of the 'pre-verbalised' stage of reasoning, where 'there are no words', and only true empathy can negate the confusion or frustration many survivors feel at trying to make the pain of experiencing an act of political violence or terrorism make sense to others. Clearly, any frameworks of resilience that attempt to shepherd people's emotions and actions through rational, linear stages are bound to fall short of helping everyone. This does not make them redundant, but it should render their promise more modest than it frequently appears in self-help and therapeutic guidance. That time does not always perform in a linear fashion, that anger and resistance may be entirely functional responses, or that positive forms of human connection are forged from awful life-changing events are surely the stuff of messy and complex reality.

References

Ahmed, S. (2004) *The Cultural Politics of Emotion*. Edinburgh: Edinburgh University Press.

Anderson, B. (2006) *Imagined Communities: Reflections on the Origin and Spread of Nationalism*. London: Verso.

Anderson, B. (2015) What kind of thing is resilience? *Politics* 35(1): 60–6.

Aradau, C. and van Munster, R. (2011) *Politics of Catastrophe: Genealogies of the Unknown*. London: Routledge.

BBC (2018) Manchester attack: Kerslake calls for families charter. *BBC News*, [online] 12 January. Available at: www.bbc.co.uk/news/uk-england-manchester-42653838 [Accessed 25/01/2018].

Becker, H.S. (1963) *Outsiders: Studies in the Sociology of Deviance*. New York: The Free Press.

Bourbeau, P. (2013) Resiliencism: Premises and promises in securitisation research. *Resilience: International Policies, Practices and Discourses* 1(1): 3–17.

Breen-Smyth, M. (2014) Theorising the 'suspect community': Counterterrorism, security practices and the public imagination. *Critical Studies on Terrorism* 7(2): 223–40.

Butler, J. (2004) *Precarious Life: The Powers of Mourning and Violence*. London: Verso.

Butler, J. (2020) *The Force of Nonviolence: An Ethico-Political Bind*. London: Verso.

Cavelty, M.D., Kaufmann, M. and Kristensen, K.S. (2015) Resilience and (in)security: Practices, subjects, temporalities. *Security Dialogue* 46(1): 3–14.

Chandler, D. and Reid, J. (2016) *The Neoliberal Subject: Resilience, Adaptation and Vulnerability*. London: Rowman & Littlefield International, Ltd.

Christie, N. (1977) Conflicts as property. *The British Journal of Criminology* 17(1): 1–15.

Crenshaw, M. (1995) Thoughts on relating terrorism to historical contexts. In M. Crenshaw (Ed.) *Terrorism in Context*. University Park, PA: The Pennsylvania State University Press. pp.3–26.

Davis, H. and Scraton, P. (1999) Institutionalised conflict and the subordination of 'loss' in the immediate aftermath of UK mass fatality disasters. *Journal of Contingencies and Crisis Management* 7(2): 86–97.

Diprose, K. (2015) Resilience is futile. *Soundings: A Journal of Politics and Culture* 58: 44–56.

English, R. (2017) The media must respond more responsibly to terrorist attacks – here's how. *The Conversation*, [online] April 4. https://theconversation.com/the-media-must-respond-more-responsibly-to-terrorist-attacks-heres-how-75490 [Accessed 29/04/2017].

Ferguson, I. (2017) *Politics of the Mind: Marxism and Mental Distress*. London: Bookmarks Publications.

Fitzgerald, J., Ali, N. and Armstrong, M. (2016) Editors' introduction: Critical terrorism studies: Reflections on policy-relevance and disciplinarity. *Critical Studies on Terrorism* 9(1): 1–11.

Giddens, A. (1991) *Modernity and Self-Identity: Self and Society in the Late Modern Age*. Cambridge: Polity Press.

Gilbert, E. (2017) Victim compensation for acts of terrorism and the limits of the state. *Critical Studies on Terrorism* 11(2): 199–218.

Ginsberg, R. (2014) Mighty crime victims: Victims' rights and neoliberalism in the American conjuncture. *Cultural Studies* 28(5/6): 911–46.

Gramsci, A. (2000) Philosophy, common sense, language and folklore. In D. Forgacs (Ed.) *The Antonio Gramsci Reader/A Gramsci Reader: Selected Writings 1916–1935*. London: Lawrence and Wishart.

Greiffenhagen, C., Mair, M. and Sharrock, W. (2011) From methodology to methodography: A study of qualitative and quantitative reasoning in practice. *Methodological Innovations Online* 6(3): 93–107.

Hacking, I. (1995) *Rewriting the Soul: Multiple Personality and the Sciences of Memory*. Princeton, NJ: Princeton University Press.

Hacking, I. (1997) Taking bad arguments seriously. *London Review of Books* 19(16): 14–16.

Hacking, I. (2002) *Historical Ontology*. Cambridge: Harvard University Press.

Hacking, I. (2004) Between Michel Foucault and Erving Goffman: Between discourse in the abstract and face-to-face interaction. *Economy and Society* 33(3): 277–302.

Harrison, E. (2013) Bouncing back? Recession, resilience and everyday lives. *Critical Social Policy* 33(1): 97–113.

Herman, J.L. (2001) *Trauma and Recovery*. London: Pandora.

Hillyard, P. (1993) *Suspect Community: People's Experiences of the Prevention of Terrorism Acts in Britain*. London: Pluto Press.

Howell, A. (2012) The demise of PTSD: From governing through trauma to governing resilience. *Alternatives: Global, Local, Political* 37(3): 214–26.

Howell, A. (2015a) Resilience, war, and austerity: The ethics of military human enhancement and the politics of data. *Security Dialogue* 46(1): 15–31.

Howell, A. (2015b) Resilience as enhancement: Governmentality and political economy beyond 'responsibilisation'. *Politics* 35(1): 67–71.

Inquest (2021) Our Mission 2018–2021. Available at: www.inquest.org.uk/inquest-mission [Accessed 12/07/2021].

Invictus Games (2014) About the Invictus Games. Available at: http://invictusgames.org/about-invictus/ [Accessed 29/03/2015].

Joseph, J. (2013) Resilience as embedded neoliberalism: A governmentality approach. *Resilience: International Policies, Practices and Discourses* 1(1): 38–52.

Kornhaber, S. (2019) When poems of resilience get twisted for terrorism, [online] 16 March. *The Atlantic*. Available at: www.theatlantic.com/entertainment/archive/2019/03/new-zealand-shooting-manifesto-poems-dylan-thomas/585079/ [Accessed 24/01/2021].

Laws, B. (2020) Reimaging 'the self' in criminology: Transcendence, unconscious states and the limits of narrative criminology. *Theoretical Criminology*: 1–19. doi.org/10.1177%2F1362480620919102.

Manyena, S.B. (2006) The concept of resilience revisited. *Disasters* 30(4): 433–50.

McGarry, R., Walklate, S. and Mythen, G. (2015) A Sociological Analysis of Military Resilience: Opening Up the Debate. *Armed Forces & Society* 41: 352–78.

McGowan, W. (2016) Critical terrorism studies, victimisation, and policy relevance: Compromising politics or challenging hegemony? *Critical Studies on Terrorism* 9(1): 12–32.

McGowan, W. (2017) In praise of forgetting: Historical memory and its ironies. By David Rieff (Yale University Press, 2016, $25.00/Yale University Press, £14.99, 160pp.). *British Journal of Criminology* 57(6): 1520–3.

Mills, C.W. (2000) *The Sociological Imagination*. New York: Oxford University Press.

Mythen, G. (2012) 'No one speaks for us': Security policy, suspected communities and the problem of voice. *Critical Studies on Terrorism* 5(3): 409–24.

Neocleous, M. (2013) Resisting resilience. *Radical Philosophy* 178(6): 2–7.

Overland, G. (2013) *Post Traumatic Survival: The Lessons of Cambodian Resilience*. Newcastle upon Tyne: Cambridge Scholars Publishing.

Pantazis, C. and Pemberton, S. (2009) From the 'old' to the 'new' suspect community: Examining the impacts of recent UK counter-terrorist legislation. *British Journal of Criminology* 49(5): 646–66.

Pitman, A. (2012) Reform of the coroners' service in England and Wales: Policy-making and politics. *The Psychiatrist* 36(1): 1–5.

Psathas, G. (2005) The Ideal Type in Weber and Schutz. In M. Endress, G. Psathas and H. Nasu (Eds.) *Explorations of the Life-World: Continuing Dialogues with Alfred Schutz*. Dordrecht: Springer. pp.143–69.

Rieff, D. (2016) *In Praise of Forgetting: Historical Memory and Its Ironies*. New Haven: Yale University Press.

Rolston, B. and Scraton, P. (2005) In the full glare of English politics: Ireland, inquiries and the British state. *British Journal of Criminology* 45(4): 547–64.

Russell, B. (2004[1946]) *History of Western Philosophy*. London: Routledge.

Sacks, H. (1989) Lecture four: An impromptu survey of the literature. *Human Studies* 12(3/4): 253–9.

Sayer, A. (2020) Critiquing – and rescuing – 'character'. *Sociology* 54(3): 460–81.

Scheper-Hughes, N. (2008) A talent for life: Reflections on human vulnerability and resilience. *Ethnos* 73(1): 25–56.

Sim, J. (2018) We are all (neo) liberals now: Reform and the prison crisis in England and Wales. *Justice, Power and Resistance* 2(1): 165–88.

Sjoberg, L. and Gentry, C.E. (2015) Introduction: Gender and everyday/intimate terrorism. *Critical Studies on Terrorism* 8(3): 358–61.

Tavory, I. and Timmermans, S. (2014) *Abductive Analysis: Theorizing Qualitative Research*. Chicago: The University of Chicago Press.

The Kerslake Report (2018) *The Kerslake Report: An independent review into the preparedness for, and emergency response to, the Manchester Arena attack on 22 May 2017*. [online] Available at: www.kerslakearenareview.co.uk/media/1022/kerslake_arena_review_printed_final.pdf [Accessed 01/06/2018].

Walklate, S. (2011) Reframing criminal victimization: Finding a place for vulnerability and resilience. *Theoretical Criminology* 15(2): 179–94.

Walklate, S. (2019) Images of atrocity: From victimhood to redemption and the implications for a (narrative) victimology. In R. Lippens and E. Murray (Eds.) *Representing the Experience of War and Atrocity: Interdisciplinary Explorations in Visual Criminology*. Basingstoke: Palgrave Macmillan. pp.73–92.

Walklate, S., McGarry, R. and Mythen, G. (2014) Searching for resilience: A conceptual excavation. *Armed Forces & Society* 40(3): 408–27.

Williams, R. (1988) *Keywords: A Vocabulary of Culture and Society*. London: Fontana Press.

Conclusion

Chapters 6 and 7 in this third and final part of the book revisited a range of theoretical and conceptual issues concerning resilience first raised in Chapter 1. This concluding chapter revisits some of the methodological issues raised in Chapter 2, focusing particularly on the process of researching resilience and some of the implications of this felt during the fieldwork and writing up stages of this project. The chapter ultimately offers some final thoughts on resilience in a reflexive capacity, including the debates it has provoked in recent years. This final reflection on the experience of working with such a ubiquitous concept hopefully gives the reader a useful insight into where to situate this book methodologically and politically in what has fast become a 'crowded field'. Some potential areas for future research are also briefly discussed, partly as a means for thinking through the possible directions that work more generally exploring issues of suffering, loss, bereavement, adversity, and community may take. These are by no means exhaustive and readers are encouraged to refer to both Chapters 6 and 7, respectively, for fuller discussions of this book's contributions to existing and ongoing theory and policy challenges.

Issues of Representation: A Methodological Note

'Mind the Gap': Discourse, NGO Practice and 'Feedback Loops'

As well as attempting to demarcate both 'general' and 'specific' features of the data as discussed in Chapter 7, researching survivors in an environment where talk of both victimisation and trauma are omnipresent throws up other methodological tensions around (mis)representation. The potential influences of cultural and policy narratives on our accounts of topics such as 'resilience' and related concepts in this project such as 'trauma' apply to both participants and researchers. Both are words used in a range of differing contexts with various meanings attached to them. Notions of cultural and linguistic signifiers, referents, or narrative are variously explored by Furedi (2007), Fassin and Rechtman (2009), and Alexander (2012) in relation to adversity responses and trauma. Furedi, somewhat cynically, notes: '[r]esearchers are busy helping

DOI: 10.4324/9781003154020-12

survivors to reinterpret their experiences through the language of trauma. Such is the power of present-day sensitivity to human vulnerability that past events can only make sense through the language of trauma' (2007: 247). The extent to which all researchers of trauma or adversity are guilty of leading participants in this way remains a moot point, but if an exploration of personal resilience is to get anywhere close to the personal then Furedi's words offer a sound methodological caution.

The difficulty in separating personal narration from cultural narrative makes it spurious to suggest that there is a 'true' or more authentic experience of resilience to be discovered, independent of its specific frame of reference. Indeed it must be acknowledged that the difficulty of teasing apart personal experiences from their immediate cultural 'prompts' is potentially exacerbated when participants are sought from an NGO whose business it is to enable individuals to identify with victimisation and trauma, albeit with the aim of enabling those individuals to work through and move beyond these identities. Following Rock (2002), we might say that individuals who have lived through trauma cannot move beyond victimhood unless they are first cast as 'traumatised victims' – that in order to become a survivor one must first define that which has been survived. Furthermore, from a political-economic perspective, NGOs require a certain level of engagement from the groups they seek to help who, in effect, become consumers of purpose-built support projects (Krause, 2014). Participants of the FfP who have experience of political violence first-hand thus represent the envisaged beneficiaries of 'terrorist victim' related projects. Thus, no matter how perceptive the researcher is, or aims to be, the reality is that some of the participants in this study were involved in the organisation for a considerable length of time and so are likely to have different frames of reference than before they attended. This is not a negative or avoidable thing but does underscore the extent to which projects such as this one are a product of particular time, place, and context-specific circumstances.

Walklate (2016) disentangles some of these tensions, identifying two predominant ways in which our understandings of victimhood and victimisation have tended to be articulated contemporarily. On the one hand, what Walklate terms the 'victim narrative' proves inadequate because it draws on data that tend to aggregate individuals into groups, focusing primarily on a macro level and so ignoring or merging agency and experience. The very existence of the FfP as a 'victim-centred organisation' (Walklate, 2016: 7), as well as relatively recent policy moves such as the introduction of an overseas terrorism compensation scheme (Ministry of Justice, 2012), suggest that both the physical, organisational site of this research, and its broader subject matter, are practical and symbolic markers of a 'victim narrative' which remains very much on the contemporary cultural and political agenda. On the other hand, the 'trauma narrative' coined by Walklate focuses intensely on individuals' experiences but then uses that fine grain insight to speak for groups, concentrating so much on one specific and often objectified micro phenomena ('trauma') that it ends up ignoring or disposing of the very individuals it has 'mined' data from. Thus, we do not need to know what it might feel like to experience terrorism, rape, tower block fires, or car accidents, since PTSD diagnostic manuals have conveniently enabled all such diversity to be subsumed under the same umbrella, leading to what Fassin and Rechtman (2009: 281) term an 'obliteration of experience'.

While this paints an extreme and dispassionate picture, the creeping discourse of trauma operates in multifaceted ways and to varying degrees with the unquestioning embrace of clinical diagnoses and promotion of related therapies at one end of the continuum, and the outright denial of medical symptoms of trauma at the other. The reality usually falls somewhere in-between. However, the use of popular psychological diagnostic, teaching and awareness-raising materials at some of the FfP's events by group facilitators, several of whom held qualifications in psychotherapy, trauma counselling, and occupation-specific training, made clear that 'trauma narratives' were actively being mobilised and made to do particular work within this research setting. One of the issues to negotiate as a researcher around recruitment stemmed from the fact that, contrary to the organisation's public image as supporting 'victims of terrorism', as well as early conversations with staff during which my own naïve assumptions about the work they did came to the fore, a closer look at the organisation's participant's 'profiles' revealed huge disparity and diversity. What was being deemed 'terrorism', 'military/paramilitary' experience and even experience of working in other emergency service roles was both rooted in concrete reality and yet made to variously bend and flex around *the practical deployment of trauma as an organising concept*. According to the 'trauma narrative', these disparate experiences all had *one* thing in common: they were all 'traumatic'; they all gave rise to 'trauma'. From a group facilitators' perspective, this made the practical accomplishment of their work (only slightly) more straightforward; after all, it is surely easier to address a group of trauma sufferers than it is a melange of civilian victims, bereaved families, retired firefighters or policemen and women, veterans, and former 'radicals'. From a researcher's perspective, this caused both conceptual and practical confusion.

The consolidation of these two narratives has, according to Walklate (2016: 11), been productive of a 'trauma creep' in which individual agency is sapped or ignored from both ends of the spectrum while homogenising or misrepresenting groups, doing 'a disservice to both individuals and collectivities at the same time'. For Walklate, this has practical, as well as symbolic, repercussions. Most seriously, it can 'silence the capacity' of individuals and groups to overcome 'the worst excesses of violence' (Walklate, 2016: 11). As well as tending to ignore the structural pre-conditions of victimisation which shape both victimisation risk and people's ability to cope (i.e. 'to be resilient') with its aftermath, this 'trauma creep' has led to a 'metamorphosis of the victim (in which being victimised and being traumatised become intertwined)' (Walklate, 2018: 2). Both resilience and trauma, then, carry with them considerable methodological and political baggage which has served, at various points during this research, to cloud the process of analysis.

216 Conclusion

Issues of representation also needed careful consideration when addressing the research questions which at first appear deceptively straightforward. How do survivors understand resilience? We cannot say for sure without asking them outright and by asking them we in turn co-produce a discursive event ('the interview') in which we make public (see Hacking, 2002) the language of 'resilience'. This is not an inherently negative or even avoidable thing, but does require distinctions to be drawn between public/private language – one set of inner actions and emotions, the other expressed outwardly. Interpreting the data here, it is more accurate to talk of 'coping mechanisms' or 'resilience resources' (Overland, 2013: 204) because of their ongoing, unfinished nature and because of their plurality than it is to talk of what survivors understand by 'resilience' or how much or little of this apparent thing they may or may not have attained.

Guarding against simply reproducing political critiques of resilience that stray from the empirical data also involves representational complexity. Possibilities for good are opened up by a range of new descriptions and we need to be as open to the fact that talk of 'resilience' among survivor groups such as the FfP can function positively for individuals and groups acting under these new descriptions (cf. Hacking, 1995: 238), fostering a sense of genuine well-being. Examples include the sense of camaraderie, catharsis, and solidarity fostered within an environment such as the Peace Centre through a shared desire to better cope. That is not to say that such 'positive' action is simply talked into being. It is equally possible that negative possibilities are enacted, such as gestures of stoicism being so strongly enacted as to offend or upset fellow survivors during group storytelling sessions who may not share such views. It may also be that nothing whatsoever is prompted by the language of resilience. All possibilities exist. Clearly, the solidarity and group 'resilience' garnered through the Peace Centre is practically organised around shared language, but it is also premised upon some fundamentally shared experiences of the body. This can be participants' own bodies or that of family or friends, but the fact that some form of trauma, mental or physical, has been visited upon the bodies of participants nonetheless provides commonality, constituting them as both biological and social (or 'biosocial') beings (Hacking, 2006).

Having warned against blindly accepting 'discourse in the abstract' (Hacking, 2004) in Chapter 1 and prompting us to look to survivors themselves for clues in Chapter 2, it is equally important that we guard against committing an obvious, though no less complex, fallacy. Namely, misinterpreting 'discourse' as something divorced from action or assuming that we can neatly 'park' the policy language of 'resilience' to one side while we get on with 'the real task' of seeing how survivors talk about their experiences as though the two were so neatly discrete. As Hacking (1995, 2002, 2004) has argued, the naming or classification of phenomena has real effects on people and vice versa. Despite a tension within much of the literature, at times suggesting a chasm between policy and practice, we must be equally poised to recognise research fields and settings where it is sometimes tricky to decipher much of a gap.

Conclusion 217

From 'Public Issues' to 'Private Troubles': Fostering a Sociological Imagination Back to Front?

Early in the project it became clear that many, if not most, participants attending FfP events were linked to particularly 'high-profile' events. As Chapter 2 has already made clear, the FfP provided an apt site at which to learn more about how survivors themselves have come to terms with the impacts of political violence, including events said to have been seminal in ushering in the discourse of resilience such as the July 2005 London bombings (see Bean, Keränen and Durfy, 2011). Several events represented in the data also pre-date the so-called resilience creep (Walklate and Mythen, 2015) by years, even decades. However, they all shared a basic feature symptomatic of our broader social and cultural response to such violence; namely, details of such events are typically widely known about in the public domain. Far from being an entirely one-sided relationship, several survivors interviewed for this research and many more whom I met with during visits to the FfP had actively spoken with the media about their experiences either in the immediate aftermath or in the months and years that followed. The Parrys themselves are an emphatic example of this. This posed a number of interesting and challenging questions during the duration of this work. Such challenges are not unique to the study of high-profile critical incidents, such as bombings or shootings.

Nevertheless, they prompt reflection on C. Wright Mills' (2000: 8) oft-cited urge to think iteratively about personal milieu and social structure — that is, to see social life as being shaped partly by personal, private troubles and partly by public, structural issues. His work is often invoked in an attempt to elevate everyday or routine practice which is seen as private to the level of collective public knowledge. It is fair to say that this elevation of private, under-researched topics or otherwise 'hidden voice' has become something of a universally valued and desirable practice within contemporary social science. Reasons for this are no doubt many, varied, and complex but include both methodological and political imperatives depending on the research topic under study and the more generalised drive towards ensuring that social science research has the potential to evidence public impact. Methodologically, however, is this always desirable? Elevating private troubles to public issues has become the traditional job of the sociologist, particularly when addressing power imbalances (*qua* Becker, 1967; Gouldner, 1971). In some ways, however, this research needed to approach the power of public visibility the opposite way around. While Mills is correct in the examples he articulates (such as unemployment), the commonly accepted 'good' of rendering such issues public runs the risk of assuming two important things where high-profile political violence and terror attacks are concerned. Firstly, that the event is not already public enough which, as Chapter 3 shows, is seldom the case here. Terrorism, by definition, is invariably highly public; this research has instead attempted to learn more about the private troubles that lay behind it, which is often overlooked in public debate (see Chapter 2).

218 Conclusion

In many cases, while bereaved families might appreciate the rendering of such violence public in general, the space for privacy and the ability to reflect on personal troubles without being exposed publicly or experiencing media intrusion is often equally valued. Secondly, it fails to take account of timing. Short-term privacy around the actual doing of the research with sufficient time to elapse between fieldwork and writing details of research up publicly are important considerations that might be overlooked if researchers are only ever urged to 'make public' their work at the earliest opportunity. In the worst case, this risks compromising trust with participants, particularly where interviews were conducted only after lengthy periods of sensitively 'gaining access' (see McGowan, 2020).

A final consideration around researching high-profile events is managing preconceptions of them before speaking with actors directly involved. As with the issue of making participants comfortable before being interviewed by spending time with them during fieldwork, the only way to truly see beyond such preconceptions is to prolong contact time with them. This in no way constitutes in-depth familiarity with participants and their everyday, personal lives but does allow time for the more practical and mundane aspects of their lives to be articulated once details of their 'event' have been established, discussed, and better contextualised.

Argumentum ad hominem: **Researching a 'Noisy' Concept**

Reflecting on some of the challenges posed while completing this book, the practical tasks of gaining access, conducting fieldwork and interviews, and trying to make sense of participant's narratives sometimes felt easier to nego-tiate than the competing intellectual voices adding to the ever-growing debates around resilience, which provided obstacles of various kinds at every turn. Of course, I am not claiming that my interpretations of my participants' lives are the correct or definitive ones, nor was it ever 'easy' hearing such complex, emotionally charged, and harrowing stories. However, unlike the obstacles associated with practical doing of the research, such as those discussed above, along with ethical and analytical dilemmas (see McGowan, 2020 and McGowan and Cook, 2020, respectively), interpreting the resilience commentaries often felt frustrating and even futile. At times, the ubiquity of resilience in both aca-demic and public discourse seemed overwhelming. Between 2010 and the pre-sent, the sheer speed with which social science literatures relating to resilience grew meant that the classification or grouping of resilience 'camps' was almost inevitable. People simply cannot read or write such voluminous amounts of work without, in some ways, succumbing to the 'practical necessities of com-plexity reduction' (Jessop, 2010: 336) and organising that work into silos. These 'influences, oppositions, agreements, new oppositions, misunderstandings, distortions, denials, surpassings, etc' make up what Sartre (1968: 39) refers to as an *area history*. As more and more people contributed their studies, books,

Conclusion 219

interviews, conference papers, think pieces, blogs, news articles, tweets, and so on, it would become easy to label the contributors as 'policy scholars', 'government researchers', 'puppets of counterterrorism strategy', 'neocons', 'liberal philosophers', 'Marxists', or 'Foucauldian discourse theorists', for example. The sometimes questionable accuracy of such labels need not detract from the categorising function they serve.

In addition to making sense of this burgeoning mass of literature is the point made in Chapter 1 – resilience is intensely contested, and rightly so. Naturally, proponents of particular philosophical and political standpoints gravitate towards one another and guard against critique in numbers, thus partly defining themselves in relation to their 'opponents' (see Collins, 1998). Collins (1998) argues in his *Sociology of Philosophies* that the occupation of intellectual space relies either on the development of an idea, raising it beyond its current watermark or, as is more often the case, the opposite – dissecting, refuting, and challenging existing ideas. Both are typically driven by intellectual networks, practical opportunism, and the demand on both sides for cultural capital. In a relatively short period (particularly 2010–15), the number of articles and books pushing typologies or policies advocating resilience further than they had previously been developed were matched by ever-more damning critiques. In many ways, this seems a healthy state of affairs insofar as ideas did not remain unchallenged for long.

However, at times during the research this perpetual political battle seemed to offer more in the way of 'noise' and distraction than helpful analysis or sound argumentation. The fact that far more of these articles, whether 'pro' or 'anti', focus on resilience in the abstract rather than on practical or concrete empirical case studies exacerbates this propensity. Such distractions were (and are) often characterised by *ad hominem* arguments, whereby the considered qualities of individual accounts (whether positive or negative) seem to be side-lined by critics who attack resilience, resilience scholars, or resilience policies based on the presumed bad character of the author and what they ostensibly stand for – sometimes a defensible move but rarely a useful one – rather than through close empirical examination. In short, 'a case is argued not on its merits but by analysing (usually unfavourably) the motives or background of its supporters or opponents' (Hamblin, cited in Hinman, 1982: 338). Such analyses also tend to rely on polemic forms of delivery in which, paradoxically, the message is often lost. It is this communicative element, rather than its criticism, which is troubling. Of course, it is perfectly reasonable to argue that the self-interests, and therefore character, of individual agents is inextricably bound up with the argument being advanced, in which case such an approach may be warranted (Hitchcock, 2007). Thinking reflexively about my own motives for and experiences of researching resilience though, the concern here is with a generalised attitude, real or perceived, towards resilience which tends to tar researchers with the same brush purely by virtue of their bothering to study resilience at all in the first place. To return to Collins

220 Conclusion

(1998), both 'sides' lose out; those attacking the dominant viewpoint begin to ignore the finer points of each other's critique, such is the assumed (though often superficial) unanimity of their viewpoint, and those defending it continues to look the other way.

The following extract, taken from an interview with Foucault just before his death, aptly captures this communicative flaw.

> Of course, the reactivation, in polemics, of these political, judiciary, or religious practices is nothing more than theatre. One gesticulates: anathemas, excommunications, condemnations, battles, victories, and defeats are no more than ways of speaking, after all. And yet, in the order of discourse, they are also ways of acting which are not without consequence. There are the sterilizing effects: Has anyone ever seen a new idea come out of a polemic? And how could it be otherwise, given that here the interlocutors are incited, not to advance, not to take more and more risks in what they say, but to fall back continually on the rights that they claim, on their legitimacy, which they must defend, and on the affirmation of their innocence? There is something even more serious here: in this comedy, one mimics war, battles, annihilations, or unconditional surrenders, putting forward as much of one's killer instinct as possible. But it is really dangerous to make anyone believe that he can gain access to the truth by such paths, and thus to validate, even if in a merely symbolic form, the real political practices that could be warranted by it.
>
> (Foucault, 1984: 383)

On the question of polemic arguments, Foucault is explicitly critical, even stating ironically that he would shut the books of polemicists immediately. He also critiques the kind of 'knowledge' produced from such discussion as not constituting a search for truth or knowledge at all but merely a crusade on the part of the polemicist to prove they were right all along – winning the argument itself becomes the focus, not grappling with the substantive problem at hand, whatever that may be.

As Anderson (2015: 64) makes clear, dealing with the generality and specificity of social phenomena requires, among other things, a 'bracketing off' of information, including the political 'noise' surrounding cognate critiques of neoliberalism. He asks: 'How do we make resilience into an object of inquiry rather than reproduce consoling accounts that repeat what is already well known in other critiques of (neo)liberalism?' (Anderson, 2015: 64). This in no way means that political critique should not be brought back into our appraisal of the given subject as a whole once analyses of our data have concluded. On the contrary – eventually situating the findings from this project within the wider political and moral economies of trauma, resilience, austerity, and NGO practice remained a key objective throughout the research process. However, as Anderson (2015: 64) succinctly puts it: 'Connections between resilience and something else – say neoliberal ways of governing – should not be the premise of inquiry, but must be demonstrated'.

Alternative frames of reference for thinking about and talking about resilience are needed; both adherents to policy narratives and critics of resilience discourse have taken their relative appraisals to their limit, reaching something of an impasse. If I were to conduct this project anew, re-approaching the research questions and fieldwork with the luxury of hindsight, I would perhaps place less focus on the language of resilience altogether. As preceding chapters have shown, what we are typically talking about when we talk about 'resilience' often boils down to age-old social problems such as harm, adversity, and violence of various stripes, and how far we are able to exercise our resourcefulness, agency, and ultimately freedom. One reason for focusing on resilience was, ironically, the enormous attention the concept was receiving within policy and critical theoretical circles. In this sense I fully acknowledge my own role, no matter how small, in making up 'resilience' (a phrase and idea of philosopher Ian Hacking's that readers who have gotten this far will be more than familiar with by now) – at least the academic noise droning on in the background. 'Resilience', for all its allure and flexibility (as presented in Chapter 7), seems almost perpetually inadequate – whether the aim is to construct psychological resilience models or to reclaim its utility from the jaws of the 'psy' disciplines (Rose, 1998), policymakers, and neoliberal economists. It sometimes seemed cumbersome and unhelpful when trying to elicit and make sense of individual survivors' journeys of suffering, strength, and coping over time. Repeatedly it was found to be unsatisfactory or inappropriate as a frame of reference or analytical concept to help make sense of human suffering and our responses to it. Arguably, it has become warped and tainted by the academic turf wars that have surrounded its use, particularly over the last decade, to the point that clarifying one's position towards the concept seems to have taken precedent over close empirical scrutiny (contra Anderson, 2015).

A concrete example of this came when attending an academic conference in early 2017 and speaking with an eminent and well-respected scholar whose work on resilience has drawn upon, and spoken to, a panoply of disciplines including criminology, sociology, philosophy, and international relations. After they had delivered their paper we spoke over coffee about various topics including their work in progress, this project, and about our relative experiences of working with and on this ubiquitous concept of resilience. Both of us shared and recognised the problem of conducting empirical fieldwork while avoiding the error of simply importing the language of that which we were initially interested in into our analyses and findings. What was even more telling, however, was the deeply reflexive account this scholar disclosed when talking about presenting at conferences. Apparently, they found themselves behaving

222 Conclusion

differently in front of predominantly policy-oriented audiences, which they would often find at conferences mostly frequented by international relations or social policy scholars, compared to supposedly more critical sociology and criminology audiences. Presenting to the latter, they felt the need to first explicitly rubbish the notion of resilience, making clear where their politics lay before even presenting their analytical arguments. In other contexts, however, they would offer a more careful and nuanced analysis if they felt less likely to be misunderstood as somehow unquestioningly endorsing whatever low opinions they assumed the audience would have of those nasty, neoliberal resilience discourses. This was an interesting exchange for two reasons. Firstly, the conference we were attending had a predominant focus on international relations and social policy and I was fortunate enough to hear this scholar's more nuanced account which I found measured, convincing, and no less critical than any I had heard previously. Secondly, it chimed with my own experiences of finding the analytical and political 'noise' generated by the term distracting, particularly so when trying to make sense of my fieldwork.

Evans and Reid's (2015: 154) view that resilience represents a politically and intellectually exhausted problématique also chimes with some of the reservations expressed in this conclusion:

> Our journey across the resilience terrain forced us to appreciate the hidden depth of its nihilism, the pernicious forms of subjugation it burdens people with, its deceitful emancipatory claims that force people to embrace their servitude as though it were their liberation, and the lack of imagination the resiliently minded possess in terms of transforming the world for the better. We too have become exhausted by its ubiquitous weight and the chains it places around all our necks.
>
> (Evans and Reid, 2015: 154)

This is certainly true of the abstract and futile debates alluded to above, which have fast become shackled caricatures, or 'images of thought' to use Evans and Reid's (2015: 158) Deleuzian parlance. In a similar vein, Reghezza-Zitt and Rufat (2015: 201) argue that 'resilience is buzzing to the point of becoming a victim of its own success'. However, in spite of such criticisms, the most pertinent observation made in the last section around representation remains – ideals of resilience, put into practice and enacted in an observable space, have produced something positive for survivors searching for a way through deeply challenging experiences. Amid all the noise generated by 'resilience', this relatively mundane, unremarkable and yet transformative process for so many survivors has ticked on in the background. If researching an area of frenzied interest and current vogue in the social sciences taught me anything, it is that we fix our gaze on such foregrounding concepts and ignore these quiet, everyday and ordinary backgrounds at our ultimate peril.

Future Research Trajectories

Facing the Emotional Consequences of Suffering, Harm, and Loss: On Sameness and Difference, Uniqueness and Commonality

Reflecting on this project's findings prompts a return to Fassin and Rechtman's (2009: 281) claim that trauma subsumes disparate phenomena, thus 'obliterating experience', under one banner. In acknowledging critiques of trauma discourse, such as Fassin and Rechtman's, we need to be careful not to replicate similar reductionism when turning to notions of resilience, recovery, or more clinical ideas around post-traumatic growth. In other words, if universalising catchall conceptualisations of trauma are too reductionist, then surely the same is true of its obverse. Space has not permitted a fuller exploration of this. As we have seen, many facets of resilience identified here boil down to broad themes long recognised in the social sciences, such as connectedness, belonging, and solidarity, which are pertinent to a range of more 'everyday' negative or adverse events than PVT. It is striking to note the overlaps in reported emotions between injured, aggrieved, and bereaved people from a whole host of events including natural deaths, road traffic accidents, life-threatening and terminal illness, to name just a few examples of suffering visited upon individuals, families, and communities every day – far more regularly than the spectacle of terrorism.

Arthur Frank's (2013) *The Wounded Storyteller*, to take one example, provokes questions around storytelling practices that resonate with the narratives analysed here. What is the function of survivor testimony? How do such testimonies shape (and are shaped by) the psychopolitics of 'self-optimization' (Han, 2017)? What is the relation between these late-modern forms of 'self-optimization' (Han, 2017) or 'self-improvement' (Hacking, 2002: 115) and the confessional practices associated with the asceticism of earlier periods? How far have consumerist ethics, mobilised through new media devices and platforms (cf. Bauman, 2007; Beer, 2008), intermingled with the confessional, the human condition, and the human need to talk and to tell? Again, in posing these more sprawling questions, there is a danger that disparate forms of coping, recovery, or resilience to/from a plethora of negative experiences are reduced to some set of essential features, realised in part through testimonial storytelling, almost irrespective of their specific nature. Like the search for trauma's essence, said to 'obliterate experience' by concreting over heterogeneity, this risk is easily replicated elsewhere. However, if future studies of emotion are to truly explore the range of human potentiality, then questioning the lines between sameness/difference and uniqueness/commonality across different adverse life course events at different and technologically changing points in history is surely an important starting point.

224 Conclusion

Further Inquiry into the Temporal Dialectics of Ontological Security

Several times during this research, individuals with clearly challenging personal circumstances have continued to evidence immense strength, perhaps even more so during times of great instability. It seems adversity can often promote inherent resilience, particularly during times of instability, where other layers of 'resilience resources' (Overland, 2013: 204) are absent or strained. In contrast, depending on individual circumstances, periods of relative stability and calm in people's lives sometimes facilitate wider sources of support at other levels (e.g. familial, communal). The individual then has 'space to breathe', reflect, think of themselves and others dear to them more introspectively. This might not necessarily be caused by obvious or spectacular adversities but could rather be simple, yet important, things such as isolation and loneliness.

Emotional setbacks, which affected all participants in this study periodically, require a degree of introspection and contemplation. Several survivors spoke of being 'blindsided' by such setbacks which often came 'out of the blue' during otherwise positive and stable periods. Again, the amount of time between a critical incident and the interviews conducted here seemed pertinent. Survivors of more recent attacks would often describe the incident itself more viscerally. Due to more recent absences from work and other forms of instability, they would perhaps rely more, perhaps even primarily, on their individual ability to just 'get on'. This was certainly true of George, Amanda, and Karen. In contrast, those reflecting on events from much longer ago have built up familiar support structures around that event, such as friends, family, partners, their faith, and so on, all of which provide strength. However, collective resilience resources such as family and friendships also allow and facilitate the recognition of adversity and the sharing of past experiences. With such recognition can come periodic challenges. Seeking the support and recognition of others also means you give yourself the space and opportunity to disclose issues rather than stoically 'soldiering on'. Seeking support in this way may be beneficial but requires sharing otherwise suppressed emotions. In some ways, those who keep a relatively closed lid on their emotions, relying instead on stoicism, appear outwardly better equipped to tackle whatever contingencies life unexpectedly throws at them.

None of this is to say that adversity or instability is desirable. This is the main criticism of resilience-based policymaking. Rather, it triggers and often brings forth particular levels of resilience over and above others at different times and according to different conditions. People still need periodic support during times of relative stability, but they may be better placed to find this at other levels as well as individually. Interestingly, it is those survivors who appear to have reached periods of stability in their lives who are invited by the FfP to share their experiences and to engage in the practice of storytelling. While offering support, this could also act as a periodic reinforcement which potentially retains

Conclusion 225

an association with a 'terrorist survivor identity' (see Chapter 6). These are all moot observations in need of further research. They need not necessarily draw on notions of resilience explicitly, but might rather key in with existing work around time and belonging (see, for example, May, 2016, 2017).

Resilience in Action: The Making and Moulding of 'Resilient' Communities

To reiterate a point made in Chapter 6 over a decade on since the financial crisis of 2008–9 and the subsequent implementation of austerity measures in the UK, it seems an apposite time to reflect on the real, imagined, and unintended ways in which resilience has been bestowed upon, expected of, or directed by notions of 'community'. Chapter 6 showed that 'community' in this context may represent something akin to Anderson's (2006) 'imagined community', but also a concrete and material one that comes into being. As this work has argued, this warrants a close examination of situated, empirical, and case study examples which may offer fresh insights for theoretical scholars to work with. Prioritising neither psychological factors over social ones and vice versa, recognising that both are important and neither 'stay still' for very long, and questioning the conception of community as a pre-existing (if imagined) entity to which resilience is bestowed, directed, or expected, this research tentatively suggests that the creation of new communities could in and of itself constitute *resilience in action*. This idea is posited in light of data collected from what we might understand as a 'survivor community'; exploring how notions of *resilience as doing* resonate and play out in other settings is one avenue to explore against a more than sufficient backcloth of theoretical 'scene setting'. This work would also dovetail and contribute to an emergent empirical literature on resilience and community (see Wright, 2016; Zebrowski and Sage, 2017).

Reappraising Violence and Its Spaces

This research journey has revealed the diversity and multifaceted potential of our responses to adversity. As productive as this has been and is, it has also revealed that there are limits to this type of approach to studying violence, harm, and bereavement — that is, from this angle. This is not because it is not fruitful to do so, as this book hopefully testifies. Throughout the book and alongside these incredible responses to adversity are also myriad sources from which violence stems and can therefore be studied. In ongoing and future work, I intend to focus further attentions on studying the social conditions and economic forms that make many of the material stumbling blocks discussed here (such as inquests, funeral arrangements, access to work and finance, and so on) operate as they do. In short, drawing out more of the material conditions for violence in its broadest sense, for the things we rely upon to negotiate the aftereffects of violence, and to investigate social welfare provision as a key component to combatting violence. This also links closely to the note on theory and method discussed in the introduction where I set out several reservations about the methodological status of qualitative research focused heavily on the collection and analysis of narrative data. Far from suggesting a lack of utility in this kind of work, or urging others to abandon it, this shift in emphasis instead simply intends to take seriously the need to explore violence not as a narrow or confined field of phenomena and study, but rather as a broad, diverse and 'essentially contested concept' (de Haan, 2008).

Conclusion

In Chapter 1, the scene was set for how the discourse of terror and our responses to it became enmeshed in actual incidents of terror. At the same time that our governments were busying themselves with communicating an omnipresent terror *threat* for political expediency, societies occasionally found themselves having to confront the exceptionally rare, though no less devastating, realities of deadly political violence and terrorism. Deadly violence of the sort alluded to in the Terrorism Act 2000, or the Civil Contingencies Act 2004, or the Counter-Terrorism and Security Act 2015, among others, is clearly not new. Nor is it even close to constituting the greatest 'existential threat' facing our society, as former UK Prime Minister David Cameron once claimed it was. Moreover, as is self-evident, only certain lives are deemed countable, indisposable, and grievable (Butler, 2004). The above legislation, and the general nationalistic mood music that serenaded 'resilience' as a stock response to public issues, was blind to so much history, to so much specificity, and to so many private troubles.

But it has also been productive of a range of unintended, or at least unforeseen, consequences for some. Indeed, some people, including some of the survivors discussed here, and including from events long pre-dating this contemporary way of urging self-optimisation, self-improvement, and self-care, have found themselves making sense of their pasts in a present where talk of resilience is familiar. Familiarity enables action of particular kinds. This need not be desirable for it to be nonetheless so. The discourse of resilience has furnished many pernicious things. It has also found a marriage of convenience within supportive and therapeutic settings, at times characterised by individual responsibility, entrepreneurialism and moral self-admonishment, at others characterised by collective reckoning, mutual aid, solidarity, and interpersonal empowerment. In this sense, and perhaps the take-home message of the book as far as resilience is concerned, is that seldom are things wholly good or wholly bad. However, as Diprose (2015) makes clear in her nuanced critique of resilience, resilience does not have to be wholly bad for it to be politically undesirable. In many ways it is a low bar to aspire to and will always remain so in societies so perennially characterised by avoidable and yet worsening inequality and harm. As a go-to solution in these macro public contexts, resilience necessarily has a different feel and character to private, local, and organic practices of agency in the face

Conclusion 227

of adversity where people's abilities to cope with difficult and often worsening structural conditions must never be assumed to shore up shortcomings in adequately resourced services, or utilised for political expediency.

This book has illustrated a complexity and nuance to resilience, acknowledging analytic elements from both its proponents and critics. In doing so, it contributes to an emergent, but growing, body of work emphasising the heterogeneity of resilience and questioning 'the subordination of resilience to neoliberal ideology' (Zebrowski and Sage, 2017: 53; see also Anderson, 2015; Howell, 2015; Sage, Fussey and Dainty, 2015; Zebrowski, 2016). Embracing the notion of 'resilience to financial crises' at the behest of global organisations such as IMF, in whose interest it is that populations respond favourably to often dire economic conditions, is quite different to reconciling those factors or moments throughout the life course that have proven to be 'turning points' for survivors of PVT. Trying to make sense of how such actors at the individual level, first and foremost, embody and contradict (often simultaneously) something akin to resilience and how this intersects with resilience across a range of other levels (the familial, the communal, the political) is, in short, an entirely different empirical proposition. Though analyses of 'resilience' at the level of discourse are critical in providing a backcloth against which to consider historical moments when concepts have found favour in particular contexts and places, it alone cannot 'build up' to a true understanding of the phenomena such discourses aim to describe. In noting the general trajectory of risk to resilience and, specifically, the conflation within counterterror legislation of risk, vulnerability, and resilience (see Chapter 1), we must respond critically to the resultant erosion of human agency and our understandings of it (Walklate and Mythen, 2015: 144–6). Moreover, we should recognise familiar aspects of this erosion, which may not necessitate the reinvention of 'new' solutions to old problems. The statement: '[p]erception and experience of risk cannot *but* be mediated by individual biography as well as dominant institutional discourses' (Mythen and Walklate, 2006: 393, emphasis in original) is as true in relation to resilience today as it was to risk yesterday (Chapter 1 explored this shift, demonstrating clear overlap rather than disjuncture). The task now, after a particularly intensive decade of 'resilience research', is to confirm, challenge, and substantiate theoretical trajectories of critique with close empirical analysis.

This book has also highlighted and problematised some inherently future-facing tendencies of the resilience agenda which have been said to promote 'insecurity by design' (Evans and Reid, 2014: 1). This dystopian imaginary may be rhetorically palpable at the level of 'big policy', but many academics have been so keen to emphasise this that the practice of looking backwards has too often been lost in the clamour. While several sociological critiques rest on the premise that resilience-based counterterrorism polices are aimed at preparing potential victims for future disaster while exculpating state and security agencies, far fewer have channelled their analytical energies into considering what resilience might look like for survivors reflecting on current and

228 Conclusion

retrospective experience. By pursuing this question, academics, policymakers, and voluntary sector organisations would surely be better placed to decide which elements of legislation and discourse pertaining to resilience actually capture the reality of living with trauma and suffering in the aftermath of PVT. As Cavelty, Kaufmann and Kristensen (2015: 8) argue:

> [T]here is theoretical as well as critical value in abandoning singular conceptualizations of resilience for an exploration of the multiplicity of subjectification processes – repressive as well as emancipatory – associated with resilience. It is necessary to move beyond positioning 'resilient subjects' simply as an effect of broader rationalities and practices of liberal governance. There is no such thing as *the* resilient subject – there is a vast variety of resilient subjects.

The task for a thoroughgoing sociological analysis of resilience in the aftermath of PVT is to begin, and proceed, with this guiding principle. To experience PVT in London is not to experience it in Paris, much less to experience it in Bama, or Gaza. This selection may seem arbitrary, but the point is that if social science is to get anywhere near an understanding of what PVT means for the people it affects, it must always question familiar frames of reference produced by universalising Western discourse (Walklate and Mythen, 2015: 178).

This research has shown, through empirical examples and analysis, how inherent resilience in a range of guises affects and moulds individuals and groups' experiences of PVT revealing that during this process a great deal of individual agency, first and foremost, is exercised and expressed. It has grappled with some of the ways in which this agency has been shaped by social structure but maintains that individual cases cannot be shoehorned into prevailing assumptions about what resilience may, or should, look like. It is not argued that there are necessarily generalisable 'hallmarks' of inherent resilience, nor that resilience is a useful concept to be deployed in all areas of policy, research, and discourse. As earlier chapters explained, resilience has been repeatedly couched as forming part of a broader and more insidious political motif when deployed as an organising metaphor in 'big policy', in which subjects are not only 'nudged' (Goodwin, 2012; Mythen, Walklate and Kemshall, 2012) towards an acceptance of 'their lot', but conditioned to perpetually expect the unexpected, even when the unexpected is already a well-established and all too familiar reality.

In relation to survivors of PVT, fewer attempts have been made to find out what these 'resilient subjects' look and sound like, rendering problematic the universal assertion that 'catastrophe has no consideration for [victim] subjectivity' (Evans and Reid, 2014: 20). This assertion may be an apt way to describe neoliberal, solution-based responses to risk and security but, equally, simplifies the complex workings of human experience. In this respect, notions of resilience may prove fruitful for survivors. The study of victims has long focused on how people become *victimised* and the myriad struggles they face, but questions of how people move beyond victimised identities are often secondary or ignored altogether (important exceptions recently include Green and Pemberton (2018) and Green, Calverley and O'Leary (2021)). This is an important and aspirational move for victims and should render questions about the merits and importance of resilience, at least in this specific context, self-explanatory, allowing for a 'bolder phenomenology of the victim' (Rock, 2002: 22) to flourish. Put differently, if resilience is, for many, a 'normal' response built on natural, innate qualities, as well as social and collective resources, which occurs in the aftermath of many critical and traumatic incidents then it clearly constitutes an important area of study which this book has taken seriously.

Resilience is not an endpoint but is processual and relational. In lieu of a definition or theory based on the findings of this book, we can at least say for certain that resilience is not a destination arrived at, but rather a journey travelled, which is likely to be travelled many, many times over during the course of a human lifetime. In light of the data and analysis presented in Chapters 3–7, coupled with the epistemological dynamism of Hacking's (1995, 2002, 2004) dialectical realism, there are two reasons for this. Firstly, people change over time – as do material circumstances which may have better enabled them to cope at certain points and not at others. Secondly, the information we have about people, and therefore ourselves, changes over time. This includes diagnoses, therapies, NGO remits, NGO terminologies, inquests, tribunals, government committee priorities, language used to describe perpetrators, language used to describe victims, precedents around victim compensation, memorialisation, remembrance practices, and so on, all of which are capable of producing, in Hackingian terms, *actions under new descriptions*. The extent to which the language of 'resilience' genuinely offers a sustained break from previous ways of talking about, and 'working with/on' (O'Malley, 2006: 52), victims of political violence more broadly might remain a moot point. We will not know this more fully without the luxury of hindsight, nor without continually comparing cases. However, the glimpse presented here, for that is all it is, into the practices of the FfP and the lives of some of its participants, coupled with the primacy 'resilience' still enjoys within the lofty echelons of international policy, should encourage us to think twice before dismissing its long-term sway out of hand.

References

Alexander, J.C. (2012) *Trauma: A Social Theory*. Cambridge: Polity Press.

Anderson, B. (2006) *Imagined Communities: Reflections on the Origin and Spread of Nationalism*. London: Verso.

Anderson, B. (2015) What kind of thing is resilience? *Politics* 35(1): 60–6.

Bauman, Z. (2007) *Consuming Life*. Cambridge: Polity Press.

Bean, H., Keränen, L. and Durfy, M. (2011) "This Is London": Cosmopolitan Nationalism and the Discourse of Resilience in the Case of the 7/7 Terrorist Attacks. *Rhetoric & Public Affairs* 14(3): 427–64.

230 Conclusion

Becker, H.S. (1967) Whose Side Are We On? *Social Problems* 14(3): 239–47.

Beer, D. (2008) Researching a confessional society. *International Journal of Market Research* 50(5): 619–29.

Butler, J. (2004) *Precarious Life: The Powers of Mourning and Violence.* London: Verso.

Cavelty, M.D., Kaufmann, M. and Kristensen, K.S. (2015) Resilience and (in) security: Practices, subjects, temporalities. *Security Dialogue* 46(1): 3–14.

Collins, R. (1998) *The Sociology of Philosophies: A global theory of intellectual change.* Cambridge: Harvard University Press.

de Haan, W. (2008) Violence as an essentially contested concept. In S. Body-Gendrot and P. Spierenburg (Eds.) *Violence in Europe.* New York: Springer. pp.27–40.

Diprose, K. (2015) Resilience is futile. *Soundings: A journal of politics and culture* 58: 44–56.

Evans, B. and Reid, J. (2014) *Resilient Life: The Art of Living Dangerously.* Cambridge: Polity Press.

Evans, B. and Reid, J. (2015) Exhausted by resilience: Response to the commentaries. *Resilience: International Policies, Practices and Discourses* 3(2): 154–9.

Fassin, D. and Rechtman, R. (2009) *The Empire of Trauma: An Inquiry into the Condition of Victimhood.* Oxford: Princeton University Press.

Foucault, M. (1984) Polemics, politics, and problemizations: An interview with Michel Foucault. In P. Rabinow (Ed.) *The Foucault Reader: An Introduction to Foucault's Thought.* London: Penguin Books. pp.381–90.

Frank, A.W. (2013) *The Wounded Storyteller: Boy, Illness & Ethics.* Chicago: The University of Chicago Press.

Furedi, F. (2007) From the Narrative of the Blitz to the Rhetoric of Vulnerability. *Cultural Sociology* 1(2): 235–54.

Goodwin, T. (2012) Why we should reject 'nudge'. *Politics* 32(2): 85–92.

Gouldner, A.W. (1971) *The Coming Crisis of Western Sociology.* London: Heinemann Educational Publishers.

Green, S. and Pemberton, A. (2018) The impact of crime: Victimisation, harm and resilience. In S. Walklate (Ed.) *Handbook of Victims and Victimology.* 2nd edition. London: Routledge. pp.77–101.

Green, S., Calverley, A. and O'Leary, N. (2021) A new approach for researching victims: The 'strength-growth-resilience' framework. *The British Journal of Criminology* 61(3): 852–71.

Hacking, I. (1995) *Rewriting the Soul: Multiple Personality and the Sciences of Memory.* Princeton, NJ: Princeton University Press.

Hacking, I. (2002) *Historical Ontology.* Cambridge: Harvard University Press.

Hacking, I. (2004) Between Michel Foucault and Erving Goffman: Between discourse in the abstract and face-to-face interaction. *Economy and Society* 33(3): 277–302.

Hacking, I. (2006) Genetics, biosocial groups and the future of identity. *Daedalus* 135(4): 81–95.

Han, B.C. (2017) *Psychopolitics: Neoliberalism and New Technologies of Power.* London: Verso.

Hinman, L.M. (1982) The case for *ad hominem* arguments. *Australasian Journal of Philosophy* 60(4): 338–45.

Hitchcock, D. (2007) Is there an *Argumentum Ad Hominem* Fallacy? In H.V. Hansen and R.C. Pinto (Eds.) *Reason Reclaimed : Essays in Honor of J. Anthony Blair and Ralph H. Johnson.* Newport News: Vale Press.

Howell, A. (2015) Resilience as enhancement: Governmentality and political economy beyond 'responsibilisation'. *Politics* 35(1): 67–71.

Jessop, B. (2010) Cultural political economy and critical policy studies. *Critical Policy Studies* 3(3–4): 336–56.

Krause, M. (2014) *The Good Project: Humanitarian Relief NGOs and the Fragmentation of Reason*. Chicago: The University of Chicago Press.

May, V. (2016) What does the duration of belonging tell us about the temporal self? *Time & Society* 25(3): 634–51.

May, V. (2017) Belonging across the lifetime: Time and self in Mass Observation accounts. *The British Journal of Sociology* doi:10.1111/1468-4446.12276.

McGowan, W. (2020) 'If you didn't laugh, you'd cry': Emotional labour, reflexivity, and ethics-as-practice in a qualitative fieldwork context. *Methodological Innovations* 13(2): 1–10.

McGowan, W. and Cook, E.A. (2020) Comprehensive or comprehensible experience? A case study of religion and traumatic bereavement. *Sociological Research Online* 26(4): 775–91 doi: 10.1177/1360780420978662.

Mills, C.W. (2000) *The Sociological Imagination*. New York: Oxford University Press.

Ministry of Justice (2012) *The Victims of Overseas Terrorism Compensation Scheme 2012*. London: Crown copyright.

Mythen, G. and Walklate, S. (2006) Criminology and terrorism: Which thesis? Risk society or governmentality? *British Journal of Criminology* 46(3): 379–98.

Mythen, G., Walklate, S. and Kemshall, H. (2012) Decentralizing risk: The role of the voluntary and community sector in the management of offenders. *Criminology and Criminal Justice* 13(4): 363–79.

O'Malley, P. (2006) Criminology and risk. In G. Mythen and S. Walklate (Eds.) *Beyond the Risk Society: Critical Reflections on Risk and Human Security*. Berkshire: Open University Press. pp.43–60.

Overland, G. (2013) *Post Traumatic Survival: The Lessons of Cambodian Resilience*. Newcastle upon Tyne: Cambridge Scholars Publishing.

Reghezza-Zitt, M. and Rufat, S. (2015) *Resilience Imperative: Uncertainty, Risks and Disasters*. Oxford: Elsevier.

Rock, P. (2002) On becoming a victim. In C. Hoyle and R. Young (Eds.) *New Visions of Crime Victims*. Oxford: Hart Publishing. pp.1–22.

Rose, N. (1998) *Inventing Our Selves: Psychology, Power and Personhood*. Cambridge: Cambridge University Press.

Sage, D., Fussey, P. and Dainty, A. (2015) Securing and scaling resilient futures: Neoliberalization, infrastructure, and topologies of power. *Environment and Planning D: Society and Space* 33(3): 494–511.

Sartre, J.P. (1968) *Search for a Method*. New York: Vintage Books.

Walklate, S. (2016) The metamorphosis of the victim of crime: From crime to culture and the implications for justice. *International Journal for Crime, Justice and Social Democracy* 5(4): 4–16.

Walklate, S. (2018) Introduction and overview. In S. Walklate (Ed.) *Handbook of Victims and Victimology*, 2nd edition. London: Routledge. pp.9–12.

Walklate, S. and Mythen, G. (2015) *Contradictions of Terrorism: Security, Risk and Resilience*. London: Routledge.

Wright, K. (2016) Resilient communities? Experiences of risk and resilience in a time of austerity. *International Journal of Disaster Risk Reduction* 18: 154–61.

Zebrowski, C. (2016) *The Value of Resilience: Securing Life in the 21st Century*. London: Routledge.

Zebrowski, C. and Sage, D. (2017) Organising community resilience: An examination of the forms of sociality promoted in community resilience programmes. *Resilience: International Policies, Practices and Discourses* 5(1): 44–60.

Methodological Appendix

This appended chapter contains information about my research questions, participants, the process of conducting my fieldwork, and some reflections on research ethics. It is typical to see this kind of methodological material removed from monographs such as this, and it is true that a lot of methodological analysis is woven into the book at various points. However, as a point of reference for readers to dip in and out of as they read through the main chapters, it is hoped that this methodological appendix provides a clear and useful roadmap to help make quicker sense of some of the 'background' work that went into the project (of course, this is never really in the background). Both the brief 'pen portraits' of my participants and Table A.1, which give a breakdown of the kinds of historical dates and incidents these survivors have experienced, will be particularly useful for readers, I think, to flick back to as they read through the interview data presented in Chapters 3–5.

Research Questions

Chapters 1 and 2 respectively considered the shortcomings of studying 'resilience' exclusively at the level of policy discourse and the need to direct our attention to survivors themselves. Reflecting these combined considerations, my first research question was:

> 1. *What do survivors of political violence and terrorism understand by resilience in the context of their experiences of trauma, both physical and mental?*

'Taking seriously' existing empirical studies around what resilience might look like, as Chapter 1 did, while remaining alert to the necessarily situated and context-specific practices underpinning them, the second research question concerned the thoughts, feelings, circumstances, or practices which might variously contribute to anything resembling 'resilience' within survivors' self-narration:

234 Methodological Appendix

2. *What fundamental 'resilience resources' (qua Overland, 2013: 204) (personal, familial, social, practice-oriented) are harnessed by survivors in the aftermath of political violence and terrorism?*

Finally, reflecting the need to better account for the temporal complexity of lived experience, contra the one-dimensional futurity of resilience policy discourse (Schott, 2015: 186), the third research question was framed as follows:

3. *To what extent is resilience pertinent in survivors' narratives of their experiences of managing trauma? (In particular, is resilience a process or are there critical moments at which resilience is stimulated and/or generated?)*

While all three questions were addressed at various points throughout Chapters 3–5, and then explored in a more synthesised and theoretically informed series of discussions in Chapters 6 and 7, the issue of 'processes' and 'moments' being stimulated, generated, and indeed challenged were considered closely in Chapter 6. There I considered two particular interviews and their participants' narratives at length as ideal-typical examples of two contrasting 'resilience narratives'.

Research Design

Negotiating Access, Building Rapport, and Getting a Glimpse of Organisational Practice

Fieldwork visits were made to the Foundation for Peace (see Chapter 2) well in advance of any of the interviews that appear in this book in order to familiarise myself with their activities and their participants, some of whom would go on to become research participants in this project. The organisation works with a vast number of survivors with wide and disparate experiences of conflict from around the world, and so it was useful to be able to access as much of this information as possible in advance of conducting interviews. The Foundation keeps a database of their participants, including some basic demographic information, which similarly aided preparation for attendance at their many events and workshops.

During this period, extensive field notes were taken in order to identify key areas of work undertaken by the Foundation and ascertain how their activities intersect with the broad aims of the charity. After a period of between 14 and 18 months, during which time many FfP participants were introduced to me and my research, in-depth interviews were used to explore individual narratives in more detail. The ongoing period of visits to the Foundation, with the support and supervision of FfP staff, allowed prospective participants who had been met during the course of this fieldwork to be approached and asked if they would like to participate in the project. Many showed great interest in

Methodological Appendix 235

the project without being directly approached and some had already made direct enquiries during earlier fieldwork visits about taking part. This elongated phase of 'gaining access' should be understood more accurately as an immersive process in which time was informally spent, and casual conversations allowed to play out, without an immediate intrusion into people's lives or a purely instrumental approach to 'data collection'. It also allowed people to express themselves 'off the record' before committing to a recorded interview, approximating something akin to Forsey's (2010) 'ethnography as participant listening' without the full immersion required to constitute ethnography as 'deep hanging out' (Geertz, 1998). While more solid participant recruitment became a realistic necessity, it was not a primary consideration for at least the first year to 18 months of the fieldwork.

Due to staff changes at the Foundation during the research, access was continually renegotiated. Changes in the way staff work may have had an impact on our working relationship, although all changes caused minimal disruption due to the fact that all staff were known and knew me and we had plenty of opportunities to meet and re-evaluate the research trajectory.

Data Collection

While ongoing visits to the Foundation proved invaluable for a number of reasons outlined above, in-depth interviews designed to document thick descriptions of participants' experiences and reflections on their biographical journeys as survivors were used as the primary data collection method. The telling of stories, personal experiences, and life histories more generally is deemed here to represent a biographical method insofar as its aim is to 'describe turning-point moments in individuals' lives' (Denzin, 1989: 7). Interviews enabled analysis to move from the more general enquiry of earlier visits to the FfP, during which words such as 'resilience', 'trauma', 'survivor', and 'terrorism' would be used and discussed by participants and staff, often in quite a general sense, to more specific personal experiences. Many of the meanings ascribed to the above terms largely mirrored government policy interpretations reproduced during FfP events. Individual in-depth interviews allowed the possibility of developing an iterative process of subjectivity-exploration in the Sartrean tradition of a progressive–regressive method (Sartre, 1968), moving forwards and backwards in time from a significant event in an individual's life (Denzin, 1989: 67). The temporality of trauma and resilience explored in previous chapters underscores the importance of this approach, in which the activities of a subject are explored multi-directionally, before and after the event in question. For example, how much time elapsed since the initial incident before an individual sought support? How have their lives differed from before this incident? How long have participants been in contact with the Foundation? What made them want to attend their events? Exploring the biographical and historical experiences of individuals in this way led to several participants recalling critical moments at which they felt fortified or at which coping was accentuated or challenged. For example, some participants turned more strongly to their religious faith in order to cope with their pain and loss. Others described becoming more involved with political activism as a way of rendering their loss meaningful in proactive ways. This emphasis on meaning-making was a salient, though heterogeneous pattern to emerge from the interviews. For others, it prompted them to talk about how physical injuries have prohibited them from pursuing the same work and leisure activities as before.

Narratives can be explored through interview techniques in a number of ways including longitudinal or repeat interviews or, more commonly, single interviews of considerable length (see Elliott, 2005: 17). Given that the interviews were likely to be conducted over a relatively short space of time, the benefits of longitudinal interviewing were deemed questionable. Research in cognitive psychology has highlighted the discrepancies of memory when recalling the same traumatic events repeatedly, with people's recall of particular memorable events changing significantly from their initial responses, meaning there is potential scope for repeat interviewing if the aim of the research was to test memory. However, it was not my intention to follow 'experimental' methods and memory of trauma was only ever one related aspect of this research. Rather than drafting identical interview schedules, observations made during fieldwork visits were revisited as points of departure before each interview. Some interviews drew upon these notes more closely than others but few, if any, followed a definitive set of prompts exactly. Relationships had already been forged with participants and most interviews were simply prompting participants to retell or expand upon stories that had been partially shared already. Differential familiarity with participants and the sensitive nature of topics under discussion meant that each interview really needed to be approached afresh. However, most interviews began by asking participants when they started attending FfP events, what brought them to this place, or something around such circumstances. This inevitably, though sensitively, led to a broader discussion about the critical incidents in question. The interviews ranged in duration from one hour to over three hours so inevitably the scope of discussion extended far more broadly than just the few questions or points of interest brought up in the form of prearranged questions.

Questions were typically based on interesting topics or patterns noticed during fieldwork and in asking about them further they would invariably feature importantly during analysis and findings, representing neither deductive nor totally inductive analysis but something closer to Tavory and Timmermans' (2014) abductive analysis (see Data Analysis section below). Each participant had his or her own way of 'settling into' the interview and this was often shaped by our previous interactions and amount of verbal contact at previous FfP events. However, the way that I conducted the interviews also developed over time. There were three main 'stints' of data collection with gaps of several weeks or even months in between which allowed for a reflection on interview practice. In initial interviews where we began by discussing the event itself, discussion often did not move very far beyond that. Jane, for example, spent considerable time explaining how the day of her attack unfolded in minute detail. In subsequent interviews where I first asked participants where they had grown up or about life in general prior to the event, participants seemed to eventually navigate to the event of their own accord as part of their broader personal and biographical background (*qua* Denzin, 1989). As well as putting people at ease, this offered insight into how prominently and where the event fitted into the overall narration of their lives. Starting interviews roughly chronologically in this way, either by asking questions about their earlier lives or simply by asking: 'So, when did you first attend the FfP?' seemed to facilitate this natural moving onto discussion of a particular critical incident but did not prohibit episodic recall of events either and so this approach was adopted for all remaining interviews.

Participant Information and Sample Diversity

The heterogeneity of the conflicts and incidents represented in this book is reflective of both the FfP's variegated participant base and, concomitantly, the result of opportunistically snowball sampling from this diverse group. While visiting the Foundation, observing its storytelling and dialogue-based events and then conducting the interviews analysed here, one of the obvious, though no less important, distinctions between interviewees which became apparent was differences in who was responsible for perpetrating extreme violence against them or their family. While these incidents span a diverse time/place range, it is possible to group or categorise them as either institutional, authorised violence committed 'from above', typically by state actors (e.g. the shooting of innocent protestors by the British military in Northern Ireland in 1972), or as anti-institutional, unauthorised violence committed 'from below', typically by non-state actors (e.g. the 2005 London bombings) (Ruggiero, 2006: 1). It is tempting to simplify this categorisation further into 'state' and 'non-state' terrorism, although this distinction is hardly useful for cases of state-sponsored terrorism or state collusion with paramilitary groups (see Green and Ward, 2004: 105–23; Chomsky, 2015). For the purpose of this book, such distinctions are nonetheless important because they have clear and palpable implications for the ways in which survivors articulated their sense of loss, injury, or (in)justice, and significantly influenced their outlook on coping, including what form coping has taken or what form they feel it should take.

Table A.1 is a participant matrix in which a basic cross tabulation/co-occurrence between the categories discussed above is presented, albeit in a truncated form. It situates interviewees according to their exposure to violent attacks and how these attacks were classified. The purpose of this categorisation is not to suggest absolute fixity to these events or label individuals only according to their 'status' as survivors of one event or another but rather

238 Methodological Appendix

to allow the reader to more easily envisage something of the diversity found within the interview sample. The consequences of victimisation for these individuals include physical and emotional adversity, personal struggles with grief and bereavement, as well as indirect impacts such as negotiating media attention and traversing a range of knock-on effects to their partners, familial relationships, and overall sense of ontological security in a range of other contexts. The information categorised in the table, while appearing somewhat 'natural', is nonetheless categorised and ordered following initial post-data gathering reflection. The decision to classify some survivors in particular ways is not neutral, nor indeed incontestable. It almost certainly taxonomises individual cases more *explicitly* than the FfP typically would. For the analytic purpose of teasing out differences or similarities within the data, it is useful and can be seen as the first stage of ordering, or even preliminarily coding, the data. From the organisation's practical point of view, such ordering may offer little benefit and in fact be seen as antithetical to the inclusivity which staff suggested was characteristic of their overall ethos. Observations made during the fieldwork phase of the research, however, revealed a more complex picture concerning the ways in which staff would have to practically negotiate contested classifications and the labels inevitably associated with different participant groups.

While 'institutional, authorized violence "from above"' and 'anti-institutional, unauthorized violence "from below"' is more nuanced, and therefore preferable, to 'state violence' and 'non-state violence' it may be seen to denote a political 'reading' of particular incidents which is at odds with the organisation's official stance of being 'non-politically affiliated'. The tensions and complexities of lexicons mobilised around violence were even more starkly illustrated where the word 'terrorism' was concerned; while its use was generally avoided unless and until it was used by staff or participants, staff themselves would switch (often unconsciously, it seemed) between the word 'terror(ism)(ist)' and words such as 'conflict', 'armed conflict', 'violence', 'political violence', etc. depending on who they were speaking to or working with. Some participants also expressed, both during fieldwork and interviews, their despair and frustration at the language of 'terrorism', or at themselves being labelled 'terrorists'. This all further underscored the notion that we can learn much more about the 'terrorism' label/the language of 'terrorism' not by focusing on settling its definition but by paying attention to the heterogeneous, contested and controversial ways/places in which it is and is not deployed (Ramsay, 2015). It also suggests the practical and ethical importance of relaying, if not adopting, the language used by participants themselves in making sense of political violence done unto them (Lynch and Argomaniz, 2015; see Chapter 2) which is sometimes pointed to in Chapters 3–5. The language used in Table A.1 enables a carefully considered taxonomy for the reader to consider while avoiding the inherent ambiguity attached to 'terrorism'.

During fieldwork, several members of staff reiterated that the Foundation is the only dedicated national charity working specifically to support survivors of terrorism and politically motivated violence. Particular emphasis would be put on this when discussing and applying for funding, such as their recently commissioned work around prevention and radicalisation which is run separately to SAN. There are other charities offering 'generic' support to a broader range of injured parties such as the British Red Cross and Victim Support, whose work is sometimes seen to be almost encroaching on the Foundation's unique remit, but these three organisations are the only ones listed in the UN's Directory of Organisations Supporting Victims of Terrorism (see United Nations, 2017). In reality, the Foundation also works with a range of other actors including former perpetrators, veterans, emergency responders, and relatives of witnesses. This became particularly apparent when trying to recruit participants not solely linked to military or paramilitary experiences. Indeed, some of these actors form the cornerstone of activities such as the Dialogue for Peace programme. This sometimes creates a somewhat contradictory and paradoxical dynamic whereby this very diversity among participants leads to fascinating and critical discussions among them within workshops of the problematic and reifying labelling of 'terrorism', 'terrorists', 'perpetrators', and 'victims' – the very labels required to publicise and 'sell' the work the organisation does. This was observed during fieldwork where certain labels and names would be used around one group of participants but then quickly changed or adjusted for another. 'The terrorism survivor', that is, the survivor of a terrorist act, is one such term – reified and rendered visible for the purposes of organisational branding, storytelling, and funding but frequently contradicted or re-rendered problematic in practice.

This presented something of a methodological obstacle during the data collection phase of the research, particularly around recruitment decisions and staff's labelling of participants as 'traumatised', at least partially for the practical purposes of delivering workshops or tailored trauma awareness events to an otherwise impossibly diverse group of individuals. This issue is reflected on in the Conclusion chapter.

Despite the usefulness of sorting the data in this way for heuristic purposes and to enable readers to more easily situate narrative extracts interspersed throughout the book, there is a danger in simplifying the messier complexity of participant's experiences. For example, some of the individuals classified as bereaved family members were also witnesses and, in one case, a witness held hostage. Furthermore, several participants had prior experience of critical incidents in the form of both 'institutional' and 'anti-institutional' violence but have been associated (in Table A.1) with the incidents which either brought them into contact with the FfP or that which they discuss at most length as having the most significant impact on their lives. These other incidents are included in the participant 'pen portraits' below and are not excluded from the analysis. Other tensions also arise. The pub bombing that killed Barry's grandfather in 1971, for example, may not be officially recognised as an instance of institutional violence in the same way the shooting of civil rights protestors in Derry in 1972 now is.

240   Methodological Appendix

Table A.1 Participant matrix 'at a glance'

	Anti-institutional, unauthorised violence 'from below'	Institutional, authorised violence 'from above'	Total
Physically injured survivors	**Chandani** (December 1983, Harrods bomb, London) **Ganesh** (July 2005, tube and bus bombings, London) **Jane** (July 2005, tube and bus bombings, London)	**Paul** (January 1972, civil rights march shooting, Derry)	4
Surviving family members bereaved	**Lynn** (October 1990, proxy bomb, Derry) **Danielle** (March 1993, Bridge Street bomb, Warrington) **Colin** (March 1993, Bridge Street bomb, Warrington) **Anne** (July 2005, tube and bus bombings, London) (eyewitnesses and ground survivors of Lockerbie) **Kevin** (July 2005, tube and bus bombings, London) (eyewitnesses and ground survivors of Lockerbie) **Stephen** (July 2005, tube and bus bombings, London) **George** (September 2014, ISIL/ISIS execution, Syria) **Amanda** (September 2014, ISIL/ISIS execution, Syria)	**Barry** (December 1971, pub bombing, Belfast) **Bridget** (January 1972, civil rights march shooting, Derry) **Liz** (January 1972, civil rights march shooting, Derry) **Kathy** (January 1972, civil rights march shooting, Derry) **Louise** (January 1972, civil rights march shooting, Derry) **Claire** (May 1976, bus shooting, Derry)	14
Eyewitness survivors	**Kelly** (March 1993, Bridge Street bomb, Warrington) **John** (July 2005, tube and bus bombings, London) **Karen** (June 2015, beach resort shooting, Tunisia)		3
Total	14	7	21

It is, however, how such violence has been characterised by Barry, his family, and campaign organisations following allegations and evidence of collusion between state and paramilitary groups (see MacAirt, 2012). This again flags up the contentious and contestable nature of classifying data in this way; it would, however, be disingenuous to participants to present it in any other way. Finally, as almost all interviews touched upon, the high-profile nature of the events discussed for this research were all covered extensively (and, in some cases, intrusively) by the mainstream media and projected around the world for weeks and sometimes months or years afterwards. Consequently, we might reasonably challenge the definition of 'eyewitness'; to play on Mythen's (2007) words, 'are we all witnesses

Methodological Appendix   241

now'? While we are not immune from seeing images of suffering and viewing it in the context of media coverage, the 'classification' of eyewitness may carry a very different significance when referring to individuals who were physically present (and, in the cases included here, in very grave danger) and directly witness to the events in question. This distinction is rendered more complex in an era when clinical manifestations of post-traumatic stress disorder (PTSD) are made possible through not only direct 'exposure' to critical incidents but also mediated, screen-based (film, television, digital) experience (Pinchevski, 2016). As Howell (2012: 216) argues: 'The key innovation in the expansion of PTSD is centred on the act of witnessing'. Space does not permit a closer exploration of this complexity, however, and eyewitness survivors interviewed here were all present at the scene of the incidents in question.

Practical considerations around access, sampling, and ethics largely overrode opportunities to balance the sample size across all six 'combinations' represented in the table, not that this was an aim of the research. Consequently, bereaved family members surviving their loved ones represent the largest group of participants interviewed by quite a large margin, although within this group the balance between 'institutional' and 'anti-institutional' violence is roughly equal (six and eight bereaved family members, respectively). Outside of this 'category', physically injured survivors and surviving eyewitnesses are almost equal in number (four and three, respectively), the latter being solely made up of witnesses to 'anti-institutional' violence. Beyond direct interviews, the more extensive period of fieldwork described above involved speaking with around 75 survivors who participated in FfP events and workshops. Both the in–depth interviews drawn on verbatim during the book, and this larger group of people whose insights often found their way into private field notes, were of ongoing significance for answering my original research questions and generally helping the project and its findings in taking shape over time.

In order to provide the reader with a little more detail on individual participants whose experiences are described and referred to throughout the book, the following provides a brief 'pen portrait' which can be cross-referenced with Table A.1.

Participant 'Pen Portraits'

Amanda

Amanda is George's partner. George's brother Peter was killed by ISIS in Syria. Peter was an aid worker and was on an aid mission to Syria when he was captured in early 2013. He was then held hostage for over 18 months before he was killed in September 2014.

Anne

Anne's daughter, Lauren, was killed on 7 July 2005 when the tube train that she was travelling on was targeted by a suicide bomber. While this was the event

242   Methodological Appendix

that eventually brought her into contact with the FfP, her and her husband Kevin were also ground survivors of the Lockerbie bomb in 1988.

Barry

Barry was almost 12 years old when his grandfather was murdered in a bomb explosion in the McGurk's Bar pub in Belfast, Northern Ireland, in December 1971. The explosion was blamed on a botched bomb assembly intended for Protestant targets. It was later established that the bomb was actually planted by Loyalist paramilitaries but victim's families are still attempting to piece together information about the event, some of which remain classified within British Army files until the 2050s.

Bridget

Bridget's younger brother Sean was shot dead by the British Army on 30 January 1972 in Derry, Northern Ireland, in what became known as 'Bloody Sunday'. The Northern Ireland Civil Rights Association organised a peaceful protest march against the British policy of internment, as well as gerrymandering and the lack of investment and equal opportunities for Catholics in Northern Ireland. The British Army opened fire on the march, shooting 28 and killing 14.

Chandani

Chandani was shopping with her sister and nephews in London on 17 December 1983 when the IRA detonated a car bomb outside the Harrods department store. They were walking out of the store when the explosion occurred, causing serious cuts and wounds to her skin and long-lasting damage to her spine.

Claire

Claire was seven years old when her older brother Ryan, who was in his early 20s, was shot dead by the British Army in a targeted operation. He had recently been released from prison and was under covert surveillance when a sniper shot him through the window of a bus.

Colin

Colin's 12-year-old son Tim was killed on 20 March 1993 in Warrington when a bomb, which had been planted by the IRA, exploded, killing Tim and three-year-old Johnathan Ball. Colin and his wife Wendy went on to found the Tim Parry Johnathan Ball Foundation for Peace where this research largely took place. A fuller account of the organisation's history is offered in Chapter 2.

Methodological Appendix 243

Danielle

Danielle was just a baby when her mother was severely injured in the Warrington bomb on 20 March 1993. Her leg was amputated and she died from a form of skin cancer a year later, which doctors believe could have been linked to her injuries. The bomb, which was planted by the IRA, killed 12-year-old Tim Parry and three-year-old Johnathan Ball. After this event, Colin Parry and his wife Wendy went on to found the Tim Parry Johnathan Ball Foundation for Peace where this research largely took place. A fuller account of the organisation's history is offered in Chapter 2. Danielle now works at the Foundation.

Ganesh

Ganesh was travelling on a tube train in London on 7 July 2005 when a suicide bomber detonated a bomb. Ganesh was shielded by several people but did sustain serious injuries. This included spinal compression, which was not diagnosed until several years later. He began attending the Foundation for Peace after a member of their staff heard him speak at a memorial service for the attack in Hyde Park.

George

George's brother Peter was killed by ISIS in Syria. Peter was an aid worker and was on an aid mission to Syria when he was captured in early 2013. He was then held hostage for over 18 months before he was killed in September 2014.

Jane

Jane was injured on 7 July 2005 when a suicide bomb was detonated on the bus that she was travelling on in Tavistock Square. She had been visiting London for the day for a work meeting. After being unable to enter the underground tube stations she decided to get a bus instead. She went on to become an active participant in the Foundation's events and has contributed to a number of public events to discuss the impact that the London attacks have had on her.

John

John witnessed one of the bombs that exploded in London on 7 July 2005. He was working in the city and was stuck in traffic opposite Tavistock Square when the bus exploded after a suicide bomb was detonated.

Karen

Karen was on holiday in Sousse, Tunisia, in 2015 where there was a mass shooting on the beach next to the resort where she was staying. She saw the

244 Methodological Appendix

gunmen moving into the resort and was forced to flee before taking refuge in a neighbouring hotel. Eventually, she was escorted to safety by a local worker and later heard police arrive at the scene and shoot the perpetrators.

Kathy

Kathy is Liz's sister and her older brother Jack was shot dead by the British Army in what became known as 'Bloody Sunday' on 30 January 1972. The Northern Ireland Civil Rights Association organised a peaceful protest march against the British policy of internment, as well as gerrymandering and the lack of investment and equal opportunities for Catholics in Northern Ireland. The British Army opened fire on the march, shooting 28 and killing 14. Her father was also seriously wounded when he went to help his son and was shot too. She was in her early teens at the time.

Kelly

Kelly witnessed the Warrington bomb on 20 March 1993 when a bomb, which had been planted by the IRA, exploded, killing 12-year-old Tim Parry and three-year-old Johnathan Ball. After this event, Colin Parry and his wife Wendy went on to found the Tim Parry Johnathan Ball Foundation for Peace where this research largely took place. A fuller account of the organisation's history is offered in Chapter 2. Kelly has continued to live in Warrington and attend the Foundation's events.

Kevin

Kevin's stepdaughter, Lauren, was killed on 7 July 2005 when the tube train that she was travelling on was targeted by a suicide bomber. While this was the event that eventually brought him into contact with the FfP, him and his wife Anne were also ground survivors of the Lockerbie bomb in 1988. Kevin worked as a social worker at the time and had some contact with emergency services during the initial response.

Liz

Liz's younger brother Jack was shot dead by the British Army in what became known as 'Bloody Sunday' on 30 January 1972. The Northern Ireland Civil Rights Association organised a peaceful protest march against the British policy of internment, as well as gerrymandering and the lack of investment and equal opportunities for Catholics in Northern Ireland. The British Army opened fire on the march, shooting 28 and killing 14. Her father was also seriously wounded when he went to help his son and was shot too. She was in her early 20s at the time.

Louise

Louise, who is Bridget's daughter, lost her uncle Sean on 30 January 1972 in what became known as 'Bloody Sunday'. The Northern Ireland Civil Rights Association organised a peaceful protest march against the British policy of internment, as well as gerrymandering and the lack of investment and equal opportunities for Catholics in Northern Ireland. The British Army opened fire on the march, shooting 28 and killing 14.

Lynn

Lynn's husband Jim was killed on 24 October 1990 in what became known as the IRA's 'proxy bombing' campaign. She was held hostage at her home while masked gunmen abducted her husband and forced him to drive a van to a British Army checkpoint that was loaded with explosives. They then detonated it, killing Jim along with five soldiers.

Paul

Paul was in his mid-20s when he was shot and wounded by the British Army in what became known as 'Bloody Sunday' on 30 January 1972. The Northern Ireland Civil Rights Association organised a peaceful protest march against the British policy of internment, as well as gerrymandering and the lack of invest-ment and equal opportunities for Catholics in Northern Ireland. The British Army opened fire on the march, shooting 28 and killing 14.

Stephen

Stephen's son Nick was killed on 7 July 2005 when the tube train that he was travelling on was targeted by a suicide bomber. Stephen later became involved in the Foundation's work and recently joined their board of trustees. He has worked more specifically on the charity's THINK project rather than their SAN activities (see Chapter 2) although he has partaken in both strands of their work.

Data Analysis: Producing Ideal Types Using Abductive Reasoning

Contrary to many 'grounded' approaches to qualitative data analysis which fre-quently claim to employ an entirely inductive logic in the generation of new the-ories, this research neither denied the existence of theoretical influences within this particular field of study nor devoted its analyses to verifying, falsifying, or modifying them. It would be at odds with the epistemological logic outlined above to deny a dialectical relationship between the two. Explicit reference to

246 Methodological Appendix

'resilience' was avoided or downplayed during fieldwork with the intention of seeing how closely the data might cohere with pre-existing influences such as media coverage, social policy, or organisational language. While explicit reference was avoided where possible, the aim was to hold existing understandings found within the literature and policy discussions loosely 'to account' while also taking seriously the possibility that participants' understandings and lexicons were shaped by its existence and use within FfP. Therefore, while many themes and subthemes were identified from the bottom-up and had little resonance with the literature and concepts discussed thus far, the analytical approach was certainly not as free from theory as a grounded theory approach proper (see Silverman, 2006: 7); nor was its ultimate aim necessarily theory generation (although see Walker and Myrick, 2006 for a fuller discussion).

Instead it adopted abductive logic which Timmermans and Tavory (2012; Tavory and Timmermans, 2014) suggest requires neither theoretical atheism nor monotheism but informed theoretical agnosticism. They take inspiration from pragmatist philosopher Charles S. Peirce who proposed a theory of logic that aimed to foster 'the creative production of hypotheses based on surprising evidence' (Timmermans and Tavory, 2012: 168). Departing from the goal of generating hypotheses in a strictly scientific/experimental sense, Timmermans and Tavory (2012) aim to reinvigorate grounded theory (*qua* Glaser and Strauss, 1967) by drawing on some of its methodological strengths while encouraging a more dialectic engagement with existing theory. This involves reading widely across multiple theoretical fields while gathering empirical data, making preliminary guesses about which theories may help explain the phenomena under study, and, as data is collected, highlighting evidence that does not fit into existing frameworks. Data collection and analysis is not approached with one fixed theory in mind, nor are existing theories somehow 'bracketed off' from processes in which they are often inherently entangled (Bourdieu and Wacquant, 1992: 225); multiple theoretical insights are brought to bear on the process as a whole which enables some to be adopted and not others. This pragmatic way of conceiving theory and its construction is a positive one and shows an inclination towards middle-range theory; the generation of theory backed up by data as a core sociological task which should help us to understand a 'broader variety of phenomena' (Timmermans and Tavory, 2012: 174). Many practical and procedural aspects of grounded theory, however, were retained (Walker and Myrick, 2006). This included making detailed field notes and memo writing, making comparisons between cases, and coding across various aspects of the transcripts. By keeping close records of field visits and observations, it was possible to revisit particular phenomena later on rather than treating their perception wholly as one-time and retrospectively imagined events.

This iterative process combined both inductive and deductive analysis (see Fereday and Muir-Cohrane, 2006) and temporally progressive–regressive features of the data (Denzin, 1989: 67). It also acted as a way of corroborating coded themes. Finally, as an analytic technique it operates in the Weberian

Methodological Appendix   247

tradition sketched out earlier, allowing for theoretical claims made in the resilience literature to be cross-referenced against empirical evidence. Weber did not advocate the abandonment of conceptualisation for investigation, that is, pure theory for pure empiricism, but rather encouraged an ongoing and iterative movement between the two (Kalberg, 1997: 232) – a principle central to this investigation of PVT survivors. While focusing chiefly on historical societies comparatively, Weber deployed this kind of synthesis to develop 'ideal types' – that is, the highlighting and grouping of essential from non-essential traits in order to 'assist in reducing ambiguity about empirical reality by providing the means to foster adequate descriptions of it' (Morrison, 2006: 347). As such, the main period of intensive data analysis, during which wider reading and regular field visits gave way to a more focused immersion in the interview transcripts, was used to order the data into *themes/sub-themes-as-ideal-typical-constructs*. The chief purpose of extrapolating ideal type constructs when analysing the interview data was to make intelligible, and to collectively order, otherwise individual patterns of purported perception and social action. They were used in relation to discrete themes/sub-themes within the data, but also individual survivors themselves whose narratives encompassed multiple features of a particular theme or feature of the data as a collective. This latter use is demonstrated in Chapter 5, with extended readings of Chandani, Anne and Kevin's interview extracts used to exemplify contrasting effects and perceptions of time through varying parts of their respective life courses that became apparent from interviews and time spent with them. Different aspects of these effects and perceptions were also evident in other interviews, or themselves typified one aspect or another found within other interviews.

Charting the development and use of ideal type constructs in the work of Weber and Schutz, Psathas (2005: 147) offers the following account of ideal types as distinct from other available conceptualisations:

> The ideal type is a construct developed by the analyst for particular purposes. It represents a selection of features or elements considered significant, essential or exemplary. It is based on or derived from observations of empirical reality and compared with that reality in its formulation but it does not purport to be a fully accurate and complete depiction of that reality in all of its features. It systematizes and organizes a number of features by drawing out or focusing on these and selectively excluding others. In the view of the analyst who develops the ideal type, empirical reality consists of multiplicities of events and activities which are manifest in a virtually chaotic and unending flow of discrete particularities thereby necessitating selection, focus and reduction in order to achieve a more coherent formulation.

Rather than suggesting that the groupings of data and accompanying observations presented in Chapters 3–6 are universally valid, ideal type constructs facilitate

248 Methodological Appendix

such data formulations for their comparative insights, to draw linkages between individual cases, and are deployed as something of a yardstick, or compass, capable of giving an impression of scales between discrete empirical cases (Psathas, 2005: 156).

Audio recorded interviews were transcribed following a technique that falls somewhere between the 'naturalised' and 'denaturalised' transcription practices discussed by Oliver, Serovich and Mason (2005). While the minute detail called for by conversation analysis, including precise time markers between conversational 'turns', was not required based partly on the modesty of the claims being made of this data (see the note on theory and method in the Introduction to the book), familiarity with the data was achieved through a thorough and accurate transcription process which made note of the main pauses, non-verbals, and emotional reactions of participants (e.g. 'sighs', 'laughs', 'pauses', and so on). This also made it easier to identify anonymised transcripts, keeping a familiar perspective on interviews that may have taken place weeks before coding the data began. Putting the abductive logic outlined above (Timmermans and Tavory, 2012; Tavory and Timmermans, 2014) into practice, an analytic technique of hybridisation combining both inductive and deductive coding, outlined by Fereday and Muir-Cochrane (2006), was adapted which begins by identifying and searching around known discussion points before generating a closer, inductive reading of the data and an exploration of purely data-driven themes. Purposefully broad but pre-determined 'nodes' which encompassed both the main research questions and recurring themes or patterns noted during fieldwork were created first as a way of initially organising the data. For example, *What is 'resilience'?*, *Turning points and processes of 'resilience'*, and *Coping resources and sources of support* acted as a starting point. Beneath these, data which explicitly related to each node was coded as sub and sub-sub nodes. For example, beneath *Turning points and processes of 'resilience'* it was clear that many turning points emerged through discussions of time, both past and present. Within this sub-node, *Effects of injuries over time* became a sub-sub node. To take another example, beneath *What is 'resilience'?* the notion of *A 'healing' process* became a general sub-node that encapsulated different kinds of description of physical and non-physical change. A sub-sub node here simply referred to *Closure*. Finally, to use one more example, *Coping resources and sources of support* contained, among others, a sub-node containing *Communal support* and a sub-sub node within this evidencing *Survivor solidarity*. Aside from the master nodes, some of the sub-nodes within them were also coded using deductive logic with familiar categories derived from the literature. This process of deductive coding, organising, and re-reading transcripts was consolidated with the inductive coding of emergent or 'surprising' (Timmermans and Tavory, 2012: 168) themes – both as 'standalone' patterns in the data and as unanticipated sub-themes which were 'coded on' (Bazeley and Jackson, 2013: 71) to previously generated codes. This resulted in a total of 78 different nodes, sub-nodes, sub-sub nodes, and so on, both deductively and inductively coded, which were then corroborated

Methodological Appendix   249

through connection to one another (Fereday and Muir-Cochrane, 2006). The process of connecting themes was completed by grouping findings for writing up – an integral part of analysis as well as presentation (Silverman, 2011: 403).

A final point of clarification concerns the use of the word 'narrative' (see again the note on theory and method in the Introduction chapter). Following the approach adopted by Jarvis (2009: 33), narrative is understood broadly to refer to an account or story of events occurring over time. Particular attention is paid within these accounts to events that were prioritised or privileged by participants. In addition, the ways in which such events are made to relate to one another within participants' recollections of the past, descriptions of the present, or anticipations of the future typically produce stories with some sense of internal coherence or plot structure, revealing something of the way survivors understand their personal experiences and life trajectories. While narrative remains a contestable and multifaceted concept, it is this sense of the word that was deemed important for the purposes of this research.

Research Ethics

The data collection outlined here did not take place until an independent review board had granted full ethical approval for the research. Conceptually, social research ethics are often sharply divorced into ethical approval processes at the institutional level and ethical practice on the part of the researcher at the individual level – a dichotomy that often ignores the relationship between the two. Guillemin and Gillam (2004) argue that while ethical requirements from an institutional review board cannot possibly regulate (or even observe) the micro ethics, pertinently referred to as 'ethically important moments', which may arise during the course of conducting social research, they do serve to reiterate the importance of ethical reflexivity on the part of the researcher (see McGowan, 2020 for an extended analysis of their work in the context of this project). In addition to the important requisites of informed consent, participant anonymity, and the safeguarding of both participants and researcher, the following are some observations about matters of ethical importance.

Interviews and group discussions observed during fieldwork around trauma and victimisation should not be confused or conflated with therapeutic group work which purposefully seeks to change, assist, or otherwise positively influence participants' thinking about their life and attitudes. Typically, group therapy assumes its role to be 'restoring' individuals to former states or enabling participants to once again integrate within society (Weinberg, Nuttman-Schwartz and Gilmore, 2005). Despite evidence that suggests that psychosocial isolation and detachment can be symptomatic of traumatic experiences (Herman, 2001), this research made no prior assumptions about participants' states of well-being; to do so would have been ethically and politically disingenuous and beyond the remit of this research. Reflexive awareness in this regard not only represents 'ethical practice as harm avoidance' but, more positively, 'ethical practice as enhancement'. In trying to discover ways in which people make sense of their own traumatic experiences and articulate the kinds of personal, familial, and social resources of significance to them in responding to these experiences, it would be counterintuitive to try and manipulate this process in ways often associated with therapy. If people naturally find within themselves the strength to respond 'resiliently' to disastrous situations, events, or periods of trauma, then what do these responses look like? What can people's lived responses retrospectively tell us about how people behaved under these circumstances, as opposed to what therapy or policy might assume people can or should do in these circumstances?

Despite the unwanted association with therapeutic intervention, some important ethical considerations from trauma-informed practice remain pertinent to all related research. Interviewers should provide a supportive environment in which empathy is not forsaken in favour of 'objectivity' and should remain alert to the potential impact of 'vicarious trauma' on themselves (Weinberg, Nuttman-Schwartz and Gilmore, 2005). Strong emotions on the part of both participants and researcher were inevitable and should not be masked or written out of the research in the belief that doing so somehow constitutes ethical research. Including the visceral and emotional reactions which accompany discussions of violence, trauma, and injustice remain key to our sociological understanding and interpretation of such phenomena (Denzin, 1984: 239; Hubbard, Backett-Milburn and Kemmer, 2001). Acknowledging this aims, in part, to respect participants' stories for what they are and how they were told rather than to 'sterilise' this element of the research.

All interview participants were identified and approached with the assistance and knowledge of the FfP, who were aware of when interviews were scheduled to take place and would ensure that a member of staff was available to either meet with those participants or speak afterwards on the phone to debrief with them. Most interviews took place on FfP premises but this was decided on an individual basis. For example, one participant (Chandani) who suffered from severe back pain as a direct result of an injury sustained some 33 years earlier found it extremely uncomfortable sitting for any length of time. Rather than having her travel for several hours on a train to meet at the FfP, the interview was conducted in her home with a member of FfP staff who was due to visit her home anyway. Some interviews were carried out in other participants' homes without the presence of a staff member but this was always at the FfP's suggestion and with their knowledge. Interviewees knew me quite well by the time we sat down for an interview following such an extensive period of building rapport through various fieldwork visits.

As Table A.1 shows, the interview sample is variegated and unequally distributed between injured, bereaved, and eyewitness survivors of both anti-institutional, unauthorised 'violence from below' and institutional, authorised 'violence from above' and there were important ethical reasons underpinning this ostensibly random selection. The number of physically injured and

Methodological Appendix   251

eyewitness survivors met during the fieldwork far outnumber those eventually interviewed. Many of these survivors had only just started attending the FfP and more were steadily being taken on by them as several violent attacks across the UK and Europe unfolded, particularly during 2016 and 2017. Aside from the very recent nature of these individuals' experiences, this also meant that less time could be spent getting to know a little more about them and building some sort of transparent rapport. Some started attending the charity's events towards the end of my data collection and fieldwork while, technically, there was still time to 'add to my interview data' – a crass way of describing such raw and harrowing experiences. Gatekeepers and I agreed that to cajole such participants into 'sit down' interviews was unethical and presented too many unnecessary risks for all parties.

Discussions with gatekeepers revealed much about how different participants' 'resilience' was perceived and described by FfP staff. They would sometimes describe an individual as 'resilient enough' or having not 'developed enough resilience' yet. Despite harbouring private scepticism at times towards the more medicalised trauma discourse sometimes adopted by staff to describe psychological harm, I bowed down to their professional judgement and even found myself assimilating my own language and attitude to theirs during such discussions. We can be as critical as we like in theory about the problematic labelling of individuals as 'scarred', 'damaged', 'traumatised', 'broken', or any other word we might believe risks stripping survivors of their agency, but, in reality, how many researchers genuinely do not believe there are risks (not to mention ethical abuses) in prizing information out of an individual still coming to terms with recent shock? More appositely, how many of them would be in a position to take full responsibility for their actions should these risks, no matter how unpalatably articulated they may be by those who endorse the medicalised language of the 'psy' disciplines (Rose, 1998), turn out to be founded and realised? The risk of causing further harm to survivors, racking up a few extra interviews at the expense of their well-being, was one neither I, nor the Foundation, were prepared to take with these incoming participants.

Entering the field, the ethics of interviewing survivors was also bound up with the *idea* (as opposed to the *object*, see Hacking, 1997: 3) of 'resilience'. I wanted the interviews to be as natural as possible, more to minimise any potential distress or setbacks for participants who may have otherwise been coping rather than to 'produce better data'. Participants were understood to be 'defended subjects' (Hollway and Jefferson, 2000) capable of telling variegated narratives, so the historical veracity of such narratives was never of primary concern. Their well-being, however, was. While there may be fine lines between 'leading' participants and facilitating spaces for the kinds of conversation to take place that they will be more comfortable with, or that *they* want to tell, Overland's (2013: 207) approach to interviewing survivors of the Khmer Rouge regime in Cambodia share some similarities with the way interviews were conducted here. Her belief that the telling of 'resilience stories' may naturally prove more

252 Methodological Appendix

useful than telling 'trauma stories' for individuals and their families led her to emphasise the importance of empathetic and affirmative interviewing. This included acknowledging stories of trauma without probing, while assisting (sometimes through silences, for example, not challenging or re-questioning turns from macabre events to more positive narratives on the part of the participant) the formulation of 'a narrative of survival'. Most importantly, it meant acknowledging 'the pain and difficulty of the potentially traumatic experience *without* full disclosure' (Overland, 2013: 207, emphasis added) being pressed for. Each participant was different in this regard. In response to the question, 'So what led you to become involved with this place [FfP]?', some would talk of life before the FfP and 'the event' implicitly, while others would spend a long time methodically and graphically describing those events in considerable detail. All interviews were followed by an FfP staff member debriefing with both participant and researcher, ensuring that any unexpected distress or disclosures that needed to be flagged up could be, though no issues presented themselves through this process. On the contrary, a gatekeeper conducting these follow-up conversations reported that a number of participants had expressed how valuable they had found the experience and even enjoyed the opportunity of talking freely and privately about their experiences, thoughts, and feelings.

References

Bazeley, P. and Jackson, K. (2013) *Qualitative Data Analysis with NVivo*. 2nd edition. London: Sage Publications Ltd.

Bourdieu, P. and Wacquant, L.J.D. (1992) *An Invitation to Reflexive Sociology*. Chicago: The University of Chicago Press.

Chomsky, N. (2015) *Culture of Terrorism*. 2nd edition. London: Pluto Press.

Denzin, N.K. (1984) *On Understanding Emotion*. California: Jossey-Bass, Inc.

Denzin, N.K. (1989) *Interpretive Biography*. California: Sage Publications, Inc.

Elliott, J. (2005) *Using Narrative in Social Research: Qualitative and Quantitative Approaches*. London: Sage.

Fereday, J. and Muir-Cochrane, E. (2006) Demonstrating rigor using thematic analysis: A hybrid approach of inductive and deductive coding and theme development. *International Journal of Qualitative Methods* 5(1): 80–92.

Forsey, M.G. (2010) Ethnography as participant listening. *Ethnography* 11(4): 558–72.

Geertz, C. (1998) Deep hanging out. *The New York Review of Books*. 45(16): 69.

Glaser, B.G. and Strauss, A.L. (1967) *The Discovery of Grounded Theory*. New York: Aldine.

Green, P. and Ward, T. (2004) *State Crime: Governments, Violence and Corruption*. London: Pluto Press.

Guillemin, M. and Gillam, L. (2004) Ethics, reflexivity, and 'ethically important moments' in research. *Qualitative Enquiry* 10(2): 261–80.

Hacking, I. (1997) Taking bad arguments seriously. *London Review of Books* 19(16): 14–16.

Herman, J.L. (2001) *Trauma and Recovery*. London: Pandora.

Hollway, W. and Jefferson, T. (2000) *Doing Qualitative Research Differently: Free Association, Narrative and the Interview Method*. London: Sage.

Methodological Appendix 253

Howell, A. (2012) The Demise of PTSD: From governing through trauma to governing resilience. *Alternatives: Global, Local, Political* 37(3): 214–26.

Hubbard, G., Backett-Milburn, K. and Kemmer, D. (2001) Working with emotion: Issues for the researcher in fieldwork and teamwork. *International Journal of Social Research Methodology* 4(2): 119–37.

Jarvis, L. (2009) *Times of Terror: Discourse, Temporality and the War on Terror.* Hampshire: Palgrave.

Kalberg, S. (1997) Max Weber's sociology: Research strategies and modes of analysis. In C. Camic (Ed.) *Reclaiming the Sociological Classics.* Oxford: Blackwell Publishers Ltd. pp.208–41.

Lynch, O. and Argomaniz, J. (2015) Victims of terrorism: An introduction. In O. Lynch and J. Argomaniz (Eds.) *Victims of Terrorism: A Comparative and Interdisciplinary Study.* London: Routledge. pp.1–9.

MacAirt, C. (2012) *The McGurk's Bar Bombing: Collusion, Cover-Up and a Campaign for Truth.* Aberdeenshire: Frontline Noir.

McGowan, W. (2020) 'If you didn't laugh, you'd cry': Emotional labour, reflexivity and ethics-as-practice in a qualitative fieldwork context. *Methodological Innovations*, 13(2): 1–10.

Morrison, K. (2006) *Marx, Durkheim, Weber: Formation of Modern Social Thought.* 2nd edition. London: Sage.

Mythen, G. (2007) Cultural victimology: Are we all victims now? In S. Walklate (Ed.) *Handbook of Victims and Victimology.* London: Routledge. pp.464–83.

Oliver, D.G., Serovich, J.M. and Mason, T.L. (2005) Constraints and opportunities with interview transcription: Towards reflection in qualitative research. *Social Forces* 84(2): 1273–89.

Overland, G. (2013) *Post Traumatic Survival: The Lessons of Cambodian Resilience.* Newcastle upon Tyne: Cambridge Scholars Publishing.

Pinchevski, A. (2016) Screen trauma: Visual media and post-traumatic stress disorder. *Theory, Culture & Society* 33(4): 51–75.

Psathas, G. (2005) The ideal type in Weber and Schutz. In M. Endress, G. Psathas and H. Nasu (Eds.) *Explorations of the Life-World: Continuing Dialogues with Alfred Schutz.* Dordrecht: Springer. pp.143–69.

Ramsay, G. (2015) Why terrorism can, but should not be defined. *Critical Studies on Terrorism* 8(2): 211–28.

Rose, N. (1998) *Inventing Our Selves: Psychology, Power and Personhood.* Cambridge: Cambridge University Press.

Ruggiero, V. (2006) *Understanding Political Violence: A Criminological Analysis.* Maidenhead: Open University Press.

Sartre, J.P. (1968) *Search for a Method.* New York: Vintage.

Schott, R.M. (2015) 'Not just victims … but': Toward a critical theory of the victim. In H. Marway and H. Widdows (Eds.) *Women and Violence: The Agency of Victims and Perpetrators.* Basingstoke: Palgrave Macmillan. pp.178–94.

Silverman, D. (2006) *Interpreting Qualitative Data: Methods for Analyzing Talk, Text and Interaction*, 3rd edition. London: Sage.

Silverman, D. (2011) *Interpreting Qualitative Data*, 4th edition. London: Sage Publications Ltd.

Tavory, I. and Timmermans, S. (2014) *Abductive Analysis: Theorizing Qualitative Research.* Chicago: The University of Chicago Press.

Timmermans, S. and Tavory, I. (2012) Theory construction in qualitative research: From grounded theory to abductive analysis. *Sociological Theory* 30(3): 167–86.

United Nations (2017) Directory of Organisations Supporting Victims of Terrorism [online] Available at: www.un.org/victimsofterrorism/en/directory [Accessed 26/07/2017].

Walker, D. and Myrick, F. (2006) Grounded theory: An exploration of process and procedure. *Qualitative Health Research* 16(4): 547–59.

Weinberg, H., Nuttman-Schwartz, O. and Gilmore, M. (2005) Trauma groups: An overview. *Group Analysis* 38(2): 187–202.

Index

Note: Locators in *italics* represent figures and **bold** indicate tables in the text.

7/7 *see* London bombings 2005
9/11 *see* September 11 attacks 2001

activism 86, 116, 171, 182, 196, 200, 236
addiction 126, 201
Adebolajo, M. 58
Adebowale, M. 58
adversity, responses to 106–110
Agamben, G. 52, 150
agnosticism 6, 246
Aguirre, B.E. 157
Alexander, J.C. 213
Ali, N. 204–205
Almedom, A. M. 33
'always-already' episteme 19
Amess, D. 59
anathemas 220
Anderson, B. 22, 175, 191, 194, 202,
    220–221, 225
anger 84–88, 168–174
Anger and Forgiveness (Nussbaum) 182
Anscombe, E. 71, 179
'anti-extremism' strategy 49
anti-institutional violence 2, 61, 135, 138,
    157, 239, 241
anti-resilience discourses 191
anti-war initiatives 128
Antonovsky, A. 32
Antonovsky's health model 32
anxiety 81, 91–94, 170–171
Aradau, C. 34
Argomaniz, J. 65
Armstrong, M. 204–205
asylum seekers refuge programme 114
Atlantic Philanthropies 54
Auschwitz 150

autism 5
awareness-raising materials 128, 215

battles 220
BBC 53, 97–98, 147
Bean, H. 19, 21–22
Beck, U. 22, 37
Becker, H.S. 178
bereavement 88–91
Big Society agenda of the 2010
    government 12
Black Humour 201
Blair, T. 20–21
Bloody Friday 54
Bloody Sunday (civil rights march in 1972,
    Northern Ireland) 87, 102, 111, 114, 141,
    151, 157, 167, 169
Bloody Sunday Justice Campaign 87,
    141
Bonanno, G. 4, 19, 33
Borough Market attack, 2017 22
bounce-back-ability 29, 200
Bourbeau, P. 166, 169, 200
Bowen, J. 54
Brassett, J. 174
Breen-Smyth, M. 197
Breivik, A. 58
Brison, S. 170
British Red Cross 176, 239
broad-brush concept 34
Bufacchi, V. 60
Bush, G 49
Butler, J. 183

Calverley, A. 229
Cambodian genocide 127

256 Index

Cambodian survivors of Khmer Rouge period 120, 127
Cameron, D. 49, 184, 226
capitalism 35, 129
car accidents 215
Carlile, 59
catastrophe society 37
Catholic working-class community 114
causal emplotment 116
Cavelty, M.D. 107, 168, 171, 174, 228
Chamberlin, S.M.E. 125
Chandler, D. 2, 39
Charley's War (Mill) 21
child abuse 5
Christianity 147
Christie, N. 199
chronic distress trajectory 33
Civil Contingencies Act 2004 25–26, 226
Civil Contingencies Era 24
civilian self- help agendas 189
civil rights 51
civil rights march 82
civil society 24–28
Cobra emergency response committee 28
codes of moral virtue 202
collective effervescence 196
Collins, R. 24, 53, 217
commission- based grants 122
communal support systems 112–120
community 12
community resilience 25, 175
compensation: awards 111; scheme for victims 112
completeness of knowledge 89
complexity governance 3–4
Comprehensive Soldier and Family Fitness programme 170
compression 132
condemnations 220
CONTEST 25
contestation 168–174
contingency planning 175
control-at-a-distance 202
Copeland, D. 59
coroners and inquests 13, 207
corroboration 70
cosmopolitan nationalism 19, 21
counter-radicalisation strategy in Europe 25
counterterrorism 1, 24, 58, 165; bounce-back-ability 24–28; hegemonic framings 52; resilience in 29
Counter-Terrorism Act 2008 59

Counter-Terrorism and Security Act 2015 226
counterterrorism policy 19, 23–24
COVID-19 pandemic 12, 190
Coxian problem-solving experts 60
Crenshaw, M. 209
Criminal Injuries Compensation Board (CICA) 110
criminal justice system 199
Crisis Cast 27–28
critical criminology 47
critical incident recovery 24–28
critical terrorism studies (CTS) 47, 49–51, 204
cultural narration 214

data collection 235–237, 246
Dawson, G. 164
decolonisation 147, 165
defeats 220
degree of anger 88
degree of scepticism 144
degrees of conscious agency 201
de Haan, W. 62
delayed distress trajectory 33
Deleuzian parlance 222
derry bombing 87, 127
dialectical realism 48, 68, 71
Dialogue for Peace programme 177
Diprose, K. 168–169, 226
Directory of Organisations Supporting Victims of Terrorism 239
discourse of futurity 38
Drury, J. 34
Durfy, M. 19, 21–22
Durkheimian analysis 24
Duty of Care for the Media 13
dynamic nominalism 48, 68, 71

Economic and Social Research Council (ESRC) 53
Emmanuel African Methodist Episcopal Church 58
emotional consequences of suffering, harm, and loss 223
emotional etiquette 153
emotional resonance 89
emotional setbacks 224
emotion-focused coping strategy 151
entrepreneurialism 226
epistemological idealism 133
Evans, B. 222

Index 257

excommunications 220
existentialism 174
exposure- isolation distinction 30
extremism 1

Facebook 95
faith-based community support 114
far-right terrorist 58
Fassin, D. 134, 213, 215, 223
fear 81, 91–94, 171
Feeney, C. 54
feminist 50
feminist-inspired scholarship 50
Fereday, J. 248
FfP *see* Tim Parry Johnathan Ball
    Foundation for Peace (FfP)
financial compensation 139
financial crisis of 2007–2008 181, 184
Fitzgerald, J. 204–205
Flaherty, M.G. 132, 158
flashbacks 38
forgiveness 151
Forsey, M.G. 235
Fostering Survivor Solidarity 13
Foucauldian genealogy 37
Foucault, M. 68, 173, 220
Foucault's cardinal axes' of ethics, power
    and knowledge 40
Foundation for Peace *see* Tim Parry
    Johnathan Ball Foundation for Peace
    (FfP)
Frank, A. 223
Fromm, E. 31
funding 28, 55–56, 122, 176–178, 198, 207,
    239
Furedi, F. 213

Gabriel, Y. 176, 182
Garland, D. 37
Gearty, C. 58
Geddes, D. 182
genealogy of resilience 20
Gillam, L. 249
Ginsberg, R. 203
Glandon, D. 33
Goffman, E. 68
Good Friday Agreement (GFA) 48, 73n1,
    138, 198
governmentality 172
Gramsci, A. 134, 196
Green, S. 229
Grenfell Tower fire 22

grief 23, 88–91
group solidarity 24, 175–181, 196–197
Grozdanova, R. 57
Guillemin, M. 249

Hacking, I. 4–6, 9, 11–12, 29, 38, 40, 48,
    63–72, 132, 146, 167, 177, 179, 191,
    208–209, 221
Han, B. C. 84
harassment 95
Haraway, D. 50
Harding, S. 50
Hardy, K. 25–26
harm and bereavement 203–205
Harrods bomb 1983 83
Hartsock, N. 50
Heath-Kelly, C. 168
helplessness 31
Herman, J.L. 128–129, 175, 190
hibernation 155
Hickey, D. 52
hierarchy of credibility 51
Higgins, Michael D. 54
Hillsborough 169
Historical Enquiries Team 112
Hogan-Howe, B. 36, 92
Holland, J. 20
holocaust 147, 165
Howell, A. 171, 191–192, 241
human resilience 208; *see also* resilience
human rights and protection 22
human/social sciences 71
human suffering 117
Humbert, C. 2
hypervigilance 38, 81, 91–94

Imagined Communities (Anderson) 22
improvisation 201
individual–familial resilience 177
individual resilience 34
informal survivor networks 118
information sharing 206
*Information Sharing Among Emergency
    Services* 13
Inherent personality 166
inherent resilience 30, 106–110
inhibitions 171
injurability 51
injury–agency, dynamics 31
institutional violence 2, 86, 135, 157
instrumentality 201
Intention (Anscombe) 179

258 Index

intersecting resilience 130
intimate terrorism 50
intrusion of privacy for survivors 95
Invictus (poem by William Ernest Henley) 188–189
Invictus Games 2014 188
Irish Republican Army (IRA) 136
Irish Republican Army (IRA) proxy bomb campaign 53, 73n1, 85, 125, 136, 142
irritability 86
Islamic State of Iraq and the Levant (ISIL/ISIS) 138
Islamist extremism 58
Islamophobia towards Muslims 148, 197

Jackson, R. 52
James, W. 201
Jarvis, L. 20, 134, 249
Jessop, B. 171
#JeSuisCharlie 12
Joseph, J. 2
Justice Against Sponsors of Terrorism Act (JASTA) 112, 206
justice–peace divide 144

Kant, I. 173
Kaufmann, M. 107, 168, 171, 174, 228
Kerslake Report 22, 206
Keränen, L. 19, 21–22
Khan, M. S. 58
Khmer Rouge genocide 127
Klein, N. 22
Krause, M. 55
Kristensen 168
Kristensen, K. 107, 171, 174, 228

Languages of Recovery within Victim Support Policy 13
Lelourec, L. 54–55
(neo)liberalism? 220
lifestyle traits 166
Lindebaum, D. 182
Lindsay, G. 147, 151
linear temporality 134
'Living with Trauma' awareness workshops 121, 124
London bombings 2005 2, 11, 19–21, 23–24, 49, 58, 83, 92, 96, 107, 110, 117–118, 127, 132, 138, 143, 147–148; Islamophobia towards Muslims 197
looping effect 123
looping effect of human kinds 66

Lorde, A. 182
luxury of grieving 88
Lynch, O. 65

MacAirt, C. 139
Major, J. 54
Manchester Arena bombing 2017 22–23, 205–206
Manchester Bee 12
Manyena, S.B. 200
market-driven capitalist environments 128
Marx, K. 173–174
Mason, T.L. 248
mass fatalities 207
mass violence 61
McGarry, R. 29, 34, 134, 200
McGurk's Bar bombing 139–141
McGurk's Bar justice campaign 97, 139, 157
media attention 95–98
memorialisation 127
mental health classifications 5
midlife crisis 99
Mill, Pat 21
Mills, C. Wright 217
moral entrepreneurialism 178
moral panic 59
moral self-admonishment 226
Morris, T. 31
Muir-Cochrane, E. 248
multidirectional memory 165
Murakami, H. 52–53, 70, 132
My Former Life 144
Mythen, G. 29, 34, 36–37, 59, 200, 240

narcissistic-obsessional tendencies 128–129
narrative analysis 7
narrativity 201
National Security Strategy, 2008 26
neatness of fit 203
negative emotions 144
Neocleous, M. 26, 39, 168–170, 192
neoliberal ideology 226
neoliberalism 22, 26, 202
Nicholson, J. 132
non-physical harm 83
non-State terror attacks 138
normalisation 201
North Dakota Access Pipeline, protest against 169
Northern Ireland Affairs Committee 155

Index   259

Northern Ireland conflict 132, 137
Nussbaum, M. 182

obesity 5
O'Leary, N. 229
Oliver, D.G. 248
O'Malley, P. 33, 37
ontological security 164, 167
organisational branding 177
Organisations Supporting Victims of Terrorism 176
Overland, G. 32, 105, 120, 127–128, 191, 201–202

Palestine 19
Paris attacks 2015 92
Parry, C. 48, 90, 121, 128, 132, 136–138, 178, 180
Parry, W. 132, 137
peace and reconciliation activities 126–128
Peace Centre 116, 128, 135, 216
Peace Foundation 64
Peer Support Programmes 13
Peirce, C.S. 246
Pemberton, A. 229
performative etiquette 153
personal narration 214
Pfefferbaum, R. L. 33
physical injuries over time 82–84
Pinchevski, A. 101
polemics 220
political and moral hegemony 50
political campaigning 86
political interdependency 190
political prisoners 142
political sociology 47
political violence 24, 64, 68, 92, 156, 197, 206
political violence and terrorism (PVT) 1–2, 50, 64; anger 84–88; anxiety 91–94; bereavement and grief 88–91; dynamically 'defining' 63–66; fear 91–94; how to (not) define 56–66; hypervigilance 91–94; individual survivors, impacts on 82–91; institutional barriers to justice 140; long-term emotional responses 91–94; making up people 66–72; media attention 95–98; narratives of survivors 49–53; personal relationships, effects on 98–101; physical injuries over time 82–84; policies 1–2, 50, 64; *a posteriori* reasoning and

post-defining 62–63; *a priori* logic and definition 60–62; short-term emotional responses 84–88; survivors and their families, indirect impacts on 91–101; survivors of 2, 6, 47–73, 81, 105, 154; Tim Parry Johnathan Ball Foundation for Peace (FfP) 10–12, 53–56
post-Holocaust discourses 168
post-traumatic stress 32
post-traumatic stress disorder (PTSD) 23, 29, 31, 70, 82, 84, 101–102, 124–125, 167, 172, 192, 241
practice-oriented support 105, 121–128
prevention-focused work 144
Professionally Developed Crisis Management and Resilience Training for the Education Sector 27
protraction 132
Proxy Bombs of the 1970s and early 1990s 54
Psathas, G. 247
psychopolitics of self-optimization 223
pub bombing in Belfast, 1971 109
pure violence 60
pursuit of peace 138

radical discontinuity 134
radicalisation 1, 62
random violence 61
rape 107, 134, 170, 201, 215
rape survivor 134, 170
reaffirmation of liberal self-sufficiency 10
reality simulation 28
Rechtman, R. 213, 215, 223
reductionism 11
reformulation of self or experience 13, 195–196
reframing 201
refugee and asylum support charity 148
Reghezza-Zitt, M. 13, 222
Reid, J. 222
religion and faith 114–115
research design: access, building rapport, and organisational practice 234–235; data analysis 245–249; data collection 235–237; participant information and sample diversity 237–239, **239–241**; participant 'pen portraits' 241–245; research ethics 249–252
research questions 223–234
resilience 1, 155, 172, 229; based policymaking, criticism 224; centrality

of 38; community debate 184; in counterterrorism 29; creep 217; defined 1–2, 166; discourse 171; elasticity of 25, 34; five framings of 191–195; group solidarity 13, 196–197; homogenous phenomenon 172; hyper-individualistic ethic 190; individual 34; individual–familial resilience 177; within military regimes and soldier fitness initiatives 26; narratives 146–156; policy and practice 205–207; policy narratives of 164; reformulation of self or experience 195–196; reformulations of self or experience 13; research 4; resisting injustice 13, 199–200; resources 105, 128; sociological imagination 217–218; solutions 27; survivor resilience(s) 200–203; syntheses of 34; tacit peer support 13, 197–198; terror and trauma 20–24; top-down strategy 172; training 166; trajectory 33; transcending the past 13, 198–199; and trauma 9
resilience-as-responsibilisation 172–173
resilience-based policy 165
resilience-based 'recovery' models 84
resilience for survivors, sources of 105–106; communal support systems 112–120; economic factors 110–112; Foundation for Peace 121–123; inherent resilience 106–110; peace and reconciliation activities 126–128; practice-oriented support 121–128; religion and faith 114–115; responses to adversity 106–110; survivor solidarity 116–120; therapy and counselling 124–126; victim compensation 110–112
resilient communities 12
resilient survivor communities 163–164; accounting for time 164–168; anger, contestation, and resistance 168–174; terrorism survivor and group solidarity 175–181
resilient survivors 5, 122–123
resistance 168–174; and resilience 12
resisting injustice 199–200
responsibilisation 10, 171
retroactive narration 146
Revolution in Military Affairs (RMA) 24
Reynolds, A. 54
Rieff, D. 136, 198–199
risk managers 169
Rock, P. 108, 157, 214

Roderick, R. 8
Ross, F.C. 154
Rothberg, M. 146, 165
Rouge, K. 202
Royal Ulster Constabulary (RUC) 139
Rudd, A. 27
Rufat, S. 13, 222
Ruggiero, V. 60
Rumsfeld, D. 25
Russell, B. 189

Sacks, H. 63
Sartre, J.P. 62, 68, 133, 174
scale of victimisation 52
Scheper-Hughes, N. 23, 29–30, 34, 191, 201
Schmid, A.P. 56
Schott, R. M. 38, 88, 158
Schutz, A. 247
Scott, T. 123
security: discourses 165; emergencies 1, 164; strategies 202
self-determination 169
self-improvement 223
self-protection 128
self-reliance/agency 202
self-supportive function 178
Self Under Siege, The (Roderick) 8
self-understanding 32
sense of coherence 32
September 11 attacks 2001 20, 23, 95, 166; state-led counterterrorism policies after 52
Serovich, J.M. 248
sexual trauma 30
sexual violence 65
Shock Doctrine (Klein) 22
Siapno, J.A. 106, 129
Smith, D. 50
social integration 202
social interactions 175
social justice 51, 171
social justice campaigning 200
social media 119
social science philosophy 47
socio-economic adversity 170
soft security 25
soldier fitness propaganda 189
state-sponsored terrorism 135, 138
State violence 156
state welfare and social solidarity 10
Stoic Art of Living: Inner Resilience and Outer Results, The (Morris) 31

Index

stoicism 9, 189
storytelling 120, 123, 154, 177
stress, abnormal degree of 85
stress-induced dermatological complaints 85
structural resilience 30
sudden deathwork 123
suicide 5
suicide attacks 138
suicide bombers 11, 83, 147, 150
survival 128
survivor 106; connotations 107; injured and non-injured 107
survivor communities 181, 225
survivor resilience(s) 200–203
Survivors Against Terrorism 12
Survivors Assistance Network (SAN) 2, 48, 64, 108, 122, 144, 176–177
Survivors for Peace 56
survivors of political violence 68
survivors of terrorism 5, 180
survivor solidarity 116–120; peer support programmes 207
survivors' propensity 93
Syria by ISIS 114

tacit peer support 197–198
Taussig, M. 69
Tavory, I. 71, 236, 246
temporal dialectics of ontological security 224–225
temporalities of (in)security and resilience 132–135; embodied proximity 145–146; narrating suffering and journeys of recovery 144–145; resilience narratives 146–147; spectacular, relating the everyday 142–144; violence 'from above' and 'from below' 135–142
terror attacks in London, 2017 22
terrorism 40, 51, 69, 164, 204, 206, 215; attacks 1–2; codify 56; deconstruction of 60; defined 51, 59–63, 66; hegemonic framings 52; ontological instability 52; survivors 175–181; victims of 51, 55
Terrorism Act 2000 57, 226
terrorism legislation 59
terroristic violence 59
terror threats 92, 134
terror–trauma–resilience 8–9
therapy and counselling 124–126
THINK 144
timelessness 134

Timmermans, S. 63, 71, 236, 246
Tim Parry Johnathan Ball Foundation for Peace (FfP) 2, 12, 64, 84, 97, 102, 106, 180, 192, 217, 234; charity 10; political violence and terrorism (PVT) 10–12, 48, 53–56; resilience for survivors, sources of 121–123; storytelling at 136
Tim Parry Scholarship 53
Tokyo gas attacks, 1995 52, 70
top-down resilience strategy 172
tower block fires 215
trauma 9, 156, 213; coping up with 196; narratives 23, 215; survivors 190; vulnerability 30
Trauma and Recovery (Herman) 190
Trauma Awareness workshops 122
trauma-informed practice 250
trauma–resilience nexus 34
traumatised victims 214

UK Civil Contingencies 24
Ulster Volunteer Force 139
Ungar, M. 109
unity of consciousness 158

Varieties of Religious Experience 201
Vaughn-Williams, N. 174
Victim Compensation 13
victimhood 69, 172, 214
victimisation 50–51, 182, 214, 238
victimology 47
victim policy 203–205
victim-related policy 191
victims 106–107; compensation 110–112; compensation scheme for 112; connotations 107; metamorphosis of 215; narrative 214; of State violence 142; of terrorism 206, 215
Victim Support 176, 239
victim support policy 206
victories 220
violence: anthology 60; as necessarily contested 63–66; perpetrators of 51; prevention- based potential 122; reappraising and its spaces 225
violent and lethal jihad 58
violent jihad 58; *see also* Islamophobia towards Muslims
vulnerability–agency dynamics 31

Walklate, S. 29–30, 34, 59, 134, 200, 214–215

262 Index

war on terror (WOT) 20, 63, 73, 134
Warrington bombing, 2000 54–55, 117, 119, 121, 127, 137, 176
Warrington Peace Centre 24
Webel, C.P. 61, 128–129
Weber, M. 57, 63, 68, 247
Weberian–Schutzian, 194
Welby, Justin 22
Welfare Reform Act in 2012 152
well-being 144
Wieviorka, M. 62–63
Wilkinson, P. 65

Williams, R. 34
Wilson, T. 51
Windle, G. 34
Wittgenstein, L. 64
Wittgensteinian language analysis 67, 71
women's advocacy 128
Wong, D. B. 31
Woolwich attackers 58
Wounded Storyteller, The (Frank) 223

Zebrowski, C. 24–25
zero-hour employment contracts 174

Printed in the United States
by Baker & Taylor Publisher Services